Carmen Sirianni was born in Brooklyn in 1947. He received a BA in philosophy from Manhattan College, and did graduate work at the New School for Social Research and the State University of New York at Binghamton, where he received his PhD in sociology. He has taught sociology at Binghamton, Brandeis and Northeastern University, where he is currently an assistant professor. For the past several years he has worked on the *Socialist Review* editorial collective in Boston. Previously, he was active in the anti-war movement, rank-and-file union organizing in New York City, and the New American Movement; he is currently active in Democratic Socialists of America. He is married to Andrea Walsh, who teaches sociology and women's studies at Clark University.

Carmen Sirianni

Verso

Workers Control
and
Socialist Democracy
The Soviet Experience

First published 1982
© Carmen J. Sirianni 1982

Verso Editions and NLB
15 Greek Street, London W1

Typeset by Comset Graphic Designs
Singapore

Printed in Great Britain by
The Thetford Press Ltd
Thetford, Norfolk

**British Library
Cataloguing in Publication Data**

Sirianni, Carmen
    Workers' control and socialist democracy.
    1. Soviet Union—Politics and government—
    1917–1936
    I. Title
    320.947   JN6524

0–86091–054–7
0–86091–754–1 Pbk

Contents

Acknowledgements

This work would not have been possible without the assistance of many people. While at the New School for Social Research, I received help and encouragement from Emil Oestereicher, who introduced me to the comparative sociology of revolutions, and Trent Schroyer, who introduced me to the critical theory of Habermas and provided some of the original suggestions from which this work developed. I also wish to thank Bill McCormick and Al DiLascia of Manhattan College, my original mentors in Hegel and Kant, Marx and Weber. Members of my dissertation committee at the State University of New York at Binghamton, James Geschwender, Terence Hopkins and Dale Tomich, provided invaluable assistance, critical insight and encouragement throughout. Geschwender and Hopkins, in particular, saw this work through from the very earliest stages. The Center for European Studies at Harvard University provided much support for discussion and research.

Many people helped type the various drafts, and I would like to especially thank Jill Friedman, Pat Doloway Terrel, Lucille Raimondo, Marilyn Churchill, Dennis Chin, Linda Schiffman and Elizabeth Bouche. Rachelle Moore at the SUNY-Binghamton library was particularly helpful in locating sources. Evelyn Meincke and Raissa Khodorkovski provided needed assistance with Russian language and materials.

Various people provided useful comments, criticisms and other forms of assistance at various stages. In particular I would like to thank Paul Breines, Anita Diamant, Robert Devlin, Robert Horwitz, Heather Hogan, Cheryl Klausner, Susan and Bob Lehrer, Charles Maier, Mark David Mandel, Bill Martin, Patrick McGuire, Lou Menasche, Chinnah Mithrasekeran, Charles Post, Peter

Rachleff, Paula Rayman, Dimitri Roussopoulos, Robert Schaeffer, Jimi Sirianni, Ella Taylor and Steve Vogel. Lew Friedland, Joel Greifinger, Allen Hunter, Elizabeth Kingston-Mann and Ralph Miliband read substantial parts of the manuscript and provided particularly valuable comments. Paul Joseph, Molly Nolan, Theda Skočpol, Peggy Somers, David Stark and Bob Wood offered valuable suggestions on the comparative aspects of my work.

Perry Anderson has provided numerous critical insights and much encouragement since the original draft was completed. I owe a very special debt of gratitude to him. And I express my appreciation to the other members of the staff of NLB for supporting this work.

Two friends did not live to see the completion of this book, but both contributed greatly. Georges Haupt provided much encouragement and critical insight while teaching at Binghamton. George Cooke knew little about its substance, yet his friendship and spirit sustained it on a very daily basis.

My dear friend Simon Rosenblum not only carefully read this manuscript instantly at every stage of its completion, but his critical insight and personal support over the years have been crucial to my own development as an intellectual, political and human being. And, as he has just reminded me, it was he who gave me the idea to write this in the first place.

Finally, to my wife Andrea Walsh I express my deepest gratitude. Her critical reading, sociological insight and personal support were invaluable throughout. She more than anyone else saw this work through from beginning to end. To her, and to my parents, Agnes and Joseph Sirianni, it is warmly dedicated.

Introduction

The history of socialism has been the history of the problem of democracy. Marx himself developed the foundations of socialist thought through a critique of the democratic heritage of the French revolution. The result was a redefinition and a radicalization of both form and content. Marx's critique and the struggles of the working classes in the nineteenth and early twentieth centuries rendered liberal democracy profoundly problematic. And yet early Marxian socialism never really rid itself of the problem. Nor have we today. From the original critiques of the anarchists to those of sociologists like Weber and Michels, this was evident. With the Russian revolution and its aftermath, it became inescapable. The future of socialism remains the problem of democracy.

This study attempts a contribution in a number of ways. First and foremost, it investigates the possibilities of revolutionary popular democracy in the early years of the Russian revolution, examining its two most important institutional expressions: the factory committees and soviets. Their emergence and development, functioning and fate are analysed within the broad context of revolutionary change. Second, it probes various aspects of Marxist and Leninist theory with a view to understanding the logic of their impact on historical developments. Lastly, it critically appropriates some of the lessons of the Russian experience for democratic socialism in the West today through a wider theoretical and comparative analysis of workers control and council democracy.

If the democratic potential of workers control and soviet democracy in the Russian revolution is still a much debated question, their significance for the revolutionary process can hardly be controversial. Nearly all historians of the revolution now agree that the committees of workers delegates elected in the factories to oversee various aspects of production and to defend the general economic interests of the workers were perhaps the most important organs of struggle created by the urban workers in 1917. They were in the forefront of the movement to defend and extend the revolutionary gains of February. And they were the earliest of the mass organizations to support the Bolshevik call for revolutionary state power. The soviets were the popularly elected organs that increasingly came to embody this revolutionary political power as they extended their authority and their actual administration of public affairs from the first days of dual power in March to the Bolshevik-led insurrection conducted in their name in October. If the factory committees and soviets were not the only major organs of mass struggle in 1917, they surely stood at the very centre of the revolutionary process.

As will be clear, I have no intention of romanticizing the experience of workers democracy, in Russia or elsewhere, or of extracting from it a revolutionary democratic mythos to serve as the pivot of socialist politics, then or now. Nor, however, do I share the more historically fashionable point of view—sometimes strangely combined with the latter approach—that the projects of popular democratization were inevitably doomed to complete failure. If analysis is to provide the insight to transform our own recalcitrant social world, then history must be reconstructed and interrogated from the standpoint of its objective possibilities at any given time. Objectivity requires a careful determination of the historically structured constraints that shape and limit human intervention and achievable options. Indeed, the burden of the historical past often reveals itself most sharply in revolutionary situations. But however structurally limited and disproportionately weighted the options might be, a range of historical choices is invariably available, particularly in revolutionary situations. The task of historical analysis is to explain how one of the range of possible outcomes came to pass, a task that raises not a few basic epistemological questions. To proceed otherwise, however, is to become mesmerized by the logic of events, by the lure of powerful personalities and conquerors in general. By refusing to examine the factors which were present in a given historical process, but were not allowed to operate, this particular school of thought also rules out a proper study of those who were defeated, and cuts itself off from an understanding of the true course of events.[1] The examination of objective possibilities and realistic alternatives is an essential moment in the logic of explanation of any critical historical investigation with emancipatory intention.[2]

As a study of the forms of popular mobilization and institution-building processes, this work draws liberally from general insights articulated most coherently in recent literature on social movements and revolutions, particularly in the writings of Charles Tilly, Anthony Oberschall, Theda Skocpol, and others. Compared with earlier sociological theories that focused on social psychological factors and often assumed that mass behaviour was irrational, recent studies have more seriously investigated the problems of mobilization and organization of scarce resources, the structural capacities for transformation, and the role of the state.[3] But since it is not my intention to offer a comprehensive theory of social movements and revolutions, I have limited references to much of the relevant literature and have sought on the whole not to engage the current debates explicitly. Questions of historical and more directly political import are of greater concern to me here. The focus on organizational capacities, structural leverage, and institution-building processes, however, in no way implies a dichotomy between structure and culture, or structure and ideology. This work definitely emphasizes structural and organizational factors. But ideology plays an important role, not as a separately determined world transformative force, but as one that interacts with popular struggle, and without which it would be impossible to understand the mobilization of organizational resources and the development of structural capacities.

As a synthetic work whose concerns are comparative and theoretical, this study offers less of the social and cultural history than is needed. The bias is not a matter of principle. And at least some of the analysis that follows will make clear that I do not think that institutional transformation and state-building processes can be understood apart from the cultural formations and the organization of the everyday life of the popular classes. Critical historical sociology must be totalizing, even if no adequate concept of structured totality can be theoretically determined a priori, and even if no single scholarly work can be adequate to the richness of historical determination. The particular constellation of relevant factors that opened up democratic possibilities, and determined their points of closure, will emerge in the discussion that follows.

The factory committees and soviets, of course, were not the only organized expressions of the popular movements for the transformation of Russian society. I have focused on them here because, despite their contradictions and the often unclear boundaries between various organizations and institutions, they became the main loci of the reality and the hope for popular democratic control in the economic and political spheres alike. The other popular organs never set democratization as their explicit organizational task; rather, whenever they were concerned with this problem, they oriented their activities towards the soviets and factory committees. But it is hardly possible to grasp the development and fate, strengths and weaknesses, of the latter apart from the other important worker, peasant, and soldier organizations. Inter-organizational ties and leadership networks provided resources that affected democratization processes positively and negatively. The political parties, which enjoyed the most continuous histories of all the organizations of struggle under the tsar and polarized the most active and committed militants, were obviously destined to play an important role in the political space opened by the February revolution, which none of them had directly brought about. The Bolsheviks, Mensheviks, and Socialist Revolutionaries were the main political contenders among the popular classes, though anarchist and anarcho-syndicalist groups enjoyed significant influence in certain areas. From the very beginning these parties were influential in the politics and daily workings of the soviets and factory committees, especially in their executive organs. The trade unions, which enjoyed a stupendous expansion in 1917 after a beleaguered and disrupted history under the tsar, also had a powerful impact on the revolution, especially since they operated in the same domain as the newly created factory committees, often competing with them directly. This parallel activity and tension will be a central theme of this study.

The urban consumer cooperatives played a much less important role in relation to the soviets and factory committees, and they were generally the most reformist of all the workers organizations. How much their activity in the sphere of distribution affected the attempts at workers control and soviet administration is a significant question, though the answer is quite unclear. The elected committees in the military also had tremendous impact on the revolution, those in the rear maintaining direct organizational links with the urban workers soviets. But as the army itself dissolved in the autumn and winter of 1917–18 and the Red Army was built up on different foundations, the significance of the committees vanished. To what extent an effective revolutionary army could have been constructed on democratic grounds is certainly a question of great import for the revolution as a whole. The proletarian Red Guards, which came to form the core of the Red Army, played a significant role in the urban revolution in general and in the protection of the workers' claims over production in particular.

Among the peasants, the most significant institution in the revolutionary seizure and distribution of land and in the everyday decisions about its use was the village communal organization, or *mir*. Its peculiar structure—especially its communal and egalitarian, but also its patriarchal, features—will be considered in terms of its effect on land distribution and use, potential long- and short-term relations to the urban economy, and the system of rural soviets that were integrated into the national political order. The peasant revolution and its organizational bases must be analysed in terms of their own potential for system-wide democratization, as well as their effect on urban developments in this regard.

The popular movements for democratization cannot be investigated without also examining the actions of the non-popular strata, or 'census society', as the Russians called it. The urban bourgeoisie, the landed nobility, the industrial administrative and technical experts, the various petty-bourgeois strata, and the state civil and military service were the major groups that acted, within and without the old and new systems, in a way that was generally hostile to the more radical demands of the masses, and often even to the moderate socialist project of democratization along reformed capitalist lines. Although this study cannot focus on the organizations of these groups to the same extent as those of the workers, soldiers and peasants, their activities did determine the parameters within and against which the popular classes had to struggle to construct an alternative political and economic order. The revolution cannot be understood without the counter-revolution. Nor can its development be separated from the international forces that aided the armed counter-revolution, determined the particular form of war-induced state crisis, and circumscribed the long-term developmental possibilities available to a revolutionary (or indeed, a non-revolutionary) government. Russian development had been closely linked to the capitalist West for decades, and the Bolshevik revolution could neither create a *tabula rasa* nor engineer an abrupt and purifying withdrawal from a world order dominated by capitalist market relations, Western technology, and powerful nation-states hostile to socialism or bent on conquest and colonial domination. The options for popular democratization must be viewed in this broader context of long-term continuities and constraints. The question of relatively short-term possibilities for revolutionary democratization cannot be broached while ignoring that 'the danger of this type of study lies in the temptation to isolate the phenomenon of overt crisis from the wider context of a society undergoing tranformation'.[4]

The emphasis on workers control in the analysis that follows should not be misunderstood. Since work is the over-riding activity in the lives of most people, and since class relations of domination are reproduced in the production process, any analysis of the potential for socialist democratization must treat this experience as central. Gone are the days when concern with the mere nationalization of the means of production by a revolutionary state sufficed for a social theory and practice aspiring to the emancipation of labour. If the democratic gains of socialist transformation are to be consolidated and extended, they cannot be interdicted from the realm of everyday life in which people produce and reproduce *themselves* simultaneously with goods and services for social consumption. Relations of domination in the work-place inevitably tend to pervade other areas of social life and ultimately threaten to undermine the democratic foundations of the polity at large.

But this central concern for workers control over production should not be mistaken for a claim that production relations must *first* be thoroughly transformed in order for political power to be effective at all. Nor does it imply that political power is unimportant. Indeed, without political power, revolutionary social transformation is simply not possible, objections of anarchists and anarcho-syndicalists notwithstanding. But what is not so simple is the relationship between political power and political democratization on the one hand and the transformation of other areas of social life on the other. Of particular importance in this regard are relations between the sexes and production relations. It seems clear that unless the latter are transformed, unless democratic and egalitarian relations begin to prevail, political democracy remains limited, and the organs of political power show a marked tendency toward autonomization. But the delicate balance and rhythm among these various processes of democratization cannot be defined a priori. Specific factors in the national and international context will determine the extent to which they can proceed simultaneously, the forms through which they can best complement one another, and the limits that might have to be set to ensure the lasting survival of the entire project of socialist democratization. In the Russian revolution, where possibilities for socialist democracy and political pluralism were quite limited, workers control within production was perhaps the most promising foundation for long-term democratization in the urban areas.

While the first part of this study seeks to determine these possibilities and limits in the early revolutionary years, the second and third parts have broader theoretical and political ambitions. Part Two critically analyses Marxist and Leninist theory with respect to the questions of workers control and technological change, political democracy and the revolutionary state, socialist bureaucracy and cultural revolution. The focus is on the theoretical formulations of Lenin, since these had the most profound impact on actual revolutionary developments and later revolutionary theory. The contradictions and ambiguities of Lenin's thought were theoretically based yet informed by the actual struggles of which they were a part. Recent critiques of Lenin have been too profound and yet not profound enough.[5] The theoretical analysis attempts to clarify some of these issues, without pretending to discuss Leninist theory as a whole.

Part Three extends the discussion of possibilities beyond Lenin's death, and provides a wider perspective on revolutionary development and democratization. Comparative analysis is particularly useful here, since workers control and council democracy were mass phenomena of international dimensions at the time, and they have recurred in a variety of forms since then. But the comparative analysis remains limited, for the study is focused on the Russian experience.[6] One question of particular relevance for socialist movements in the West today, however, is considered in some detail, namely the organizational forms of workers control in socialist transformation and the heritage of councilist theory in the writings of Gramsci and Pannekoek.[7] This is the subject of chapter 11.

Studies of the objective possibilities of democratization are essential to historical analysis and political practice. Yet a work such as this, which endeavours to offer explanations for the failure of popular democratic institutions to survive an attempted socialist transition, is limited by the absence of lasting and thoroughgoing examples of successful socialist democratization against which to compare. Comparative historical analysis can provide only a partial understanding of the factors required for such democratization. To be sure, experiences from all over the globe are now to hand, and these can afford us insights about past, present, and future developments. Yet none is without serious contradictions and limitations. The task of identifying the reasons for the deformation and demise of popular democratic institutions in one country is thus difficult, and must remain tentative. But incomplete empirical knowledge is not the only reason for this. Rather—and responsible theorists and activists must admit this openly—we still do not know under what conditions genuine socialist democracy can flourish. We really do not yet know whether it is truly possible, especially in its more radical forms. Marx's conception of a 'free association of producers' can serve as an impetus for analysis, but hardly as its touchstone. What are the specific institutional contours that might make possible the rational use of collective resources (including advanced technology) in a way that is consistent with active participation in collective decisions, a high degree of individual freedom, and relatively equal work and life opportunities? Platitudes about transformed human beings with completely new values and unbridled technical capacities, about complete decentralization and the liberatory warmth and simplicity of face-to-face democracy, about the explosive release of potential that will accompany the end of capitalism or the state, will not bring us one step closer in theory or practice to a society in which real human beings can democratically and collectively control a material and social world that is inevitably recalcitrant, existentially threatening, and extremely complex. Only if we openly recognize that as yet we have no complete solutions to the problem of socialist democracy—and that no easy solutions exist—can we proceed with the task of developing a historically grounded and empirically relevant theory of it.[8]

This work is, hopefully, one step in that direction, but its limits are defined at least partly by those of a general theory itself. And this, in turn, points to the horizons of our actual experience in a world that has yet to be successfully transformed along democratic socialist lines.

Such limits pose certain problems of analysis and warrant extreme caution in ascribing a causal role in the fate of socialist democracy in Russia to any set of factors. But only the positivist would despair of the task altogether, escaping into untestable assumptions about what is and is not possible. The critical historian and social theorist must recognize from the outset that answers to the most difficult questions will be tentative, and must depend on the progress in the transformation of the world in which we live. This is the irreducibly practical and experimental dimension of any truly critical theory. We must proceed, as Habermas has noted in a different context, according to the 'logic of justified hope and controlled experiment'.[9] Social theory, historical analysis, and political practice must inform one another in the process of actively testing the anthropological and social-organizational potential of the human species. Our understanding of the past and present is reciprocally and inextricably linked to our transformation of the future.

Part One

Popular Democracy and the Russian Revolution

The following chapters analyse the factory committees and soviets from their inception during the February revolution against the tsar to the end of the victorious struggle against the armed counter-revolution in 1921. A separate chapter considers the peasant revolution up to roughly the same time, when Soviet leaders introduced the New Economic Policy to consolidate the worker-peasant alliance, eroded by several years of forcible grain requisitions. These were years of intense struggle on many fronts—political, economic, military. The victory of the Bolsheviks was never certain, the gains of the popular classes never secure. Inaction and reaction posed continual threats. Even after the seizure of power in October, the new regime faced serious opposition and sabotage, the cumulative effects of wartime economic disintegration and an autocratic political heritage, and—after only a few months of peace with Germany—an armed counter-revolution supported by the Allied powers. The complex history of these struggles has been recounted many times. The presentation that follows is organized primarily along thematic lines within the broad chronological demarcations represented by the February and October revolutions, and the period of civil war that began in mid-1918. It ends with the decisive rebuff of the Workers Opposition and the armed suppression of the Kronstadt revolt for soviet democracy and workers control, the ideals of the October Revolution itself.

The Factory Committees in Early 1917

In the middle of February 1917 few expected that the scattered strikes throughout the city of Petrograd would lead to the downfall of the tsar. Resentment against the deprivations of the war was mounting, and the government looked increasingly unstable. Rasputin had been assassinated. The workers' representatives on the War Industries Committees had recently been arrested. The war itself was going badly for the Russian troops. The cities were dangerously short of food and rationing had just been instituted in the capital. But hardly a socialist leader thought revolution possible in the circumstances. Not long before Lenin had lamented that there would be no revolution in his lifetime.

On 18 February, however, the large Putilov works went out on strike, and the owners responded with a lockout four days later. But it was not until women workers took to the streets in a massive show of strength on International Women's Day that the strikes began to spread, becoming virtually general by 25 February. The Bolshevik Vyborg District Committee, which days later was to impel radicalization, urged the women not to strike until May Day, but to hold an orderly demonstration. However, the women refused to heed this directive, and the strikers joined up with the bread riots of housewives and others. Calls for bread were soon overshadowed by demands for peace and an end to the hated autocracy. When the regiments called out to quell the disorders fraternized with the strikers, the revolution was all but secured, at least in the capital.[1]

Spontaneity and History

The February revolution had begun without the direction of any party, as nearly all contemporary accounts, including those of

Trotsky and Sukhanov, attest. Indeed, the Bolshevik leaders in Petrograd tried at first to curb the movement, and the Menshevik Skobelev called for the repression of the strikes before they brought chaos. But to characterize the revolution as simply spontaneous would be misleading. Although no party planned and directed the popular movement of February, the revolution did not simply erupt *ex nihilo*. The consciousness that underlay it was the product of years of struggle and education by organized revolutionaries—an active elite of Bolsheviks and Mensheviks, Socialist Revolutionaries and Anarchists. Militants from these groups not only helped radicalize the movement that led to the downfall of the tsar, but articulated the demands that became central to the entire revolutionary process.[2]

Several days after the Petrograd strike had become general, the organizational forms of the new order began to emerge. In the political sphere, initiatives to establish a Soviet of Workers and Soldiers Deputies competed with efforts to form a Provisional Government of bourgeois democratic parties. The dynamic between these two centres of political power would define the revolutionary process of 1917. In the economic sphere, workers established factory committees (*fabzavkomy*) in the industrial areas throughout Russia. Their creation was also largely spontaneous; they often grew out of the committees set up to conduct the strike itself. When in his April Theses, Lenin issued the call for dual power in industry (via soviet control), it was already a reality in many places, effected mostly by non-party workers and through the factory committees rather than the soviets. It was only in May that Lenin endorsed the spontaneously created factory committees as the organs of this dual power. But while the party leadership lagged behind these developments for some two months, many rank and file Bolshevik militants and local party committees were involved in the factory-committee movement from its outset or shortly thereafter. In the election to the First Electricity Works of Petrograd on 2 March, for instance, the workers elected ten Bolsheviks to the twenty-four-member council, although in most committees Mensheviks, SRs, and non-party workers greatly predominated in the early weeks. The soviets, although dominated by a Menshevik and SR leadership that was generally hostile to

workers control at the plant level, likewise aided in the early formation of factory committees. This was especially true of the Labour
Section of the Petrograd Soviet. But the soviets in Moscow,
Saratov, Omsk, Kiev, Ekaterinoslav, Archangel, Ivanovo-
Voznesensk, in the Donbass and Volga regions and elsewhere were
also quite active in this process. On 7 March, for example, the
Petrograd Soviet issued this call: 'For the control of factory and
shop administration, for the proper organization of work, factory
and shop committees should be formed at once. They should see to
it that the forces of labour are not wasted and look after working
conditions in the plant.'[3] In some cases, elections to factory committees took place before or simultaneously with soviet elections,
and soviet delegates sometimes formed the core of the committees
as well. The soviets encouraged the formation of factory committees to broaden their base and to aid in the establishment of locals
in the now fully legal trade-union movement. However, many, if
not most, factory committees had a quite different conception of
their functions, as we shall see.[4]

Although the factory committees were created from scratch during the spontaneous wave of strikes in February and the weeks
following, they were not without precedent in the Russian workers
movement. In the 1890s strike committees and strike funds had
arisen first among the Jewish workers of Western Russia (forming
the basis of the Bund: the Social Democratic Jewish Workers Party) and later spread to other industrial centres. Even earlier, in the
1870s and 1880s, workers sometimes elected deputies to negotiate
with management and government authorities. In general, however, tsarist authorities cooperated with the owners in crushing any
permanent forms of workers representation, at the plant level and
beyond.

With the growth of labour unrest around the turn of the century,
however, the Ministry of the Interior recommended in May 1901,
that permanent labour delegations be permitted within the plants.
Two more years of protest and massive strikes finally convinced the
government to issue a law on 10 June 1903 allowing for factory
elders (*starosti*) in industry. Workers were to nominate representatives, but only with the owner's permission, and final selection of a
starost from each department rested with management. Even then,

the *starosti* were permitted to raise questions and complaints only within the framework of existing regulations. They could not even meet and function as a group. The system was bound to flounder. Most employers declined to obey the law, and most workers, not to mention the Social Democratic Party, rejected this form of paternalistic representation.

The other form of patriarchal-bureaucratic representation of these years was initiated by Sergei Zubatov, chief of the Moscow Division of the Okhrana (secret police). It was designed to allow limited workers representation on economic questions in an effort to encourage them to abandon their political aspirations. Zubatov's intent seems to have been to create a legal trade-union movement consistent with a reformed monarchy, and his protégés not only helped to organize the workers but even provided them with strike funds. Thus, even though the elected factory committees and district associations operated under police supervision, Zubatov's Societies for Mutual Aid became quite popular among the workers of Moscow, Odessa, Kharkov, Kiev, and Minsk—so popular that the Social Democratic Party decided to participate in them, while simultaneously striving to unmask their police sponsorship and manipulation. By 1903, however, these societies had become dangerous enough in the eyes of employers and government alike to warrant their liquidation. Indeed, it was a Zubatov offshoot, Father Gapon's Union of Russian Factory Workers, that sparked the protests and rebellions of 1905, and another government-sponsored body investigating the causes of labour dissatisfaction, the Shidlovsky Commission, that provided the organizational basis, through its elected worker representatives, for the first Petrograd Soviet of Workers Deputies in 1905.[5]

Truly independent workers committees sprang up throughout the industrial centres of Russia in 1905, and in some places developed into city-wide bodies of workers representatives—soviets. These committees also constituted the basis of the nascent trade-union movement. While all these workers organizations were involved in the general political struggle to establish a parliamentary democratic government, they tended to focus on economic issues like the right to organize and the fight for the eight-hour day. The soviets had little intention of becoming the bases of revolutionary self-

government, and where they did assume limited government functions it was only out of the exigencies of continuing the general
strike, or, as in Moscow, the desperate insurrection against government repression. The workers committees in the plants acted
primarily as strike organs, and scarcely thought of workers control.
The nascent trade unions, after a brief period of toleration, were
decimated by tsarist repression and the severe economic recession
that followed the defeat of the workers movement and the struggle
to establish a constitutional republic.[6]

The workers' economic struggle was once again partially legaliz-
ed before the war, and trade unions and locally elected factory
committees, often under Bolshevik leadership, waged a number of
quite militant struggles in the 1912–1914 period.[7] Russia's entry into the war dealt a severe though temporary blow to this process.
Many Russian workers, like their European counterparts, put aside
their class demands and rallied under the flag of patriotism.
Labour organizations were again decimated, partly by renewed
tsarist repression and partly by the call-up of many workers to the
front, especially the more militant. Many large plants were even
militarized, the workers legally treated as mobilized soldiers. By
1915, however, strike activity had resumed again, but the strike
committees did not become permanent organs. In the summer of
1915, legal worker representation at the plant level was again revived under the system of War Industries Committees, which was initiated by the Constitutional Democrats (Kadets) and the Oc-
tobrists, two liberal bourgeois parties, in an effort to free Russian
industry from the constraints of tsarist bureaucracy. Workers
representatives, elected in two stages beginning at the plant level,
were to sit in a special section on the War Industries Committees,
but their proportion of votes was minimal. Although the
Bolsheviks boycotted the committees on the grounds that they fur-
thered the aims of an imperialist war, all sections of the Social
Democratic Party participated in the plant elections, which provided the first opportunity since the beginning of the war for public
meetings and open political debate.

The Labour Group of the Central War Industries Committee—the 'central workers group'—under the leadership of the Menshevik Kuz'ma Gvozdev also tried to revive the old factory elder

system, and this met with some success, despite the fact that many of the more politically militant workers opposed it. With these two forms of factory-based election in existence in many places, the Bolsheviks began to push for a new workers soviet, this time with representatives from all of Russia. Lenin opposed the idea, and the party's propagation of it ceased. However, it was revived once again at the end of 1916, this time by the now radicalized central workers group, which had moved to the left under the pressure of rising unrest in Petrograd and elsewhere. The group was arrested after calling for the full democratization of the state, and the War Industries Committees were disbanded, but not before Gvozdev had circulated an appeal, in January, for all workers to elect factory committees.[8]

Thus, only a month before the first strike wave, which toppled the tsar, the idea of factory committees was in the air, and a system of factory-based elections to the War Industries Committees had been functioning since the middle of 1915. The February revolution may have been 'one of the most leaderless, spontaneous, anonymous revolutions of all time',[9] but the forms it took in the early days were at least partially a result of the revolutionary tradition of 1905, the limited system of factory-based elections, and the propaganda of the central workers group. The rapidity and intensity of response were based on the workers' prior mobilization.[10] In subsequent months the Russian workers would display an organizational capacity that was truly impressive, though hardly surprising in view of what they had been able to accomplish in the brief periods of relaxation of tsarist controls. Nevertheless, relative to the challenges a rapidly developing revolution was to impose, these organizational traditions were weak and discontinuous, and factory organization had hardly broached the question of workers control of production either practically or ideologically.

The Utopian and the Mundane

Workers involved in the factory-committee movement of early 1917 have often been described—by supporters and detractors alike—as utopian and visionary.[11] While it is true that their visions of socialism and workers control were quite vague in the first months after February, it can hardly be doubted that the overthrow of the tsar had engendered 'almost apocalyptic hopes'[12] among broad segments of the urban working class. The Russian workers movement was permeated with feelings of relief and deliverance from all past oppression, and with the spirit of creating something altogether new—the spirit of utopianism.

However profound these apocalyptic and utopian aspirations may have been, the workers concentrated their attention on changing the concrete conditions of factory work and proletarian life. These conditions had always been little short of wretched, even in comparison with those of their European counterparts. But the war aggravated the misery, even for those workers whose sought-after skills enabled them to keep pace with galloping inflation. Labour discipline and controls on labour mobility were tightened, and recalcitrant workers could be sent to the front (though the labour shortage limited such disciplinary measures and afforded leverage for both political and economic opposition). Mandatory overtime increased enormously, the meagre protective legislation was abrogated, and illness and mortality rates soared. Housing, always in short supply, became even scarcer, and fuel shortages left not a few poor urban dwellers frozen to death before they could return for another tedious stint at the bench. By the end of the war food itself had become scarce, and the queues began to wind their way through the working-class districts. As one French historian put it, 'for the Russian workman to live meant simply not to die.'[13] Lists of quite simple and basic factory demands were drawn up throughout Russia: an eight-hour day, elimination of piece-work in favour of a daily wage, equal pay for women, an end to personal searches, boiling water for meals, installation of canteen and toilet facilities, improved ventilation in the factories, tools to be furnished by the firm instead of by the workers, weekly payment of wages, abolition of child labour, management to be polite to the workers, two weeks pay in case of dismissal, and an increase in pay. In the metal and textile factories, where militancy was often greatest, the demands were still more basic.

The demand for the eight-hour day was the most insistent of all in the early weeks of the revolution. It had been part of the Social

Democratic programme since 1898, and had been central through-out the stormy months of 1905. In 1917 it was one of the first issues that threatened to tear apart the hastily constructed coalition of bourgeois liberals in the Provisional Government and the reformist socialist leadership of the Petrograd Soviet. And, indeed, it threatened to alienate the workers from their Soviet leaders, who did not press the issue vigorously until the workers in many plants in Petrograd and Moscow simply stopped working after eight hours. An agreement with the Provisional Government on 10 March did recognize the eight-hour day in the capital, and as the news spread, workers elsewhere pressed the demand with similar in-sistence. But the owners soon reneged, arguing that the shortened day threatened to disrupt war production. The Soviet leaders ac-cepted this rationale, and many workers seemed to do so as well, with the added compensation of double pay for overtime in many places. But the issue remained alive, especially as the justifications for continuing the war began to lose cogency in face of the repeated defeats of the Russian armies over the next few months.[14]

The motives behind the creation of the factory committees were concrete and pragmatic for the most part. The workers were in-terested primarily in maintaining their living standards and ensur-ing the security of their jobs. 'Workers control' did not mean out-right seizure and workers self-management. The Russian word for control is weaker than the English and implies inspection, check-ing, and supervision of the production process, but not its domina-tion or complete management. In the months after the February revolution, workers control was instituted for various reasons.[15]

To begin with, the workers were concerned simply to keep pro-duction going. Control was established to prevent sabotage and lockouts by the employers, and as the months went by the latter seemed ever more calculated and politically motivated. In June, the number of workers laid off due to plant closures jumped dramatic-ally. The owners claimed a shortage of fuel and raw materials, but even if this were true, the history of Russian labour relations understandably led workers to suspect a plot to destroy their move-ment. They intervened to help make sure that materials were on hand, that machines were kept up, that orders were met, that liquid capital did not suddenly evaporate, and that administrative personnel performed their tasks responsibly. When they suspected foul play or incompetence, it was quite common for workers to fine administrative and technical personnel and try to replace them with others. Besides dealing with sabotage, closures, and suspected incompetence, workers were forced to intervene to start up production in those plants that had been deserted by their staff (sometimes generals and other despised tsarist officials) during the February revolution.

The supervision of administrative and technical staff was also profoundly bound to the developing sense of dignity among Russian workers. The demand that management be polite to workers had been a leitmotiv in the protest of the past decade, especially among the younger, more literate, urban-born. In the immediate pre-war years, workers often demanded that management stop using the familiar forms of address, which were a sign of the old, humiliating feudal relationships. Women actively rebelled against the rudeness, obscenity, and sexual exploitation rampant among foremen and managers. Both men and women began to define themselves as 'persons' and 'workers', that is, as equal and/or superior (as a class) to those in authority over them. No longer would they tolerate being treated as animals, slaves, children, machines, or commodities—all common designations or self-perceptions that they now strongly resented. The factory committees of 1917 added to this new sense of dignity and afforded them a means of enforcing such demands as the abolition of personal searches and petty fines. Indeed, many of the numerous expulsions of managerial personnel occurred solely because they were not respectful enough to the workers. Though there was virtually no serious violence, such abusive overseers were often ceremoniously carted off in wheelbarrows and dumped in the river, or found themselves subject to mock arrest and designated for service at the front. In some cases staff were required to perform some manual task as part of their normal duties—an implicit, although not yet coherently articulated, attempt to begin breaking down the strict division of labour in the factory. Rage does often precede theory. But, on the whole, it does not seem to have preempted practicality. Most dismissals of higher staff occurred on a case by case basis, and often only after a 'trial' before the factory committee in which the accused could defend himself or promise to rectify his behaviour. Ninety percent of the charges brought by the workers committees on the railroads, where there were many dismissals, were regarded as just by the Provisional Government's own minister of ways and communications. Some supervisors were declared 'not guilty', and many who 'repented' their previous behaviour were permitted to stay on. Most others were later asked to return if serious technical difficulties arose. There were few, if any, complete purges, and the committees seem to have been interested mainly in establishing relations of mutual trust so that production could proceed in an orderly and dignified fashion.[16]

In addition to ensuring that production continued and that administrative personnel treated the workers respectfully, the factory committees also supervised the hiring and firing of workers themselves. Job security was a constant concern, as was draft-exempt status, and one of the workers' first acts was often to find and destroy the 'black books' management kept on them. Job security and dignity were also linked to the committees' active disciplining and even firing of workers who were disruptive or who stole from the factory. In no way did the establishment of a factory committee mean licence for workers. And, in fact, the committees were to take a more active role in disciplinary matters as conditions deteriorated.

The committees were also intended to act as trade unions in the many places where none yet existed, or where the local's ties to the central bureau made it too unresponsive to the immediate needs of the workers. They bargained on wages and demanded to see the accounts to justify increases. They organized wildcat strikes or militant sitdowns to prevent layoffs. They also bargained on conditions, and often directly intervened to change them. Indeed, some committees claimed a say over nearly every aspect of factory life. If food rations or clothing were distributed in the factory, committees often became involved. And they took an active interest in improving the cultural lives of the workers, establishing libraries and discussion groups within the factories. In this, as in other matters, their activities often overlapped with those of the neighbourhood soviets, from which they were at times indistinguishable. And how-

ever meagre their achievements may have been in the area of education, it is undeniable that the workers set up committees not only
for material survival but for cultural development as well.
Although protection of their jobs and standard of living was the
primary motivation for workers control, an underlying passion for
dignity, self-improvement and general democratization was un-
mistakable. After years of extreme managerial abuse, social exclusion, and political repression, this is hardly surprising. Even among
the more politically conservative workers in the plants and on the
state-run railways, economic democracy seemed but a natural extension of the political democratization of February.[17]

It can hardly be said, however, that the demand for workers control in the early stages of the revolution was motivated by an
ideological or practical commitment to socialism. In fact, after the
first agreements on the eight-hour day and the limited recognition
of the factory committees on 10 March, relative peace returned to
Russian industry for a few months. Most strikes were averted
through last-minute negotiations, and the committees generally
came out fairly well. Despite continuing tensions, the apparently
common interest of owners and workers in industrial peace and increased production tended to predominate. Even in some of the
most radical plants, the factory committees took as one of their
main goals the raising of productivity to ensure the provisioning of
the troops at the front—partly out of patriotism for their newly
democratized nation, partly for fear that the troops might otherwise turn counter-revolutionary, and in some cases partly because
of the incentive of special bonuses. During the period of relative
labour peace that lasted until May, the rate of private industrial investment rose sharply compared with preceding months.[18]

This tendency toward cooperation with the owners, however,
was always unstable, and tended to be disrupted both by the war's
deterioration of the economic situation and by the rising politiciza-
tion of the workers. As conditions worsened in a particular plant,
the committees took desperate measures to protect their livelihood.
Some simply forced wage increases and raised prices for their products indiscriminately. Others sold machinery to buy raw
materials, or distributed their strike and pension funds among the

workers. Committees sometimes denied each other credit. One account tells of a committee that sold fuel to another committee (both apparently *de facto* managers at that point) for four times its normal price. Many seem to have viewed themselves as new shareholders who regarded the means of production as property they were entitled to dispose of as they saw fit. Workers attending the Third Factory Committee Conference of Petrograd in September, indifferent to their fellow workers elsewhere, attempted to prevent orders from being placed with plants outside the capital. Such actions can only be understood as rather desperate attempts by individual workers or groups of workers to protect their livelihood by whatever means were immediately available. As Marc Ferro concludes, workers saw control as a means for bettering their condition, not for fundamentally changing it according to some socialist or anarchist ideal, which 'appeared in their demands only rarely or as a distant goal.'[19]

Although the motivation for the factory committees was initially defensive and pragmatic, the main goal being to guarantee effective production under normalized, albeit reformed, capitalist relations, the idea rapidly took root that workers control was the school for a system of self-management that would arise with the socialist revolution. One of the early statements to this effect came from the factory committee of the huge and militant Putilov metal works in Petrograd on 24 April, less than two weeks after its election by more than 90 per cent of the workers: 'While the workers of the particular enterprises educate themselves in self-management, they prepare themselves for the moment when private ownership of the factories will be abolished and the means of production will be transferred into the hands of the working class. This great and important goal for which the workers are striving must be kept steadfastly in mind, even if we are carrying out only small details in the meantime.'[20]

Although Bolsheviks and unaffiliated sympathizers dominated the main committee at Putilov, this linking of control to the development of socialist self-management did not derive from party doctrine. Neither Lenin nor the party had yet even declared support for workers control through the factory committees. Nor had all rank-and-file Bolsheviks waited for Lenin's April Theses to be convinced of the urgency of socialist transformation.[21] For some of the more militant workers involved in the committees, the relation between workers control and socialism must have seemed quite obvious. And as economic conditions deteriorated in the coming months, the practical tasks facing the committees made it even more so. Organized propaganda by the Bolsheviks and anarcho-syndicalists somewhat later played a significant, if not always consistent, role in this regard. But a little power over production often leads to demands for more, and under the conditions of 1917, the logic of the struggle began to unfold relentlessly in this direction.[22]

Organization and Composition

The factory committees spread rapidly during March. By the end of the month they existed in nearly every sizeable plant in Moscow and Petrograd, and were especially strong in the state-owned metallurgical works run by the Artillery and Naval Departments. In Baku, where there had been a relatively strong pre-war committee tradition, nearly every plant recreated one soon after February. Within a month, 'almost every major rail station, section and service had its workers committee.'[23] Before long they appeared in every industrial centre of European Russia, although there are no figures on exactly how many plants had committees in the early months or how extensive their functions were.

Under the pressure of continued strikes, the Petrograd Owners Association worked out an agreement with the Soviet on 10 March to permit the formation of factory committees elected by equal, secret, and universal suffrage. The agreement, however, strictly circumscribed the functions and rights of the committees:

'a) to represent the workers in a given enterprise in their relations with government or public institutions; b) to formulate opinions on questions pertaining to the socio-economic life of the workers in a given enterprise; c) to settle problems arising from interpersonal relations of workers in a given enterprise; d) to represent workers before the management in matters concerning labour-management relations .... The removal of foremen and other administrative officials without examining the case in the chamber of conciliation, and their subsequent more violent removal (by physical force) are prohibited.'[24]

Such restrictions did not accord with the actual functions of the more militant committees even in the early weeks of the revolution. The Provisional Government realized that more would have to be done if relative peace were to be maintained within the factories. In an attempt to ensure class harmony by integrating the factory committees into the existing economic and political order, the government granted them legal recognition on 23 April, simultaneously ceding a few important concessions beyond the 10 March agreement but limiting their functions to the representation of workers in disputes and to cultural and educational affairs. The law protected committee members from dismissal without an appeal to the factory arbitration commission (which was composed of equal representation of management and workers), or other proper jurisdictional negotiation. It also provided factory space for committee meetings. However, some of the most important questions were left for arbitration between the committee and management. For instance, the law did not spell out the conditions under which elected members would be released from work, nor did it set guidelines on the time and place of elections. Committee and general assembly meetings during working hours were explicitly forbidden—a severe limitation, since many workers continued to work beyond the eight-hour shift. It made no mention of the more important questions of the power of the committees in hiring and firing, or in inspection of the company's books and correspondence—areas of committee jurisdiction already approved by the 15 April conference of workers in factories under the Artillery and Naval Department. Major areas of dispute between the management and the more active committees thus remained unresolved. The latter simply ignored the new law and created their own guidelines for workers control. Workers who had been less bold took legalization and legitimation by even the bourgeois cabinet as a signal to form such committees. Government recognition, which the owners accepted only reluctantly, had backfired, fostering the spread of the committee movement without effectively restraining the more militant committees. The weapon of cooptation, always double-edged, cut in the workers' favour this time.[25]

Evidence about how the factory committees were organized is sparse. Some general statutes on organization were drawn up at the Second Conference of Factory Committees of Petrograd and Its Environs, held in August. According to these statutes, the various workers organs in the factory were: the general assembly, or gathering of the workers and white-collar employees as a whole; partial councils, representing the various departments of the factory; the factory committee; and special committees set up by the factory committee. Ten subjects for the special-control committees were listed: mediation of conflicts, wages, distribution of labour power, cultural and educational activity, deferment of military service, finance, technical questions, working conditions, food, and raw materials. The general assembly was the highest organ and had full power over the others. It could be overruled only by the Central Council of Factory Committees.[26] Half of all the workers in the enterprise had to participate in the elections for the committee to be valid. If the rate of participation fell below 50 per cent, however, a temporary committee could be elected, and the rules did not stipulate any limitations of tenure or function of such temporary committees. The number of workers on the committees was to vary with the size of the work-force. The factory committee was to be the executive organ of all the workers of the enterprise. The right of the general assembly to convene relatively frequent elections (every six months) at the initiative of the workers and the right to recall all or part of the committees at any time were designed to prevent the committees from becoming independent of the general assemblies.

These statutes arose from experience as much as from ideal theories. In reality, of course, there was great variety among the committees. Not all of them formed subcommittees for all the various realms of activity, nor did they all involve themselves in these activities, especially at first. The larger plants did seem to develop separate committees in the shops, Putilov containing forty-six such committees that kept regular contact with one another. The white-collar employees seem to have been generally organized into separate committees, and even formed their own Central Council of Elders of Employees, representing some 50,000 employees from 200 firms by May. Some groups of employees were integrated into the general assemblies of workers later in the year.

Some workers committees used the nomenclature 'council of elders,' symbolizing continuity with both the patriarchal and traditionalist village organization and the paternalistic modes of factory representation permitted under the tsar. But the general tendency was away from such older names and toward the common designation 'factory committee.'[27]

It does not seem that the committees were always constructed according to meticulous democratic procedure. Behind-the-scenes negotiations by the political parties or manoeuvring in the soviet executive committee sometimes determined the composition of the committees, and membership was sometimes put to a vote only if the parties failed to agree on their relative degree of support. In some instances delegates were named to the committee or the assembly from outside the factory itself, as in the case of the Svetlana electrical factory, where the Central Council of Petrograd Factory Committees intervened: 'It is almost exclusively women who work there. It is to be regretted that their understanding of the situation is weak, and so is the workers' sense of organization and proletarian discipline .... It has been decided to delegate a comrade from the first reserve regiment to the general assembly of women workers.'[28]

Such intervention, however, did not necessarily imply the manipulation of the workers in the plant, nor does it seem to have been generally opposed. Even in the case of Svetlana, it is unclear whether the delegate was given any special power. Although there certainly were cases in which instant recall was utilized, the relative stability of committee members suggests that it was not common.[29] While it is no doubt an exaggeration to argue that the general assemblies approved every action of the committees beforehand,[30] the contrary assertion by John Keep that 'the situation was generally one which favoured manipulation by the leadership and hindered efforts to assert control from below'[31] seems much too extreme. There may indeed have been demagoguery, but the general assemblies often asserted themselves against their elected delegates, rectifying both substantive positions and formal procedures. Indeed, the factory committees were probably the most democratically responsive organs the Russian workers ever had.

Skilled male workers dominated the committees almost everywhere, for many reasons. First of all, the skilled workers knew much more about how the plant actually ran, a competence upon which any effective control over management would have to rely. With knowledge came the confidence that they could indeed run the factories if need be—even better than their bosses, some felt. Literacy also tended to be greater among the skilled than the less skilled, especially recent peasant recruits and women. And literacy was essential if the committees were to negotiate with management, check on their accounting procedures, and supervise overall operations. The cultural and educational functions the workers expected of their committees also required at least basic literacy. Moreover, skilled workers had the longest and most continuous political traditions, including, for many, experience dating back to 1905, and for a smaller core, membership in one or another branch of the Social Democratic Workers Party, the smaller anarcho-syndicalist groups, or even the Socialist Revolutionary Party. Organizational activity, within and beyond the factory gates, was nothing new for many of them. Their knowledge, skill, and organizational traditions were resources upon which the committees could draw in the workers struggle to control production. Finally, many of the skilled workers (especially in metals and machinery) were impelled to activity in response to the new forms of technology and labour control (for example, electric and pneumatic lathes, scientific management, piece rates) that had been increasingly introduced during the war.[32]

The relation between these skilled male workers and the rest of the work-force, however, was hardly unproblematic and never had been. In the decades before the war, peasants flowed to and from the factories in tempo with the cyclical spurts of Russian industrialization. In the four-year period of rapid expansion before the war, the industrial work-force grew by some 30 per cent, and in Petrograd and the metal industry the increase was closer to 50 per cent. This expansion and influx continued during the war. Russian industry became even more highly concentrated. Four-fifths of Petrograd's industrial work-force, which doubled during the war, were concentrated in factories of more than 500 workers. Metals, mining, and chemicals, in particular, expanded enormously throughout the country. Ties to the villages had grown distinctly weaker after the turn of the century, but even in 1917 peasant themes pervaded the culture of recently proletarianized workers, and even some of the more settled and hereditary urban work-force. The latter, however, tended to view the *chernorabochie* (black workers) as backward-looking and superstitious, passive and fatalistic, crude and ignorant, and prone to drunkenness and wife-beating. Such perceptions contrasted with their own evolving self-consciousness as active, cultured, and dignified. These dichoto-mies, while they had a definite basis in reality, proved far too simplistic, as women and less skilled peasant recruits proved time and again, especially just before the war and at crucial junctures in 1917 (most notably February and July). As Reginald Zelnik has argued, the consciousness of recent peasant recruits must be understood as 'a uniquely volatile and dynamic *mixed* con-sciousness that combined a peasant resentment against the vestiges of Russian feudalism (i.e. serfdom) with a proletarian resentment against capitalist exploitation in the factories—the proportions, of course, varying with different segments of the labour force and at different points in the business cycle.'[33] In the pre-war years and after the upswing in militancy after 1915, a revolutionary working-class consciousness was being forged in a process of struggle that did not wait for full certification of hereditary proletarian status. And the peculiar combination of peasant and worker rebellion at times led the recently proletarianized to even more radical visions than their more urbanized counterparts. Politically, the activities of these different sectors were not always in sync, and the more skilled proletarian veterans often complained about peasant-worker and feminine indiscipline during strikes and demonstrations. In periods of revolutionary upsurge, however, the relationship tended to be more complementary than conflictual, especially in the most mili-tant sectors, where the distinctive combination of elements was most pronounced.

Within the representative organs in the factory, however, there were bound to be conflicts. On questions of wages, discipline, and layoffs, there were often differences among the various sectors. The less skilled pressed militantly for policies that would reduce the wage gap between categories, which had widened during the war (this was a major concern of their conferences in 1917), and heated debates on this question often erupted in the general assemblies. The democratic structure of committees, however, seems to have enabled the less skilled to narrow the gap considerably, even though the committees themselves were mainly composed of skilled workers.[34] The committees took an active role in worker discipline, especially as they assumed more responsibility for production in general, and conflict with the less skilled workers seems to have been greater than with the skilled. This is hardly surprising, given the relative absence of an urban industrial culture, the inevitable persistence of very different peasant work rhythms and habits, and the peasant's renowned *buntarstvo*, or rebelliousness against all forms of authority. The less skilled and more recently proletarianized seem to have been more impulsive in demanding the dismissal of technical and administrative personnel, for instance, and this sometimes led to conflicts with the factory committees. Nor did the economic deterioration of the latter part of 1917 ease the problem of discipline. And the relations between the skilled committeemen and the less skilled were particularly difficult when layoffs were involved. Even before October, the committees played a role in deciding who would be dismissed, and almost invariably it was the less skilled who were first to go. As soldiers began to return from the front, it was often argued that women, who now constituted 43 per cent of the industrial work-force, up from 23 per cent before the war, should be dismissed first. Such patriarchal patterns had deep roots in Russian culture, and were often reinforced by the male-dominated revolutionary organizations.[35] Women themselves, however, were not always ready to press for equal pay, and it is unclear how much they resisted relinquishing their jobs to the returning men, often their own husbands. They did make their voices heard in general-assembly meetings, but it is difficult to tell whether the democratic structures of the factory committees, dominated as they were by skilled male workers, helped to reverse the tendency of women to be less organizationally active than their male counterparts—a tendency that was itself less pronounced where the women were more highly skilled.

Workers control was thus a complex and contradictory process. Skilled male workers dominated the factory committees, largely as a result of their own privileged position within the inherited industrial division of labour and within Russian political and cultural life relative to other workers. The less skilled and women-workers seem, on the whole, to have accepted the leading position of the skilled men within the factory committees, since it was the latter who possessed the very scarce resources of skill, literacy, confidence, and organizational experience that were crucial if the goals of workers control were to be secured. That acceptance was pragmatic, and fraught with conflict over some of the most basic questions facing the workers. While the skilled men in the committees at times pursued their own narrow goals at the expense of other workers, the trend in 1917 was not towards narrow corporatism. Many of the leading skilled militants themselves pressed for a reduction of wage differentials. Such egalitarianism partly reflected historical conditions that had moderated past differences and restricted the development of a labour aristocracy.[36] But it was also true that hereditary working-class culture and ideology contained profoundly egalitarian and universalistic elements. Skilled workers were internationalist, and there were few ethnic antagonisms in the workers movement. The Bolshevik Party, whose most solid core was made up of skilled male workers, consistently pushed for a narrowing of differentials throughout 1917. And within the working class as a whole, it was these workers who had the most profoundly democratic consciousness in regard to the legitimate source of authority.[37] Such relative egalitarianism was no doubt encouraged by continuous pressure from the less privileged workers, as well as by a political situation that became increasingly open to working-class intervention and militant cooperation by workers and peasants-in-uniform, skilled and unskilled, male and female. But the consistently democratic and universalistic organizational structures that emerged in the factories in the wake of the February revolution played an important and relatively autonomous role in determining the complex inter-relationships among workers and in fostering an egalitarian dynamic.[38]

Control and Coordination

The factory committees came under attack from the employers from the very outset. Even the most minimal forms of control were resented. Some managerial staffs even abandoned their plants at the inception of a committee, though the vast majority stayed on and attempted to subvert workers control however they could. At first they opposed the legalization of the committees but later used the April law to restrict their functions. Committee members were harassed to make them hold their meetings after work, and those elected to higher coordinating organizations, or who served on special delegations away from the factory, were not infrequently refused pay and threatened with the loss of their military deferments. Eventually the owners tried to develop a concerted policy to prevent permanent workers representation and intervention in production, and even threatened to fine those in their ranks who yielded to such demands. The committees, for their part, were not always successful in resisting the manoeuvres of management. At the Skorokhod shoe factory, for instance, the committee was unable to extend its supervision over accounting, since no one would explain the system in use. In other cases, the owners were able to withdraw large accounts of liquid capital abroad despite the workers financial control commissions, or to ship goods, fuel, and raw materials without the prior approval of the committees. The committees seem to have been more successful in matters of wages, working conditions, and control over hiring and firing.[39]

These conflicts, and the committees' response to them, produced a heterogeneous movement. In a few plants, factory committees tried to continue production on their own. In others, management and councils barely coexisted. In still others, compromises were worked out, lines of authority were more clearly drawn, and sometimes workers received production bonuses, tying them more firmly to the capitalist management. On the whole, however, the antagonistic coexistence of the owners and factory committees eventually began to contribute to economic collapse, especially given the already existing shortage of fuel and raw materials. One response to this situation by the local committees—a necessary one if the workers-control movement was to protect and extend its gains—was to attempt to coordinate the various factory councils into local, regional, and national federations. An analysis of these efforts reveals some of the strengths and weaknesses of the movement for workers control in 1917.

As Paul Avrich has noted, 'almost from the moment of their inception the Petrograd factory committees sought to establish an interfactory organization.'[40] On 13 March factory-committee representatives from the twelve largest metal works of the Artillery Department, employing some 100,000 workers, met in Petrograd to demand an eight-hour day and government recognition of workers control. It seems, however, that no coordinating organ was set up at this time. A month later, on 15 April, a similar conference in Petrograd drafted a set of prototypical rules and functions for factory committees. These went beyond the March statements and provoked the government's response of legalization and attempted cooptation. Although the rules stated that the factory committees were to be consultative until socialization of the economy could be achieved, they were nonetheless quite bold in demanding representation in all areas of production, examination of all official documents, and the right to dismiss members of the administration who could not guarantee 'normal relations with the workers'. The conference also made plans to form a Chief Centre to coordinate the factory committees of the state sector.

A conference in Moscow on 8–9 April was much more moderate in its call to strengthen factory committees, without significant control functions. Similar conferences in the provinces also tended at first to be more moderate than in Petrograd. Many, however, set up coordinating centres and established links with the major cities, and some even attempted to set up mutual-aid organizations with the peasants. Committees in some areas, for instance, took the initiative to organize the production of nails out of scrap metal to exchange with the peasants, and the Bolsheviks, in line with their anti-war policy, urged a general reconversion to peacetime production (of farm implements for example). A conference of committees held in Kharkov on 29 May was even more radical than some of the Petrograd conferences. One delegate called for a national organ independent of the trade unions. Resolutions were passed stating that the factory committees should become organs of the revolution. And a number of non-Bolshevik delegates, perhaps under the influence of anarchists in that city's factories, even proposed that the committees should seize the factories outright and manage production themselves.[41]

The first major steps toward general coordination of the factory-committee movement were taken in Petrograd. Rank-and-file committee members from some of the larger metal works—mostly Bolsheviks acting, as far as is known, without directives from higher party organs—began to plan for a city-wide conference in April. The Putilov factory committee sent out a general call on 29 April. The organizational bureau that prepared the conference was composed of four Bolsheviks, one Left SR and a Menshevik-Internationalist who later joined the Bolshevik party. The delegates who assembled for the First Conference of Factory Committees of Petrograd and Its Environs from 30 May to 5 June represented 367 committees and 337,464 workers, some 80 per cent of the 400,000 workers of Petrograd. Most of the delegates were from the larger plants and particularly those concerned with war production, though more than one-fourth were from smaller plants in chemicals, leather, and printing. The major debate centred on the issue of state control by the Provisional Government (supported by the Mensheviks) versus workers control through institutions composed primarily of workers (supported by the Bolsheviks and Anarcho-Syndicalists). The Bolsheviks, whose influence on the factory committees had grown rapidly in the preceding weeks due to their newly espoused support for workers control, won every major vote by resounding majorities. The resolutions called for 'the complete regulation of production and distribution of goods by the workers' (that is, by organs in which at least two-thirds of the seats were held by workers), the opening of all commercial books, the formation of a workers militia, universal labour duty, an end to the war, and transfer of political power to the soviets.[42]

One of the major achievements of the Conference, however, was the formation of a Central Council of Factory Committees for the city of Petrograd. The Mensheviks, who opposed the formation of a factory-committee centre independent of the Central Council of Trade Unions, voted against the proposal, as did the Anarcho-Syndicalists, who feared the overcentralization of the movement. But the conference approved the proposal and elected nineteen Bolsheviks, two Mensheviks, two SRs, one Interdistricter (Trotsky's group), and one Anarcho-Syndicalist to the twenty-five member council. Later in the month, the Organization Bureau of the state artillery enterprises was merged with the Central Council. The functions of the Council were to include directing the acquisition of fuel, raw materials, machinery, and markets; the distribution of financial and technical information; and the establishment of a committee to aid the peasants (mostly by providing farm implements). Members of the Central Council, which was in more or less permanent session, also participated in various government boards and state agencies concerned with labour, defence, and supply, although usually only to demand two-thirds representation for itself.

The formation of the Central Council of Factory Committees contributed dramatically to the coordination of the committee movement, not only in Petrograd but throughout the country. As Roger Pethybridge has noted, 'in many of the large Petrograd enterprises the committees worked out carefully how their productive capacity could be geared to the restricted supplies of coal, and reported their findings to the Central Council of Factory Committees so that it could coordinate fuel rationing in the city and prevent the closure of some plants.'[43] The Central Council formed an engineers' section to dispense technical information to those committees requiring assistance. It helped arrange for the transfer of funds from one enterprise to another in order to prevent shutdowns. Thus, despite the often strong factory identification of workers, as, for instance, 'Putilovtsy' or 'Treugolniki', both the Putilov and Treugolnik factory committees, in collaboration with the Central Council, provided money and materials to keep the Brenner plant open.[44] The Council also began active registration procedures to gauge the condition of equipment, the number of workers, stocks of fuel and raw materials, the quantity of finished products, and the type of military production—the latter with a view to as smooth and rapid a reconversion to peacetime production as possible. Similar coordinating centres were formed within the city's districts, and activists moved continuously between factories arranging for mutual assistance.

The Central Council of Petrograd also played an important national role. It dispensed delegates and information to numerous cities, and similar centres began to develop relatively quickly, in addition to some that already existed. By the end of June there were at least twenty-five city and district factory-committee centres.[45] By October, at least sixty-five industrial centres had some kind of coordinating council, and more than one hundred conferences had met to discuss the common problems facing the committees. The councils performed numerous functions related to production and prevention of closure, and some set up departments that began organizing exchange of farm equipment with the peasantry and coordinating food supplies. The Central Council of Petrograd received constant requests for assistance from the provinces and acted as a *de facto* national centre while it prepared for a nation-wide conference in October. At the first All-Russian Conference of Factory Committees, which met in Petrograd shortly before the seizure of power, representatives from forty-nine industrial centres were on hand. The conference voted to set up an All-Russian Central Council, and carefully apportioned representation for the various industrial regions. But the demands of the armed struggle intervened, and the delegates rushed back to their localities without having elected the All-Russian Council.

The coordination of the activities of the factory committees had serious deficiencies, however, in view of both the daunting tasks confronting the workers movement in the area of production and the quickening pace of the revolution after the initial period of relative political peace. The Central Council of Petrograd Factory Committees frequently complained of a lack of resources with which to meet all the demands made upon it. The local committees did not send enough personnel, Central Council member Skrypnik complained at the second city-wide conference in August. And the fewer the factory delegates who came to conferences and served on the Central Council, the more these positions were open to nomination from other organizations, such as the parties, unions, and soviets.[46] The dues promised at the First Conference had been forthcoming from only about one-fifth of the committees represented, and thus the Conference decided overwhelmingly to impose a 1–4 per cent deduction on wages. Antipov complained that many workers still did not know that the Central Council existed. A Council report in early October noted that only seven of the eleven district (*raion*) councils in the city were operating effectively and keeping contact with the Central Council, which began to publish its own journal, *Novyi Put'*, only on 15 October. Many other cities, including Moscow, lacked city-wide coordination altogether, though some of the centres that did exist grouped together the more important factories in the area. Their effectiveness is difficult to assess. Instances of local parochialism and 'shopism' were quite numerous. And on the national rail network, the Central Line Committees constantly complained of occupational parochialism among the various services and districts, and had an extremely difficult time enforcing decisions of the line congresses and maintaining overall coordination.[47]

Such evidence, however, should not be taken to imply that particularism and economic fragmentation were inherent or inevitably destructive traits of the movement for workers control.[48] We should not ignore or belittle the very impressive degree of coordination and solidarity achieved in the short and turbulent months between the February and October revolutions, nor the enormous attention given the question by committee militants. As October approached, the committees were coordinating their activities at an accelerated pace and on an ever broadening scale. But more important, we should not describe as *inherent* features of a movement that was shaped by a complex set of inter-relationships within Russian society and the revolutionary process itself. The movement for workers control in 1917 drew upon a very weak organizational base in its attempt to effect coordination. The trade unions were not only relatively disorganized in the early months after February, but were for the most part hostile to workers control. Trade-union activists, not to mention top-level officials, often refused to support the committees' attempts at coordination, thus further splintering the already scarce organizational resources available to the workers. The committees were able to draw upon the networks and resources of the Bolshevik party, and this undoubtedly aided the coordination of the movement. The great majority of factory-committee centres were initiated by local Bolshevik militants, many of whom were in contact with factory-committee leaders in Petrograd, or local party committees in the more important industrial centres. But the Bolshevik party was not only ideologically inconsistent about the role of workers control in the revolutionary process, but was also relatively disorganized itself, particularly at the inter-city, provincial, and national levels. That its organizational resources proved adequate to the seizure of power should not blind us to the very serious problems that plagued the party in many respects. Some of these organizational conflicts overlapped with trade-union/factory-committee divisions. Political differences also impeded factory-committee coordination, and criss-crossed other lines of conflict. Where Mensheviks and SRs predominated in local soviets or in the factory committees themselves, they often resisted the formation of separate coordinating councils for the committees. This is one reason why no such centre was formed in Moscow, though there were a number of more localized councils within and around the city. Bolshevik predominance on many of the coordinating councils that did exist in turn kept away less radical activists, or those suspicious of Bolshevik intentions, as Bolsheviks on the Petrograd Central Council themselves admitted.[49]

These organizational and political problems were compounded by the mounting disintegration of the communication and transportation networks, always insufficient in this country of such vast size and widely scattered industrial centres, and now subject to the added strains of war, revolution, and political animosity among workers. Under such conditions it became increasingly difficult to convene delegates from dispersed locales, or for delegates elected to coordinating centres to maintain close contacts with their consituents. The symbiotic dynamic of fragmentation and bureaucratization was henceforth in force. Where industry was more concentrated geographically, as in Petrograd, committees could be more successful in rapidly developing coordination with their own resources. The more dispersed, variegated, and smaller character of Moscow industry contributed to coordination difficulties. Moreover, a basic aspect of the revolutionary process must not be forgotten, namely, that as long as political power remained in the hands of the Provisional Government and its ministries, and production continued under the impetus of private profit, the costs of coordination through independent factory-committee centres could be as real as the benefits were uncertain. Short-term sacrifices, especially under the economic conditions of 1917, which provided such small margin for the misdirection of material and human resources, were that much more difficult to rationalize since the long-term results were so unsure. Until these issues of political and economic power were resolved, there would be a powerful impetus for committees and general assemblies simply to optimize their own factories' economic situation, and for individual workers to do the same. That there was so much effort at coordination in 1917 testifies both to the contradictory demands of economic survivaland to an emerging consciousness of the requirements of reconstruction on new foundations.

2

Trade Unions, Parties and Workers Control

Although the factory committees arose spontaneously in the early days of the revolution, their fate was soon linked to that of the other major labour organizations existing before February: the trade unions and political parties. These too developed rapidly once the economic and political struggle of the working class received full legal sanction for the first time in more than a decade. Both had a longer and more continuous, albeit disrupted, history. Although neither the unions nor the parties had ever had much to say about workers control in the past, the emergence of the committees made a response to this issue requisite. And their responses, conditioned by their own organizational structures and by their conceptions of the nature of the revolution, had an enormous impact on the fate of the movement to establish a society based on democratic control of the means of production by the workers.

Trade Unions and Factory Committees

Before 1905 trade unions were outlawed and severely repressed by the Russian autocracy. The massive strikes of that year, some of which bordered on outright insurrection, along with the middle-class reform movement, forced the government to legalize unions and to sanction the legitimacy of economic strikes. But the unions had little chance to develop into stable organizations. In the heated struggles of 1905 they had been overshadowed by the soviets, in both the political and economic spheres. In the fifteen months of legalization they enjoyed after the March 1906 decree, they grew exceedingly rapidly. At least seventy-one unions were formed in Petrograd, another sixty-eight in Moscow. Nationally there were as many as eight hundred. But by the time of Stolypin's coup in June 1907, only a tiny fraction of the working class had been enlisted, perhaps 6 per cent of Petrograd's workers, 16 per cent of Moscow's. Between 1907 and 1911, police repression and economic recession decimated the unions. They quickly revived in the immediate pre-war period under the impetus of renewed industrial expansion, intense militancy, and occasionally tolerant government policies, which provided opportunities for organization while excluding significant chances for material advancement.[1] Despite renewed rapid growth, however, once again only a small percentage of the workers (indeed far less than in 1906–1907) actually joined unions before wartime repression smashed most organizations once again. During the war, discontent was channelled into the War Industries Committees, or expressed itself in the sick fund organizations that provided perhaps the closest links between underground party and union militants and the rank and file.[2]

Despite considerable intermittent potential for union organization, therefore, the unions were unable to develop stable structures and a vibrant engagement in working-class life and struggle. A small but important core of working-class leaders with union experience had emerged, and many would play significant roles in the revolutions of 1917. The vast majority of these militants were, like the activists of the factory committees, skilled, male, and usually urban-born as well. But organizational networks were extremely thin or non-existent for most of the pre-revolutionary period. Cultural and recreational activities for workers were more likely to be organized by government bureaucrats and liberal philanthropists than class-conscious union militants. And, as Isaac Deutscher has noted, 'in suppressing trade unionism, tsardom unwittingly put a premium on revolutionary political organization'.[3] Militants most willing to take the risk of illegal activity were drawn to the parties. And rank-and-file workers, including those who became involved in unions, came to look to the parties for tutelage in both political and economic struggles. The Mensheviks recognized the need for political guidance, but hoped to build a relationship on the German model, which excluded outright party domination. The Bolsheviks, however, despite their changing attitudes to work in mass organizations, never wavered from a theoretical position that strictly subordinated the unions to party control. On the eve of the February revolution, however, neither could fail to recognize that the locus of the organized struggle of the working class lay within the parties and not the unions.

The overthrow of the tsar brought the full legalization of the unions, and they began to grow at a phenomenal rate. By May, perhaps one and a half million workers had been enlisted in some two thousand unions, and by October the membership figure reached at least two million, or more than 50 per cent of the workforce in industry, transport, and mining.[4] Such growth, however, was quite loose and disorderly. The early months saw myriad jurisdictional disputes, and craft organization flourished despite the efforts of Bolsheviks and Mensheviks alike. In the Petrograd metal industry alone there were twenty-four independent unions. At the First All-Russian Conference of Trade Unions in June, one delegate complained frankly that many unions were in a state of 'extreme disorder and anarchy', and that many members even in Petrograd and Moscow did not understand their purpose.[5] Political conflicts often aggravated the disorder and fragmentation, as was the case on the rails. And, though much progress towards consolidation and industrial organization was made over the course of the year, Marc Ferro's description of the unions as a 'veritable tower of Babel' is hardly an exaggeration.[6] In addition to the confusion in the union movement, many of those enrolled were simply paper members who did not even pay dues, let alone participate in union activities. And the central bureaux had even less connection with the rank and file. Many were phantom organizations performing few if any real functions. Others were formed on the morrow of February by small coteries from underground days, which then remained dominant regardless of the orientation of their constituent unions. On the whole, organizational statutes were democratic. Some, however, contained clauses conducive to party domination, as in Petrograd, where the central bureau was pledged 'to ensure concerted action with ... the political party of the proletariat.'[7] The Menshevik argument for 'parties' in the plural had been rejected, an ominous sign for the union movement.

The organization of the unions was not only top-heavy and bureaucratically embrangled, but also suffered from many of the deficiencies that plagued the factory committees. There were constant complaints of lack of dues, administrative experience, personnel, and office space. There were even cases of theft. The All-Russian Central Council of Trade Unions, formed in June, lacked permanent quarters and was unable to convene full plenary meetings due to transport difficulties. Its journal appeared only twice before October. In August the Moscow central bureau appointed a committee of five to find permanent premises, and in December, the task still not accomplished, a new committee, this time with fifteen members, was named. The support of the parties and soviets, and the existence of prior networks of trade-union activists, however thin and fragmented, enabled the unions to convene a nationwide conference in June. But a full constituent national congress was able to meet only in January of the following year.[8]

The weakness of the unions was exacerbated by the ability of the factory committees to coalesce much more quickly and to respond directly to local grievances. In the first months of the revolution, workers were hardly wont to wait for the outcome of the often protracted negotiations between employers and unions. In Petrograd, for instance, the unified union of metal workers was able to reach agreement with the Association of Manufacturers only in mid-August. The factory committees were able to take more direct action, and even then many strikes occurred without their direction. The unions competed more successfully with the committees where artisans predominated, where industry was more dispersed and shops smaller. And their position relative to the committees in economic struggles seems to have improved during the year. Conflict-resolution commissions were established, though they had to compete with similar commissions established earlier by the soviets, and sometimes even by the factory committees. But economic deterioration and political polarization increasingly undermined the basis for industrial legality, and brought struggles for control to the forefront. Not only did conciliation committees increasingly lose their relevance, but even the strike as a weapon of struggle declined in significance as October approached.[9]

The unions considered the existence of independent factory committees as the organizer of the local work-forces and leader of militant actions or negotiations anathema. The only rationale for the committees was as local cells of the unions. The role of the committees should be to check on the fulfilment of agreements negotiated by the unions, not to make such agreements independently. Even less was it to take direct action to force changes at the work place. The proper channels were to be respected, and all workers were to act under the aegis of union organization. To help ensure this, factory-committee elections were to be conducted by the unions. Independent coordinating councils of factory committees, of course, were viewed as illegitimate rivals of the unions' central bureaux.

The great majority of factory committees seem to have recognized the need for close cooperation with the unions—in principle. The general sentiment among the committees was not one of hostility toward trade-union organization. Like the unions, most committees nourished hopes for unified labour organizations, and in fact required their members to join the relevant trade unions. Indeed, the existence of committees no doubt accelerated the development of industrial forms of organization in the unions. Very few committee activists expressed principled hostility to trade unions as such, and a good number went so far as to agree that the committees should be incorporated into the unions on the latter's terms. The Moscow committees were a case in point. In July 1917 their city-wide conference acknowledged the right of the unions to supervise committee elections. Whether the unions were actually able to perform this role is unclear, though it seems that in cases of dispute over policy, the committees were elected and re-elected much as they had been all along. Nor did the committees in Moscow form a city-wide centre.[10] Even in Petrograd, the more militant committee movement called for the closest collaboration with the unions, though it rejected the complete subordination sought by the trade-union central bureau, and maintained an independent coordinating centre. In practice, however, most committees jealously guarded their autonomy of action and refused to be disciplined by the unions, especially on issues of control. The relations between them varied greatly, and the dynamic interaction was extremely complex. As the unions, under pressure from the committees, increasingly developed industrial structures and recognized control issues, a greater basis for cooperation emerged. But as the economic situation deteriorated, and extensive controls through direct action seemed necessary to the local committees, cooperation became more difficult, or more cumbersome trade-union procedures simply proved inadequate. A similar dynamic was at work at the higher levels of the committee and union movements, and would become more pronounced after October.[11]

Political differences in the workers movement also partly determined the relation between factory committees and unions. In the early weeks of the revolution Mensheviks dominated the higher levels of most union organizations. Because of their relative moderation during the war and their leadership in the War Industries Committees, their party had remained more nearly intact. The Bolsheviks, on the other hand, were subject to severe police repression and refused to collaborate in efforts to increase war production. Their organizations had been decimated as a result. A small underground apparatus existed on the eve of the February revolution, but many of the major leaders were in exile. Those still in Russia had decided to concentrate their activity in the early weeks on rebuilding the party apparatus. When they participated in the formation and re-activation of the unions, they often did so in a rather heavy-handed and tactless manner, substituting abstract polemics for real organizational work, as was admitted by Tomsky, a leading Bolshevik trade unionist and future chairman of the All-Russian Central Council of Trade Unions. Hence, in the early months of the revolution, the trade unions, with some exceptions, were under Menshevik leadership. Organizational manoeuvres in preparation for the Third All-Russian Trade Union Conference in June, when the political leadership of many of the unions had already begun to change, prolonged Menshevik dominance and assured them a majority in the All-Russian Central Council of Trade Unions formed at the conference. Factory committees, on the other hand, reflected the radicalization of the rank and file much more closely. They were the first major workers organs to come over to the Bolshevik party on a mass scale. Once they did, they were not about to allow themselves to be subordinated to moderate trade-union officials.[12]

Mensheviks and State Control

The Mensheviks considered the February revolution a bourgeois revolution ushering in a period of prolonged capitalist economic development and liberal democracy. While the workers had played an important role in the upheaval, a result of the weakness of the bourgeoisie, they were not to become the dominant class. Socialism could come to Russia only after further capitalist development had created an adequate industrial basis, giving rise to a proletariat that was not only the major class in society, but also possessed the political and technical competence to assume control over the state and the economy. Until then, the Mensheviks held, the working class was to struggle to strengthen bourgeois democracy, and specifically to fight for a Constituent Assembly that would permanently establish labour's freedom to organize to improve its economic conditions and to compete freely in the political arena for eventual hegemony. In the absence of a bilateral democratic and non-annexationist peace, this perspective also implied support for the Western democracies against the Central Powers, since only the victory of the former could guarantee the international political conditions for the eventual victory of democratic socialism. The major economic tasks of the working class therefore were: to build industrial trade unions as permanent legal organizations representing the entire working class; while these would eventually struggle to improve the conditions of labour, they were first to focus on raising productivity, because of the economic crisis and the need to prosecute the war; and to establish state control over industry.

In pursuing the latter objective, the Mensheviks and their SR allies in the Petrograd Soviet pressured the Provisional Government to establish broad state controls over the economy. This policy was endorsed against considerable opposition from most of the owners, who wanted the Provisional Government to do all it could to increase production, but nonetheless resisted controls in their own industries. In May the government announced the formation of an Economic Advisory Council and a Supreme Economic Committee. These were to be composed of representatives from the employers associations and the Provisional Government on the one side and from the trade unions, soviets, and cooperatives on the other, in a proportion of approximately three-to-one in favour of the former. The government's delay in implementing these decisions and the continued obstruction of the owners, however, doomed them to relative ineffectiveness in stemming the disorganization of the economy.[13]

Given their conception of the revolution, the Mensheviks argued vigorously against workers control and an independent movement of factory committees. At the First Conference of Petrograd Factory Committees, the Menshevik Minister of Labour Skobelev put his party's case: 'the regulation and control of industry is not a matter for a particular class. It is the task for the state. Upon the individual class, especially the working class, lies the responsibility for helping the state in its organizational work.'[14] The entire democratic bloc, Skobelev said, must participate in economic control. The Menshevik Dalin expressed a similar view: 'The factory committees must see only that production continues but they should not take production and the factories into their own hands...If the owner discards the enterprise, it must pass not into the hands of the workers but to the jurisdiction of the city or central government.'[15]

At the Third All-Russian Conference of Trade Unions in June these arguments were repeated more ardently. Factory committees must become local cells of the trade unions and their elections should be supervised by the latter. The committees' primary role is to enforce labour legislation and collective agreements negotiated by the unions. Under no conditions were the committees to assume control functions, for that could only lead to further economic disorganization, since committee control implied the dominance of parochial interests over the interests of the democracy as a whole. The unions and the committees could effectively defend the interests of the working class only if they shunned control functions.[16]

Anarcho-Syndicalists and Workers Control

The anarcho-syndicalists exerted significant influence among the workers and within the factory-committee movement in 1917. They were the most consistent proponents of the committees, and the

Bolshevik participation was to some extent a response to the rising influence of anarchism among workers in the early months of the revolution. The anarcho-syndicalists saw the existing trade unions as bankrupt bureaucratic forms designed to harmonize class interests and suppress the self-activity of the masses. Their whole history had conditioned them to party domination. The committees, on the other hand, were 'the very best form of workers organization that has ever appeared...the cells of the future socialist society.'[17] These cells, the anarchists maintained, should be fully developed in the current period, so that at the moment of the revolution they could begin to assume full control functions. Many anarcho-syndicalists argued for the immediate expropriation of all the large productive and financial establishments. Others, such as Grigorii Maksimov, however, argued that the workers were not technically and administratively competent to run industry on their own. But this did not justify a prolonged transition period during which workers control would be limited to the functions of mere checking and accounting, as Lenin's schema seemed to maintain. Rather, Maksimov and the largest group around *Golos Truda* in Petrograd called for total workers control, meaning genuine control over hiring and firing, work rules, hours and wages, and the very process of production itself. Such active control would help train the workers, and hasten the day when complete expropriation and self-management could be achieved.[18]

While the anarcho-syndicalists were relatively clear about workers control at the plant level, their conceptions of how to coordinate local workers organs were quite vague. They were firmly opposed to a statist revolution and a top-down centralized system of workers control. At the First Conference of Petrograd Factory Committees they argued against the formation of a central council, fearing that it would stifle local initiative, although two prominent anarcho-syndicalists, Maksimov and Bill Shatov, became members after it was formed. In September, A. Grachev elaborated a schema in *Golos Truda* which began from the premise that, in a complex industrial society, the social fabric was one and indivisible and that all factory committees and agricultural communes had to be closely interconnected.[19] But neither Grachev nor other anarcho-syndicalists ever clearly specified the institutional arrangements for this overall coordination. They offered merely a glib dismissal of the argument that the factory committees might pursue particularistic interests. They talked in general terms of a free federation of autonomous communes, but offered no specific conceptions as to how conflicting local interests could be mediated, how inequalities among communes and committees could be overcome, how nationwide planning and coordination could be achieved. Their conceptions of local and regional coordination were always vague, their arguments for complete decentralization always voluble.

In their support for the committees and in their general radicalism, the anarchists had a considerable impact on the workers movement. Tomsky, for instance, warned the Bolshevik Party that 'by fencing ourselves off from the anarchists, we may fence ourselves off from the masses.'[20] Their influence was significant among the bakers, river transport workers, the Donetz miners, the food industry workers, postal and telegraph workers, and to a lesser extent the metal and textile workers, printers and railwaymen. Geographically, their largest concentration was in the militant working-class district of Vyborg in Petrograd and among the sailors and workers of Kronstadt. But the weakness of their organizations and the predominance in the early months of the anarcho-communists, who were more concerned with random expropriations than with strengthening the factory-committee movement, prevented the anarchists from becoming even more influential. The anarcho-syndicalists, who condemned the terrorism and expropriations of the anarcho-communists, reached the peak of their strength only after the arrival from exile of many of their leading thinkers. *Golos Truda*, the first anarcho-syndicalist paper, did not appear in Petrograd until August. By that time the factory-committee movement in Petrograd stood solidly behind the Bolsheviks, who almost completely dominated the city's only factory-committee central organ.[21]

Bolsheviks and Workers Control

The Bolsheviks' relationship to the workers-control movement was much more complex than that of the anarcho-syndicalists or

Mensheviks. The latter, in accordance with the Marxist orthodoxy of the time, had sketched out a relatively neat conception of capitalist development and revolutionary stages. This schema quite unambiguously delimited the role of workers control at the point of production during the developmental stage through which Russian society was said to be passing. The anarcho-syndicalists, on the other hand, took an unambiguously revolutionary stand, expressing principled hostility to the trade unions and characteristically avoiding the problem of coordination. The Bolsheviks had no such neat schema. The party was confused and divided about the significance of the February revolution. Many Bolsheviks, like the Mensheviks, foresaw a relatively prolonged period of capitalist development in the wake of the fall of the tsar. Others believed that it was time to put the socialist revolution on the agenda. With Lenin's return to Russia in April, the left-wing position prevailed, though not without considerable struggle. Even then, serious contradictions and ambiguities remained on crucial matters of theory and practice. One of these was workers control.

Although Lenin called for the beginning of the second, socialist stage of the revolution when he arrived in Russia, he did not believe that socialism could be achieved in Russia without an intervening transitional period. The revolution for which he called would transfer political power to the proletariat and peasantry. It would be a 'revolutionary democratic dictatorship of the proletariat and the peasantry', constituted through popularly elected soviets. In the economic sphere, Lenin argued in his April Theses, 'it is not our immediate task to "introduce" socialism, but only to bring social production and distribution of products at once under the *control* of the Soviets of Workers' Deputies.'[22] Monopoly capitalism in its imperialistic stage had created the basis for socialism on a world scale: the concentration of production, large-scale banking institutions, the corresponding concentration of the working class. It likewise created the necessity for socialist revolution by producing inevitable wars and misery for the vast majority of people. Capitalism, however, had not developed evenly on a world scale. In Russia, the concentration of industry and the proletariat was very pronounced, while the concentration in agriculture and its technical base lagged far behind. These developments explained how revolution could begin in the 'weakest link' of the world capitalist system.

But socialism could not be completely established in Russia without the ultimate victory of the revolutionary forces in Europe and the support of the poorest strata of the peasants in Russia itself. Russia would have to pass through a transitional period. After his return, Lenin began to define the nature of this transition period with greater precision. Under the influence of the writings of Mikhail Lur'e (Larin) on the wartime state-regulated German economy, Lenin began to conceive of the transition as 'state monopoly capitalism under the dictatorship of the proletariat'. This formula suggested that the relations of production would, with certain exceptions, remain basically unchanged (and therefore capitalist), but political power would be in the hands of the revolutionary proletariat, which would regulate production and distribution for the overall needs of society and would create the basis for subsequent full socialization.[23]

Where did workers control fit into this schema of state monopoly capitalism under the dictatorship of the proletariat? Lenin's pre-1917 writings contain scarcely a reference to workers control or self-management at the point of production. There is certainly no systematic treatment of such problems in his work.[24] Lenin, like most of the European Social Democrats, seems to have assumed that socialism meant only centralized state control of production. His first pronouncements on his return to Russia stressed state control of production through the soviets, which were to become the basis of the new revolutionary state. By then, however, a movement for control based on the factory committees had already arisen, and many rank-and-file Bolshevik workers had taken an active role in it. Indeed, independent of any directives from higher party organs, Bolshevik militants had taken a step that was to become crucial for the development of the revolution. They had linked the fate of the party closely to the committee movement. The Bolsheviks were the only major party to do this, and as a result benefited enormously from the popular support and increasing radicalization associated with the committees. The latter became the first major mass organizations to support Bolshevik positions, and supplied a steady influx of party cadre. The support of Lenin and other party leaders for the factory committees in May was largely the recognition of a fait accompli.[25]

Lenin and the Bolsheviks' conception of workers control and of the party's relation to the factory-committee movement, however, was often ambiguous, even contradictory. In his first articles in *Pravda* on workers control (16–17 May), Lenin called simultaneously for control by the soviets, by the committees, and by the major political parties. This he saw as the only alternative to bureaucratic control by the bourgeois state. 'The workers must demand the *immediate* establishment of *genuine* control, to be exercised by the workers themselves.'[26] On 25 May Lenin elaborated on this: 'The only way to avert disaster is to establish effective workers control over the production and distribution of goods. For the purpose of such control it is necessary, first of all, that the workers should have a majority of not less than three-fourths of all the votes in all the decisive institutions and that the owners who have not withdrawn from their business and the engineering staffs should be enlisted without fail; secondly, that the shop committees, the central and local soviets, as well as the trade unions, should have the right to participate in the control, that all commercial and bank books be open to their inspection, and that the management should supply them with all the necessary information; third, that a similar right should be granted to representatives of all the major democratic and socialist parties.'[27]

At the First Conference of Petrograd Factory Committees, which met in the Tauride Palace between 30 May and 5 June, Lenin himself appeared as the champion of workers control and the factory committees, and the vast majority of the delegates were Bolshevik sympathizers. The party pushed for the formation of a Central Council of Factory Committees independent of the trade unions and responsible to the local committees. There was great opposition at the conference to the integration of the committees into a centralized bureaucratic framework, whether of the trade unions or of the existing state. Naumov, a rank-and-file Bolshevik worker from the New Parviainen Factory who was elected to the Central Council of Factory Committees, expressed the sentiments of many at the conference when he said that 'control must be created from below and not from above, created democratically and not bureaucratically, and I call upon you to take this mission upon yourselves. Only we workers can achieve what is necessary for our future existence.'[28] The conference passed a resolution on workers control similar to Lenin's outline of 25 May: workers representatives from the soviets, trade unions, and factory committees were to constitute two-thirds of the membership of all central organs of economic control, and the factory committees as well as the trade unions were to participate in local control.[29]

It is significant that about the time of the First Conference of Petrograd Factory Committees, the emphasis in both Lenin's writings and the party's official pronouncements on workers control shifted away from Soviet state control and fell upon the independence of the factory committees from the trade unions. Exactly how the system of control was to operate, however, remained ambiguous. Instead of proposing a clear-cut schema of democratic representation and accountability resting on the rank-and-file workers acting through their local committees, the Bolsheviks offered a hodgepodge that was to include representatives from the committees, the unions and the soviets. The relationship of these delegates to one another and their accountability to the rank and file was never articulated. The implicit assumption, as in much of Lenin's theory and practice after the revolution, seems to have been that bureaucratic control would be countered simply by the presence of a majority of workers or workers representatives on the central control boards. Nor did the rank-and-file workers demand a more precise formulation. They were content with the defeat of the Menshevik proposals for state control and the attempts to subordinate the committees to the unions.

In his *Pravda* article of 4 June Lenin again shifted ground. Defending the party against charges of syndicalism, he reasserted that control would be directed by the soviets. *The factory committees received no mention.*[30] Later that month, at the Third All-Russian Trade Union Conference, the party's position shifted even further. Milyutin, the Bolsheviks' chief representative at the conference and Lenin's major spokesman on workers control throughout 1917, argued, to the dismay of the Bolshevik factory-committee militants present at the conference, that not the factory committees but the Soviet of Workers and Soldiers Deputies and the trade unions were the primary instruments of control. According to the 'Theses on the Role and Relationship of the Trade Unions and Factory Committees in the Regulation of Industry' presented by the Bolsheviks at the trade-union conference, the unions and the committees were to have distinct functions, but the latter were to be strictly subordinate to the former. The factory committees were to become the cells of the unions. Economic control commissions were to be attached and responsible to the central administration of the unions, although composed of members of the committees. Conferences of the factory committees were to be convoked by the unions and no longer by the Central Council of Factory Committees. The latter was not even to have independent financial support—a position clearly designed to undermine its existence. Workers control on a nation-wide basis was to be effected by central commissions of the All-Russian unions. At the level of national economic planning, majority representation in the Provisional Government's Economic Council was to be allotted to trade-union and soviet officials.[31]

These contradictions in party policy and practice persisted throughout the year. At the Second Conference of Petrograd Factory Committees in August, the Bolsheviks upheld the independent existence of the Central Council of Factory Committees, and planned the formation of a national coordinating council. Yet they seem not to have channelled significant resources to make it an effective economic centre. Instead, they utilized it primarily as a weapon of political struggle to gain control of the unions, to stage political demonstrations, and to help organize the insurrection.[32] At the first All-Russian Conference of Factory Committees just before the seizure of power in October, the Bolsheviks once again took a strong stand in favour of the committees. The Bolshevik resolution, passed by the Conference, stated that 'the task of workers control cannot be fulfilled by the kinds of workers organizations which have existed up to the present time [presumably the unions], but by...the factory committees and *their* local unions, the local councils of factory committees.' (My emphasis.) The Central Council of Factory Committees was to be strengthened as an economic centre and charged with the elaboration of a general economic plan for the demobilization of industry, the distribution of fuel and materials, and other tasks basic to economic reconstruction. The unions' control functions were to be limited primarily to the labour market. The factory committees had the right to dismiss administrative personnel and, after consulting with other local committees in the same industry, could go so far as to confiscate the enterprise if the owners failed to meet their responsibilities.[33] This latter issue was to become crucial immediately after the seizure of power. Despite his belief that capitalist relations of production could not be abolished immediately, and that the working class had to be content with soviet regulation of capitalist industry and with a form of workers control limited to the 'most precise and most conscientious *accounting* of the production and distribution of goods', Lenin nonetheless called for the nationalization of major syndicates such as oil, coal, iron, steel, and sugar. And other leading party representatives supported the right or necessity of confiscation at factory committee conferences. As a result, many, if not most, committee militants believed that the party was committed to a decisive transformation of capitalist property relations and to extensive intervention in the management of industry.[34]

How can we account for these contradictions and ambivalences in Bolshevik policy? One common explanation is that the Bolsheviks were simply deceitful and manipulative, carefully trimming their slogans and resolutions to suit the audience. Though they had no genuine commitment to the factory committees, they needed their support in the struggle for power.[35] There may well be some truth in this. The Bolsheviks were not above manipulation in the committees and at the various conferences, and party leaders sometimes took positions that seemed motivated primarily by the nature of the audience they were addressing. But such an explanation has its limits. Not only does it greatly overestimate the degree to which higher party officials sought to mask their real positions, but it directs attention away from the social context in which these positions developed, including those of Lenin himself.

An analysis less dependent on the calculating intentions of a small coterie of party leaders must recognize several basic and inter-related features of the revolutionary process within which various tactical decisions were made. To start with, the party itself was not unified, even at the higher levels. Even if it had been, it would still have been unable to impose a monolithic position on the rank and file. Relatively august members of the party hierarchy not infrequently presented different, often flatly contradictory, positions at the same conference. At the First All-Russian Factory Committee Conference, for instance, there was a broad range of Bolshevik opinion, although none of the veteran leaders took positions as radical as those of some of the members of the Petrograd Central Council of Factory Committees.[36] Some of the differences in the party undoubtedly reflected the fact that certain Bolsheviks, and apparently nearly all the best-known veteran militants, were affiliated mainly to the unions, while others were most active in the committees.

But the committee movement itself was far from completely unified and coherent. Its organizational boundaries were never clearly delineated, nor did it command a well-developed or consistent conception of the role of workers control in the coming revolution. The movement was of very recent origin, and a good number of its chief advocates were quite young. Indeed, they seem to have been not only younger and less politically experienced than Bolshevik trade-union leaders, but less articulate as well. At the factory-committee conferences, for instance, trade-union leaders were often called upon to give major reports. And most factory committees accepted in theory the need to form united organizations with the unions, even if they did not necessarily agree on the terms, and even if the realities of struggle often impeded close cooperation. There were serious differences on the Central Council of Petrograd Factory Committees itself. It was a member of the Central Council, Glebov-Avilov, who presented at the Third Trade Union Conference the main Bolshevik theses that would have subordinated the committees to the unions and put the Central Council itself out of business. And it was another of the leading members of the Central Council, Vlas Chubar, whose proposal to limit the committees' activities to workers affairs and leave economic regulation to the state was rejected at the First All-Russian Factory Committee Conference.[37] The divisions and differences that pervaded the workers movement and its organizations cut right through the Bolshevik party as well. The latter, indeed, became the powerful political force it did in 1917 not by careful recruiting policies and strict discipline, but by a virtually open-door policy that was bound to foster conflicting currents. As one recent commentator has noted, 'centrifugal tendencies dominated party life in 1917...Anarchic attitudes to higher authority were the rule of the day.'[38] If party leaders had had a more consistently favourable policy on workers control, they might have influenced the movement differently. But they certainly would have been unable to unify the various conflicting tendencies within the party around such a policy. Another Bolshevik member of the Central Council of Factory Committees, the 22-year-old Naumov, vividly revealed the party's situation when he said in disgust, after a disagreement over political tactics in June, 'let it [the party] be completely undermined. It is necessary to trust only in oneself and in the masses.'[39] No wonder party positions on workers control were often attempts to square a circle rather than to impose a line.

In the light of some of the economic developments in the post-October period, it is difficult to avoid the conclusion that the party's relative neglect of the Central Council of Factory Committees considerably undermined the possibilities for a more democratic and coherent policy of economic reconstruction. The committee movement developed quickly in 1917, and showed mounting signs of coordination and maturity. It came to recognize the complexity of many of the problems of control and management, of worker discipline and technical expertise. And within the Central Council of Petrograd Committees a small group began to develop plans for demobilization and reconversion, and for a democratic system of economic management and accountability. Party leaders, however, seem to have lent very little assistance to these efforts. Relatively few organizational resources were directed towards developing the Central Council into an effective economic centre. It seems to have been used for strategic political purposes rather than to have been the recipient of party resources for its own pressing tasks of coordination. As a result, the workers movement would face October without a coherent democratic strategy for economic reconstruction.

As regrettable as such decisions may appear with hindsight, we must not forget that they occurred in the heat of a political struggle in which time itself was a scarce factor and the party's own resources were strained. Virtually all party committees and workers organizations constantly complained about the shortage of competent and effective activists, not to mention material resources. The Bolsheviks were better organized, and progressively more effective at fund-raising and recruiting than their major competitors for popular urban support. But their costs of mobilization were nonetheless considerable, given all the tasks they faced and all the competing claims on those resources. One goal was inevitably as central as it was uncertain: political power. Only a state power favourable to the working class could provide the basis for the realization of the proletariat's more radical economic demands. Tactical decisions about the factory-committee movement must be evaluated in this context, even though some of them were neither inevitable nor without their own serious costs for the future of the workers movement. Similarly, decisions to mask differences or to tailor certain positions to particular audiences of factory-committee and trade-union representatives may have shirked or even exacerbated certain problems. But the Bolsheviks could neither quickly and easily facilitate consistent collaboration between the committees and the unions nor imagine revolutionary political and economic power without them.

Finally, Bolshevik contradictions and ambivalences on the issue of workers control in 1917 can be understood only in light of the theory that informed party policies and the historic struggles that provided the practical context for the development of theory in the years prior to the revolution. When the tsar was overthrown in February, no major party figures, including those on the left wing, had given much thought to the problem of workers control. There was not a single sustained analysis of the concept in all of Russian Marxism. This is hardly surprising, since the issue had not been a major one in the Russian workers movement, and the political struggle against autocracy and then war consumed so much of the efforts of Bolshevik and Menshevik leaders alike. Faced with new opportunities in 1917, therefore, Bolshevik leaders had to improvise on workers control, and under circumstances that were not particularly favourable to systematic theory. Nor did their efforts enjoy unambiguous guidance from the movements that were then emerging. But the theoretical heritage that was brought to bear on the problems of the day did contain decided elements of productivism, statism, and political authoritarianism. These aspects of Bolshevik, and particularly Leninist, theory will be analysed in detail in subsequent chapters. What is important to note here is that even in a highly fluid situation open to conscious improvisation, the underlying assumptions of Bolshevik theory tended to impede recognition of the need for more careful analysis and a consistent policy on the issue of workers control at the point of production and systemic economic democracy. The Bolsheviks did not remain ambivalent simply because the movements themselves were often confused and contradictory. Their own theoretical preconceptions helped sustain confusion, ambivalence, and even hostility to workers control. And the organization of the factory-committee movement suffered as a result.

3
Power and the State: February to October

Political power is ultimately the central problem of every revolution. The movement for workers control, initially motivated by relatively limited pragmatic aims, increasingly came to realize this in the course of 1917. Its own rhythms were, indeed, in continual interplay with the shifting constellation of political authority and public policy, administrative capacity and coercive power. After the overthrow of the tsar in February, unitary political power was never re-established. The old administrative and police apparatus had crumbled, but the liberal democratic politicians, who saw themselves as the rightful heirs of government, now inherited the fruits of their own historic weakness and timidity in resisting the autocracy. Though they were able to establish a Provisional Government to carry out democratic reforms and, most importantly in their own minds, to prosecute the war more effectively, they had not made the revolution. That had been the work of the masses of workers and soldiers in Petrograd. And just as the latter did not wait for the liberal parties to take decisive action against the hated autocracy, so did they not wait to establish their own organs of power: the soviets. Even though these soviets did not claim official authority, and even though their original moderate leadership hoped to phase them out with the birth of a democratic republic, it was to them that the popular classes accorded the legitimacy of the February revolution. And under the conditions of 1917, this unofficial authority was progressively transformed into actual administrative and coercive power. Such dual power is inherently unstable. Without a solution to the problem of war that had brought down the autocracy, the Provisional Government was doomed, and with it the moderate socialist leadership that persisted in propping it up.

The System of Dual Power

The weakness of the Provisional Government was signalled in its very formation. On 27 February, at the height of the mass disorders in Petrograd when the troops had finally begun to fraternize with the demonstrators, and when a soviet of workers and soldiers had already begun to form in a room in the Tauride Palace, a committee of the Duma opposition chose an adjoining private conference room to discuss the future of the government so as not to violate the tsar's prorogation order of the day before. This timidity had characterized the liberal opposition since the great shock of 1905–06, when it came to fear the peasant and proletarian masses even more than it hated the autocracy. Given the class-based system of elections, the Duma's legitimacy had never been particularly strong in the eyes of the popular classes. The fact that it had ceded revolutionary initiative to them and their leaders, while continuing to press for a constitutional monarchy despite popular outrage at the idea, hardly enhanced that legitimacy. Indeed, legitimacy could have been attained only with the support of the Petrograd Soviet and a commitment to a republic based on universal suffrage—a prospect the bourgeois politicos were not enthusiastic about, preferring a liberal dictatorship that could effectively prosecute the war and tutor the ignorant masses in their civic responsibilities.[1]

With the agreement of the Soviet, a liberal cabinet was formed, although Trudovik socialist leader Alexander Kerensky joined it as an independent. Following Petrograd's lead, similar committees and liberal local governments stepped into the vacuum left by the disintegrated tsarist administration across the country, though nearly everywhere they were confronted with parallel organs of soviet power. The institutional base of local zemstvos and dumas, on which the official authorities built, was relatively weak. And the Kadet party, which dominated the new regime, was small in numbers, poorly organized, and appealed to a relatively narrow constituency of privileged, middle-class, and professional people. The new government's ability to administer, to mobilize public support, and to claim the legitimacy of the democratic revolution was, therefore, severely handicapped from the outset.

The Petrograd Soviet of Workers and Soldiers Deputies was both the major competitor of and prop for the Provisional Government in 1917. Initiative to establish the Soviet came from the workers, for many of whom the soviets of 1905 were still a living memory, and from various socialist leaders. Elections in some shops took place at least as early as 24 February, either spontaneously or at the urging of rank-and-file Menshevik, Bolshevik, SR, and anarchist militants. However, these actions were either disrupted by the police or remained localized until the Central Workers Group of the old War Industries Committees, led by the Menshevik Gvozdev, were released from prison on 27 February. At the initiative of this group and of Menshevik and Trudovik factions of the Fourth Duma and several Menshevik officials of the legal trade unions and cooperatives, a Provisional Executive Committee of the Soviet of Workers and Soldiers Deputies was formed. This committee immediately issued an appeal to the workers and soldiers to elect deputies to the city soviet, and most did so on the next day. The system of representation, however, was loose. Large factories were to elect one deputy per 1,000 workers, but smaller factories could also send delegates. Military units were to send one delegate per company (approximately 250 men), which was clearly disproportionate to the workers' representation. There was hardly any check on credentials at first. This mode of representation permitted a situation in which the larger Petrograd factories, representing 87 per cent of the city's work-force, elected 424 delegates, while the smaller factories, representing only 13 per cent of the work-force, sent 422. By mid-March there were some two thousand soldiers delegates compared with the workers' eight hundred plus, even though the number of workers was considerably larger than the number of troops stationed in the city. This system of representation, and the formation of the Provisional Executive Committee by the moderate socialist parties, insured domination by the latter.[2]

In the ensuing debate on state power, some on the left demanded that the soviets take full power immediately. This position, while enjoying support in the more militant areas of the city, was in the minority among workers, not to mention the troops and the socialist leaders.[3] Even the Bolsheviks, divided at first, came to support the *poskol'ku-postol'ku* formula, which meant that the Soviet would support the Provisional Government as the only legal authority insofar as it did not violate its agreement with the Soviet to protect freedom, institute basic democratic reforms, and attempt to negotiate a democratic, non-annexationist peace. 'There is no dyarchy', asserted Steklov, a leader close to the Soviet majority, 'there is only the influence of revolutionary democracy on the bourgeois government, to submit to the latter the demands of the revolutionary people.'[4] This abdication of power was prompted on the one hand by quite realistic fears of armed counter-revolution and on the other hand by the ideology of the majority socialist parties. The Mensheviks, in particular, who took the lead in the Soviet, saw the working class as too small and not competent to run the state on its own, while the peasants were essentially hostile to socialism. Any attempt to establish a revolutionary government of workers, or workers and peasants, would be crushed by counter-revolution, just like the Paris Commune. Even were it to succeed temporarily, it could only do so through dictatorial methods antithetical to socialist goals. A soviet government dominated by the working class could play no role in the transition to a genuinely democratic socialist society, or even in ameliorating the immediate problems of war and economic disorganization—unless, some admitted, there was a socialist revolution in Europe. But even those who were less dogmatically committed to a rigid stages theory of revolutionary development estimated the chances of socialism in Europe as close to nil. They therefore chose to support a bourgeois government that was at least formally committed to the establishment of a democratic republic, but to remain outside that government so as not to compromise their independent socialist leadership of the working class.[5]

Within the next few weeks soviets were established in all the major cities and garrison towns of Russia. In Moscow, the Bolsheviks took the initiative shortly after events in Petrograd became clear, though this did not yield them a majority. Nor were they able to get the workers and soldiers to form a joint soviet, as in Petrograd. The SRs feared the radicalizing influence workers might have on the soldiers, though in other cities joint councils were established precisely to provide the basis for a moderate majority. As the war dragged on, however, this strategy would backfire. The method of representation, similar to the Petrograd arrangement, often accorded a disproportionate influence to soldiers and the workers of smaller factories. In the Moscow Workers Soviet the number of white-collar and professional workers considerably exceeded that of the factory workers. A good number of soviets were formally constituted as Workers, Soldiers and Peasants Soviets, though the genuine peasant component was not very substantial. Peasants tended to confine their activity to the village and local *volost* level, while the SR intelligentsia delegated themselves as peasant representatives at higher levels. Some soviets, especially those of the *raion* or city districts, were not constituted on the basis of class or occupation, but represented all inhabitants equally. By June there were more than five hundred soviets throughout the country, and by October some nine hundred.[6]

Already in March the soviets took steps to effect cooperation and coordination on a broad scale. After several regional conferences, a national conference of Workers and Soldiers Soviets convened on 29 March, and in May elections were held for the First All-Russian Congress of Workers and Soldiers Deputies. The Congress, which met in June in Petrograd, claimed to represent some twenty million people, though methods for establishing representation were quite loose and irregular. Frequently, soviets simply claimed to represent all the working population of a specific locale, regardless of whether all were organized to vote in elections. And the problem of forged mandates was not uncommon.[7] The more than 1,000 delegates from over 300 soviets elected a 250-member Central Executive Committee, whose composition was overwhelmingly Menshevik and SR, and remained so until the revolution in October. This Central Executive Committee, however, had no real powers over the local soviets, though it did develop the rudiments of an alternative administration, with departments for virtually all areas of social and economic life—from health and international affairs to justice and economic planning. This administration was built primarily on the foundation of the Petrograd Soviet's Executive, which employed hundreds of people in various capacities. Indeed, the All-Russian Central Executive Committee was led by the more prestigious and strategically located Petrograd Executive, which dominated the entire Soviet system and set the pace of the revolution. Even in the formal provisions for representation in joint meetings with the Executive of the Peasants Soviets, which was established in May at the All-Russian Congress of Peasants' Deputies, delegates from the Petrograd area had overwhelming predominance.

Soviet organizations proliferated at the local level. At the *raion* or district level within the urban areas, soviets were established spontaneously or in conjunction with city soviets and factory committees. The social geography of certain districts was such that the committees and *raion* soviets often merged, or their organizational boundaries were never clearly delineated. But the soviets tended to assume a wider range of functions than the committees. They involved themselves in economic struggle and organization, often providing community resources for the organization of unions and factory committees. They engaged in bargaining and mediation where the committees and especially the unions were slow to develop, although the larger the plant, the more likely it was that a factory committee would assume such functions itself. In addition to political activity, armed defence, and liaison with soldiers and peasants, the *raion* soviets were particularly active in general neighbourhood and social affairs: food provisioning and rationing, housing, care of widows, unemployment aid, communal kitchens and nurseries, the struggle against alcohol, gambling and theft, domestic quarrels (including battered wives), local justice, recreation and culture (libraries, theatre, lectures, youth groups). Under the conditions of 1917, their ambitions far outran their accomplishments, but they were central to the organization of daily life in revolutionary Russia, much more so than the city-wide soviets.[8]

In April an Interdistrict Conference of Soviets uniting the various *raion* soviets of Petrograd was established at the initiative of the Executive Committee of the city soviet. The latter's motivation in this was not to make the city soviet more representative and responsive to local rank-and-file initiative, but to create an intermediary organization for the more effective implementation of its own decisions. However, this proved impossible, since the *raion* soviets, even those that were in political agreement with the Menshevik and SR leadership of the Executive Committee, were jealous of their local autonomy and suspicious of the imposition of decisions from the centre. As the Executive Committee turned its attention toward the construction of an All-Russian soviet network, the Interdistrict Conference of Soviets was suspended in early June. It was reconvened only in mid-July, when the Executive Committee tried to enlist its help in disarming the workers involved in the armed street battles of the previous week. By this time, however, the Interdistrict Conference had moved to the left, and it refused the order, demanding that the Executive Committee be reorganized to include participation by *raion* soviet representatives. Until this happened, the Interdistrict Conference would consider itself a rival independent centre of soviets, with rights to convene executive and plenary sessions of all *raion* soviets and to participate in the executives of the workers and soldiers sections of the city soviet.

In Moscow, a similar conflict developed between the executive of the city soviet and the district soviets. The Menshevik leadership of the city executive insisted on central direction and the right of city-wide delegates to cast the deciding votes in their district soviets. The district soviets, on the other hand, wished to inject greater democracy by having representatives from the districts in the Soviet and its Executive, and by requiring the latter to issue regular reports to the district soviets concerning its activity. The view of the Mensheviks in the Executive Committee won out, although the *raion* soviets continued to radicalize much faster than the city soviet.[9]

Participation and Oligarchy

Despite various irregularities in their methods of representation, the soviets were highly democratic in that they provided mechanisms for frequent election and recall of delegates. These formal procedures enabled the rank-and-file workers and soldiers to keep the pressure on their soviet leaders, and ultimately to transform their policies and leadership in the process of protecting and extending the gains of February. But formal mechanisms of control were scarcely enough to assure strict accountability or participation on a regular basis. At every level of the soviet system, effective power gravitated to executive committees and their even smaller bureaux. In the major city soviets and in the various provincial and national organs, intellectuals exercised predominant influence. Workers and soldiers participated more effectively in lower-level soviets, although those who took on executive responsibilities were likely to be full-time party functionaries, or to become such after accepting paid positions.

The Petrograd Soviet's Executive Committee dominated policy formation from the very beginning. As its own membership rose beyond a practical number, it created a special seven-member Bureau (later expanded), which met daily, discharged most matters before the Soviet, and was empowered to make emergency political decisions on its own, requiring subsequent ratification by the Executive Committee. Important decisions could thus be made without the participation or control of the general assembly. In August, for instance, the Executive took the extremely controversial step of participating in the Moscow State Conference without discussion in the plenary. And when the Executive decided in July to arrest Bolshevik leaders and stop their press, an entire month went by before the Workers Section of the Soviet met to discuss these decisions. Although both of these incidents occurred during the low point of popular participation, for several months there had been a marked tendency towards less frequent plenary sessions, which in the early weeks after February took place almost daily. When plenary sessions were held, they were often poorly attended. This was true even at the *raion* level, with constant complaints by full-time cadre about the apathy of the delegates, and counter-complaints by the delegates about the usurpation of too much power by the executives.[10]

How can these tendencies towards oligarchy be explained in such democratically conceived popular institutions that provided for relatively easy recall and re-election? One root of the problem lies in the manner in which many soviets and executive committees were formed, though this in turn reflects the peculiar organizational and ideological heritage of the Russian workers movement. The Petrograd Soviet was established at the spontaneous initiative of workers and soldiers and the efforts of a small group of socialist intellectuals, but its executive was essentially a self-constituted group of the latter whose leading core scarcely changed at all through more than six months of social and political turmoil. Members were continually coopted onto the Executive and its various organs on the basis of party affiliation, thus reducing the percentage of those elected by any constituency, and often even excluding the constituencies from effective participation in debates. At Shlyapnikov's suggestion, for example, the Petrograd Executive permitted each of the numerous parties and organizations, including major unions and cooperatives, to send two delegates. The choice of delegates was to remain with the outside organization, so that, ironically, elected Bolshevik leaders like Shlyapnikov were themselves replaced by those of higher party standing, like Stalin and Kamenev. The general assembly, in turn, approved of the principle of cooptation.[11] This revealed the lack of clarity of its own conception of democratic accountability, and the general recognition in the workers movement of the leading role of the parties. Nor was Petrograd exceptional, though not all soviets followed its lead. In Saratov nine of the twenty-four members of the soviet executive were appointed as early as March.[12]

The soviet democratic structure was therefore quite loose, drawing in delegates from various kinds of organizations and constituencies according to no consistent principle of equal representation, and open to direct nomination by outside organizations to its chief decision-making organs. Such phenomena reflected on the one hand the very sudden blossoming of soviet and other popular organs without any institutional basis for regular mechanisms of democratic control and, on the other hand, the relative strength and continuity of parties compared with other forms of popular organization. The heritage of struggle under the autocracy was reasserted in the very structures of popular participation after the fall of the *ancien régime*. Even at the grass-roots level, party organization often proved crucial, if not indispensable. *Raion* soviets were sometimes formed directly out of party committees, from which they were often indistinguishable, or were maintained only by the the continual efforts of cadre from the various parties.[13]

The relative organizational superiority of the parties lent the ideological outlook of their leaders added significance. The Mensheviks and SRs, for instance, did not utilize the Interdistrict Conference of *raion* soviets in Petrograd to help democratize the city soviet, since their policies were hinged on the eventual dismantling of the soviets and the replacement of dual power by a unitary parliamentary structure for the entire nation. The Bolsheviks, despite their commitment to soviet power, neither developed a clear conception of institutional accountability nor decisively purged themselves of ideological and practical tendencies toward party domination. Once they achieved majorities in the Petrograd and Moscow Soviets in September, they lost interest in schemes to make the city soviets more responsive by according the *raion* soviets a more active and coordinated role.[14] The Bolshevik party's attitude toward the Interdistrict Conference thus paralleled its attitude toward the Petrograd Central Council of Factory Committees. And, as John Keep has pointed out, Bolsheviks, Mensheviks, and SRs alike tended to operate according to an implicit tenet that revolutionary mass organizations required no checks and balances, no separation of powers.[15] Indeed, such notions were seen as 'bourgeois.' In *State and Revolution*, Lenin would make this a central principle of the revolutionary state, thereby legitimating the already manifest tendencies toward centralized power.

Effective control over delegates and real possibilities for participation in organizational work were further impeded by the generally low cultural level of the popular classes and the paucity of administrative and communication skills. The average deputy to an urban soviet (not to mention the average worker) lacked administrative skills, although this did not always rule out effective organization. Delegates from the military tended to be even less competent, with the exception of those who came from urban backgrounds or from the ranks of NCOs. In fact, the military delegates to the Petrograd Executive Committee seem to have vanished before long, overwhelmed perhaps, as were their worker counterparts, by the party intellectuals.[16] Some 60 per cent of the population in 1917 did not have even basic literacy skills, though peasants, women, and older people were disproportionately deficient. In some industries, such as machine construction, metals, and printing, literacy rates ranged from 75 to 95 per cent, but in others, especially those with a high proportion of women such as cotton, literacy could drop to a mere 50 per cent. The lower the skill and literacy level among workers, the lower was the rate of participation in general.[17] Even for the relatively simple tasks performed by the *raion* soviets, there were constant complaints about the scarcity of competent people. As a result, many delegates and executive committee members 'wore two hats', carrying out responsibilities not only of the soviet but of other organizations, such as factory committees. The lack of skills exacerbated the tendency to turn to local party committees for assistance, and the parties, in turn, often siphoned off the more capable for work at higher levels.[18] The political and organizational heritage of tsardom was thus reinforced by socio-cultural factors, even as massive grassroots efforts sought to smash that legacy.

Participation problems were further aggravated by a scarcity of time. Most workers continued to work beyond the eight-hour shift, six days a week, and women remained mainly responsible for housework and childcare. Ordinary delegates were usually not paid for time spent in meetings, and were thus forced to rationalize their commitments. Such time pressures, and the unwieldy nature of large plenary sessions, which often seemed more like mass demonstrations and pep rallies than deliberative meetings, encouraged the concentration of effective everyday power in small executive organs, the members of which were paid by voluntary subscriptions. Before October, of course, the soviets had no official powers of taxation, and this severely limited their ability to perform administrative tasks and make more rational use of the skills that were available. The tendency of full-time, paid delegates not to want to return to their former employment—a tendency noted often in labour movements since Robert Michels's classic study of German Social Democracy[19]—was exacerbated by general socio-economic instability. Workers were more likely to get laid off by factory administrations than by soviet executive committees, especially since the latter expanded as the economy spiralled downward. Regularly paid functionaries thus sought to protect their positions, and drew institutional support from other organizations—again, most notably, the parties.

The more unstable and insecure daily life became, the less able were soviet constituencies and general assemblies to exert regular control over their full-time staff. People were too busy struggling to survive to attend meetings on a regular and frequent basis. Attendance at assembly meetings declined, and plenaries were held less often. But it would be wrong to conclude from statistics on attendance and frequency of meetings that a one-directional and irreversible trend towards bureaucratization of the soviets had set in.[20] Even though there was a noteworthy decline in *raion* soviet general assembly meetings in Petrograd, for instance, they still occurred at least weekly (on the average) in September and October. Nor is the proportion of general assembly meetings to meetings of executive bureaux itself a simple and direct indicator of popular power, which can be determined only in relation to the effective mechanisms for control of important policy decisions and not by crude statistics on the frequency of meetings. Indeed, constant mobilization through daily or near-daily general assembly meetings, especially under adverse socio-economic conditions, could create greater possibilities for elite manipulation (and inefficiency) than less frequent, regularly scheduled meetings that might be better attended and capable of conducting a general review of the activities of executive members and staff. The conditions for sustained participation were not favourable, but the possibilities for various forms of democratic control had not been irretrievably lost.

The nadir of popular participation seems to have been reached in July and August, due to a convergence of factors whose relative significance is not completely clear. In Petrograd, fear and a sense of isolation among the militant workers after the July repression and the unleashing of the right-wing Black Hundreds surely played a part. As class and party polarization increased, the more militant workers may have shifted the focus of activity to the Bolshevik party. After General Kornilov's attempted march on the city in late August, a renewed burst of activity and participation occurred, as workers saw the gains of February threatened, and also perceived the chance of extending the revolution with the support of the moderate socialist forces. In Moscow as well, there was renewed interest and participation after the Kornilov threat. July and August were also months of vacation for many, of temporary plant closures and travel to the countryside for the five major religious holidays of the late summer period.

In general, it seems that crisis spurred participation, sometimes dramatically, since it was then that participation made the most difference. Attendance at Petrograd Soviet plenaries in September and October are a case in point.[21] In addition to all this, it cannot be forgotten that dual power itself, and the lack of formal authority and resources inherent in it, constantly impeded the effectiveness of soviet activity, and hence fuelled a feeling that participation was a waste of time. The October revolution would resolve this duality, but would also create obstacles of its own to popular participation and control.

Finally, the soviet system of representation was heavily weighted toward the urban areas. The peasantry, as we shall see in chapter 6, was deeply involved in the revolutionary process, but tended to confine its activity to local problems, particularly the distribution of land. Peasant soviets developed more slowly, and, like their urban counterparts, were dominated by their executive-committee members. At the lower levels, these were often quite similar to traditional village leaders, primarily older male heads of households. But above the village and *volost* level, the threads of genuine representation wore extremely thin. Despite formal accountability to periodic congresses and conferences, in reality the higher levels of rural soviet organization tended to be an extension of the power of urban soviets and their executive committees. And in the national soviet structure, as we have seen, rural delegates were overwhelmed by their urban counterparts, and particularly by leaders from the capital city of Petrograd. The reasons for this are as simple as they are fundamental to Russian socio-economic structure and development. Russian villages were for the most part isolated and self-enclosed entities, and the horizons of their inhabitants scarcely extended beyond local boundaries, except to resist unfavourable terms of exchange for their produce, or the taxation and conscription policies of the state. Supra-local organization was impeded by the poor system of transportation and communication. Villages and local soviets could scarcely maintain permanent delegates to provincial congresses, or effectively oversee the policies of those elected or coopted onto higher executive bodies.

At the national level, permanent contact of delegates among themselves and between them and their constituencies was even more difficult. For the rural areas, there was no core soviet to provide the sort of permanent organizational base the urban soviets had in Petrograd. The Socialist Revolutionary Party, for its part, lacked strong rural organizations, despite its claim to be the sole representative of peasant interests and its often highly inflated rural membership figures.[22] The political dominance of the city, if not the dictatorship of the proletariat, was an inevitable short-term consequence of the socio-economic legacy of Russian development, even if revolution opened up long-term possibilities for the progressive integration of the peasantry into national political life.

War, Power and the Failure of the Moderate Socialists

From the very beginning most soviets were dominated by moderates of the Menshevik and Socialist Revolutionary parties. In Petrograd and Moscow, their dominance continued uninterrupted until September, and in the All-Russian Central Executive Committee it lasted right up until the October revolution. As leaders of unofficial organs of dual power that were supposed to phase themselves out of existence, they were in an extremely delicate position, especially since the official government was from its inception so weak in legitimative, administrative, and coercive resources. The continuation of the war rendered that position nearly impossible, but the fate of their leadership was ultimately sealed by their own ideological commitments.

As democratic socialists who had struggled for years against the autocracy, the Menshevik and SR leaders were committed to basic democratic reforms. They vigorously supported the establishment of trade unions and the rights of labour to bargain collectively. They fought for the establishment of labour exchanges, unemployment insurance, social security, an equitable system of food rationing, and state economic controls. They likewise looked forward to an equitable distribution of the land and to an early non-annexationist peace. And they supported the establishment of a democratic republic on the basis of universal and equal suffrage. It was the Mensheviks, however, who were the ideological and practical leaders of the socialist coalition. And their conception of the current phase of the revolution at home, like their estimation of the international conditions for democratic and revolutionary development, placed them in the arduous position of mediating conflicts between the workers and the bourgeoisie, of postponing democratic and rural reforms, and of restraining and even repressing the actions of their own constituencies.

As early as March, for instance, the Petrograd Soviet urged a return to work before any agreement had been reached with the Provisional Government on the basic questions of the day: peace, land, and an eight-hour day. Only direct mass action and a threatened general strike forced at least a formal commitment on this last issue. Likewise, the Soviet stood behind the government's attempt to limit workers control to the general representation of workers interests and to cultural and educational affairs. Much effort was directed to the establishment of labour mediation boards to prevent strikes and the disruption of production. As workers and soldiers increasingly took to the streets in angry demonstrations against the government's inability to solve the most pressing problems of the hour, the Soviet began to exercise a greater role in directly restraining them. In the April demonstrations over the publication of Foreign Minister Milyukov's note revealing the government's continued imperialist war aims, it was the Soviet that finally established order. From then on, the socialist leaders of the Petrograd Soviet found themselves compelled to enter the Cabinet to prop up the Provisional Government, whose continued existence had now become questionable in the eyes of the popular classes in Petrograd and elsewhere. By taking this step, however, the moderate socialist leaders simply reproduced another form of dyarchy in the heart of the legal government itself, without thereby making the latter significantly more effective.

In June, the Petrograd Soviet Executive used its own coercive powers to reschedule a mass demonstration, only to be subsequently embarrassed and frightened at the extent to which the parading masses had supported radical Bolshevik slogans for an immediate end to the war and the assumption of sole authority by the soviets. In early July, with spiralling inflation, a further reduction in food rations, and the ordering of sections of the Petrograd garrison to the front in the desperate offensive against the Austrians, mass demonstrations exploded into armed confrontation, and the Soviet leaders marshalled loyal troops to repress those who wanted the Soviet itself to assume power and put an end to the perceived threats of counter-revolution. Among the latter were not only the movement of troops out of Petrograd, but the transfer of industry itself, which would undermine the role of the capital's proletariat in the revolutionary process. The blood of four hundred workers and soldiers now stained the hands of the Soviet leaders. The counter-revolutionary orgy that followed, though moderated by the Soviet leaders, further contributed to their own loss of support—a loss that proved decisive in the summer months of 1917. With the march of General Kornilov on Petrograd in late August, and its defeat through armed militancy, infiltration by workers and soldiers from the city, and the obstruction of railworkers, the revolution took a decisive turn. The Putilov workers, in a burst of revolutionary labour discipline, had produced three weeks' output of cannon in three days, and the Petrograd working class was now armed for the final battle. The Kerensky coalition government was more isolated than ever, even from the right, though it was now tainted with counter-revolution in the eyes of the masses. The Soviets of Moscow and Petrograd finally gave majorities to Bolshevik resolutions calling for soviet power. The Menshevik and SR leaders, however, in greater disarray than ever, continued to gamble on a new coalition with the bourgeois parties. The majority of leaders were simply unable to discard their rigid ideological schemata, despite the rumbling in the factories and barracks.[23]

Under the conditions of 1917, the mediating efforts of the Mensheviks and SRs were doomed to failure. It was the war and their attitudes towards it that made their position untenable. As long as the war continued, the progressive disintegration of the Russian economy and transport system could not be effectively halted, state measures of economic control notwithstanding. As long as some ten million peasants were in uniform, the land could not be equitably distributed—not to mention the effect the shortage of peasant manpower had on the decline in agricultural production and the provisioning of the cities. How, they thought, could the speedy election of a permanent Constituent Assembly be called in such a state of national crisis, or the nationalities question be properly dealt with while the country's borders were invaded by the armies of the Central Powers? Everything the Mensheviks and SRs tried to do to establish a stable bourgeois-democratic order hinged on the attainment of an early peace settlement. But such a peace was not to be had, and the reasons derive to a considerable extent from the ideological commitments of these parties.

Like most other European socialist parties, the Mensheviks had split on the issue of the war. On the one side, there were the Defencists, who justified the need to defend one's country in case of attack and to press on to victory as the only sure defence. The father of Russian Marxism, Plekhanov, and a number of other prominent Mensheviks fell into this camp. But the majority of the party upheld some form of internationalist position, which looked to an early settlement of the war through the concerted activity of all socialist parties and the pressure of the international workers movements on their respective governments. These were the basic principles endorsed at the international socialist conferences at Zimmerwald and Kienthal in 1915 and 1916, and they were the principles embodied in the Petrograd Soviet's 14 March 'Appeal to the Peoples of the Entire World'. But such appeals were rather vague about what to do in the absence of a general peace. With the arrival of the group known as the Siberian Zimmerwaldists, led by Tsereteli, however, the position that came to be known as Revolutionary Defencism was elaborated. It dominated the politics of the Mensheviks until just before the October insurrection, when the Left Menshevik Internationalists, led by Martov, achieved a formal majority in the party.

The Revolutionary Defencists held that the peace must be a general negotiated peace without annexations or indemnities, and must be based on the right of self-determination of all peoples. But until such a general settlement could be negotiated, the *revolution* in Russia had to be defended by force of arms. This, they held with the utmost sincerity, was in no way a traditional nationalist position, since their platform renounced the imperialist aims of all the warring states, including Russia itself.[24] The peace had to be a general one, since only this would guarantee the renunciation of imperialist designs on both sides. A separate peace with Germany was explicitly ruled out, for such a peace would simply strengthen the Central Powers in their fight against the bourgeois-democratic powers in the Allied camp, and it was only in a world dominated by such bourgeois-democratic governments that the Mensheviks could envisage the full development of a democratic socialist movement and revolution. Any settlement that gave the Central Powers the edge over the Allies could only lead to an autocratic world order in which the safety of the revolution in Russia would be in jeopardy. For these reasons, the German offer in May for a separate peace was turned down by the Soviet Executive Committee.[25]

But the Mensheviks had no effective way to implement their policy of revolutionary defence and general negotiated peace. First of all, the democratization of the army, to which the Mensheviks acceded in order to protect the revolution from reactionary elements in the officer corps and to guarantee the support of the troops in the capital, made it nearly impossible to implement an effective military strategy, even if the Russian armies had otherwise been capable of this, which is itself highly doubtful. Second, given their conception of the bourgeois nature of the revolution, both the conduct of the war and the negotiations for peace were left in the hands of the bourgeois ministers of the Provisional Government. Even after the resignation of Milyukov in the first major crisis of dual power in April, when the workers and soldiers clamoured for stricter Soviet control over foreign policy and the moderate socialists agreed to enter the Cabinet, the Foreign Ministry was placed in the hands of a liberal sugar magnate from Kiev, Michael Tereshchenko, who was hardly an ardent advocate of a democratic peace. But more general factors doomed the Menshevik strategy. 'No matter how one sifts the evidence', concludes Rex Wade in his thorough study of the Russian peace efforts, 'a general peace appears to have been out of the question in 1917.'[26] Once the United States had entered the war in March and German submarine warfare had proven a failure, any chance of the Allied governments seeking anything but complete victory had vanished. The Mensheviks, although they regarded the war as imperialist, were rather naive on this score. They placed their hopes on the willingness and ability of European socialists to pressure their governments to the peace table. The Mensheviks' influence on the European socialists was not inconsequential, and plans for an international socialist conference at Stockholm were laid during the Europeans' visit to Russia in April. Whether such a conference would have been able to bring the warring states to the negotiating table is another question, but one that remained academic in view of the Allied governments' refusal to issue passports to their socialist delegations. The inter-allied socialist conference that finally met in London in August was considerably less effective, and revealed fatal divisions among the various labour and socialist parties.[27]

The ideology of the majority Mensheviks had driven them to a near-impossible situation. As the peace terms of the Brest-Litovsk treaty in 1918 would reveal, some of their fears about the consequences of a separate peace were not unfounded, though an earlier settlement might have made them less onerous. Indeed, it is perhaps somewhat ironic that it was not an international socialist revolution that would save the new soviet regime from destruction by the capitalist powers (especially Germany), as the Bolsheviks argued in 1917, but the decisive victory of the Allies over the Central Powers. Although the Revolutionary Defencist prognostications were realistic, their general estimation of the political possibilities was fatally deficient. By the time of the London Conference, if not sooner, they should have realized that an internationalist socialist strategy would not work. But what the Mensheviks and SRs failed to recognize was that US entry also created the possibility for Russian withdrawal without crippling the Allied cause. In other words, American participation in the war broadened the political options available that would not fundamentally violate their overall ideology. But they did not see this, even when it became obvious, in the summer and autumn, that the Russian army was virtually unable to contribute to the war anyway. The June military offensive, which the Mensheviks approved in the interests of defending the revolution, proved this decisively. But it is indicative of their general lack of political initiative that they did not use this offensive—their one trump card—to attempt to extort promises of negotiations from the Allies. The latter, for their part, recognized after the miserable failure of this offensive that the Russian army would be of little further help in the war.[28]

The inability of the Mensheviks and SRs to end the war or mitigate the economic crisis, however, led to the growth of strong left wings in both these parties. Already on his return to Russia in May,

Martov, the leader of the Internationalist left wing of the Menshevik party, had taken a position on the war that provided a realistic alternative to the fruitless policies of the majority. He proposed to give the Allies an ultimatum to begin negotiations, and if they did not, to negotiate a separate peace for Russia. Such an ultimatum would have the best chance of motivating the working classes of Europe to pressure their respective governments to the negotiating table. If this did not work, Russia would pull out, and the army would be purged of counter-revolutionary elements so as to be able to defend the revolution from attack effectively. After the disastrous military offensive in June and the restoration of the death penalty in the army in July, the Left SRs took a similar position.[29]

By the summer, the left wings of these two parties had proposed alternatives on political power as well. They called for a coalition government of socialist parties to consolidate 'the revolutionary democracy' and lay the foundation for a Constituent Assembly. The positive revolutionary role of the bourgeoisie had played itself out, Martov argued, and it had now become the tool of counter-revolution and Allied imperialism. Although the bourgeois stage of the revolution had not been transcended, the bourgeoisie had to be excluded from political power, which should now pass to the soviets and other democratic institutions, purged of their bourgeois leadership and led by a coalition of Mensheviks, SRs and other democratic parties. The Left SRs, though hardly committed to Martov's rather contorted notion of remaining within the confines of a bourgeois revolution without the bourgeoisie and, indeed, of preparing the social basis for the regeneration of a more progressive bourgeoisie, gave vigorous support for a socialist coalition based on soviets and other popularly elected bodies.[30]

From the complex and shifting deliberations among the parties in the weeks following the Kornilov march, no unambiguous conclusion can be drawn as to the realistic possibilities for state power before the October insurrection finally placed the Bolsheviks at the helm of a Soviet government. But much evidence suggests that a coalition of socialist parties, based primarily on the soviets, would have been possible if Martov and the Left Mensheviks had been able to act decisively on their positions. Indeed, if there ever was a chance for the establishment of a relatively democratic and pluralist socialist government in Russia, its best opportunity would seem to have been after Kornilov and before the formation of a third coalition government with the Kadets on 25 September, and the subsequent decision on insurrection taken by the Bolshevik Central Committee. Had Martov moved decisively to negotiate a socialist coalition, even if he had to threaten or actually split the Menshevik party, he would have been in a relatively strong position. His views had probably gained a majority in the ranks of the party by September, and a majority of Menshevik and SR delegates originally supported his proposal for a socialist coalition at the Democratic Conference. The Internationalists had also won control of the All-Russian Central Council of Trade Unions in September. The crucial party apparatus of Petrograd was theirs, as well as those in Kharkov and the Donetz Basin. On 10 September, the Moscow organization came out for an all-socialist government, and the party centre was beginning to move. In October Dan, who had become the official party chief after Tsereteli fell ill, finally made the shift, and had been wavering for over a month.[31] The Left SRs, who by the autumn had become a major force, particularly among the troops and in numerous provincial organizations, would probably have supported a socialist coalition. They had been firmly committed in principle to a pluralist socialist government that would respect democratic freedoms and civil liberties and would begin to resolve the questions of war and the equitable distribution of land. Even the majority SR leadership, which was not committed to the Menshevik dogma of bourgeois revolution, raised the possibility of a socialist coalition in July, only to be rebuffed by their Soviet partners.[32]

A socialist coalition government would have clearly received the support of a majority of Bolshevik leaders in September, though it would no doubt have eventually had to include Bolshevik ministers. Lenin's post-July position, which saw the moderate socialists as hopelessly counter-revolutionary and even called for abandoning the slogan 'all power to the soviets', had not won a majority in the party hierarchy, and the broad masses of party workers and soldiers remained opposed to it. After the defeat of Kornilov, hopes for a united revolutionary democracy had risen enormously among the masses.[33] Thereafter, Lenin not only reversed his previous stand on soviet power, but proposed on several occasions that a soviet coalition of Mensheviks and SRs, or one including the Bolsheviks, could proceed to resolve the problems of the day, while the contenders competed peacefully among themselves for political influence.[34] Even if Lenin's moves were primarily tactical, as many of his critics, as well as Trotsky, concluded, he and others on the left wing of the party would not have been in a strong position to undermine such a coalition, since it would have enjoyed the overwhelming support of the popular classes. These issues were to come to the fore again after the seizure of power in October, although clouded by the question of the legitimacy of the insurrection. Deeply entrenched attitudes, and fundamentally different conceptions of revolutionary transformation among all the parties involved, cast serious doubt on the long-term possibilities for a broad socialist coalition under the arduous circumstances of economic disintegration and capitalist sabotage, foreign invasion and devastating peace terms, counter-revolution and peasant resistance to central authority. But what was probably the best opportunity passed in September, because the Left Mensheviks, slow to gain dominance, remained timid and perhaps deeply feared taking responsibility for a revolution that hardly looked as if it would remain within the bourgeois limits they had defined in theory. By the time they had gained control of the party apparatus and were ready to act, their working-class support had largely deserted them for the Bolsheviks.

The Demise of Dual Power

After the Kornilov fiasco, the days of dyarchy were numbered. The failure of the Mensheviks and SRs to constitute an all-socialist coalition government resulted in the formation of one final and feeble bourgeois coalition. The scanty legitimacy the Provisional Government had commanded to begin with had now vanished completely in the eyes of the popular classes. Promises of a Constituent Assembly could no longer even begin to fill the void of Russia's missing bourgeois parliamentary heritage. The always tenuous prop of the Soviet leaders was being kicked loose by soldiers, who were beginning to vote with their feet on the war, and by workers, who were continuing to take in hand the basic tasks of managing the economy and society. The edifice of dual power was crumbling. The official government was displaying its incompetence and paralysis daily. The soviets were irreversibly assuming *de facto* administrative power, even as some (though steadily fewer) continued to shy away from the ultimate political implications. The Provisional Government had failed to provide. Under the conditions of 1917, it could not administer. It could not command authority. And it could not coerce compliance.

Coercion is the ultimate bulwark of state power. And the Provisional Government never possessed a fully operational or reasonably reliable coercive apparatus. At the local level, the old tsarist police force had disintegrated in the wake of the February revolution, and workers in many cities raided the police stations, arsenals, and weapons factories to secure arms. At first the Petrograd Soviet Executive Committee, fearing a counter-revolutionary attack, approved such moves. But it soon recoiled from the idea of dual coercive power, and ordered the formation of unified city militia under the command of the legal government. All attempts to disarm the workers or effectively subordinate them to government authority failed however.

The workers militia, or Red Guards, remained the sole armed power in the workers districts, and were closely tied to the factory committees and *raion* soviets. In Petrograd, the Vyborg district alone is said to have possessed half the weapons available to the entire city militia, including those districts staffed primarily by middle-class people. Service in the workers militia was determined by lot, guaranteeing a constant turnover and thus the participation and training of as many workers as possible. Young workers in particular participated enthusiastically, though the number of women was extremely small. Some seem to have been paid by the firm, though the owners no doubt had grudgingly to admit the service performed in guarding property. There are even cases, however, of workers hiring military experts to train them at the factory owner's expense! Besides preventing theft and maintaining general order in the factories and working-class districts, the Red Guards ensured the safety of striking and demonstrating workers, and backed up the factory committees' demands for inspection and control of production with the force of arms. Attempts to disarm them, even after the July events in Petrograd, proved a failure, and after the government was forced to enlist their help against Kornilov, they were armed as never before. Their local influence was decisive in protecting and extending the gains of February, even though by October they numbered only seventy to a hundred thousand countrywide, and fifteen to twenty thousand in the capital.[35] Far more crucial to the ultimate balance of power, however, were the garrisons stationed in the major cities and the troops at the front. The Petrograd garrison alone numbered between 215,000 and 300,000, from one-half to three-fourths the number of industrial workers in the city. As V.I. Nevsky, a leader of the Bolshevik military organization noted, 'no matter how well-armed the working class is, the triumph of the revolution without the participation of the huge military mass is impossible.' And later he added, 'to win the Petrograd garrison was to win first place in the revolution.'[36]

Within a year after the war's outbreak, Russia's troops had begun to show severe signs of disillusion and rebelliousness. They were far more poorly equipped and supplied than their foes, and less competently led. Discipline was severe and arbitrary, and the traditional haughtiness and insolence of the Russian nobility, from which the officer corps was predominantly drawn, was especially pronounced in the service. Thus, when the February revolution overthrew the tsar, it was greeted with glee by almost all the troops. The yearning for peace had become general, and the new regime held out hope for an early settlement and the democratization of society.

On 1 March N.D. Sokolov, a Menshevik member of the Petrograd Soviet Executive Committee, met with a score of elected representatives of the Petrograd garrison to discuss what the revolution meant to the troops. There was very little disagreement in the exchange that followed. The soldiers were unanimous in their belief that far-reaching change was required, and a number of resolutions were drafted. These became the basis of Soviet Order

#1—an order Trotsky later called 'the single worthy document of the February revolution.'[37] This order recognized the troops as full legal citizens who, when not on duty, had the private and political rights of all other citizens: assembly, debate, information, and so on. Previously, Russian soldiers had not been allowed to enter tramway carriages or restaurants, had to ride third-class on the railroads, had to address officers at all times as 'Your Excellency', while being addressed in the familiar form of the second person. The soldiers, much like the urban workers, were demanding basic human dignity and respect. Order #1 also sanctioned the formation of elected soldiers committees on all levels from the company on up, and set the committees under the political leadership of the Soviet to which they were to send their representatives. Orders of the Provisional Government were to be obeyed only if they were sanctioned by the Soviet. All arms were to be under the control of the elected committees, and under no circumstances surrendered to the officers. It is no wonder, then, that Kerensky is reported to have said that he would have given ten years of his life for that order not to have been signed.[38]

Although discipline did not collapse immediately, no longer would the troops stand for the old forms of obedience. When the Soviet Executive Committee subsequently tried to limit the rights of the troops at the front, it was already too late. Even as the further election of officers was forestalled, many units refused to obey orders that were not first sanctioned by their elected committees. In the early months, however, these committees were dominated by SRs, and in some cases even formed at the initiative of the officers, who were now being promoted through the ranks, since much of the old officer corps was decimated in combat. Under the initial reflex of patriotic fervour, the elected committees helped reestablish discipline, and the slogan of the day was 'soldiers to the trenches, workers to the factories'. But after the crisis of Milyukov's note in April and the failure of the Austrian offensive in June and July, demands for immediate peace mounted and discipline began to crumble. The reintroduction of the death penalty was now but an ineffective ploy that signalled counter-revolution, and units began to desert—perhaps a million soldiers left the front and returned to their villages to get a piece of the action of land redistribution. Henceforth they would not march on a revolution supported by urban workers and troops in the rear.

After the Kornilov attack, the troops in Petrograd and neighbouring Kronstadt stood solidly behind the Bolsheviks and Left SRs, and the Petrograd Soviet, which had come under the radicals' control in September, organized its own Military Revolutionary Committee to prepare for the final battle. With a vengeance reflecting more than three years of massacre and deprivation, the rallying cry now went up 'the bourgeois to the trenches, the bourgeois to the factories'. The seizure of power itself, however, was almost bloodless in Petrograd. In Moscow there was considerably more resistance, though the outcome was never in doubt. No protracted struggle took place anywhere in the country. War and the February revolution had left the Provisional Government with no effective force with which to defend itself.[39]

In the economic sphere, the first few months after the February revolution were ones of relative stability, labour peace, and optimism, as was noted in chapter 1. Most looked forward to the consolidation of a democratic republic and the economic gains that had recently been won. Despite the militancy with which the workers had pressed their demands and the constant vigilance they demonstated through their factory committees, labour relations showed many signs of stabilizing. Unlike the pre-war period, in which labour's struggles were obdurately resisted and often ended in complete defeat, the workers were now winning numerous gains.[40] Complete freedom of organization and the right to strike were finally achieved after long years of struggle. Real wages, which had dropped considerably in the last half of 1916 and early part of 1917, began to rise once again.[41] The eight-hour day was won in many places, even though workers often agreed to work overtime to keep up war production and to obtain overtime pay. Most strikes were avoided through last-minute negotiations. The owners, for their part, sometimes looked favourably on the factory committees, especially when the latter cooperated in disciplining the workers—although in general they preferred to deal with the trade unions. They also looked with some hope to the Chambers of Conciliation that were set up as a result of the 10 March agreement with the Soviet. Reflecting this new mood of optimism, the rate of private industrial investment had risen considerably.

This did not last long. The war continued to wreak havoc on the Russian economy, as it had done in the preceding years. And at the centre of many of the economic problems was the progressive disintegration of the railway system, so important in a country of such vast size, now cut off from a number of important sea routes. The war continued to strain the already inadequate rail system beyond its capacity. Locomotives and rolling stock were breaking down much faster than they could be repaired or replaced. By October only 26.1 per cent of locomotives were usable. Under these conditions, supply of many of the necessities for consumption and industry was becoming increasingly doubtful. Petrograd was especially hard hit because of its distance from the centres of food, fuel, and raw materials production. By late summer, the capital was being supplied with bread on almost a day-to-day basis. The average per capita portion of meal dropped month by month, and by October many areas of the country faced famine. Fuel deliveries, especially to Petrograd industry, also began to dwindle, as coal production dropped and the rails faltered.

On 10 September the Petrograd Trade Union Council predicted that more than half the city's industry would face closure in the next few weeks if fuel deliveries were not increased.[42] Plant shutdowns had begun to rise dramatically across the country. From March to May, only 18,000 workers had been thrown out of work as a result of shutdowns. In June, the number jumped to more than 38,000 and in July to more than 47,000. In August and September another 61,000 workers were laid off. In Petrograd alone some 40,000 were out of work by October, 25,000 of them from the metallurgical plants. In the Urals almost half of all factories had closed, in the Donetz Basin 10,000 miners were idle, and in the Moscow region some 50,000 textile workers were likewise idle.

The reason given by the owners for most plant closures was the shortage of fuel and raw materials, although deliberate attempts to bring the workers to their knees were often disguised in these terms. Indeed, the evidence for concerted closures is overwhelming. Such intent was expressed openly in the bourgeois press, and even the Menshevik press had to admit on occasion that its designated revolutionary class was consciously undermining production. The government itself was forced to intervene, even to the point of sequestration, in some of the numerous cases of deliberate sabotage claimed by the factory committees. Examples included the concealment of fuel and materials, the unnecessary delay of orders, the refusal to make technical improvements when capital was available, the transfer of liquid capital abroad, and collusion with the banks to deny or delay loans. In August a suspicious wave of industrial fires swept Petrograd. For those who continued to work, real wages began to fall once again. Nominal wages in some areas rose as much as 500 per cent, but inflation outpaced them considerably. In the last half of 1917, real wages fell on average to some 62.8 per cent of their pre-war level.[43]

In this concerted attack by capital, the factory committees were singled out for special attention. Particularly after the suppression of the July revolt in Petrograd and the repression of the Bolshevik party that the new Kerensky regime carried out in its wake, the owners were emboldened in their attempts to limit workers control to the norms established by the 23 April law or, in some cases, to eliminate it altogether. In mid-August the Second All-Russian Congress of Employers met in Petrograd, and one of its chief aims was to devise ways to limit factory-committee interference in management. The Committee of United Industrialists announced plans to discontinue wages for time spent by committee delegates in meetings, and an end to military deferments for them, since their work could no longer be said to contribute to production for the war. Some even called for the militarization of the factories, as in the days of the tsar.

The Petrograd Manufacturers Association began a stepped up campaign for the open shop and the introduction of piece-wages. More and more cases were reported of factory-committee members actually being refused pay and a place to meet, and of members of the Central Council of Factory Committees being harassed by their employers.

In the midst of this general attack on the working class by organized capital, three other developments converged, which tipped the balance decisively towards revolution. On 21 August Riga fell to the Germans and rumours spread of the impending evacuation of industry from Petrograd. The workers saw this as a deliberate attempt to crush their movement once and for all by dispersing them to other locations. On 23 August the Menshevik Minister of Labour Skobelev issued the first of his famous circulars, threatening the factory committees with judicial proceedings if they interfered in hiring and firing. This was particularly ill-timed, since it appeared to the committees that the Menshevik Minister was in direct league with the owners. If this were not enough, news of Kornilov's march on Petrograd was made public on 27 August, and the revolution of February was for the first time directly threatened by armed counter-revolution. The next day, as the workers armed themselves to defend the city, Skobelev issued a second circular calling for the limitation of factory-committee meetings to non-working hours and the deduction of committee members' pay for the time they missed. The committees responded by soundly condemning the circulars in separate spontaneous protests and at the Third Conference of Petrograd Factory Committees, which was organized within the fortnight. On 31 August the Bolsheviks received their first majority in the Petrograd Soviet, and Moscow followed suit five days later.[44]

Under these conditions, the spiral of attack and counter-attack, of owner resistance and direct intervention in production by the workers, proceeded at a mounting pace. Workers were beginning to lose faith in the willingness or ability of the owners to keep production going. Even less did they believe in their desire to end the war and convert to peacetime production. No plans for reconversion seemed to be in the offing. As the economy spiralled downward, there was little room for real concessions, and union-led strikes became increasingly irrelevant and unsuccessful. After years of repression, the short and war-wracked months of 1917 provided scant opportunity for the development of stable trade unions with a tradition of organizational discipline and collective bargaining that might have inspired a minimal degree of mutual trust between labour and capital. By the late summer, control issues had become predominant. In Petrograd, factory committees took an active role in preventing strikes, and even disciplining strikers, since the major issue had become maintaining production and preventing further layoffs—indeed, preventing the virtual collapse of industry. Committees increasingly extended their control functions, as passive checking and supervision shifted to active involvement in hiring, firing, and discipline, procurement of fuel and raw materials, and even entry into administrative boards. Their ingenuity was often extraordinary, as when an arms factory in Petrograd dug a canal to a nearby estate (against the landlord's protest, of course) to harness water power for production.

The committees themselves, however, often hesitated to assume full-scale management functions, but the pressure from the rankand file was becoming irresistible. At factory committee conferences and in general assembly meetings the demand for nationalization and full-scale workers control was increasingly heard. As of October, most committees had not been able to extend their control to all aspects of production, though in the state-run factories, which did not enjoy the same freedom of shutdown and where political and economic democracy were more closely linked, control was more thorough. But under the conditions of owner sabotage and economic breakdown, the limits of workers control became further evidence of the bankruptcy of dual power in the factory. Although many, including the more skilled and politically active workers, shied away from the idea of displacing the capitalists for fear of what might happen to production, the realities of everyday struggle were leading them to do just that.[45]

Direct sequestration by the workers and full-scale self-management were rare before October. In Petrograd and Moscow there were perhaps no more than three cases, and countrywide not much more than three dozen or so. Most of these seem to have been in relatively small firms, and some were led by anarchists. But the factory-committee conferences repeatedly rejected anarchist proposals for direct, uncoordinated seizures and slogans calling for 'the factories to the workers'. In the larger plants, in particular, there was strong recognition of the need for coordinated action and planning, even though many would eventually be pushed to the point of nationalization from below. The workers wanted state sequestration when the capitalists no longer seemed capable of managing. In the early months this meant take-over by the Provisional Government, but by September calls for nationalization were linked to the revolutionary state power of the soviets. Without the latter, most workers had come to believe, capitalist sabotage and war-induced disintegration could not be stopped.[46]

The factory committees were, not surprisingly, the most active of all the workers organizations in the preparation of the uprising. Because of the Bolsheviks' support of workers control, the committees had been the first workers institutions to come over to the party. At the First Petrograd Conference of Factory Committees in late May and early June, the Bolsheviks had received resounding majorities for all their resolutions, although the committees in Moscow and other cities were not Bolshevized until later in the summer. They were very active in the July rebellion, in the general strike that greeted the delegates to the Moscow State Conference in mid-August, and especially active in preparations for the defence of Petrograd against Kornilov. The Central Council of Factory Committees took an active role in the Military Revolutionary Committee of the Petrograd Soviet, which coordinated the seizure of power, and was energetic in organizing the vigilant armed guard that the committees' militia kept over the city throughout October. When the Bolshevik Central Committee sounded out the masses' psychological readiness for the uprising, it was Skrypnik, a Bolshevik member of the Central Council of Factory Committees, who argued, against the objections of trade-union leaders Shmit and Shlyapnikov, that the masses were indeed ready. If the party did not act now, Skrypnik pleaded, they would go over to the anarcho-syndicalists. The trade-union leaders, even the Bolshevik ones, were more conservative than the rank and file. This estimation was, by and large, correct. The workers and soldiers were ready, and even the Bolshevik trade unions played little organizational role in the uprising, although some contributed funds and many individual leaders actively participated in the preparations.[47]

By October the Bolsheviks and their allies among the Left SRs dominated virtually every major city and garrison town soviet. Their rise had been breathtaking. At the time of the February revolution they numbered perhaps as few as 23,000 in a country of 160 million, with only 2,000 or so in the capital. Of course, many workers in the early months hardly knew the difference between

Bolsheviks and Mensheviks, and voted more on the basis of personal activism than factional label. Even as late as the summer, many militants hoped to reunite the two wings of Russian Social Democracy, and joint party committees persisted in many areas, despite all the calls by party leaders for a decisive split. But the issue of the war eventually made the dividing line plain for workers, soldiers, and peasants alike. Only the Left countenanced the direct seizure of the land for which the peasants had longed for generations. Though the latter did not participate in the seizure of political power, they would not move against it either. Exact estimations of Bolshevik growth are quite hopeless, as Robert Service has most recently noted, but it is clear that their rise was enormous and irreversible.[48] Even the July repression only momentarily interrupted it, and no important leaders or significant numbers of rank-and-file cadre were lost.

Many in Petrograd, however, were chastened, and would approach the next armed confrontation only with careful organization, and with the mantle of legitimacy, for most workers desperately wished to avoid civil war. In the eyes of the popular classes, this legitimacy rested above all with the Soviet, and Bolshevik reports indicated that they would respond to its call, but not to that of the party alone. Mass meetings in the factories and barracks throughout the Petrograd area passed resolutions calling for the long-delayed Second All-Russian Congress of Workers and Soldiers Deputies to form a government. The Military Revolutionary Committee of the Petrograd Soviet, whose leading force was the new Presidium chairman Leon Trotsky, planned the insurrection to coincide with the Congress, even though Lenin condemned concern for legitimacy as 'utter idiocy' and 'sheer treachery'. But the tactic proved effective. The Second Congress ratified the insurrection, which was staged under the slogan, 'the All-Russian Congress is in danger.' Workers and soldiers in the rear met the act with enthusiastic support in most areas, and the troops at the front had been neutralized. At 2:35 in the afternoon of 25 October, Trotsky opened the emergency session of the Petrograd Soviet: 'On behalf of the Military Revolutionary Committee, I declare that the Provisional Government no longer exists.' In many ways, it hardly ever had.[49]

4
Organizing a Revolutionary Economy

The Second All-Russian Congress of Soviets 'hereby resolves to take governmental power into its own hands', read Lenin's manifesto 'To All Workers, Soldiers, and Peasants'. Despite the opposition of Mensheviks and SRs, who walked out of the Congress in protest, the vast majority of delegates approved of soviet power and the tasks that Lenin set before them: 'The Soviet authority will at once propose a democratic peace to all nations and an immediate armistice on all fronts. It will safeguard the transfer without compensation of all land—landlord, imperial, monastery—to the peasant committees; it will defend the soldiers' rights, introducing a complete democratization of the army; it will establish workers control over industry; it will ensure the convocation of the Constituent Assembly on the date set; it will supply the cities with bread and the villages with articles of first necessity; and it will secure to all nationalities inhabiting Russia the right of self-determination.'[1]

The thunderous applause that interrupted the reading of this manifesto was but one sign of the enormous legitimacy the new government enjoyed in the eyes of the popular classes. But when the cheering stopped, the tasks set forth stared the revolutionary forces starkly in the face. Peace would not come quickly or without great cost. The land would be radically redistributed, but the cities would not so easily be fed, nor would the peasants themselves secure straightaway the conditions required for economic improvement and socio-political development. And from the outset the new regime would face organized counter-revolution on the economic, administrative, and military fronts, though the latter would reach serious proportions only in mid-1918. Under these conditions, and given the limited support or outright opposition of the moderate socialist parties, the new democratic soviet state would undergo profound transformation, and within a few short years the infrastructure of a totalitarian party-state would be firmly in place. These developments will be analysed in subsequent chapters. Our present concern is the urban workers movement, and particularly the attempts to democratize economic relations while stemming the collapse of Russian industry. The possibilities were severely circumscribed, though the options finally chosen were not strictly predetermined. But even as the chances for democratic economic development seemed to flower as never before, the legacies of political autocracy and economic backwardness, of war and revolutionary crises, relentlessly reasserted themselves.

Legalization of Workers Control and Conflict of Interpretations

Within a day or two of the seizure of power, Lenin had drafed a set of regulations on workers control, which were discussed at a meeting with representatives of the Central Council of Factory Committees and the trade unions and then submitted to the Council of Peoples' Commissars, the new revolutionary cabinet, as the basis for a new law.[2] The draft called for '*workers* control over the production, storage, purchase and sale of all products and raw materials...in all industrial, commercial, banking, agricultural and other enterprises employing not less than five workers and employees (together), or with an annual turnover of not less than 10,000 rubles.' Control was to be exercised by a general assembly of all workers or an elected factory committee having access to all information concerning the enterprise. The decisions of the workers and their elected committees were to be binding on the owners and administrators. Paragraph five, however, gave the trade unions and their congresses the right to annual factory-committee decisions, and paragraphs six and seven stated that in any enterprise important to the state (and this was defined as practically any enterprise), the factory committee was 'answerable to the state for the maintenance of the strictest order and for the protection of property'. Lenin's draft was admittedly incomplete, and paragraph eight promised that 'more detailed rules on workers' control shall be drawn up by the local Soviets of Workers Deputies and by conferences of factory committees, and also by committees of office employees at general meetings of their representatives.'

More detailed instructions on workers control were drafted during the next two weeks, but not by the local soviets or factory-committee conferences. First, Larin and Milyutin were commissioned to draw up a new law, but their draft was rejected because, among other things, it did not make factory-committee decisions binding on the owners. Then Lenin's draft was given to a commission of the Commissariat of Labour under Shlyapnikov, and then to a Commission of the All-Russian Central Executive Committee of Soviets (CEC) composed of three Bolsheviks and two Left SRs. When the final draft was presented to the CEC on 14 November, the lively debate that had been simmering behind the scenes finally burst into the open. Trade unionists such as Lozovsky, Larin, and Gastev stood for strong top-down centralization and trade-union authority over the factory committees, a position most trade-union leaders shared. The factory-committee representatives vigorously protested such conceptions, although it is unclear what role they played in the official debates. Milyutin now came out in opposition to Lozovsky, calling for full support for the 'free spontaneity of the masses'. The final version was a compromise between these various positions.[3]

The new statute on workers control approved by the CEC on 14 November repeated the basic aspects of local control contained in Lenin's draft. The factory committees' decisions were to be binding on the owners, who, however, could appeal these within three days to the higher organs of workers control. The latter were to be formed in every large city, *guberniya*, and industrial area, composed of representatives of the trade unions, factory committees, and workers' cooperatives, and were to be subordinate to the soviets. The highest organ of workers control—until a promised meeting of a Congress of Soviets of Workers Control—was to be the All-Russian Council of Workers Control, which was to make binding decisions for all lower organs. This All-Russian Council was to consist of representatives from the following organizations: five from the All-Russian Central Executive Committee of the Soviet of Workers and Soldiers Deputies, five from the All-Russian Central

Executive Committee of the Soviet of Peasants Deputies, five from the All-Russian Council of Trade Unions, two from the All-Russian Union of Workers Cooperatives, five from the All-Russian Council of Factory and Shop Committees, five from the All-Russian Union of Engineers and Technicians, two from the All-Russian Union of Agronomists, one from every All-Russian union having less than 100,000 members, two from every All-Russian union having more than 100,000 members, and two from the Petrograd Council of Trade Unions.[4]

The first effect of the new law was to legitimate the factory committees' struggle against sabotage by those owners and administrators who remained in their plants. It was therefore greeted favourably by the committees and ratified at the Fifth Conference of Petrograd Factory Committees on 16 November.[5] The trade unions objected to the law because it gave further impetus to the class struggle at the plant level. It was inevitable that the struggle against sabotage, under existing conditions, would develop into broad intervention into the production process, and the unions would have a difficult time controlling this.[6] But the 'compromise' law was clearly weighted in favour of the trade unions at the higher levels of control, where they comprised the majority of delegates on the All-Russian Council of Workers Control, as against the relatively slight representation of the factory committees. Some unions, according to the schema set forth in the new law, were doubly and trebly represented. Trade-union leaders such as Lozovsky recognized the significance of this and urged the unions to 'enter the institutions created by this decree in order to regulate the matter of control....'[7]

The All-Russian Council of Workers Control met only twice before it was absorbed into the Supreme Economic Council (SEC) on 5 December. At the first meeting, on 28 November, the trade-union spokesmen continued to argue their more moderate interpretation of workers control in opposition to the factory-committee representatives present. Their numerical superiority allowed them to empower a commission to draft a set of instructions (in opposition to that being circulated by the Central Council of Petrograd Factory Committees)[8] to be issued to all workers control organs, which would more clearly specify the prerogatives and limits of local control. The commission was headed by Lozovsky, a leading opponent of the committees. The set of instructions, which came to be known as the Counter-Manual, was read at the second and last meeting of the All-Russian Council of Workers Control on 5 December and, without having even been discussed, published in *Izvestiya* a week later.[9]

The overall intent of these General Instructions on Workers Control was to curtail the functions of the committees in relation to the owners, the unions, and the state. Article 7 stated that 'the right to issue orders relating to the management, running, and functioning of enterprises remains in the hands of the owners.' The committees were explicitly forbidden under any circumstances to confiscate an enterprise and run it themselves, though they could petition the government for this. They were now subordinate not to the local councils of workers control, but to trade-union Commissions for Calculation and Distribution, whose members were to come from committees and local unions from other firms in the same branch of industry. These control commissions were also to have the right to force new elections on the factory committees if they did not approve of their composition or policies, and to propose the closing of unprofitable plants—both of which could become powerful weapons against any opposition at the plant level. In effect, as Uwe Brügmann notes, the intention of these instructions was nothing less than to turn the factory committees into powerless organs of the union control commissions.[10] The latter were to be subordinate to economic policies set by the state and its newly decreed Supreme Economic Council.

The factory committees themselves, however, were not at all amenable to this interpretation of workers control, and set to work developing and disseminating instructions of their own. Matvei Zhivotov, a Bolshevik worker, chairman of the factory committee at the '1886' power station in Petrograd, and an active member of the Central Council of Petrograd Factory Committees since its formation, made known his displeasure with the trade unionists' intentions at the first meeting of the All-Russian Council of Workers Control. He said that 'it is where we are, in the factory committees, that instructions are elaborated which arise from below to envelop all branches of industry; these are the instructions of the workplace, of life, and hence are the only instructions which can have any value. They show what the factory committees are capable of and, therefore, they should dominate everything which concerns workers control.'[11]

This was exactly the premiss of the first set of instructions on workers control issued by the Central Council of Factory Committees in late November and distributed throughout the Petrograd area. These instructions, subtitled the 'Practical Manual for the Implementation of Workers Control', saw workers control as a direct transitional stage to complete workers self-management at the plant level and in the economy as a whole: 'Workers control over industry, as an integral part of control over the whole economic life of the country, should be understood not in the narrow sense of a simple revision, but on the contrary, in the broad sense of an intervention in the employers' decisions concerning capital, stocks, raw materials and finished articles in the factory; effective supervision over the profitable and expedient execution of orders; the use of energy and labour power; and participation in the organization of production itself on a rational basis, etc., etc.'[12]

In effect, the basic rights of the owners were to be transferred to the committees until complete nationalization—the explicit goal of the instructions. Commissions were to be set up in each factory for the organization of production, the demobilization and reconversion of industry, and the supply of fuel and raw materials, with the tasks of each of these commissions spelled out in considerable detail. The commissions were permitted to consult with technicians and other experts, but the latter were to have no independent power. The committees were to unite into local, regional, and national federations in order to plan and coordinate the economic life of the country as a whole. The latter intention was a direct repudiation of the All-Russian Council of Workers Control, created by the 14 November law, in which committee representatives were in a decidedly minority position.

Shortly after the Practical Manual was issued, the Central Council of Factory Committees, probably in response to the 'Counter Manual' of the All-Russian Council of Workers Control, drew up a

Model Statute for Factory Committees and a new draft of detailed instructions to the 14 November decree, and these were published in mid-January in *Novyi Put'*, the journal of the Central Council. Whereas the first set of instructions had generally alluded only to the 'broad intervention' of the factory committee in the owners' decisions, paragraph 34 of the new Model Statute now explicitly stated that 'instructions and acts of the administration of the owners relating to the operations of the enterprise cannot be put into effect without the knowledge and consent of the Factory-Shop Committee.' The factory committee's decisions were to be binding on the owners and administrators, and violation would lead to the committee's proposing nationalization. Similar to the Practical Manual, the new draft instructions envisioned the integration of local committee control into a general economic council system. Local People's Economic Councils were to be formed in districts, cities, and regions. The directing boards of these councils were to be elected at factory-committee conferences, and eligibility was to be based solely on committee membership. A Supreme People's Economic Council was to stand at the head of this council system, elected at annual congresses of the local councils. It was to be answerable for its activity to the highest standing body of the political council (soviet) system, the All-Russian Central Executive Committee.[13]

The great majority of factory committees themselves rejected the more moderate instructions of the All-Russian Council of Workers Control in favour of those drawn up by the Central Council of Petrograd Factory Committees. A city-wide conference of committees from the metal industry, for instance, declared that the instructions of the All-Russian Council 'shackled the hands of the workers' in their revolutionary struggle against capital, while the Petrograd Central Council's guidelines 'allowed the workers great room for self-activity and made them the practical rulers of the factories.' Even in areas outside of Petrograd, where the committees were often not as strong relative to the trade unions as they were in the capital, the more radical instructions seem to have been more frequently followed. The Council of Workers Control of the Central Industrial Region (Moscow province), for example, published the official rules of the All-Russian Council, but in such a way as to sabotage their very intent. The crucial paragraphs of this document prohibiting confiscation, intrusion into management, and financial control were omitted from the text and replaced by a laconic reference stating that the committees did not have such rights. In a widely distributed brochure, the entire text was chopped up, and as a preface, the paragraph was added from the Practical Manual that interpreted workers control 'in the broad sense of intervention' in management. In case the intent was not clear enough, an example of workers control was given that could only be construed as full intrusion into the prerogatives of management. Almost all the workers organizations of the Ukraine, including the trade unions, took the Instructions of the Petrograd Central Council as a basis for workers control. The Kharkov metal workers issued their own set of guidelines, for instance, stating that the control commission 'reviews and decides all questions connected with the activity of the industrial enterprises'. Even the Bolshevik Central Committee and the Commissariat of Labour had occasion to refer inquiring factory committees to the Practical Manual.[14]

Class Struggle and Self-Management

The extension of workers control in the months after October was a product of continued economic deterioration and the deliberate and concerted sabotage by Russian capital. Most owners met the new regime with trenchant hostility, and the primary focus of their attack was directed at the factory committees' encroachment on their managerial prerogatives. As soon as the 14 November law on workers control was promulgated, a wave of protests was heard from industrialists in all parts of Russia. The mine owners in the Urals and in the South threatened to close down all the mines. The Petrograd Manufacturers' Association threatened to do the same (and set up a special committee to decide which plants to close), especially if workers adhered to the instructions elaborated by the Central Council of Factory Committees. A meeting of the All-Russian Congress of Manufacturers' Associations in Moscow on 7–9 December issued a statement protesting 'active intervention' in the affairs of management. The banks soon came to an agreement with the owners to limit funds to all firms controlled by the committees. Individual capitalists began to abscond with liquid assets and attempted to conceal stocks of raw materials and finished goods. Some, with foreign parent companies, stored such stock in their embassies or in Red Cross buildings. Others withheld or postponed wage payments in an attempt to bring the workers to their knees.[15]

Sabotage, plant closures, the withholding of wages, and reluctance to reinvest led to an escalation of the factory committees' struggles to control production, and in the months that followed hundreds of firms were taken over spontaneously by local groups of workers. Indeed, the vast majority of the firms that were nationalized in the first eight months of the new regime were seized by local workers organizations independently of the central government. Looking back on this in 1922, the Bolshevik Savelev noted: 'The overwhelming majority of firms were forcibly nationalized, resulting above all from so-called punitive considerations, and only a minority out of considerations of state or economic necessity. In general over 70 per cent of the firms were confiscated or nationalized because of their non-fulfilment of the decree on workers control, or because the owners closed their firms or abandoned them. Thus, the first period of the development of the revolution was characterized by the lack of a strictly thought-out plan of nationalization; to a large degree this was a spontaneous process.'[16]

The government and the trade unions attempted to prevent such spontaneous expropriations. In accordance with Lenin's dominant conception of the transitional period as state capitalism under the dictatorship of the proletariat, the Bolshevik regime supported the retention of the private owners in most cases. The November law on workers control and the Counter Manual's official instructions reflected this outlook. The Supreme Economic Council often intervened to discourage unauthorized seizure by threatening to cut off funds to such firms. On 1 February the Council of People's Commissars explicitly forbade expropriations without SEC approval. Most unions likewise tried to prevent such actions, or, where they occurred, to bring the new workers management under the control of their Commission for Calculation and Distribution. But these efforts were to little avail, as workers continued to take over plants into the summer of 1918, and the SEC was usually forced to officially recognize the *de facto* situation.[17]

Management of the factories expropriated from below was usually effected by a collegial board elected by the factory committee. The majority of the management board were workers (mostly committee members), but representatives from the technical and administrative personnel also usually participated. The new management itself continued to be supervised by the factory committee. Depending on the constellation of forces in the local area, the latter was answerable to the local Council of Workers Control, the local People's Economic Council, the trade union Commission for Calculation and Distribution, the Central Council of Factory Committees (in Petrograd), or only to itself. By mid-1918, factory committees directly participated in the management boards of more than three-fifths of all plants, excluding those in the Urals and Donetz basin (where sequestration from below was even more extensive than elsewhere). In factories of five hundred to a thousand workers their participation rose to 74 per cent, and in those of more than a thousand it was nearly universal.[18]

The question whether extensive worker participation in management was effective is not simply and unambiguously answered. The Russian economy continued to deteriorate in the first months after the revolution, and what stabilization was achieved was again disrupted by the exigencies of the Civil War in the summer of 1918. Many have concluded that workers control and management directly contributed to economic disorganization, since the committees were incompetent and careless, incorrigibly parochial, hostile to technical personnel, undisciplined, and short-sighted.[19] While there is no dearth of evidence to support this view, any general evaluation of workers control must take into account not only the vast amount of evidence that runs counter to it, but also the context in which the workers struggled to maintain production, as well as the relative feasibility of alternative methods for stemming economic collapse under the extremely difficult conditions, which the workers, for the most part, did not themselves create. Viewed in this light, as well as from the standpoint of the struggle for dignity and democracy, workers control in revolutionary Russia appears as a component of economic reconstruction and long-term development considerably more effective and feasible than is often recognized.

In regard to the utilization of technical expertise, the committees' attitudes did not change from 1917. While there were abuses on both sides that reflected long years of antagonism, most factory committees attempted to establish relations of mutual trust and clear lines of authority. The actual dismissal of technical personnel was handled on a case-by-case basis, and instances of actual violence were relatively rare. While some anarchists called for mass repression of intellectuals and specialists, most workers seem to have ignored such ravings.[20] All the instructions issued by organs of the factory committees called explicitly for the retention of the specialists, and the Petrograd Central Council of Factory Committees was active in establishing a special section for them.[21] Though there was much resentment against the privileges of the *spetsy*, there was no general effort to level their salaries. As in most aspects of workers control, practical considerations tended to predominate over rage, ideology, and even serious political antagonism.

The technical experts were generally very hostile to workers control. Many went out on strike immediately after October, and the All-Russian Union of Engineers (which represented, however, only a small fraction of the elite of university-trained engineers) forbade its members to participate in the organs of workers control. How effective such sanctions were is unclear, though most engineers did not engage in actively disruptive behaviour such as strikes. Nor were they, for the most part, deeply wedded to the capitalist class. Rather they were highly conscious of their own separate interests as people who had to sell their labour-power to survive. They favoured much stronger state controls over the economy than did the bourgeoisie. In fact, many of them had engaged in radical politics during their student days, and by 1914 a very considerable percentage of students in the technical institutes and even university programmes came from the less privileged urban and rural strata and had to struggle to support themselves through school. Moreover, many of those working in production had never been able to get diplomas. As a result, many were ready to cooperate with a revolutionary government, though only on terms that protected their material position, their personal safety, and the practical role of their expertise in production.[22]

Their hostility to workers control, though strong, was not universal, and many factory committees managed to work out mutually acceptable relations. Most specialists had little choice but to cooperate in some fashion, since they had to earn a living, though in the early weeks many seem to have taken money from the bourgeoisie in exchange for sabotaging production. The government could have discouraged resistance to workers control more effectively by introducing compulsory labour service for *spetsy* earlier than it finally did, in December 1918. But coercion, most realized, would hardly suffice, and the factory committees made serious efforts to circumscribe the power of the specialists while protecting them in the execution of their delegated functions. The lines of authority were extremely difficult to work out in practice, and abuses persisted on both sides. The committees' own energetic attempts to ensure discipline and increase production created an important basis for mutual respect and cooperation, though the harsh conditions of 1917–18, as well as the legacy of managerial abuse, generated enormous tensions between the workers at the bench and *all* organs and personnel exercising disciplinary and managerial functions. However, neither the general attitudes of the workers, nor factory committee behaviour, nor the various forms of *spetsy* hostility manifested in 1917–18, can be said to have inevitably doomed economic reconstruction on the basis of some form of workers control. The process was inevitably conflict-ridden, but the exercise of control was not fundamentally irrational, nor was the comportment of the experts completely incorrigible.[23]

The broader question of labour discipline and productivity under workers control is also complex. There are numerous contemporary accounts that link workers control with the decline in productivity both before and after October. In March 1918, Shlyapnikov, the Commissar of Labour, presented a graphic report to the Soviet Central Executive Committee which described how workers often refused to carry out unpleasant instructions until the factory committee met on the spot to confirm them. He complained: 'If the shop committee attempts to control the repair shops, it is immediately disbanded and another committee is elected. In a word, things are in the hands of a crowd that, due to its ignorance and lack of interest in production, is literally putting a brake on all work.'[24] A report from the factory committee itself at the Putilov works in Petrograd noted that 'under the pretence of political struggle and economic demands a struggle of particular groups is taking place which is directed against the workers organizations and even against individuals. There occur strikes and the loosening of discipline on the basis of petty-bourgeois demands. These are entirely lacking in any collective feeling.'[25]

Undoubtedly, similar situations existed in many plants, and it is beyond dispute that productivity in Russian industry fell dramatically in the initial months after October. But whether workers control as such was a major factor in this is open to considerable doubt. First of all, the owners themselves not only continued to sabotage production, but deliberately undermined worker incentive by withholding pay, sometimes for weeks at a time. Bank officials sometimes collaborated with them in freezing employee wage accounts.[26] Such actions help explain why workers were less than enthusiastic about maintaining discipline while the old owners were retained and the incentive of private profit officially upheld by the Bolshevik government. Indeed, the Supreme Economic Council itself was known to have cut off funds from firms where workers took over production without authorization from higher authorities. The factory committees had a difficult time convincing workers to produce under conditions of dual power within the factories, and hence vigorously supported nationalization of one sort or another. Once achieved, nationalization seems to have had an important positive impact on productivity.[27] In addition, conflict among workers' organs, such as factory committees and unions, sometimes led to confusion and lack of consistency in work directives, especially since the unions often opposed active intervention in production. This confusion was often magnified at higher levels of state organization. The period of disorganization on the rails that Shlyapnikov described, for instance, was dominated by intense competition between rival unions for management of the rail system. Only after several months of struggle was Vikzhel (the All-Russian Executive of Railwaymen), which had opposed the initial single-party cabinet and then the disbanding of the Constituent

Assembly, replaced by a union more favourable to the Bolsheviks and more accurately reflective of rank-and-file political sentiments in its executive committee (Vikzhedor).[28] Such intense political conflicts, especially those concerning the basic legitimacy of the new government itself, inevitably had a deleterious effect on discipline and productivity.

But the decline in productivity that continued beyond the October revolution had more profound causes. The rail system, after all, had begun to disintegrate well before the workers exercised any power over it. The major reason for this was the enormous demands placed on it by the war. As a result, deliveries of fuel and raw materials were constantly delayed, and by October production was regularly interrupted. Simon Zagorsky, a professor of political economy at the University of Petrograd during these years, estimated that during a normal working day of eight hours, workers might actually work only six, or even four, hours because of such delays.[29] The consequent demoralization was considerable. Moreover basic productive machinery was breaking down. Spare parts could not be purchased because the war had interrupted normal foreign trade. A significant number of skilled urban workers had been drafted. Numerous mines had been flooded, and important industrial centres occupied by foreign troops. In fact, industrial productivity had steadily declined since mid-1915.[30] Now, in order to reverse this decline, many factories were attempting to reconvert to peacetime production. Even under normal conditions of supply, completion of such a process might take anywhere from nine to fifteen months, and would involve temporary layoffs of large numbers of workers.[31]

But perhaps the most important factor affecting the productivity of the Russian worker in the early months of the new regime was the simple lack of proper nutrition, which was leading many to the brink of sheer physical exhaustion. Insufficient deliveries of grain, a problem before the revolution and, indeed, one of the factors that helped radicalize the masses in the final months of the Provisional Government, reached crisis proportions in the winter of 1917–18.[32] Bread rations were often as low as a quarter of a pound per day, and seldom rose above a half pound, compared to more than two pounds before the war. The average daily calorie intake of workers doing heavy labour in Petrograd fell from 1705 in October, to 1162 in December, and to a low of 771 in January, only to climb to 1000–1100 in March and April. The estimated number of calories per day required by a worker doing heavy labour was 3600, for moderately heavy work 3100, and for light work 2600.[33] This calorie deficit, coupled with other nutritional deficiencies, had a profound effect on the ability of the average worker to continue working at his or her normal pace. Indeed, many were forced to leave their factory jobs to roam the countryside for food or return to their old villages for a plot of land or family assistance. Others simply became too ill to continue working regularly. The resulting high turnover in many plants further reduced discipline, incentive, and productivity. Those who stayed at the bench became increasingly dependent on food parcels from relatives in the countryside. And ration delays and reductions frequently occasioned angry strikes and protests.[34]

Despite all these factors, however, it is significant that the steady decline in productivity seems to have been arrested within a few months. In a broad survey covering numerous factories from various regions, Lomov concludes that January 1918 was the low point in productivity. Rates of output and productivity began to climb steadily after that, in some cases quite dramatically. By the spring, a number of factories were producing at or beyond their 1916 levels, and a few had even achieved the peacetime levels of 1914, despite the continuing food shortages and the reduction of daily working hours from an average of ten to eight. In some factories, production doubled or tripled in the early months of 1918, and the Gartman works in Lugansk delivered thirteen locomotives in March, compared with only three per month during the autumn of 1917. Many of the reports explicitly credited the factory committees for these increases.[35]

A corollary of the profound demands for dignity expressed through the factory committees in 1917 was the widespread concern for workers self-discipline after the October revolution. General assembly and factory committee meetings across the country passed resolutions and established rules for what was variously referred to as 'self-discipline', 'self-control', 'self-compulsion', and 'self-creation'. Plants with a high percentage of unskilled, recently proletarianized workers and women, as well as those dominated by highly skilled male veterans, pledged themselves to demonstrate that they were no longer the intimidated workers of tsarism, and did not need to be compelled by the capitalist stick to produce. Even loftier ideals were sometimes expressed, as when the Moscow Council for Workers Control declared in January 1918: 'Each worker must be given the possibility to develop the worth of his full individuality; each worker should be allowed to work as he sees fit. Unless there is particular urgency, one should not interfere with his work, for it is then that disadvantageous effects on collective production are to be feared.'[36]

In the circumstances, reality could hardly meet the aspirations. The factory committees preferred to use methods of education and persuasion for those who repeatedly violated work rules. Comradely courts were established in many plants, and workers were often required to give public explanations for such infractions as lateness and absenteeism. If the workers disliked the rules that were established, the chief committee of the Ryazan-Urals railroad commented, then they should compose others. But if persuasion and public pressure did not suffice, the factory committees did not shrink from more coercive measures. On some sections of the rails, workers who were absent without an acceptable excuse were immediately dismissed. The factory committee of the Radiotelegraph Factory in Petrograd suspended workers for a week if they left work prematurely, and the committee at the Nevka textile mill brought workers to court for a mere five minutes absence from the bench. In fact, Milyutin had occasion to remark that the workers were often overly harsh with each other. Work norms were often strictly enforced, and many factory committees, after much initial reluctance, decided to re-introduce piece-rates. This generated a good deal of conflict, reminiscent as it was of capitalist methods of exploitation and control.

Indeed, the committees often came under fire for their disciplinary measures, especially from the less skilled and more recently proletarianized workers, who not only were relatively unused to industrial work routines, but were disproportionately subject to temporary or even permanent layoffs because of shortages and reconversion adjustments. Relative stability of employment, a necessary condition for the inculcation of self-disciplined industrial work habits among such workers, was lacking. The factory committees themselves often helped to designate those to be laid off, though in some instances they first tried to share out the work available. But, however much conflict there was between committees and workers over disciplinary questions, the workers resented other, less collectively imposed norms even more. Factory committees were not frequently voted out for enforcing discipline and imposing sanctions. And, in fact, of all those competing for control over the workplace in matters of discipline, including the old owners, state appointees, and various trade-union organs, it was the factory committees that exercised the greatest influence among the workers. Perhaps this helps explain why Shlyapnikov, who issued such a critical report on railway discipline in early 1918, subsequently became a leader of the Workers Opposition movement to restore local, democratic workers control.[37]

The System as the Solution

As factory-committee militants recognized early in 1917, democratic solutions to Russia's economic crisis required more than mere local action in individual factories. The extent to which coordination on a broad scale was achieved, or was even possible, however, is a matter of considerable dispute. Nor are the causes for the parochialism that did exist clear and unambiguous. Many have concluded that particularistic and centrifugal tendencies were inherent in the movement for workers control, and that some form of authoritarian centralization was thus inevitable.[38] The available evidence, however, presents a much more complex picture, and suggests not only that the centrifugal tendencies had broader causes, but also that the possibilities for democratizing the urban economic system in the initial period after October, while far from ideal, were considerably greater than the stark dichotomy of fragmentation from below or coordination from above would suggest.

The evidence for particularistic behaviour by workers and factory committees is plentiful. Skilled workers sometimes used the committees for their own personal advantage. In Shlyapnikov's report it was noted that some railroad repair shops used cars to house their workers and families. Theft from factories was not uncommon. Stocks of fuel, materials, and even machinery were sold for personal gain, or, more commonly, simply to feed the workforce. Some committees refused to share their fuel reserves with others, or to coordinate efforts to obtain more. This was often the case with food as well. Some committees accepted orders they could not fulfill in order to create a hedge against possible layoffs. Others resisted layoffs required by demobilization until new non-military orders were guaranteed. The exact extent of such behaviour is impossible to gauge, though it would be reasonable to conclude that parochial and particularistic concerns presented a constant problem for economic reconstruction. Many workers seem to have developed a sense that their particular factory was the collective property of its own work-force, although those with a more tenuous relation to the factory would often try to take what they could get immediately and split.[39]

In assessing the role of the factory committees in these developments, however, many other factors must be considered. The committees operated in a broad context of economic disintegration, disruptive class struggle, organizational conflict, and confused and ineffectual state formation that fundamentally defined their responses and circumscribed their options. That their attempts at coordination were not always successful cannot be simply imputed to tendencies inherent in the institutions themselves.

First of all, some of the shortsighted actions of individual committees were no fault of their own, but rather a necessity under the circumstances. For instance, in the early weeks the new regime took no steps to make sure that factory committees attempting to manage production could get credit to buy fuel and raw materials and to pay their workers. The 14 November decree on workers control did not recognize the committees as juridical agents entitled to borrow from the banks. It was only on 6 December, a full six weeks after the seizure of power, that the Council of People's Commissars published a draft decree empowering the local soviets to grant such status to the committees. Moreover, the private banks were in league with the owners in often refusing credit to the committees. This began to be rectified only later in the month, with the nationalization of the banks and the SEC's assumption of responsibility for finance, though the latter itself often obstructed the flow of funds to the committees.[40] Thus, the committees often had no choice but to sell some of their machinery or other stocks in order to pay their workers and obtain what was necessary to keep production going. And as long as the government refused to take decisive nationalization measures, competitive market calculations continually reasserted themselves.

Although the dire economic circumstances forced many workers to take desperate measures for their own survival, such as stealing from the factories and selling finished goods, machinery, and even scrap metal for a loaf of bread, the factory committees generally took strong measures to prevent this. With the dissolution of the old police and judicial apparatus, the loss of authority of the owners, the loose and often distant organization of the unions, and the initially feeble and often unpredictable activity of the new state cadre, the factory committees remained the most effective organs in limiting the extent of such behaviour. Despite the shareholding mentality among some workers, there were no widespread moves to institute profit-sharing or other forms of collective capitalist property. All the official proposals for confiscation by the factory committees took some form of broad social ownership. Perhaps this was not true for some of the smaller factories hoping to go it alone, which, Marc Ferro has hypothesized, reproduced a village mentality of collective property.[41] But this was clearly not the case in the larger plants that dominated the committee movement, or on the rails and in the factories that had come under state management before 1917.

In many areas committees were quite active in preventing situations in which each committee had to fend for itself in competition with others in order for its workers to survive. The Central Council of Factory Committees in Petrograd was especially involved in containing parochial and competitive tendencies. That Petrograd industry did not completely collapse after October was primarily the result of its energetic efforts. For instance, it actively strove to make arrangements to distribute all fuel in the area rationally and equitably. According to a plan proposed at the Fifth Conference of Petrograd Factory Committees in mid-November, all fuel reserves in excess of three months' requirements would be transferred to the Central Council's fuel commission and distributed to firms classified into four ordered emergency categories. Between 22 November 1917 and 20 January 1918, it arranged for eighty such transfers of fuel reserves, amounting to approximately thirty thousand tons. Of course, individual committees sometimes refused to cooperate, and the Central Council, not being an officially sanctioned body, had no means by which to force the more favourably situated plants to aid their fellow workers. The Fifth Conference also commissioned a group of forty-five workers from various types of firms to go to the Donetz Basin to attempt to procure more fuel, but this project ended in failure due to local political and economic developments and the disruption of transportation. This last factor remained a constant obstacle to all committee efforts at coordination. A similar commission was established to procure raw materials, and the Central Council was active in the delivery of various items (machine oil, drugs, kerosene, yarn) from Petrograd to the provinces and to Finland. On 1 January 1918 a Bureau for Statistics and Registration was established, and the Central Council's technical advisory committee was active in supplying expertise in such matters as engineering and finance.

In two other crucial areas—the demobilization of Petrograd industry and the partial evacuation of the city in early 1918 in face of the threat of an assault by German troops—the committees were especially active. The First All-Russian Conference of Factory Committees, held just before the revolution, called for an immediate demobilization plan, and the Central Council of Factory Committees set up special demobilization commissions. These had to make many hard choices, since their decisions often resulted in layoffs. But the Central Council actively assumed this responsibility. And the Sixth Conference of Petrograd Factory Committees in February voted to subordinate the particular demobilization bureaux of each factory to the general direction of the demobilization commision of the regional People's Economic Council (see below). The First Regional Conference of Factory Committees of the Urals, which met 1–4 December 1917, also called for a general demobilization plan to which all local committees would be subject.[42]

One of the clearest examples of the attempts by workers organizations to coordinate their movement and develop a coherent system of self-management was in the Urals. Certain local characteristics permitted the development of a system that was both relatively democratic and efficient. Most firms had been quickly taken over by the workers and nationalized, thus reducing the possibility of structurally induced conflict between capital and labour as well as the problems that might thus result: sabotage by the owners, lack of incentive and participation by the workers, constant disruptions of production over questions of authority and control. In addition, there seems to have been much less conflict between the unions and the committees than in many other areas, with both supporting nationalization and some form of workers self-management. But another important factor, in a period when regional and national inter-relationships were in a general state of disruption, was that the Urals constituted a relatively self-contained economic area producing much of its own coal and ore, and hence less heavily dependent on imports. Reconversion problems were also minimal. All these factors contributed to the development of a local economic system that was in many ways ideal. On 7 January 1918 delegates representing some three hundred thousand workers from the nationalized firms met in Petrograd and worked out the following schema. Workers in every mine and plant were to elect a managing council of twenty-five to sixty persons, which would include representatives of the technical and administrative personnel. This body would elect from its members an executive organ of three to fifteen people. On the basis of direct elections, higher organs of authority would be constituted all the way up to a Central Mining Council. Explicitly spelled out in the statutes approved by the conference was the right of recall, which rested with the workers of the organization from which the delegate was elected. Both state organs and trade unions *as organizations* were excluded from representation in this system.

The economy of the area was maintained throughout the winter and spring of 1918 on the basis of this system of workers self-management. Productivity rose steadily, and by the end of May 1918 it had surpassed that of the previous year. A report presented at the First Congress of People's Economic Councils in May noted that state administrative authorities themselves felt it necessary to intervene to 'rectify' the decisions of workers management boards only twice in a period of nearly five months.[43] These developments were especially promising, for the area was considered in many respects a technological and cultural backwater, where peasant traditions were particularly pervasive and resistance to authoritarian forms of labour discipline particularly explosive.

The initiative displayed by the various factory committees and their conferences and coordinating organs attests that parochialism and competitiveness were opposed by very significant countertendencies. From the early days of the February revolution, the committees attempted to break out of the narrow framework of 'control in one's own hut', as the highly critical trade-union leader Gastev once characterized workers control.[44] Many of the committee militants fully understood the need to generalize the struggle for democratic control beyond their particular workplaces, if workers self-management was to become a comprehensive system that could lay the foundations for collective and individual liberation. But perhaps the greatest indication of this is the effort of the Central Council of Factory Committees, beginning on the very day after the revolution, to form a national economic council system organically rooted in the democratic control of each workplace.

On 26 October several representatives of the Central Council met with Lenin at Smolny, along with various trade-union leaders, and presented an outline for a Provisional All-Russian People's Economic Council. This was to be composed of two-thirds workers representatives from the factory committees, trade unions, and Soviet Central Executive Committee, and one-third from the owners and engineers organizations. Each division of the Provisional Council would be overseen by a control commission composed exclusively of representatives of workers organizations, and together these would form a control commission over the highest organ. It would be vested with the regulation of industry, agriculture, and transport, and would be authorized to requisition and confiscate private firms. Lenin, however, brushed aside consideration of this proposal in favour of discussing his draft regulation on workers control, which, it will be recalled, legitimated dual power at the plant level—a fact the committees themselves took for granted and were already striving to transcend—and subordinated the committees to the unions. It also failed to invest the committees with the power to borrow money, and thus partially undercut their ability to fight sabotage and, if necessary, to manage production themselves.[45]

On 3 November the Central Council issued a circular announcing that it was initiating steps to form an All-Russian Council for the Regulation of Industry. The new plan derived largely from a proposal put forth by P.N. Amosov several days earlier, which would have combined the Provisional Government's economic regulating organs with the organizational structure of the factory committees and workers cooperatives, but would have excluded the trade unions.[46] The latter point was a result of the escalating conflicts between the unions and the committees over the extent and organizational structure of workers control. In the new situation of revolutionary urgency, the committee leadership had concluded that the unions were too distant from the rank and file, and thus too timid in the struggle against capitalist sabotage. The Central Council of Factory Committees announced that the decision of the First All-Russian Conference of Factory Committees to cooperate with the unions in matters of control had been 'definitively abolished' as a result of the transformation in the political and economic situation.[47] Shortly after promulgation of the law on workers control of 14 November, the Central Council issued its famous 'Practical Manual for the Implementation of Workers Control', in which again it spoke of the necessity for local and regional federations of factory committees and their unification into a statewide system of management. Significantly, this set of instructions no longer mentioned the massive inclusion of representatives of the owners, or of the old economic regulating organs, whose own concerted sabotage was at its peak. Nor did it mention integration of the committee movement into any existing state institutions, or into the All-Russian Council of Workers Control, which had just been set up.

For at least another month and a half, members of the Central Council struggled to win approval of their conception of how the economy as a whole could be managed on the foundations of the factory committees, as opposed to other, less democratic and less representative organizations. The second set of instructions on workers control issued by the Central Council contained a similar set of proposals, this time specifying that local, regional, and national People's Economic Councils were to be elected solely by factory-committee conferences. Eligibility was to be based solely on committee membership, with all other persons serving in purely advisory capacities. What is significant about this proposal is that itwas issued *after* the regime's official proposal for a Supreme Economic Council had already been approved (1 December), and as we shall shortly see, it differed considerably on the crucial questions of election, composition, and accountability. The same differences were again evident in the discussions leading to the formation of the regional People's Economic Councils later in the month, with representatives of the Central Council of Factory Committees insisting that power and control should rise from below and members of the regime and the trade unions forcing through proposals that opened the way for manipulation and control from above.[48]

Councils of the National Economy

In early November the Council of People's Commissars established a commission to draft a decree for a Supreme Economic Council. The commission was composed of both left and moderate Bolsheviks, though the decisive influence seems to have been that of Bukharin. His suggestion that predominance in the new economic council should be accorded neither workers nor capitalists, but the commissariats that had been hastily established after the seizure of power out of the former Provisional Government's economic committees, was taken as the basis of further work. In Bukharin's conception, the council was designed 'as an organ under the Council of People's Commissars, and for issuing instructions on workers control'. Objections to this conception were voiced from a number of quarters. The Central Council of Factory Committees wanted a council with real powers over the economy, without the parallel existence of economic commissariats, and saw it as being built upon and responsible to the factory committees. The All-Russian Central Council of Trade Unions wanted trade-union dominance, and the All-Russian Union of Engineers wanted half the seats in the new organ. The Left SRs, for their part, favoured granting the peasants and cooperative societies up to one-half the seats, and subordinating the council not to the Commissars but to the Soviet Central Executive Committee. The final proposal, drafted by Bukharin, Savelev, Larin, and Milyutin, was approved by the Central Executive Committee on 1 December after a speech by Lenin in its support, but not until Lenin had convinced the CEC to grant the new council fairly extensive powers.[49]

The Supreme Economic Council, subordinate to the Council of People's Commissars, was to have as its goal the regulation and coordination of the entire economy, with 'the right to confiscate, requisition, sequester, and consolidate various branches of industry, commerce, and other enterprises in the field of production, distribution, and state finance.'[50] It was to be composed of representatives from the All-Russian Council of Workers Control and the commissariats, with experts in an advisory capacity. In other words, it would be dominated by representatives of the upper echelons of the trade unions, party nominees, and technical and administrative experts, with a slight representation from (and no accountability to) the factory committees. Economic departments of the local soviets were to be subordinate to the SEC. Policy was to be set by a seventy-to-eighty-member Plenum, and daily business conducted by a Bureau of fifteen. Characteristic of the decree, however, is its complete lack of clarity about the relations between the new council and the economic commissariats, which would continue to exist alongside it. The SEC was charged on the one hand with directing and coordinating the work of the commissariats, and on the other with simply preparing measures for them. This lack of clarity would soon become the basis for jurisdictional confusion and conflict, and the eventual truncation of the authority of the body now being invested with regulation of the entire economy.

At the first plenary meeting of the SEC, Osinsky, its chairman, vowed to bring the economy under centralized direction. The meeting approved the creation of special committees to direct each branch of industry, which soon became known as *glavki* (chief committees) and *tsentry* (centres). These were gradually organized in the major industries, usually on the foundations of pre-existing committees for industrial regulation established under the tsarist and Provisional governments. On 25 December the chairman of the SEC was given the authority of a commissar in order to make the new organ more effective. Its first major task was to take over the old State Bank. Members of the Central Council of Factory Committees were coopted, including three into the first Bureau of fifteen (Chubar, Antipov, and Amosov) and one (Antipov) into the first presidium of five. Special effort was made to draw into the work of the *glavki* and *tsentry* trade-union officials from the corresponding branches of industry. And the Commissariat of Labour, Trade, and Industry likewise transferred some of its divisions to the new organ in order to avoid unnecessary duplication of work.[51]

The efforts to bring some degree of centralization and coordination to the Russian economy through the SEC were, however, mostly in vain during the early months of its existence. It had little influence over the spontaneous process of nationalization by the factory committees, despite its control of finance, fuel, and raw materials. On 27 April the SEC issued its second decree outlawing 'wildcat nationalization', since the order of 16 February had had virtually no effect. As Osinsky himself later recalled, 'the nationalization of industry was going on in an uncontrollable fashion and we were unable to establish even regular connections with socialized factories.'[52] This was often the case with commercial and financial institutions as well. In part, this was a consequence of the general disruption of the economy, and the lack of cooperation of some technical and administrative experts. On the other hand, the factory committees showed little allegiance to an economic centre that was imposed from above and over which they had little control. The official institutions were thus able to draw only minimally on the resource of legitimacy in what would have been, in any case, extremely difficult tasks of coordination. The organ that enjoyed the greatest legitimacy among the factory committees of Petrograd and elsewhere—the Central Council of Factory Committees— received no official sanction in its existing form or in its projected national form. As a result, its energetic attempts to effect coordination immediately after October, and to induce the more favoured committees to make temporary sacrifices in the interests of maintaining production in other factories, were inevitably considerably impaired. Nor did the SEC compensate for its deficiencies of legitimacy by an effective deployment of resources. Its leadership, and Osinsky in particular, seems to have resisted its transformation from a deliberative body into a real central economic authority, thus resulting in a high degree of what William Rosenberg has called 'institutional superficiality'.[53]

This lack of decisive action made it that much easier for the economic commissariats to entrench themselves. Or perhaps it could be put the other way around: government support for the commissariats tended to prevent the SEC from being able to encompass more economic activity than it did. On 19 January 1918, for instance, the SEC won the right to inspect all economic orders before they were issued, but failed to subordinate the economic commissariats to itself. This conflict emerged again at the First Congress of People's Economic Councils in the late spring, and on 1 August 1918 the SEC was explicitly deprived of the right to control or reorganize the commissariats. The resulting jurisdictional confusion was stunning. In the areas of internal and external trade, in finance, food distribution, and other spheres, SEC departments competed for authority with the commissariats, and issued counter-orders. The SEC became effective only later in the spring, as it was increasingly demoted to a *de facto* commissariat of industry, and leadership passed to a more determined and efficient administrator, Alexei Rykov. In the context of such limited legitimacy, near-paralytic ineffectiveness, and bureaucratic confusion at the centre, it is hardly surprising that many factory committees resisted official orders, or simply went their own way in their efforts to keep their plants going and their workers fed. As one worker put it, 'not being an anarchist, when I see the confusion at the centre, I involuntarily become one.'[54]

The Supreme Economic Council did not reflect the factory committee leaders' conceptions of what a central economic coordinating organ should look like. On the one hand, it co-existed with the economic commissariats, thus allowing for jurisdictional conflicts and guaranteeing ineffectiveness. On the other hand, it was composed of delegates who were in no way accountable to the rank-and-file workers in the factories. When their plans for democratic control of economic coordination were rejected by party leaders, however, they transferred their struggle to another level. A few days after the approval of the SEC by the Soviet Central Executive Committee, the Petrograd Central Council of Factory Committees submitted a plan for the organization of regional People's Economic Councils (PECs). This draft argued for the consistent application of an economic council system, in which conferences of factory committees, of workers in transport, commerce and agriculture, would elect regional councils; these, in turn, would elect the Supreme Economic Council at their yearly congresses. The SEC was to operate as an umbrella organization, coordinating the activities of the relatively autonomous regional councils and the local councils contained therein. The PECs were to encompass all the economic activity in their respective areas, and thereby supersede other organs previously concerned with economic questions, such as the commissariats. Factory committees and similar organs were to be the basic order-giving cells of the projected system, except in areas where expressly forbidden by the coordinating councils. Regional/horizontal integration was to take precedence over vertical integration.[55]

Although this draft was taken as the basis for further work by the SEC, the plan for regional councils that was finally approved by a very narrow margin differed considerably from what the factory committee leaders had in mind. The democratic principle was not recognized in any consistent fashion. Although central coordination was to be achieved through the SEC's *glavki* and *tsentry*, jurisdictional confusion between these and the commissariats and local soviets was not reduced, and responsibility for work rules and the organization of the labour market was shifted to the trade unions. In practice, however, the organization of the PECs varied considerably, depending on local conditions and the relative strength of existing organizations. The Moscow Region PEC, for example, allowed experts and even capitalists a decision-making function, while the Northern (Petrograd) region and the Urals only accepted them as advisors. The Northern Councils formed primarily on the basis of local soviets exhibited greater centrifugal tendencies than those formed at the initiative of factory committees or conferences representing all workers organizations. The PECs themselves became arenas for further conflict among organizations. In the Northern Region PEC, for instance, members of the Central Council of Factory Committees continued their struggle to strengthen the committees as local cells of economic management and coordination, while union leaders looked to their own organizations in these matters.

On the whole, however, the creation of the People's Economic Councils severely curtailed the powers of the factory committees, even in the Petrograd area. Departments were created to oversee the activities of the committees and to mediate conflict with the owners. When firms were spontaneously nationalized by the workers, the latter's collegial management boards were often displaced by administrative councils set up by the PECs, or by the *glavki, tsentry* or production departments of the SEC itself. The factory committees were then demoted to inspecting the fulfilment of instructions from higher organs, checking the activities of the owners for possible criminal violations in economic matters, and regulating workers' affairs in the factory.[56]

In many places, of course, such control over the factory committees was not achieved immediately; nor was the strict subordination of the regional and local PECs to the SEC, as was intended in the founding statute. By May there were PECs in seven regions, thirty-eight *guberniyas* and sixty-seven *uezds*. In most places they had arisen from local workers organizations, and their connections with the SEC remained relatively loose in the early months. Despite the SEC's control of such matters as finance, the local councils were often able to find ways around SEC directives. Conflicts persisted into the spring, as the Left Communists and Left SRs attempted to give ideological articulation to demands for strengthening the power and initiative of the lower organs—but to no avail. For its part, the SEC began to establish effective control in the late spring, when it created its own Workers Control Section and began to take over the management of more and more factories. The nationalization decree of 28 June 1918 was the climax of this process, depriving the regional economic councils of much of their *raison d'être*. In December of the same year they were formally abolished.[57]

Committees and Unions, Party and State

The First All-Russian Trade Union Congress, which met in Petrograd 7–14 January 1918, was the occasion for the official delineation of the organizational and political relationships between the factory committees and trade unions, and between the unions and the state. The Bolsheviks had a solid majority at the congress, and tended to be better represented than their rivals in the lower echelons of the union structures. Speaker after speaker from the party's leadership repeated the same theme: the workers of the factory-committee movement lacked the discipline, experience, organization, and indeed the class consciousness appropriate to the proletariat as a new ruling class. The committees pander to the whims of the workers, Arskii argued, while the unions make more demands on them. The committees are unable to assess the interests of the class as a whole. Ryazanov went so far as to slander the committees, charging that 'in the majority, they cooperate with the owners', even though he and others continued to argue against both nationalization and the more radical interpretation of the law on workers control set forth by the Central Council of Factory Committees. The committees, it was further claimed, were aberrations that arose after the February revolution only because the trade-union movement was unusually weak. Now that the unions had developed, they should absorb the undisciplined and parochial committees. The resolutions approved by the Congress duly noted these points. The trade unions were to champion the interests of the working class as a whole, against the sectional interests of workers in particular factories or trades. The committees and all local control commissions were to be subordinate to the unions, and control was not to imply socialization and workers management. The local control commissions were to be subordinate to the local Councils of Workers Control, and, ultimately, to the All-Russian Council of Workers Control. The latter's moderate set of instructions on workers control (the Counter-Manual) was to guide all control activities, and was appended to the set of approved resolutions.[58]

By and large, the Mensheviks at the congress agreed with the Bolsheviks about the relation between the unions and the committees, although they continued to articulate their general political line and to argue for the inclusion of all strata of the 'democracy' in the state regulating organs.[59] The few Anarcho-Syndicalists present repeated the critique of the trade unions they had upheld throughout 1917, urging the workers to abandon these 'living corpses' and 'organize in the localities and create a new Russia...without a boss in the trade union.'[60] Maksimov proposed the formation of democratically elected economic councils linked in a federalist structure, without distortion by trade-union or state representation: 'The aim of the proletariat was to coordinate all activity, all local interest, to create a centre but not a centre of decrees and ordinances but a centre of regulation, of guidance—and only through such a centre to organize the industrial life of the country.'[61] Others in the Bolshevik ranks defended the committees, and attempted to attribute their often parochial behaviour to confusion and disorganization at the centre. But leading members of the Central Council of Factory Committees do not seem to have been present to articulate an alternative.

The resolutions on the relation between the unions and the state and the party, presented by Zinoviev, were designed to curb the independent initiative of the working class. The October revolution, he argued, had created a new situation, placing the working class in political power, and a trade-union movement preoccupied mainly with defending the economic interests of the workers was henceforth inappropriate. The unions could protect the long-term interests of the proletariat only by fully subordinating themselves to the state and party that represent those interests.[62] Such total subordination to the party and the state would not impede the creative initiative of the workers themselves, delegates were assured. As Weinberg noted, arguing for the priority of increasing production: 'Look at those organizations which are now being created in every city, notice how they carry out work together with the trade unions and factory committees. They distribute questionnaires to the masses, inspect enterprises and draw greater and greater numbers of workers into this work. Here we have a genuine creativity.'[63]

Gastev, presenting a resolution that was approved nearly unanimously, argued for the industrial reconstruction of Russia on the basis of foreign capital investment, the fullest implementation of the Taylor system in an effort to raise work discipline and productivity, and the distribution of labour power solely according to the demands of industry, without regard for possible layoffs. The reorganization of industry had to be accomplished not according to any criteria of social justice, but exclusively in the light of the need to raise production.[64] The primary function of the unions was to participate in the organization of production with this goal in mind. But they were not themselves to manage production, which would continue under private ownership, albeit with state controls. They were to take part in state regulatory organs, with the promise that they would be gradually and automatically transformed into state economic organs as a result of such cooperation.

These theses were confirmed and clarified at the Fourth Conference of Trade Unions in March. The unions were to continue their tasks of regulation, control, and the registration and distribution of labour power, with a view to increasing production. They were to work closely with the Commissariat of Labour, whose decisions were to be binding in the area of labour. However, the Commissariat was to be guided in its policies by the unions, and aided in its practical work by collegia of union representatives, who it was thought, would serve as an antidote to bureaucracy. A resolution approved at the conference stated that 'all decisions of principle of the higher organs of the trade unions (congresses, conferences, etc.) are binding upon the Commissariat of Labour. All legislative proposals and special binding decisions concerning the conditions of labour and production must be preliminarily approved by the appropriate organs of the trade unions.'[65] But the unions had no way to enforce this, and the Second All-Russian Congress of Commissars of Labour in May explicitly repudiated the mandatory character of trade-union advice.[66]

The Bolshevik position on the relation of the unions to the state was stridently criticized from both left and right, within the party and without. The anarchists flatly rejected any state authority over workers organizations. The Mensheviks, at the extreme right of the First All-Russian Congress, likewise rejected the Bolshevik theses, since they saw the new regime as temporary, expecting that it would soon be succeeded by political arrangements more conducive to capitalist development. The independence of workers organizations like the unions would therefore have to be preserved. The Left SRs agreed with the Bolsheviks that the unions should be subordinate to and eventually incorporated into the state, but insisted that the state was essentially the soviets and not the Council of People's Commissars, which often acted independently. Lozovsky, the chairman of the Central Trade Union Council, who was expelled from the party just before the Congress for expressing such views, argued that the unions could not defend the economic interests of the workers, a task still required at this stage of the revolutionary coalition of workers and peasants, if they were merged with the state, which represented both these classes and was often the employer of labour. The unions, he said, while generally supporting the regime, must have the right to criticize it as well. And he repeated the Left SRs' rebuke of the Council of People's Commissars. From the left wing of the Bolshevik party, Tsyperovich argued that as long as production was not entirely socialized, there could be no complete identity of interests between the workers and the state, and that the workers would need independent organizations to articulate and struggle for their interests. But these criticisms were ignored by party leaders. The right to strike, for instance, while not expressly forbidden, was deliberately not approved in principle.[67]

The First All-Russian Congress of Trade Unions of January 1918 thus marked an important step in the subordination of the factory-committee movement to the trade unions and, through them, to the state, which was in practice being ruled by the Council of People's Commissars. In recompense, trade-union personnel began to staff economic regulating organs at all levels, but never were they accorded major policy-making powers in their capacity as union representatives. In their attempts to ensure party control, the Bolsheviks began to use the national apparatus, captured at the First Trade Union Congress, to bring the non-Bolshevized unions into line. Their tactics included the creation and recognition of rival unions, the deprivation of strike funds and control of welfare benefits, the breaking up of union meetings, the appointment of union officials from above, and the recall of officials elected by the rank and file at union congresses. The Commissariat of Labour had the power to ratify all trade-union collegia assigned to work in its various committees. And the Central Council of Trade Unions itself depended on the state and the party for funds—which considerably undermined the influence of the local union structures. Nor did the Bolsheviks shrink from the use of more directly repressive measures (arrest, reduction of rations, preferential supply of food and other articles of consumption), although these became common only during the Civil War. Some unions andgroups of workers resisted this control, and as early as the spring of 1918 there were protests against the lack of union independence.[68]

In mid-February 1918 the factory-committee representatives of Petrograd met at their sixth city-wide conference to consider a collective response to the decisions of the trade-union congress. While the delegates strongly rejected the accusations hurled against the committees at the union congress, they also declared that the working class could no longer afford the disunity and competition of the two types of organizations. Since the trade unions had begun to give strong support to the new soviet regime, and since they had begun to place the organization of production in the centre of their work, albeit reluctantly and under strong pressure from below, the committees now saw a real basis for unification. But only under certain conditions. To begin with, the unions would have to abandon the principle of voluntary membership, since all workers had to take part in the decision-making processes associated with the building of socialism. Next, the factory committees, which were to become the local cells of the trade unions, must retain their functions of control and regulation, while the distinct function of the union apparatus proper would be to defend the workers' economic interests and to regulate the labour market. The executive organ in the factory would continue to be the factory committee, elected by all workers and employees. The highest organ of each union would be the Conference of Factory Committee Delegates from each branch of industry, and this conference would elect the union's executive organs. The latter would be reformed to encompass all the functions of the Central Council of Factory Committees.[69]

This plan for the incorporation of the factory committees into the trade unions repeated the essential points of an informal agreement (pending approval by the committees themselves) between the

Central Council of Factory Committees, the executive board of the Metalworkers' Union, and a number of other unions prior to the Sixth Conference. In no way did it reflect the complete capitulation of the factory committees. Rather, under the constraints imposed by the recent development of the economic regulating institutions, the conference decision reflected the intention of the committees to penetrate the unions both ideologically and in terms of personnel. As Falk Döring convincingly argues, 'with this resolution, the factory committees understood themselves to be claiming direction and leadership inside of the unified workers organizations.'[70] The committees had no intention of 'burying' workers control, as the Soviet historian Anna Pankratova has written.[71] Conference delegates continued to voice support for the more radical Instructions on Workers Control issued by the Petrograd Central Council, and defended the right of the committees to confiscate firms if necessary. This, and much in the other proposals, ran counter to the decisions of the Trade Union Congress the previous month. And the sixth and last factory-committee conference of Petrograd, in its proposal for planned demobilization, also called for the nationalization of all large industry and the trustification and syndicalization of smaller firms.[72]

Though many committees and leading fighters for workers control intended to carry on the battle within the unions and the newly established economic regulating organs, by late winter 1918 their own conceptions of control had clearly been defeated. They now had to compromise, and to shift the terms of their struggle. Once the shift was made, the terms for realizing some form of economic democracy were never quite the same. The general socio-economic conditions for economic democracy were not very favourable, and would become even less so over the next three years. But the socio-economic conditions alone do not account for this original defeat. Nor do the internal weaknesses of the movement itself.

At the time of the October revolution, the factory-committee movement, despite serious deficiencies, had achieved a notable degree of organization and coordination. With the seizure of power, this accelerated rapidly, the coordinating councils helping to maintain production and organize the exchange of scarce resources. The Central Council of Petrograd Factory Committees was the leading economic organ not only of Petrograd, but probably of the entire Russian economy.[73] In August 1917, when no one else was talking in such terms, it had recognized the need for an economic apparatus ready to function once political power was finally won.[74] This was not achieved, as much for reasons relating to the larger process of revolutionary change and the responses of the parties and unions as for those relating to the inherent weaknesses of the factory-committee movement itself.

Immediately after the seizure of power, however, the Central Council proposed a series of specific proposals for economic coordination, and these, though somewhat confused, were democratic, relatively clear on questions of authority, notably detailed, and never mindlessly impractical about the need to employ administrative and technical experts from the old regime. Indeed, it was the Central Council that took the earliest and most decisive action in these matters, and then provided a crucial core to staff the actual regulating organs, even though the latter did not conform to their own conceptions. That the SEC, for instance, did not simply discuss itself into obscurity was due largely to the presence of Central Council leaders.[75] Granted, these leaders were not completely effective, nor even totally united. But their effectiveness, and the coordination they achieved, compared favourably with that of the unions. Though it is impossible to determine such questions exactly, it does seem that in October union organization was hardly superior to that of the committees. The executive of the Central Council of Trade Unions, for instance, seems not even to have met for nearly an entire month after the revolution.[76] In the practical struggle against sabotage and the development of workers self-discipline, the committees were much more effective than the unions. Under conditions of intense class struggle in the factories and the relentless pressure from below to keep production going, the factory committees were clearly the most effective and legitimate organs in the eyes of the rank and file, even though conflicts between the committees and workers (particularly the less skilled) were often quite serious. On the practical questions that were most pressing for the workers and for the maintenance of production after October, the committees were, if anything, considerably more organized and effective than the unions.

The Bolshevik party, however, decisively threw its weight behind the unions after October, and gave little support to the factory-committee leaders' conceptions of economic reconstruction and institutional accountability. That the Bolsheviks did so was not simply because of their realistic assessment of possibilities for managing the economy under revolutionary conditions, since the relative costs of their policies were high. Nor, however, do they seem to have acted primarily out of an inherent drive to straitjacket the workers movement. Attempts at realistic assessment and desire for party dominance were both involved, but the role they played in this shift toward the unions can be understood only in the wider context of political, organizational, and ideological divisions and legacies in the workers movement, as these were brought to bear on a revolutionary situation of extreme urgency.

The Bolshevik party was clearly the most important organizational factor in the post-revolutionary context, particularly once it controlled the major levers of state power. But it was nonetheless divided, its own organizational capacities still quite limited. There had been serious splits and resignations from official posts on the right wing of the party over the insurrection and the talks on coalition, and the issue of the Constituent Assembly still loomed as a potentially explosive factor in the early weeks. This helps to explain not only why the party leadership (and Lenin in particular) chose to rely on the young leftists from the Moscow Regional Bureau of the party in the construction of an economic apparatus,[77] but also why conciliation with trade-union leaders, who were predominantly from the moderate wing of the party, was such a priority. In addition, many of the top union leaders were still Mensheviks who opposed the new regime politically but whose support in economic matters was both important and possible on certain terms—terms that ran counter to those of the factory-committee leadership on the basic issues of nationalization and the extent of worker intervention in production. From the standpoint of party leaders, although the committees had shown more vigorous support for Bolshevik political positions than the unions in 1917, their organizational links to the party hierarchy were more tenuous. Union organizers were generally older and had a more reliable tradition of close cooperation with and tutelage be party leaders, Bolshevik and

Menshevik alike. Their access to the party leadership was also much greater, and as a result, it was largely through them, it seems, that appraisals of the economic situation and the causes of disorder were filtered. A few factory-committee leaders did have access to the party leadership, but the latter's promised support for factory-committee conferences to debate the issues publicly and contribute to the official definition of workers control and economic regulation never materialized. Thus, despite the enormous organizational growth and relatively greater coherence and effectiveness of the factory committees in matters directly pertaining to production in the last months of 1917, the organizational heritage of tsardom continued to exert strong political pressure, to restrict the process of discussion, and to provide the dominant definition of the situation.

This bias in the production of knowledge relevant for strategies of economic reconstruction was complemented by Lenin's own strong ideological commitment to the definition of the current stage of revolutionary development as state capitalism under the dictatorship of the proletariat. This implied the retention of capitalist property relations in major industries, and hence state intervention to contain mass incursions on the basic prerogatives of the owners and to prevent spontaneous nationalizations. Thus Lenin, who again and again waxed eloquent on the need for popular initiative in economic matters, implicitly limited that initiative to the boundaries set by the state capitalist formula. He was hardly being cynical when, for instance, he said at the Third Soviet Congress in January 1918:

'In introducing workers control, we knew that it would take much time before it spread to the whole of Russia, but we wanted to show that we recognize only one road—changes from below; we wanted the workers themselves, from below, to draw up the new, basic economic principles....

Soviet power does not know everything and cannot handle everything in time, and very often it is confronted with difficult tasks. Very often delegations of workers and peasants come to the government and ask, for example, what to do with such and such piece of land. And frequently I myself have felt embarrassed when I was that they had no definite views. And I said to them: you are the power, you do what you want to do, take all you want, we shall support you, but take care of production, see that production is useful. Take up useful work, you will make mistakes, but you will learn.'[78]

In the context of a previously favourable reference to 'the transition to confiscation of the factories, after workers control had been introduced',[79] this speech must have seemed like official ratification of the factory committees' encroachment on the power of the owners and their inchoate socialization of the means of production. Yet Lenin returned time and again to the conception of workers control as basically accounting and checking on the decisions of others, primarily the retained capitalists. This was true from the very first day of the revolution, when he commissioned Larin to negotiate for major state capitalist projects in some of the industries in which workers control had proceeded furthest, to the spring of 1918, when the workers themselves had finally defeated such projects. Such conceptions were reflected in his draft law on workers control, though Lenin seems to have remained somewhat to the left of those who issued the moderate instructions interpreting the law. But he refused to lend official support to the Central Council of Factory Committees' more radical instructions. Nor did he ever vigorously campaign for a fundamentally different conception of control and accountability than that officially instituted—as he often did when he had serious disagreements with party leaders on other issues. And on a number of occasions he repeated the theme that 'the accounting and control of the amount of labour performed and the distribution of products is the *essence* of socialist transformation, once the political rule of the proletariat has been established and secured.'[80] His support for the dominant trade-union positions was not simply practical compromise, but was founded on his own profound, if sometimes ambivalent, ideological positions.[81]

Again, however, it must be emphasized that the ideology of party leaders such as Lenin itself reflected the legacy of practical struggle in the Russian workers movement. Autocracy and war, the basic rights of labour to organize for concrete material improvements— these were the questions that dominated the movement before 1917. Workers control had hardly been an issue, even if the dignity of labour had been. And it was only quite unexpectedly that the party had to face the problems and possibilities of a socialist revolution. The sudden blossoming of a movement for control after the fall of the tsar, and its progressively greater organizational and ideological coherence in the late months of 1917, were hardly enough to reverse or transform the major ideological orientations party leaders had developed in the earlier period. Even those on the left wing of the Party who did not share the ideological commitment to state capitalism, and who would soon mount a strong attack on Lenin's policies, had no coherent alternative conception of economic democracy and institutional accountability in the early phase of post-revolutionary development. Osinsky, Bukharin, and other nascent Left Communists, who were very well situated in the planning and establishment of the SEC, had no clearly developed economic ideas to complement their political radicalism. Instead of directly confronting the possibility of top-down centralized control, they chose to avoid it, and failed to make a common front with the leaders of the Central Council of Factory Committees.

Thus, even as the latter took decisive action to effect coordination and establish a national economic centre, Lenin brushed aside their proposals as not immediately relevant, and the regime stumbled through precious weeks before it came up with another proposal. Instead of officially legitimating—even conditionally, until more representative structures could be elaborated—the role of the Central Council, which was probably the most effective and prestigious organ in such matters to the workers at the bench, Bolshevik leaders constructed a Supreme Economic Council that was short on both effectiveness and legitimacy. The party's lack of ideological preparation and its organizational deficiencies helped produce an economic superstructure riddled with bureaucratic confusion and contradictions, despite the fact that Central Council members argued strongly that clear lines of competence, authority, and accountability were necessary. Indeed, it was the party's very disorganization that in some ways made the Central Council's schemes even more relevant in practice. Yet the leading Bolsheviks had always expected that the party would (and should) provide the basic elements of organizational coherence. The confusion, delay, ineffectiveness, and limited legitimacy of the official apparatus contributed significantly to economic disintegration, as did the commitment to state capitalism and the obstacles to the committees' incursions into the prerogatives of the owners. Lenin's conception of state capitalist forms as a transitional stage, while understandable given Russian economic backwardness, and while not necessarily completely inappropriate to socialist politics in principle, was not realistic given the intensity of class struggle at the point of production in 1917 and the legacy of capital-labour relations prior to the February revolution. By January 1918, Larin, the mastermind of such projects, was himself expressing strong doubts about the willingness of the Russian bourgeoisie to cease their sabotage.[82] Many union leaders gradually came to this position as well. To the factory-committee militants, who stood in the most direct line of pressure from both owners and rank-and-file workers and were themselves often reluctant to take over production, it became clear much more quickly that such state capitalist arrangements with limited control by the workers were not feasible.

The Bolshevik party's economic choices in the months following October were not determined simply or even primarily by the internal weaknesses and practical ineffectiveness of the factory committees. Nor were they dictated by the resistance of the experts, whose eventual willingness to cooperate with the new regime and with worker-management boards offered considerable promise for a more democratic alternative. In the construction of an economic superstructure, the revolutionary government had to employ the *personnel* of the old Provisional Government apparatus. But this apparatus had been neither effective nor stable enough to *structurally* predetermine the institutional form of the new economic regime.

Because of the nature of the evidence and the hypothetical character of the question, it is impossible to determine with any degree of certainty whether the practical economic costs would have been reduced if the party leadership had tried to implement the proposals of the factory committees. Many signs—worker discipline and coordination, the disruptive effect of dual economic power and bureaucratic confusion, the unnecessary delays and indecisive action, the very promising development of a council system in the Urals, and more—suggest that economic disorganization could, indeed, have been less. But the trade unions would have had to have been integrated into the system, since effective economic reconstruction could never have been accomplished as long as there were serious splits among the major labour organizations. The leaders of the factory committees generally realized this throughout 1917 and early 1918, except for a brief period of extreme alienation immediately after October, when the unions appeared much too timid in the struggle against sabotage and too ready to tie the hands of the committees at the point of production. Only the anarcho-syndicalists, it seems, failed to recognize this need for committee/union cooperation, and this condemned them to irrelevance, except in their sporadic role of leading worker protest. Had major party leaders thrown their weight behind factory-committee conceptions of economic reconstruction, it is not at all inconceivable that enough union leaders would have reluctantly given their support so that the system could have worked—at least as well as the one instituted. The party leaders' influence among the union officials was considerable. Nor would the latter, any more than the leading committee militants, have long persisted in divisive and destructive policies simply for the sake of organizational loyalty. With the unions' increasing support for the Bolsheviks and recognition of the need for nationalization, the possibility of union/committee cooperation in the construction of more democratic regulating organs was enhanced. At the least, the party could have supported the convocation of a joint national trade-union/factory-committee congress to discuss the basic issues and the grounds for unification that might have been most consistent with economic democracy. Instead, the leadership coopted prominent committee militants into the new regulating organs, gave virtually no official support to a national meeting of committee representatives (which, as a result, never came off, despite plans for it), and lent massive aid to the convocation of a union congress that would ratify its own confused conceptions of economic regulation and legitimate them through the broad inclusion of union representatives.[83] Given the organizational and ideological legacies of tsarism, perhaps the party leaders could not have been expected to do otherwise.

But if the practical costs of the party's actions are difficult to determine, the effect of its actions on the possibility of some form of system-wide economic democracy are rather clearer. The greater the bureaucratic conflict and confusion, the more the party's own power relative to other organizations grew, thus giving practical substance to the theoretical positions of party dominance put forward at the First Trade Union Congress and implicit in much party-activity earlier.[84] Had the committee leaders' conceptions of an economic council system been instituted, there would inevitably have been considerable bureaucratic aspects to it, because of many of the factors already discussed in relation to prior committee and soviet development, and because conditions during the civil war were to deteriorate even further. But such a system could have provided the institutional infrastructure and legitimation for more consistently democratic development when conditions became more favourable. The ideological impediments to such an idea among the party leadership were enormous, as the debate between Lenin and the Left Communists in the spring of 1918 would reveal.

The Left Versus Lenin

By late winter and early spring, the Russian economy had fallen into deeper disorganization, and the peace terms of the Brest-Litovsk treaty with Germany brought it to the very brink of disaster. The demobilization of Russian industry was chaotic, despite the efforts of the Central Council of Factory Committees, the Commissariat of Labour, and a plan approved at the First All-Russian Trade Union Congress. The unions and the factory committees often refused to cooperate with each other, and the PEC of the Northern Region set up its own demobilization commission to work with similar bureaux in each factory, although the Council of People's Commissars had assigned the Petrograd Metalworkers' Union primary responsibility for demobilizing that industry. Some of these conflicts were eventually healed as the PEC assumed authority, but the factory committees themselves, fearful of losing their jobs and resentful of administrative control, sometimes resisted its orders. Those owners who remained in their plants often sabotaged plan-like demobilization, as did some of the old bureaucrats now working for the Soviet government. Petrograd industry was especially disrupted, since so much munitions production was located there, and as of 1 January 1917 88 per cent of Petrograd workers had been employed in war-related jobs. In addition to the problems of demobilization, the German threat to the city in early 1918 led to the partial evacuation of industry and workers to other parts of the country. The logic behind this decision was to prevent industry from falling into German hands, to limit the amount of unemployment in the city itself, and to begin locating industry closer to the sources of fuel and raw materials. The factory committees opposed the evacuation but seem to have taken considerable initiative once the process had begun. In all, some thirty-eight plants with sixty-four thousand workers were relocated by the end of April, although not without some panic and loss of machinery on the waterways. Many of the relocated plants were unable to resume full production for several months.

As a result of all these factors, unemployment reached crisis proportions. In Petrograd alone, even after partial evacuation, close to one-half of the industrial work-force remained jobless. The Commissariat of Labour reported a national total of 342,500 registered unemployed as of 1 April 1918, although the actual figure was undoubtedly much higher.[85] Returning soldiers pressured the unions for employment in the trade they had worked in before the war. Women were pushed out of their old jobs. Councils of unemployed workers formed spontaneously in many areas, and often took drastic measures to provide some security for their members. In Kaluga, for instance, an unemployed council taxed all those employed and exercised control over the few open positions. In Tver, workers who received any income outside work, even if it was from the work of members of their own family, were dismissed. Such councils, of course, put pressure on the government to provide jobs, but public projects succeeded in absorbing only a small percentage of the total number of unemployed. Nor did the Labour Exchanges set up by the trade unions with the approval of the Commissariat of Labour make a significant difference. They grew up too slowly, were plagued with a shortage of funds, and lacked vigorous state support. Insurance for the unemployed was also quite inadequate. The government had passed a law on 11 December providing for an average day's pay for each day lost in all areas where the population was more than twenty thousand. But the owners were to assume the responsibility of payment, and most begged off with the excuse that they were unable to meet the costs. The practical effect of the decree was therefore next to nil. With the lack of work and adequate insurance, many workers began to return to the countryside. The major cities were beginning to depopulate, Petrograd losing one million inhabitants by the spring, Moscow one-half million. The industrial proletariat had declined from around three and a half to two and a half million by the summer of 1918.[86]

The Brest-Litovsk peace terms, ratified by the Soviet government in March 1918, left the Russian economy in a worse position still. More than a quarter of its arable land and total population were ceded to German control. Some 90 per cent of the sugar industry was lost, as was 70 per cent of iron, steel, and coal. Some factories were resettled in Russian-controlled areas, but these remained few in comparison to the total. The Fourth All-Russian Congress of Soviets, which met in mid-March and ratified the treaty, called upon the working population to increase its activity and self-discipline, and to build solid organizations capable of stemming the economic disorder. But the Congress left ambiguous the *social forms* the activity and self-organization of the workers should take. This was shortly to become the focus of the debate over economic policy in the Bolshevik party.

In his political report to the Seventh Party Congress on 7 March Lenin had begun to define what he meant by worker self-activity and organization with his phrase 'learn discipline from the Germans'.[87] On 12 March he elaborated in *Izvestiya*: 'Yes, learn from the Germans! History is moving in zigzags by roundabout ways. It so happens that it is the Germans who now personify, besides a brutal imperialism, the principle of discipline, organization, harmonious cooperation on the basis of modern machine industry, and strict accounting and control. And that is what we are lacking. That is just what we must learn.'[88]

This is what he intended to introduce into every workplace in Russia. In 'The Immediate Tasks of the Soviet Government', written later in April[89] and widely distributed in pamphlet form, Lenin argued that the dictatorship of individuals is perfectly consistent with socialist democracy. The history of bourgeois revolutions proves that the dictatorship of individuals is often the instrument of dictatorship of revolutionary classes, he said, without attempting to reconcile this with his belief that the socialist revolution differs decisively in that its goal is the political and economic rule of the vast majority of the population. Indeed, Lenin continued, the technical organization of industry itself *requires* the social form of dictatorship within the labour process: '...it must be said that large-scale machine industry—which is precisely the material source, the productive source, the foundation of socialism—calls for absolute and strict *unity of will*, which directs the joint labours of hundreds, thousands and tens of thousands of people. The technical, economic and historical necessity of this is obvious, and all those who have thought about socialism have always regarded it as one of the conditions of socialism. But how can strict unity of will be ensured? By thousands subordinating their will to the will of one.'[90]

If 'class consciousness' is ideal, Lenin continued, this subordination will be relatively mild. But ideal or not, *'unquestioning subordination* to a single will is absolutely necessary for the success of processes organized on the pattern of large-scale machine industry.'[91] The workers were permitted 'the airing of questions at public meetings' as long as they exercise *'iron* discipline while at work.'[92] Later in the article, he characterized this dictatorship in the work process as 'purely executive', but made no attempt to clarify what powers of election and recall the workers were to have either in the individual workplace or in the larger economic regulating institutions if the problem of bureaucracy, which he himself recognized, was to be counteracted. The orders the dictators would execute were simply those of the Soviet government.[93]

The primary tasks of the hour, then, were accounting, control, and strict labour discipline: 'Keep regular and honest accounts of money, manage economically, do not be lazy, do not steal, observe the strictest labour discipline—it is these slogans, justly scorned by the revolutionary proletariat when the bourgeoisie used them to conceal its rule as an exploiting class, that are now, since the overthrow of the bourgeoisie, becoming the immediate and principal slogans of the moment.'[94]

Indeed, Lenin continued, their fulfilment was the *'sole* condition' for the salvation of the country, and, given Soviet state power, the *'sufficient* condition for the final victory of socialism' (Lenin's emphasis).[95] The essential goal was to raise the productivity of labour. The distinctive feature of socialism was its ability to achieve this: 'In every socialist revolution, after the proletariat has solved the problem of capturing power, and to the extent that the task of expropriating the expropriators and suppressing their resistance has been carried out in the main, there necessarily comes to the forefront the fundamental task of creating a social system superior to capitalism, namely, raising the productivity of labour, and in this connection (and for this purpose) securing better organization of labour.'[96]

In order to raise the productivity of labour, industry itself must be developed, along with the educational and cultural level of the people. But the Soviet government should not shrink from using methods previously associated with capitalism, namely, Taylorism and piece-work. Lenin argued: 'The Russian is a bad worker compared with people in advanced countries. It could not be otherwise under the tsarist regime and in view of the persistence of the hangover from serfdom. The task that the Soviet government must set the people in all its scope is—learn to work. The Taylor system, the last word of capitalism in this respect, like all capitalist progress, is a combination of the refined brutality of bourgeois exploitation and a number of the greatest scientific achievements in the field of analysing mechanical motions during work, the elimination of superfluous and awkward motions, the elaboration of correct methods of work, the introduction of the best system of accounting and control, etc.'[97]

In addition to piece-work and Taylorism, the Soviet government must pay high salaries to the bourgeois experts. Admittedly, this is a step backward from the principles of the Paris Commune, where the wages of the highest paid were not to exceed those of the average worker. But such a retreat was necessary, if the services of such experts were to be employed for the benefit of the people. Taylorism and piece-work, however, were *not* similarly designated as unwelcome but unavoidable compromises.[98]

Referring to the continuity of his present theses with his thinking even before the revolution, Lenin told the Soviet Central Executive Committee on 29 April that what he was proposing was essentially the introduction of state capitalism on the German model. Attempting to claim democratic approval for his policy, he argued that the concrete propositions of 'The Immediate Tasks of the Soviet Government' were 'nothing but a development of the resolution' on mass activity and self-organization approved at the Fourth Soviet Congress, although they were nothing of the sort.[99] State capitalism was to be introduced by any means necessary: '...our task is to study the state capitalism of the Germans, to spare *no effort* in copying it and not to shrink from adopting *dictatorial* methods to hasten the copying of it. Our task is to hasten this copying even more than Peter hastened the copying of Western culture by barbarian Russia, and we must not hesitate to use barbarous methods in fighting barbarism.'[100]

Since the major enemy was petty proprietorship, anything that could be done to introduce the centralized forms of state capitalism would be an advance. Indeed, it would be Russia's 'salvation', and would make the further development of socialism 'easy' and 'assured'. It would be 'a sure guarantee that within a year socialism will have gained a permanently firm hold and will have become invincible in our country.'[101] The fear that social forms like this could evolve in a capitalist direction, now that the proletariat possesses state power, is 'so ludicrous, such a sheer absurdity and fabrication',[102] nothing short of 'utter theoretical nonsense'.[103]

It was the Left Communist faction of the party that harboured just such fears, and attempted to articulate a theoretical justification for them in a debate that lasted several months. Led by such figures as Bukharin, Osinsky, Radek, Uritsky, Pyatakov, and Smirnov, this faction officially constituted itself during the debate on the peace settlement with Germany, although its roots lay in the Left Bolshevism of 1917, and in Bukharin's case, in pre-revolutionary leftist opposition to Lenin. In February and March 1918 the Leftists argued vociferously against acceptance of German peace terms as a capitulation to imperialism and a sellout of the European, and especially the German, proletariat, and urged a revolutionary guerilla war instead. Having lost on this question, they shifted their emphasis to a critique of Lenin's newly elaborated economic policies.

The most articulate expression of the Left Communists' position on economic questions came in Osinsky's articles in their theoretical journal *Kommunist,* which appeared in Moscow after suppression of their Petrograd daily of the same name in March.[104] Under capitalism, Osinsky argued, labour is organized essentially for the needs of accumulation and profit. In the interests of preserving their own labour-power, workers tend to resist this complete subordination to accumulation, while capitalists employ whatever methods they can to perfect it. Anything that isolates the workers from one another as separate owners of their commodity, labourpower, tends to serve the purpose of accumulation. Among such devices are the decomposition of the labour process into fragmented tasks, the introduction of Taylorism, piece wages, premiums, profit sharing, and so on. In proposing the use of some of these very same methods of labour organization and motivation in the interests of increasing the productivity of labour, Lenin forgets their essential connection to the exploitation of labour. The introduction of such measures, Osinsky continued, would tend to destroy the solidarity of the working class, for the very same reasons that they do under capitalism. Workers would be encouraged to view themselves primarily as peddlers of their labour-power, competing against one another and elevating their individual interests over those of the class as a whole. 'The worker is encouraged to make as much money in a day as possible, and for other things he has neither the time nor the interest.'[105] The social relations of the workplace organized in this manner tend to discourage any concern with general social tasks outside of work, promote the formation of a labour aristocracy, the physical exhaustion of the workers, and the general passivity of the class as a whole.[106]

Osinsky expressed as much concern as Lenin with the urgent need to raise the productivity of labour if the revolution was to secure its material foundations. But, he argued, Lenin and others tended to confuse labour productivity with labour intensity. The latter is, certainly, one aspect of labour productivity, but less important than the two other essential factors: 1) the general condition of the means of production, their proper organization, functioning, supply, etc.; 2) the skill of the workers. Piece wages can increase the intensity of work, but can hardly influence these more basic factors. And, aside from the negative consequences already mentioned, they tend to divert attention from the primary task of reorganizing production and exchange. For, he asked, 'is not the lack of all these things, the obstruction and wearing out of the machines, the disorder in the factory apparatus, the constant interruptions of production because of the lack of materials, fuel etc.—are not these among the most important causes—or perhaps the most important cause—of the falling productivity of the factories and of labour?'[107] It is these objective factors, above all, that demoralize the workers and encourage carelessness, since theirwork is constantly interrupted, tasks must be continually repeated unnecessarily, and workers often have to move from plant to plant with little overall stability in their work relations and patterns. Indeed, Osinsky argued, these objective factors alone account for perhaps two-thirds to three-quarters of general labour productivity, and any attempt to shift the burden to labour intensity by introducing piece wages will lead to the exhaustion and mechanization of the proletariat itself.

It was not work discipline as such that the Left Communists opposed, but such discipline under capitalist authority relations inside the plant and by the use of typically capitalist methods. Osinsky argued that production norms, in connection with hourly wages that allow the workers a 'normal' existence, are not only admissible but required by the dignity of all those who would be energetic in producing for society's needs. To work regularly and without carelessness and inattention is a matter of occupational and class respect and a citizen's general duty. Such production norms must be set by workers organizations themselves, and violations must be dealt with by work mates and by 'comradely courts of justice'. Democratically reconstituted People's Economic Councils should have authority in establishing such norms. The trade unions should regulate and shorten the length of the working day so as to eliminate existing unemployment, since lengthening the working day in a situation of rising unemployment as the regime was proposing, was completely absurd. For, as Osinsky concluded, 'if the proletariat itself is not in the position to create the prerequisites for a socialist organization of work, then no one can do it in its stead, and no one can force it to do it.'[108]

Concerning the role of technical and other experts in the organization of production, Osinsky was no less forthright in distinguishing himself from the proposals of Lenin and other party leaders. It must be fully recognized from the start, he argued, that the Russian

proletariat—or, for that matter, the West European proletariat—lacks sufficient technical knowledge and general education to be able to adminster a socialist economy completely on its
own. Although the goal of a socialist society is to break down the
capitalist division of labour and generalize such competence among
the workers, the current tasks require that we base ourselves on the
division of labour inherited from the old society. The experts from
the old regime must be utilized to the fullest, and the workers must
set themselves the task of learning from them in the process.

But this must be done in such a way that real power over production remains with the proletariat. These bourgeois specialists
should be encouraged to work both by the payment of the higher
salaries required and by the introduction of general labour duty for
them. But their connections with the bourgeoisie *as a class* must be
decisively severed. Under no condition should their remuneration
take the form of obligation notes or shares (as under the old
regime, as well as in the various state-capitalist proposals of the
new), since these simply perpetuate the material and psychological
connection of the experts to finance capital. The technicians and
administrators must understand that they are simply employees of
the soviet state, and be discouraged as much as possible about the
possibilities of a return to capitalism. Only then will their work and
their tutelage consistently promote socialist aims. The engineers of
the city electricity works, of the streetcar and water transport
systems, of the state factories and mines, have already begun to
work in this fashion, argued Osinsky, and the resolute nationalization of all large-scale industry would further promote this process.
In their executive functions (in contrast to their legislative and advisory functions), the technical and administrative experts must be
autonomous to a considerable extent: the workers must abide by
their directions in the normal course of production. However, these
experts are to be nominated only by the workers management itself
and confirmed by the regional People's Economic Council. They
are not to be appointed by higher state institutions, and they can be
removed on initiative from below.[109]

Only the resolute completion of the nationalization of large-scale
industrial and financial institutions, Osinsky continued, could provide the framework for the conscious construction of socialism by
the working classes themselves. But for nationalization to be a true

step toward socialism, an extensive network of democratically organized People's Economic Councils must be formed (or re-formed), from the local level to the Supreme Economic Council, with emphasis on the development of coherent regional councils. Until now, Osinsky admitted, the SEC has been a top-heavy organization dominated by the trade-union bureaucracy and state representatives—and a relatively ineffective one at that. But the main reason for this is that it has been 'hovering in the air', cut off from vital democratic economic councils at the regional level and below. Its activity has been absorbed in administrative details because it has not delegated its work to lower organs.

The Kharkov regional council, before its destruction by the German occupation, provided a living example of how such a net-work of regulatory institutions could work. This council embraced some eighteen local councils, and superseded all the economic administrative authorities of the region, including the com-missariats, in food, supply, transport, agriculture, finance, and labour, thus eliminating much of the conflict and confusion of overlapping economic authorities. Besides these areas and other general departments concerning technical, statistical, and legal matters, the council was organized into a series of production departments (coal, iron ore, salt, chemicals, metals, and so on). The boards of these departments were staffed with up to two-thirds skilled workers from the respective branches of production and up to one-third engineers and white-collar employees. The workers and employees were elected at regional congresses of the factory committees and trade unions, although later this power was transferred to the district councils. These elected boards constituted the Plenum of the regional council. The heads of the production department were elected by the Plenum, and in their common meeting they formed the Bureau of the council, which administered its daily activity. If all regions were so organized, argued Osinsky, the SEC could begin to function as a true centre organically linked to the localities. It should be elected at the congresses of these local organs, and at least two-thirds of the members of its plenum should come from them. Such an arrangement would complete the democratic-centralist character of the entire system, as opposed to its current bureaucratic-centralist organization. A centre like this would thus be free of day-to-day details and could concern itself primarily with the development of guiding principles, general production plans, and cost estimates and instructions, while retaining only the power of the purse.[110]

Nationalization of all large industrial and financial institutions under such a system of economic councils, according to Osinsky, would eliminate the confusion and conflict associated with the system of dual power in the factories, where formal authority rested with the owners, actual power with the factory committee. Such a system would also eliminate the dualism and confusion in accounting, registration, and financing, and thus remove many of the possibilities for sabotage. It would likewise—and Osinsky reiterated this point again and again—preclude syndicalism and separatism among the individual factories. Although workers would have a decisive two-thirds majority in the management boards of each factory, only half of these would come from within the particular factory, the other half from the PECs, the Workers Soviets, and the trade unions. The workers are to understand that the means of production belong not to the workers of each particular factory, but to the working class as a whole. As long as the organs regulating the economy are democratically constituted and organically linked to the rank and file, they can function in the interests of the entire class. Each particular factory management is to have a significant degree of independence, but it is also strictly subordinate to the regional economic council, which examines its production plans and cost estimates to make sure that it is operating within the framework of the authorized plans. In fact, syndicalist tendencies have primarily been the result of the lack of organic connections and the bitter experience of fruitless requests for aid from the overburdened central administration.[111]

'The emancipation of the working class must be the act of the working class itself.' Osinsky repeated this famous tenet from Marx's Inaugural Address to the First International, and offered his detailed outline to provide the social and institutional framework most conducive to that conscious process of self-emancipation. His two-part article in *Kommunist*, like other pieces by the Leftists, elaborated even further on questions of finance, pricing, the relation between town and country, workers' wage demands, and the possible objections to this system. But the details need not concern us here. What is important is that a relatively coherent and articulate alternative to Lenin's was being put forward in the Bolshevik party itself in the spring of 1918, and its authors viewed it as both more principled and more realistic. Indeed, they argued that the adoption of the Leninist proposals would threaten the very basis of the revolution.

The state-capitalist organization of industry, Osinsky held, would open the way to forces threatening the revolution from without and within. Proposals were being advanced to transform factories legally into state property and to form state trusts. Out of this would come stock companies, a large percentage (up to one-half) of whose shares and yearly dividends would be distributed to capitalists to obtain their cooperation; alternatively, they would receive bonds on which they would receive a fixed percentage. Such arrangements would permit the penetration of 'nationalized' industry by foreign capital, and inflect the development of the Russian economy in the direction of a full restoration of capitalism. But the threat from without was not the most perilous. The real menace was that these economic forms would vest all power and initiative in the old captains of industry, state representatives, and the trade-union bureaucracy. Practically every impetus from below would be stifled, the organization of production subordinated to the needs of profit. This would imply not only authoritarian relations within the factory, where power would remain in the hands of the capitalists, experts, and state appointees, but also the organization of labour-power for the most intensive use possible. This would involve, of course, material incentives, piece-work, and Taylorism. The working class would be urged to view its social tasks primarily in terms of the election of its political leaders and discipline at work. In daily life in production, it would become a passive element, a mere object, an atomized mass of privatized interests. With the vitiation of its social interest and the restoration of dictatorial power in the workplace, the political dictatorship of the proletariat would itself eventually degenerate:

'The stick, which is brandished over the workers, will be in the hands either of a social force that is under the influence of another social force or of the proletariat. If this stick is in the hands of the soviet power, then the latter will have to draw support from another social class (e.g. the peasantry) against the workers, and in this way will destroy itself as the dictatorship of the proletariat. Socialism and the socialist organization of work will either be built by the proletariat itself, or it will not be built at all; but then something else will be erected, namely state capitalism.'[112]

The programmes put forth by Lenin and the party leadership, which Osinsky sarcastically called socialism à la Morgan-Rockefeller, would undermine the revolution itself and would lead to 'bureaucratic centralization, the rule of various commissars, the deprivation of the independence of the local soviets, and in practice the rejection of the type of "state commune" administered from below.'[113]

Lenin, as already noted, considered such gloomy analyses to be 'utter theoretical nonsense.'[114] State-capitalist economic forms, under the dictatorship of the proletariat, would assuredly lead to socialism. His arguments against the Left Communists, however, evinced caricatured distortion of their positions, evasiveness, and bitter invective more than principled confrontation and clarification of opposing positions. Their theses, he argued, were '*absolutely nothing but* the same petty-bourgeois waverings' of other enemies of the revolution, from Martov on the left to Milyukov on the right.[115] All shared the same doubts 'from the standpoint of deciding not on paper but in practice whether the hardships on the road to socialism are worthwhile.'[116]

In effect, Lenin argued that anyone who disagreed with his proposals on state capitalism, labour organization, and discipline lacked the determination to struggle through the present difficulties and was 'thoroughly imbued with the mentality of the declassed petty-bourgeois intellectual.'[117] By selectively quoting Osinsky's article so as to make it appear that the Left Communists opposed all labour discipline, and not just discipline under capitalist authority and by capitalist methods, he was able to avoid confronting their concrete proposals for work norms and self-discipline by democratically elected workers organizations.[118] Completely misrepresenting their position on the need to appropriate the knowledge of the bourgeoisie and their experts, but only under conditions that severed this knowledge from the bourgeoisie *as a class*,

Lenin caricatured them as wanting instead to give these experts lessons: 'But what do you want to teach them? Socialism, perhaps? Teach socialism to the merchants, to businessmen? No, take on the job yourselves, if you like. We are not going to help you, it is labour in vain. It is no use teaching these engineers, businessmen and merchants. It is no use teaching them socialism.'[119]

At only one point in his continuing polemic against the Left during the spring did he even mention their central criticism of his proposals, namely that the introduction of capitalist authority and labour discipline would diminish the initiative, activity, and self-organization of the proletariat. And his reply was simple: such claims 'are a terrible disgrace and imply the complete renunciation of communism in practice and complete desertion to the camp of the petty bourgeoisie.'[120] Why? The closest thing to an answer that he gave was that the vanguard of the proletariat supports the introduction of labour discipline and the petty bourgeoisie opposes it. The workers have confidence in the ability of proletarian state power to control these authorities. On the democratization of the economic regulating organs through which such control was to occur—not a word. On Osinsky's quite specific proposals on how to reform the economic councils at all levels so as to make them both more efficient and more subject to popular control—not a word. On the warnings that Lenin's propositions would lead to the atomization of the working class, the narrowing of its interests to the most favourable sale of its labour-power, and eventually to its physical exhaustion—nothing.

Labour and Economy, Spring 1918

Amidst these debates on the proper road to socialism, the regime was attempting to bring together a general economic programme. At its heart early in the spring were efforts to establish state-capitalist trusts. It will be recalled that on the very day of the seizure of power Lenin had approached Larin with such proposals, and meetings with various groups of capitalists had begun in December. The first plan, offered by the influential industrialist (and prominent benefactor of right-wing causes) Alexis Meshcherskii, sought the creation of a huge metal trust, the 'Russian National Association', which would employ some three hundred thousand workers and be responsible for 50–60 per cent of all railway-car construction. It would be capitalized at 1.5 thousand million rubles. One-third of the shares and votes on the administrative board—corresponding to the percentage of already nationalized firms in the trust—were to go to the government, with the remaining two-thirds distributed to the shareholders of the non-nationalized firms. In the course of negotiations, the government laid claim to 40 per cent, then 50, and 80 and finally 100 per cent. In return for their investment and cooperation, the former shareholders were to receive non-voting bonds equal to one-tenth of the original capital and to be guaranteed annual receipts of 4 per cent. In either case, the factories were to be managed by bourgeois specialists. The regime likewise re-opened negotiations to effectively denationalize the banks and return them to the control of their former directors. This plan, which reportedly had won the approval of Lenin and Trotsky, represented the financial counterpart to similar moves in heavy industry. The motivation of Meshcherskii and the other industrialists engaged in negotiations with the regime was to forestall nationalization until the unstable government could be overthrown by force.[121]

Several state-capitalist combines were set up early in 1918. Lenin himself referred approvingly to agreements in the leather, textiles, and sugar industries, where the owners retained one-third of the posts in the respective *glavki* and *tsentry* administering the industries.[122] And many other Bolshevik leaders, including some in the trade-union hierarchy, were quite enthusiastic about such projects. Gol'tsman, Gastev, Oborin, and Kozelev, all top officials of the various metalworkers' unions that would have been affected by the Meshcherskii project, supported it on the grounds that it was the only way to attract foreign capital and credit to Russian industry. Gol'tsman and Gastev were themselves leading proponents of industrialization at all costs throughout the early years. (Gol'tsman, for instance, said on one occasion that 'none of us should be thinking about whether we are promoting socialism or capitalism. That is legalism—let us stop analysing.')[123] But the rank-and-file workers in the metal industry reacted to the project quite differently, notwithstanding Lenin's insistence that no class-conscious worker could possibly fear capitalist authority in the workplace as long as soviet political power was upheld.[124] Workers in Meshcherskii's own plants staged a protest and demanded immediate nationalization. A conference of delegates from several affected plants met on 17 April to demand that the negotiations be broken off, and the trade-union leaders were forced to call an ad hoc conference of metal workers in Moscow on 19–22 April to discuss the matter. This time Gol'tsman's arguments were countered by those of the Left Communist Kosior, and the conference voted that the regime should break off the negotiations—a decision which, apparently unknown to the conference, had been taken a few days earlier. The metal industry should be fully nationalized instead. Mass pressure from below and the ideological challenge of the Left had brought the downfall of one of Lenin's most cherished projects.[125]

With the defeat of the Meshcherskii project, demands for the completion of nationalization became ever more irresistible. A metalworkers conference in mid-May repeated its earlier demands, as did a conference of representatives of the already nationalized industries. The First All-Russian Congress of Councils of National Economy passed a resolution on 3 June calling for the 'systematic nationalization of whole branches of industry' beginning with metals, engineering, chemicals, oil, and textiles, as well as the nationalization of all the banks. But little was done by the authorities. Even in metals, where the decision to nationalize had been taken in mid-April, little further progress had been made by late June. Of the 521 nationalized firms of which the SEC had a record, 24 per cent had been taken over by the local workers organs, and 51 per cent by regional People's Economic Councils, where the influence of local organs was often very strong. Only 20 per cent were the product of action by the SEC or the Council of People's Commissars, the rest having been state-owned before October.

Most banks, the commercial fleet, and all foreign trade had been nationalized, but not a single industrial branch. Entire industries had been taken over in the Donetz basin, South Russia (smelting), and Baku (oil), but these were disrupted by political and military developments in these areas.[126] It was only the fear that important Russian firms might be transferred to German ownership to protect them from future nationalization that prompted the regime to move decisively on 28 June and nationalize all large-scale industry. Henceforth, all such industrial and commercial enterprises were to be considered state property, and were to be administered by the various departments of the SEC. Until special instructions were issued for each enterprise, the former owners were to lease them rent-free and receive income from them provided that they continued to administer and finance them.[127]

While rank-and-file pressure from the workers and Left Communist struggle within the party had been relatively successful in the conflict over nationalization and state capitalism, the results were much more ambiguous concerning the structure of management of industry itself. In early March, after Larin and Milyutin had displaced Osinsky and other Leftists, the SEC issued an order calling for the *glavki* and *tsentry* to set up managerial troikas in all nationalized firms. These were to be composed of an administrative director, a technical director, and a government commissar. All decisions of the first two members were to be binding on the factory committee and could be overridden only by the government commissar. Workers, employees, and technical delegates from the factory, along with representatives of the Central Council of Trade Unions and local soviets, could participate in an advisory council. This order was aimed directly at undermining the power of the elected worker managements in those firms that had been sequestered by local workers' organizations, although it probably did not begin to take effect for some time.[128] In mid-May, Lenin proposed another model for the metal industry, whereby the metal conference (consisting of 50 per cent workers representatives and 50 per cent engineers and administrators) would elect a provisional management council for the entire industry, to be supplemented at the initiative of the SEC and the Central Committee of the Metalworkers' Union.[129]

The situation on the railroads was still different. In March Shlyapnikov had issued a very critical report on the effect of self-management, and Lenin came out for dictatorial control by appointed commissars. Several days later, on 23 March, the Council of People's Commissars, without even submitting it to the Soviet

Central Executive Committee for ratification, issued a decree granting the Commissar of Ways and Communications full power over all railways. A collegium of representatives, elected at the railworkers' congresses and confirmed by the Council of People's Commissars and the Soviet CEC, was to convene under the commissar, but in no way interfere with his dictatorial authority. Thus workers delegates were to function only in an advisory capacity, and even then had first to be approved by higher administrative authorities. On each particular line there was also to be a commissar with dictatorial powers, either elected by the workers or appointed from above. In either case, he was answerable only to the highest commissar, and the actual manner of appointment was dependent on his tractability in regard to the latter.[130]

The Left Communists, Left SRs, and railworkers met this new decree with a wave of condemnations and protests. A rank-and-file movement called the Alliance of Workers Representatives sprang up in many places and articulated many typically Leftist demands. Vikzhedor, the executive board of the railworkers union, immediately submitted an alternative plan that would have vested overall power with an elected collegium. The regime, however, rejected it out of hand, even though Lenin continued to bait the Leftists with their lack of an alternative to the new rail decree. But the protests did not subside, and soon the Commissar of Ways and Communications found himself overburdened in this supercentralized management system. As a result, the commissar submitted a new decree to the Soviet CEC on May 31, calling for the resumption of functions by the local rail councils. The district commissar was still to have unlimited powers, but the councils were to be protected against arbitrary nominations and dismissals. In addition, twice-yearly district workers congresses were to elect collegia to advise the district commissars. Clearly, this revival of council organs at the lowest levels was an extremely limited form of workers control, but it was an advance over the March decree, and further protests against its restrictive character were of no avail.[131]

It was only with the First All-Russian Congress of People's Economic Councils, which met from 26 May to 4 June in Moscow, however, that general principles for the management of nationalized firms were finally worked out. Present were more than one hundred voting delegates from the SEC, and regional and local PECs, along with some one hundred and fifty non-voting delegates. The Presidium of the SEC presented a proposal authorized by Lenin himself for strictly centralized management through government-appointed commissars. Lomov, arguing for the Left Communists, noted regretfully that 'we are by every means—by nationalization, by centralization—strangling the forces in our country. The masses are being cut off from living creative power in all branches of our national economy.'[132] Andronikov, a trade unionist from the Urals, where support for the Left was very strong, put forth a proposal that the workers elect two-thirds of the management, one-third of which was to be nominated by the appropriate trade union. The latter would likewise nominate the remaining one-third from among the technical and administrative personnel. But the power of the centre would not be threatened, since the *glavki* and *tsentry* would retain the right to disband particular management boards. This proposal was accepted by the Section for the Organization of Production. Lenin, however, upon hearing of this anarcho-syndicalist 'stupidity', began a massive campaign of party pressure among the delegates, and although unable to convince the congress of his own preferred proposal, forced a compromise. Two-thirds of the management boards, including the technical personnel, were to be appointed by the regional PECs, with the SEC having the right to veto all appointments. The trade unions could propose up to one-half of these. The remaining one-third was to be elected by the trade-union members in the plant. However, it seems that in practice the regional PECs and the trade unions often relinquished their right to appoint members to the managerial boards, leaving representatives of the workers who were already there in a majority. Thus, even amidst a system designed to assure effective control from above, the factory committees often played the most dynamic role in managing the nationalized firms.[133]

In the early spring of 1918 a consistent policy in regard to wages, work discipline, and organization also still remained to be worked out in practice. By the time of the October revolution, most Russian workers had shifted to hourly wages, although with considerable gradations according to skill, industry, location, and other factors. Many in the party took it for granted that wages would be equalized after the revolution, although no theorist seems to have dealt with the problem directly. An early decree limited the salaries of commissars to about that of an average skilled worker, in accordance with the spirit of Lenin's *State and Revolution*, and the Commissar of Labour set the equalization of wages as a general principle. But most wage agreements, which according to a decree of 29 December had to be approved by the Commissar of Labour, continued to recognize distinctions based on skill, and sometimes on difficulty or danger.[134] And with the continued decline in productivity immediately after revolution, the issue of piece-wages arose once again. Although some factory committees and trade unions supported a return to piece-rates as the only real solution to this problem, most seem to have opposed it. As a resolution passed at the Railworkers Congress in January 1918 held, piece-rates would drive the workers to physical exhaustion and increase unemployment, thus further contributing to the problem rather than helping solve it.[135]

As the economic crisis intensified, however, especially after the signing of the Brest treaty, many trade-union leaders began to shift their opinion. Others, such as Lozovsky, maintained their opposition, arguing that the introduction of piece-wages within a system of continuing private ownership and profit would only intensify the exploitation of the working class. But such objections were overridden, and the All-Russian Central Council of Trade Unions, after deliberations with the SEC, the Commissariat of Labour, and Lenin himself, issued a decree on 3 April approving the use of piece-rates and bonuses, provided a minimum wage was guaranteed and a maximum limit set to prevent the exhaustion of the workers.[136]

In May, following the ratification of these principles by the Second All-Russian Congress of Labour Commissars and the Soviet Central Executive Committee, the Trade Union Council issued further instructions, mandating the classification of all work by skill, complexity, precision, training and experience, importance, and difficulty, and the payment of wages accordingly. All such scales had to be approved by the Commissariat of Labour and the appropriate All-Russian trade-union councils.

The new policy permitted the full payment of wages only to those who fulfilled strict production norms set by the authorities. Those falling short were to have their wages reduced by one-third, with the stipulation that the so-reduced wage in the lowest category conformed to the minimum standard of living set by the Commissariat of Labour. The number of gradations varied from industry to industry. In metals it was fifteen, in leather as many as twenty-six. While the highest rates paid were supposed not to exceed twice the lowest, this was often disregarded in practice. Women were to be paid as much as men, but again, this was seldom observed, as women received some 10 to 45 per cent less than men doing the same work, even in industries where women predominated. In addition, the Commissariat often set the minimum wages below what was necessary for a worker to subsist, and set production norms very high. In the metal industry, for example, the norms were first set at 85–90 per cent of the average productivity before the war. As Brügmann notes, however, in conditions of long years of war and malnutrition, ill-functioning and disrepair of the means of production and supply, such norms could be met only if the workers drove themselves to the point of damaging their health.[137]

Under such pressure, productivity did begin to increase, in some places two and three times. But this did not prevent the regime from raising the norms again at the end of 1918, arguing that the extremely meagre wages were 'perniciously high' and were leading to the formation of a labour aristocracy. In January 1919, for instance, minimum norms in the metal industry were increased 150 per cent. Due to the difficulties of calculation of overfulfilment on an individual basis, however, the unions switched to a collective system of bonuses about the same time.[138]

On the issue of Taylorism, Lenin's viewpoint also gradually won out over opposition from all parties, including the Left Communists and moderates such as Lozovsky and Ryazanov. The 3 April decree of the Central Council of Trade Unions formally recognized it, and the Soviet Central Executive Committee and the First Congress of People's Economic Councils later followed suit. Influential trade-union leaders such as Gastev, whom Lozovsky once justly characterized as the 'poet of Taylorism' and who later went on to found the Central Labour Institute in Moscow, whose goal was the extension and propagation of Taylorist research and principles, argued in the spring of 1918 that struggle against Taylorism meant struggle against the workbench itself.[139]

The Left was considerably more successful on the question of actual work discipline. At the end of March, Lenin had come out in favour of transferring responsibility for discipline from the workers organizations to independent organs. His fear was that under a system of state capitalism in which workers would still be taking orders from owners and their managers, the unions and factory committees would be too soft on workers who violated established work rules. But many union leaders, not to mention factory-committee militants and rank-and-file workers, resisted this. And the 3 April order 'On Work Discipline' issued by the Central Council of Trade Unions, while it set out specific rules regarding work time, breaks, meetings at work (which were forbidden except for elections to the factory committees and soviets), and a schedule of fines up to expulsion from the plant, left the enforcement of these rules to the factory committee, which was the local cell of the trade union. These principles were reiterated at the Second Congress of Labour Commissars, where trade unionists predominated, and at the First PEC Congress in late May and early June. Strict discipline had to be observed but the old forms of supervision avoided. Self-discipline would arise only if the initiative remained with the workers' own organizations.[140]

5

The Peasantry
in Revolution

In 1917 some 80 per cent of the people of Russia were peasants. The great majority of them eked out a living from year to year on small, inefficient plots of land that they either owned, held in communal tenure, or rented from the landed nobility. Some had little or no land at all and were forced to work for a wage on the large estates or the farms of the richer peasants. But the formation of an agricultural proletariat was not well advanced, and the working class of the cities had no real parallel on the land. Although the urban-oriented and urban-based Bolshevik party came to power with at least the passive support of most sections of the peasantry, the revolutionary coalition of workers and peasants was racked by many problems. The most immediate of these, as we have seen, was the organization of an effective system to feed the cities under conditions of severe disruption in industry and transport, which aggravated the tendency of the peasants to retreat to their self-enclosed world of largely subsistence farming.

Behind the pressing problems of urban-rural exchange lay the long-term prospects of the modernization of agricultural technique, the transformation of the social relations of production in the countryside, and the development of the institutional and cultural conditions for the integration of the peasantry into a national democratic polity. The Soviet government's early peasant policies presented a peculiar blend of rigid economic exigency on the one hand and grand ideological illusion on the other. They did help save the new regime from military defeat and complete urban disintegration, but at the price of the profound alienation and introversion of the peasantry and the estrangement of the only major peasant-oriented party that supported the seizure of power and the socialist transformation of Russia. The price was indeed heavy, and perhaps not entirely unavoidable. In any case, the legacy of the years of civil war deeply affected the options available in the twenties, and set the stage for Stalin's brutal and authoritarian collectivization.

Serfdom, Emancipation and Crisis

Until 1861 the vast majority of Russian peasants had been serfs. For several hundred years they had been bound to the land, performing labour service (*barshchina*) or providing payment in money or kind (*obrok*) to the master of the estate on which they lived, whether noble, church, or state. In the more fertile areas, where grain production was often aimed at the export market, labour duty with their own tools and livestock tended to predominate. In the less fertile regions, where both the peasants' share of the land and the average size of the holdings were considerably larger—although still barely sufficient for subsistence in most cases—obligation took the form of *obrok*, which was obtained through home handicraft production or employment in town industries. In the early part of the nineteenth century, however, the peasants, who had never quite accepted that the land did not belong to those who worked it, became increasingly rebellious. Tsar Alexander was finally forced to recognize that 'it is better to abolish serfdom from above than to wait until it begins to abolish itself from below.'[1]

In the interests of social stability and the development of a modern military force that would not again suffer humiliation as in Crimea, the tsar had been able to override the nobility's opposition to emancipation.[2] But the landlords decisively influenced its implementation at the local level. To begin with, they were to receive compensation for the land turned over to the freed serfs. The latter had to advance 20 per cent of this payment, the state advancing the remainder. These advances were to be repaid over a period of forty-nine years at an annual interest rate of 6 per cent. In addition, the land was often sold at prices considerably in excess of current scales especially in the less fertile regions, where the peasant share of the land was higher. In the black-earth regions, the peasants' share of the land actually decreased by about 25 per cent, and it was often the best land that was detached from their holdings. Access to pasture, forest, and stream was heavily dependent on landlord rentals. The reform, so 'well adjusted to the differential interests of the gentry in the two regions,'[3] hardly satisfied the needs of the peasantry, and hunger for land remained chronic. It is no wonder that the original proclamation was met with a confused combination of anger and disbelief. Indeed, some peasants felt it was a fabrication of the landlords, and awaited the real decree of the tsar.

But no benevolent decree was to follow, and the peasantry was condemned to worsening misery for the rest of the century. Decreasing grain prices on the world market and rising taxation to pay for state-financed industrialization played no small part in this—indirect taxes alone rose from 16.5 million rubles in 1881 to 109.5 million in 1895.[4] The size of the average plot of land per male peasant dropped from 4.8 *desyatins* in 1860 to 2.6 in 1900.[5] Such conditions encouraged the retention of various forms of labour service alongside the emerging capitalist relations in the countryside. But perhaps the most important factor in the mounting agricultural crisis was the communal system of land tenure itself, which had been strengthened by the terms of the Emancipation Act.

The *mir* or *obshchina*, as the village commune was known, generally consisted of all the peasant households of the village, and was governed by the *skhod*, the assembly of all male heads of households. Although its roots may go back hundreds of years, as its Slavophile proponents claimed at the time, its most important functions date from the early years of the eighteenth century, when a government-imposed 'soul tax' encouraged the practice of repartitional land tenure. Control over the land was vested in the commune, and each household had the right to an allotment. The commune periodically repartitioned or reallocated the land on the basis of family size in order to equalize economic opportunities and the ability to pay the soul tax, the responsibility for the collection of which it had assumed. In addition, it functioned as a general organ of social control within the feudal system, although its autonomy in strictly village matters was extensive. The land, however, was cultivated individually, not by the village as a whole, though common rights existed over pasture and forest lands. On the principle of three-field crop rotation, the *mir* divided the fields into strips and distributed these to the individual household, making some attempt to equalize the number, quality, and distance from the village of the many strips.[6]

The Emancipation strengthened the *mir* by making it responsible for the redemption payments as well as general taxes. Enclosure and consolidation of one's strips were extremely difficult, as was withdrawal by the individual peasant from the commune. Repartition continued in most areas throughout the century. In sixty-six districts of European Russia, for instance, 88 per cent of the communes repartitioned their land between 1897 and 1902.[7] Household partitioning was another important equalizing mechanism among peasants, especially in the face of government attempts to limit land repartition. Where land was scarce, technology primitive, and the threat of famine constant, such arrangements may have been a rational economic response by both the commune and its individual members.[8] But the overall impact was to retard the modernization of agriculture. The commune could, indeed, spread improved techniques rapidly and widely, but it was often difficult to persuade a majority to adopt them.[9] Nor did the government provide incentives for modernization through the *mir*. The nobility, on the other hand, did not make the transition to a rational system of capitalist agriculture, preferring instead to lease plots to land-hungry peasants. Tenants generally rented for short periods, and thus tended to exploit the soil to exhaustion. And the entire system encouraged rapid population growth, since an increase in the size of the household was a means of augmenting the family allotment. The result, however, was a decrease in the amount of land per person, even though the (often communal) purchase and leasing of non-allotment land was on the rise. The nobility, which had hoped that the strengthening of the *mir* would exercise a conservative force over the peasants and prevent the formation of a dangerous agricultural proletariat, was soon threatened by a peasantry that had never given up the idea that the land should belong to those who till it.

By the turn of the century peasant unrest had reached crisis proportions. In 1902 seven provinces in south-central Russia came close to full-scale revolts, as the peasants pillaged and burned manor houses. Minor revolts continued for the next few years until, in 1905, under the impetus of a disastrous war, the urban strike, and political movements, the peasants set out to destroy their dependence on the nobility once and for all. Acting collectively on the basis of the traditional solidarity and relative institutional autonomy of the *mir*,[10] they organized rent and labour strikes, seized the landlords' grain and husbandry, felled their forests, and—more commonly as the year progressed with few concessions—violently drove them out, seizing all their valuable possessions and burning their estates to the ground. The *mir*, instead of acting as a conservatizing force as the nobles had hoped, now became the main instrument of revolutionary activity. As Geroid Robinson has noted, 'it is probably not a matter of pure coincidence that among the twenty *guberniyas* in which the landlords suffered the heaviest losses during the disturbances of the autumn of 1905, sixteen show a predominance of repartitional tenure over hereditary holding by individual peasant households.'[11] That summer an All-Russian Peasants' Union was formed to give expression to peasant demands. The Union supported the convening of a Constituent Assembly that would abolish all redemption payments and transfer all land to the peasantry free. Only those who tilled the soil without hiring labour would be able to share in what was viewed as essentially a repartitional commune on a national scale. The Union's second congress in November 1905 declared that if peaceful means did not suffice to bring about the desired goals, a general agricultural strike should be organized in conjunction with a general workers strike. If all failed, a popular uprising would be inevitable. But peasants in numerous districts had already gone beyond the legal steps and had taken matters into their own hands.[12]

The government responded to the disturbances with very severe repressive measures. In a telegram to one of the governors, the minister of the interior, Durnovo, urged 'the sternest measures to bring the disorders to an end: it is a useful thing to wipe the rebellious village off the face of the earth, and to exterminate the rebels themselves without mercy, by force of arms.'[13] With the return of troops from the east, repression was eventually successful. But the rebelliouns had taught the government and the nobility alike that the *mir*, far from promoting social stability, had done just the opposite. The peasants lacked a strong sense of private property, and this had to be inculcated. As the First Congress of Nobles proclaimed: 'the commune—there is the enemy!'[14] It had to be destroyed.

That is exactly what the legislation enacted in the wake of the disorders attempted to do. Every peasant head of household, whose rights were now to supersede those of the family as a unit, had the right to claim his allotment as his own private property, to have it consolidated as far as possible into a single plot, and to withdraw from the commune. Peasants living in communes that had not made a general distribution in the past twenty-four years had the right to all the land in their possession. In communes where redistributions had been made within the past twenty-four years, those who possessed more than their share were entitled to purchase the extra amount at the price set at Emancipation. Both these clauses directly favoured the more well-to-do peasants. All redemption payments, the arrears of which by 1900 exceeded the average annual assessment, were cancelled. The commune and the household head lost control over the mobility of their members, thus allowing a freer flow of permanent workers to the cities. Individuals were directly to assume the burden of taxes. In 1910 all allotments in communes that had not reallocated their land since 1887 were automatically converted into private holdings. Entire villages could enclose individual holdings by a two-thirds (and later a simple majority) vote of their eligible members. The aim was the creation of 'secure individual ownership,' for only this, said Stolypin, the initiator of the reforms, could create the incentive to work and improve both the land and the peasants themselves. The regime was now wagering on the 'strong and sober' to provide the bulwark among the peasantry itself against all future attacks on the property of the nobility.[15]

The reforms, however, did not succeed fully. Of the 12.3 million peasant households in 1905, 9.5 million lived in communes. By 1916, only 2.5 million of the latter had individualized their titles, and many of these had been officially coerced.[16] Some of the 'separators' were clearly the more well-to-do peasants, others the village poor who used the opportunity to abandon farming altogether. By 1910, the great majority who were to leave had already gone, indicating some restabilization of communal tenure. The land was still cultivated mainly in the traditional fashion of three-field rotation and division into strips, as the degree of consolidation lagged considerably behind the separations. Even fewer peasants actually moved out of the villages to establish fully private homesteads. The reforms were most successful in the south, southwest, and west, but the major grain-producing areas of the Russian heartland remained solidly communal, somewhat less differentiated than before, and antagonistic to both the separators and the nobility—a 'compact phalanx of so-called "middle-peasantry"'[17] who in 1917 would finally finish the job they had begun in 1905.

Movement, Party, and State in 1917

The peasants played no part in the disorders that toppled the tsar in February, although once the deed had been done, most of them clearly supported the formation of a democratic republic. Their initial demands on the new government were rather moderate: lower the land rents, forbid the selling of land until the Constituent Assembly, make sure all fields are sown, control the wages of agricultural labourers, confiscate state and crown lands. The peasants had not abandoned their belief that the land should belong to the tillers, but in the early weeks of the new government only a minority pressed for the immediate confiscation of the landlords' estates without compensation. For the most part, their early activity remained confined to legal pressure and petitioning. A framework was established for this when the government set up a Central Land Committee on 21 April, and a system of local land committees from the regional to the *volost* levels 'in order to prepare the way for land reform and to draft provisional measures to be adopted pending the settlement of the land question by the Constituent Assembly.'[18] The Central Committee, which was appointed and non-peasant in composition, commanded broad but vague powers of recommendation. Although it quickly moved to abolish the widely hated Stolypin reforms, its activity was closely tied to the official policy of the Provisional Government, which hoped to postpone all other essential land questions until the Constituent Assembly was convened. The provincial and district (*uezd*) land committees had broad powers to settle disputes among peasants and landlords, and could stop proceedings that they deemed would lower the value of landed property. They could also request that the Central Committee confiscate the property of speculators, although this was not done automatically. Some of these rights could be delegated to the *volost* committees, which represented several villages and were the only committees in the entire framework to be democratically elected.

'The history of the agrarian movement consisted...in the progressive annexation of complete control by the cantonal [*volost*] committees until, in October, the superstructure was left entirely devoid of material or political significance.'[19] Indeed, some of these local committees had arisen quite spontaneously and had never been well integrated into the system designed to establish a *modus vivendi* between the peasants and the nobles, at least temporarily. But even those set up within the legal framework soon began taking measures that were semi-legal at best. In the latter part of the spring, the *volost* committees began increasingly to dictate rules on the 'proper' use of land both to the landlords and to the higher land committees. Landlords were forced to cease using war prisoners on their estates, and to lease their land at low rates fixed by the committees, which often kept the rents for their common purposes. They also fixed rates for labour on the estates, set an eight-hour day with special rates for overtime, and restricted the nobles to hiring local labour. Forests and unsown land were requisitioned, as were livestock, seed, and agricultural instruments. The rhythms of peasant revolt closely followed the agricultural production cycle itself.[20] Committees that resisted the will of the peasants were simply replaced, and individual peasants were forced to abide by their decisions. Those who had withdrawn from the *mir* under the Stolypin reforms were forced back in, although their return seems often to have been voluntary.[21] The *mir* as an institution, which had not by any means been destroyed during the Stolypin era, now experienced a general revival. But even in those areas where communal tenure had never existed or had long vanished, the peasants were rebelling against the landlords with equal vigour.

The local land committees achieved virtual control in most areas by September 1917. In their structure they reproduced the patriarchal relations of the *mir* and the household, though the war had significantly enhanced the participation rights of women and younger males.[22] Richer peasants were excluded from some committees, though it is difficult to determine how widespread this phenomenon was. The poor peasants apparently exerted strong influence on some committees, but, as in 1905, the leadership of the movement remained with the middle peasants. Soldiers on leave and those who had deserted or had been sent to the villages for political reasons had a radicalizing effect on some committees, as often did workers' delegations from the cities. Peasant soviets also began to form, although their development lagged considerably behind the land committees at the local level. They were more numerous in the provincial urban centres, where intellectuals and party organizers, especially the SRs, took the lead in their formation. Indeed, the First All-Russian Congress of Peasants' Deputies met in May, before there were many local soviets to speak of, and the link between local and higher organs remained extremely weak throughout 1917. Separate soviets of agricultural workers, advocated by the Bolsheviks, were formed only in a few localities, most notably in the Ukraine and the Baltic provinces.[23]

The Socialist Revolutionary Party, which dominated the organized political activity of the peasant movement throughout 1917, played a complex and contradictory role. Legatee of the nineteenth-century populist faith in the peasantry, the party held that progress toward socialism could be made by cultivating the egalitarian and communal aspects of the Russian *mir*, and that an intervening stage of capitalist development in the countryside and class struggle among a highly differentiated peasantry was not necessary, as the Russian Marxists generally believed. Their basic land programme, written by Viktor Chernov for their founding convention in 1906 and essentially unchanged through 1917, reflected ideas that were widespread in areas where the *mir* remained strong.[24] It called for the 'socialization of the land,' which meant that the land was somehow 'to belong to all the people', but not to be the 'property' of the state, the organs of local self-government (which would administer the land fund), or those who had a right to its use by virtue of their willingness to till it themselves. This was designed to prevent the formation of class divisions in the countryside, while providing the space for the gradual development of collective forms of cultivation. The latter would perhaps take decades, and could and should be accomplished through purely voluntary means, as a result of the peasants' own recognition of the technical and economic advantages.[25] The programme got no more specific than that. There were no detailed recommendations about the equalization of land among unequally endowed communities. No specifications were made for the distribution of land to individual households or collectives. And, most significantly, no attempt was made to analyse how such relationships on the land could coexist with capitalist industrial development in the cities and a bourgeois-democratic political order—both of which the SRs saw as a necessary stage following the coming revolution.

The SR position was put to the test in 1917. The party with far the largest base of popular support entered the Provisional Government, and assumed direct responsibility for its land policy when Chernov became minister of agriculture in May. The party's commitment to radical land reform was strongly reaffirmed at the First All-Russian Congress of Peasants' Deputies, where the SRs enjoyed uncontested dominance and the original agrarian platform was adopted virtually unchanged. In addition, the delegates resolved to transform the land committees into organs of local self-government that would accomplish 'the most speedy and final liquidation of all survivals of the order of serfdom remaining in the countryside.'[26] But the catch in the SR policy was epitomized in Chernov's first speech as minister of agriculture, when he said: 'Naturally in the Constituent Assembly, the land question will occupy first place.... The Socialist Revolutionaries (the party of Kerensky and Chernov) have attacked any kind of extra-legal seizures and outrages and have therefore instructed the peasantry to prepare for the Constituent Assembly.... The most systematic slogan seems to be "Land through the Constituent Assembly".'[27]

As the war dragged on, however, and as the Constituent Assembly was repeatedly postponed, this became an increasingly untenable position. Chernov was well and truly caught in the middle. While he did not believe that any equitable and final solution could be achieved before the Constituent Assembly, he saw the land committees as exercising *de facto* control until then, the landlords thus being deprived of the material advantages of their soon-to-be-abolished property rights. On 16 July Chernov issued an instruction empowering the local committees to go 'quite far' in satisfying peasant needs, as long as these did not endanger the national economy; more specifically, it gave them the right to manage all land not being cultivated by the owners.

Chernov was opposed not only by the Kadets in the coalition, who had consistently resisted confiscation without compensation, but by the Mensheviks as well; and Tsereteli, as minister of the interior, called for the arrest of all peasants involved in 'arbitrary' land seizures. Not even the leaders of Chernov's own party in the Provisional Government supported him. Bureaucratic impediments were thus continually placed in his way as he attempted to mobilize the official apparatus to support popular peasant demands. Indeed, in both agricultural and industrial policy, the government was an ineffective and bureaucratic mess. The ministries of agriculture, supply, and the interior were ever embroiled in jurisdictional conflicts.[28] The supply apparatus lacked the administrative capacity to deliver sufficient goods from the cities, or to procure grain. And as long as the prices of urban goods for peasant consumption could not be controlled, nor their production significantly augmented, the peasants would choose to hoard, consume, or distill their grain—or even destroy it—before they would deliver it to the State Grain Monopoly at fixed prices. The central authorities could not maintain effective accountability over the local food committees, and the peasants resisted the authority of local organs that were not democratically constituted. The old tsarist apparatus, which had penetrated the villages only minimally in any event, had disintegrated, and the new *volost zemstvos* could barely establish themselves without peasant support. Confusion and ineffectiveness were the rule in the areas of local administration, adjudication, and coercion.[29] As government willingness to resort to direct coercion mounted, its ability to employ troops to quell peasant revolt declined. The war had ensured that there would be no repetition of 1905.

The peasants themselves were increasingly estranged from a policy that was such a confused and contradictory mixture of admonishments of restraint and encouragements of semi-legal encroachment on the landlords' rights. The left wing of the Socialist Revolutionaries, which had originally coalesced around the issue of the war, began to take distance from the leadership and to support direct action. Already in May, the Kazan Peasant Soviet, led by the Left SRs, urged the local land committees to take over all privately held land but to postpone parcelling it out until the demobilized soldiers could participate fully in the process. By July this was accomplished. Actions like these helped the Left to achieve mass support among the peasantry and wide influence in the soviets and land committees, especially in the provinces of Kherson, Kharkov, Ufa, Kaluga, and Pskov. But by late summer and autumn even the peasants in Right and Centre SR strongholds could no longer be restrained from directly seizing land for their own use.[30] With the October revolution in Petrograd, these actions received the full sanction of the new government.

Lenin and the Peasant Question

Lenin had been concerned with the problem of the Russian peasantry from the very beginning of his revolutionary activities. Indeed, his earliest known written work (1893) was entitled 'New Economic Developments in Peasant Life.' In *The Development of Capitalism in Russia* (1899), one of his most careful if highly flawed analytical works, he strove to trace in great detail the evolution of the social relations of the Russian countryside, the complex intermixture of corvée and capitalist labour, and the rising class differentiation among Russian peasants.[31]

His purpose, of course, was ultimately political: to determine the relation of the peasantry and agrarian revolution to the workers movement and the general development of socialism in Russia. In 1902 he dráfted an agrarian programme for the Social Democratic Party that called for the abolition of all redemption payments and quit-rents, of collective liability through the *mir*, and of restrictions on the free disposal of land. Other demands included the restitution of all previous redemption payments through the confiscation of monasterial and royal estates and a special land tax on the landed nobility, the restitution of all lands withheld from the peasantry at the time of emancipation, and the elimination of all remnants of the feudal system everywhere. The achievement of these demands was seen as part of the democratic revolution that would stimulate the development of capitalism in the countryside. Only then could the class struggle freely develop, and the material and social conditions for an agrarian socialist movement be prepared. The two revolutions were still strictly separated in Lenin's mind at the time. Nationalization of the land was therefore inappropriate, for this and other reasons; large landed estates using capitalist methods had to be further developed, not broken up. Small property was to be encouraged not against more advanced capitalist forms of agriculture, but only against the remnants of serfdom.[32]

The revolutionary movement of 1905, in which the peasantry directly and forcefully attempted to confiscate landlord estates in many areas and the Peasant Union raised the demand for the transfer of all land to the people, transformed Lenin's approach to the agrarian problem. He now admitted that in 1902 he had underestimated the breadth and depth of the movement against the remnants of feudalism, and had lagged behind the peasants' own demands for their complete abolition through nationalization. At the end of 1907 he reflected on this:

'That mistake [of the 1903 programme for the restoration of only the lands cut off at Emancipation] was due to the fact that while we correctly defined the *trend* of development, we did not correctly define the *moment* of that development. We assumed that the elements of capitalist agriculture had already taken full shape in Russia, both in landlord farming (minus the cut-off lands and their conditions of bondage—hence the demand that the cut-off lands be restored to the peasants) and in peasant farming, which seemed to have given rise to a strong peasant bourgeoisie and therefore to be incapable of bringing about a "peasant agrarian revolution." The erroneous programme was not the result of "fear" of the peasant agrarian revolution, but of *an over-estimation of the degree* of capitalist development in Russian agriculture. The survivals of serfdom appeared to us then to be a minor detail, whereas capitalist agriculture on the peasant allotments and on the landlords' estates seemed to be quite mature and well-established.... We rectified that mistake by substituting for the partial aim of combating the *survivals of the old* agrarian system, the aim of combating *the old agrarian system as a whole*. Instead of purging the landlord economy, we set the aim of *abolishing* it.'[33]

The Bolshevik adoption of the demand for complete nationalization of the land still did not imply that the revolution had reached its socialist stage. Neither the objective nor subjective preconditions for this had developed far enough yet. But the revolutionary actions of the peasants convinced Lenin that it was not the bourgeoisie that would lead a bourgeois revolution in Russia, nor even the bourgeoisie in alliance with the proletariat, but rather an alliance of the proletariat and the peasantry under the leadership of the former. The 'revolutionary-democratic dictatorship of the proletariat and the peasantry'[34] would create the conditions for the full development of a capitalist economy and bourgeois political freedom—themselves conditions for the proper development of a socialist movement—over an entire historical period. Nationalization of the land (while retaining individual tillage, as the peasants desired) would clear the way for an 'American type' peasant agriculture. This would lead to a more rapid development of the productive forces, and would have more progressive cultural and social effects in the rural areas than the Prussian Junker model, which preserves elements of feudal bondage and retards the introduction of the most advanced technology. The Stolypin reforms would lead down the Prussian path. 'In the Russian revolution,' Lenin concluded, 'the struggle for the land is nothing else than a struggle for the renovated path of capitalist development. The consistent slogan of such a renovation is—nationalization of the land.'[35]

In 1917 Lenin developed this programme further. Contrary to the SRs, he urged the peasants not to wait for the convening of the Constituent Assembly, but to take direct action and confiscate the nobles' estates, livestock and instruments *immediately*. This was to be carried out in an orderly way, so that agricultural production would not be detrimentally affected. The confiscated land was to be organized by democratically elected peasant soviets and other organs of local self-government, until the Constituent Assembly or a popularly empowered Congress of Soviets could determine a

more equitable distribution of the nationalized land. Such nationalization would represent the culmination of the bourgeois-
democratic revolution on the land, and would free the class struggle
from all feudal remnants: 'The more determined and consistent the
bourgeois-democratic agrarian reform in Russia in general, the
more vigorous and speedy will be the development of the class
struggle of the agricultural proletariat against the well-to-do
peasants (the peasant bourgeoisie).'[36]

But no longer did Lenin see the bourgeois-democratic phase of
the revolution as lasting indefinitely, for an entire historical period.
By the time of his return to Russia in April 1917, he had adopted a
position virtually identical to Trotsky's theory of permanent
revolution. Trotsky had argued after the 1905 revolution that in
any alliance with the peasantry the working class had to maintain
hegemony for itself, since the peasantry is incapable of playing an
independent political role in capitalist society. The revolutionary
government led by the proletariat, however, could not limit itself to
establishing the conditions for capitalist development and
bourgeois democracy, as Lenin's earlier formula had stated, since
'the political domination of the proletariat is incompatible with its
economic enslavement. No matter under what political flag the
proletariat has come to power, it is obliged to take the path of
socialist policy. It would be the greatest utopianism to think that
the proletariat, having been raised to political domination by the
internal mechanism of a bourgeois revolution can, even if it so
desires, limit its mission to creation of republican democratic conditions for the social domination of the bourgeoisie.'[37]

The moment for the dictatorship of the proletariat, Trotsky
argued, depends not on the level of development of the productive
forces of any particular country—for in the age of imperialism national economies are not self-contained entities—but on the level of
political development of the proletariat, the general class relations
in that society, and the possibility of socialist revolution in Europe,
which would permit direct state support by the European proletariat of its economically less advanced allies in Russia.[38]

His acceptance of the prospect of permanent revolution in Russia
led Lenin to view the agrarian problem in a new light. 'Under these
circumstances', he argued in the September 1917 Postscript to the

Agrarian Programme of Social Democracy in the First Russian Revolution, 'the question of the nationalization of the land must inevitably be presented in a new way ... namely: nationalization of the land is not only "the last word" of the bourgeois revolution but also *a step towards socialism*.'[39] Nationalization of the land not only would clear the soil of all remnants of feudal bondage and open the way for the free development of the class struggle in the village, but would immediately put on the agenda the question of the viability of small-scale commodity production in agriculture, and the organization of collective cultivation of the more technically developed landed estates that were to be confiscated. In a *Pravda* article written in anticipation of the First Peasants' Soviet Congress he argued: 'We cannot conceal from the peasants, least of all from the rural proletarians and semi-proletarians, that small-scale farming under commodity economy and capitalism *cannot* rid humanity of mass poverty, that it is necessary to *think* about going over to large-scale farming conducted on public lines and to *tackle this job at once* by teaching the masses, and in turn learning from the masses, the practical expedient measures for bringing about such a transition.'[40]

Nationalization of the land and its parcellization will not deliver the peasants, especially the majority, from their misery, since 'you cannot eat land. The millions of households that have no horses, implements, or seeds will gain nothing from the transfer of the land to the "people".'[41] Lenin therefore urged the separate organization of the rural proletariat and semi-proletariat—of all who must sell their labour, even part-time—to protect their interests from the richer peasants and to prepare the organizational basis for the collective tilling of the soil. Soviets of Agricultural Labourers should be set up, and model farms managed by them with the aid of agronomists should be established on the large estates. The outcome of the revolution itself depended on the movement of the poor peasants.[42]

Although Lenin recognized in late June that separate organizations of agricultural labourers had developed in only a few locales, and although he had earlier expressed uncertainty about the extent of class divisions in the village, he was generally optimistic on these matters.[43] But he insisted again and again that however desirable such developments might be, they could not be forced or decreed from above: 'This work must be done by means of friendly persuasion, without anticipating events, without hurrying to consolidate "organizationally" that which the representatives of the rural proletarians and semi-proletarians have not yet fully realized, thought out, and digested for *themselves*. But it most be done, and a start must be made at once everywhere.'[44]

As Engels had argued in *The Peasant Question in France and Germany*, socialists have no intention of forcefully expropriating the small peasants; the advantages of mechanized socialist agriculture can be made clear to them only by the force of example.[45] In the meantime, Lenin told the First All-Russian Congress of Peasants Deputies, the landed estates must be taken over and organized 'according to the will of the majority.'[46] If the peasants, including the poor, decide to keep their small farms and parcel out the confiscated estates, then the Bolshevik party must go along with it, for, '*provided the proletariat rules centrally*, provided political power is taken over by the proletariat, the rest will come *by itself*, as a result of "force of example," prompted by experience.'[47] Shortly after the seizure of power, then, Lenin argued that, on matters of agricultural policy the Bolsheviks would have to cede to the demands of the peasants and their Left SR representatives during the transition to socialism.[48]

Revolutionary Aftermath

On the evening of 26 October the Second All-Russian Congress of Workers and Soldiers Deputies passed the decrees on land drafted by Lenin. Largely based on the SR programme and the Model Instruction drawn up earlier by the Peasant Congress, it went a long way in recognizing the immediate aspirations of the peasants and legitimating their revolutionary deeds. All estates of landlords, the imperial family, monasteries, and churches were confiscated without compensation, and until the Constituent Assembly met to determine final distribution, they were to be transferred to the *volost* land committees and the district (*uezd*) peasant soviets. The transfer was to be orderly and without damage to property. 'The right of private ownership of land is abolished forever. Land cannot be sold, bought, leased, mortgaged, or alienated in any manner whatsoever.'[49] All underground resources, minerals, petroleum, coal, salt, and forests and water of national importance were to be transferred directly to the state for its exclusive use. Intensively cultivated land, such as orchards and nurseries, were to remain undivided and managed by the state or the local commune, as were stud farms, state and private farms for breeding thoroughbred stock, depending on their size and importance. All inventory and livestock of confiscated lands were to be turned over without compensation to the state or commune, but the inventory of small landholding peasants was not to be touched. All citizens, regardless of sex, were entitled to use the land as long as they did not hire labour, and such use was to be determined by norms of consumption or labour, depending on local conditions and at local option. Each village was to be completely free to determine the form of land utilization (separate farms, collective, etc.). The land, however, was to be subject to periodic redistribution depending on population and production increases, with compensation for those who improved their plots.

The Fundamental Law of Land Socialization of February 1918, which finalized most of these provisions, shifted the power of land distribution to the soviets, partly because of the continued influence in many of the land committees of the SRs, who strongly opposed the Bolshevik/Left SR government. But in practice neither the soviets nor the land committees but the village communes primarily effected the redistribution of land after October. The communes had experienced a general revival, and now even spread to areas that had been non-communal. The membership base of the *mir* was broadened with the legally recognized right of all citizens to the use of the land and the return of the Stolypin separators. Formerly landless peasants and returned urban dwellers were admitted. On the whole, however, the *mir* continued to function rather traditionally, granting full rights of participation only to male heads of households. By 1920 nearly all peasant households working the land had been drawn into communes.[50]

The total amount of agricultural land (excluding non-arable and forest lands) taken from the gentry, state, and church estates and from the richer peasants was about thirty million *desyatins*. The manner of distribution varied from area to area, and there seem to have been few adjustments between communes and *volosts*. In some cases, all land (including peasant allotments) was pooled and divided up according to the number of consumers per household. This 'black redistribution' (*chernyi peredel*), however, was relatively rare, as was the redistribution of only the newly acquired land, which the Right SRs favoured. Most common was the redistribution of the new land, plus strips taken from richer peasants, which went primarily to the poorest.[51] In the vast majority of cases, however, the norm of distribution was the number of consumers, not the number of male workers, though the latter were often pro-rated as having greater consumption requirements. Redivisions continued throughout the period of War Communism, even though the government attempted to strictly limit them in cases not associated with technical improvements. The inventory and live-stock were usually divided up along with the land, including the meticulous re-allocation, in one case, of the former lord's grand piano and stud bull.[52]

The redistribution of the land, stock, and inventory in the years 1917–20 resulted in considerable social levelling and an aggregate downward shift among the peasantry. The percentage of peasants without land fell by half, to about 6.6 per cent in 1919 and 4.5 per cent in 1920. Horseless households declined slightly, but still remained at about one-quarter of the total in 1919. Households at the other end of the scale, with more than ten *desyatins* also declined, from approximately 5.1 per cent in 1917 to 1.59 per cent in 1919. Significantly, those with more than eight *desyatins*, the average amount estimated as necessary to produce a surplus, fell from 7.9 per cent to 3.1 per cent in these same years. The proportion of peasant households that were well off (more than sixteen *desyatins*) was a negligible .16 per cent, and large peasant farms of more than twenty-five *desyatins* represented only .01 per cent. The share of livestock of the more well-to-do households also dropped, so that, for instance, those with three or more horses fell to 2.5 per cent in

1919. The groups with the largest increase were those just above the very bottom, with less than four *desyatins* of land (72.2 per cent) and one horse (60.5 per cent in 1919)—middle peasants relative to the others, but poor by any absolute standard.

The levelling was primarily the result of the egalitarian tendencies within the commune in these years, which clearly prevailed over the tendency of the richer peasants to dominate the affairs of the *mir* so as to enhance their own economic position. The general downward shift in the size of landholdings and livestock was due to the increased number of households. This, in turn, was a result of the entry into the *mir* (and its land pool) of formerly landless peasants, urban returnees, and newcomers driven out of the cities and smaller towns[53] by the food shortages, and the increased rate of family partitions that accompanied the decline in patriarchal authority and the claims of younger males (often returning servicemen) and some women for their share of the land, as well as the desire of the larger households with more land to protect themselves from partial expropriations.[54]

Crisis and the Bolshevik Response

The honeymoon between the Bolsheviks and the peasants that followed the decree on land soon ended, however, as the cities faced the very real threat of starvation in the spring of 1918. Inadequate food supply had been a problem before the Bolshevik takeover, and indeed, had been one of the main causes of the February revolution. The reasons were manifold, though all war-related: lack of manpower due to the mobilization of 40 to 50 per cent of all able-bodied adult village males, the disruption of transport and grain-producing areas due to war activity, the interruption of imports of farm implements and fertilizer, and the decline of civilian industrial production. The Provisional Government had failed to arrest this process. After October, industrial production continued to decline, the demobilization of industry was slow and chaotic, and major grain-producing areas were occupied by the Germans. In addition, some areas had experienced major crop failure in 1917.

By January 1918 only 7 per cent of the grain supplies allotted to Petrograd and Moscow were actually being delivered. Although the figure increased in the next few months, by April it was again down to 6 per cent, and it fell even lower in May.[55] Emergency measures had to be taken if the cities were not to starve, and if industrial production and the proletarian social base of the revolution were not to disintegrate altogether.

The immediate crisis became the occasion not only for temporary emergency measures to save the cities, however, but also for the grand political and ideological illusion that the villages were suddenly ready for the second, socialist stage of the revolution. Lenin blamed the food shortage exclusively on the *kulaks* (rich peasants) who refused to deliver their surplus to the cities at the fixed prices set by the grain monopoly. As early as February 1918 he declared his confidence that 'the working peasantry will declare unsparing war on its *kulak* oppressors.'[56] In early March he told the Seventh Party Congress 'how the peasants, for all their prejudices and all their old convictions, have set themselves the practical task of the transition to socialism. This is a fact.'[57] The stage of economic coalition with the bourgeois-democratic elements among the peasantry was over, he repeated in June. 'Serious famine has driven us to a purely communist task. We are being confronted by a revolutionary socialist task.'[58]

In May the Commissariat of Supply was granted extraordinary powers, including the right to use armed force, to dissolve local food authorities, and to ferret out the large stores of grain the kulaks were supposed to be hiding, as well as a monopoly over the distribution of all prime necessities. The latter were *not* to be given in exchange for grain, but distributed to the poor peasants, who in turn were forcibly to seize grain from the rich.[59] Armed detachments of workers were to aid the commissariat in these tasks, as well as to educate the working peasantry and organize them against the kulaks. According to Lenin, these measures represented nothing short of 'fighting for the bases of communist distribution and for the actual foundations of a communist society.'[60]

But the most significant step in the party's instigation of the 'second stage' of the agrarian revolution came on 11 June 1918 with the formation of the Committees of Poor Peasants (*kombedy*). These were to be formed at the village and *volost* level to aid the food agencies in procuring food from the kulaks. All other peasants were eligible for membership, including peasants from other districts, as well as urban workers. The latter—no doubt because they were armed and many were party members—exercised a disproportionate influence in the leadership positions.[61] The *kombedy* were promised free grain for their own needs if they requisitioned all the grain designated by the procurement agencies by 15 July, a 50 per cent discount up to 15 August, and a 20 per cent discount thereafter, as well as discounts on other necessities. By autumn, more than one hundred and twenty thousand people had participated in them, and they existed in the majority of villages under Soviet control.[62] Their importance, according to Lenin, could not be overestimated: 'Comrades, the organization of the poor peasants is the key problem in our internal construction work, and even in our whole revolution.'[63]

The *kombedy*, however, fell far short of the tasks ascribed to them by the Bolsheviks' urban-oriented models of class struggle. Lenin claimed that two and a half times as much grain was delivered to the state procurement organs in the latter half of the year, but there is reason to doubt that this was simply the result of *kombedy* activity. Most historians seem to agree with Narkiewicz's view that 'the Committees of Poor Peasants were extremely unsuccessful in requisitioning grain.'[64] They may have had some influence in redistributing the land more radically but this does not seem to have been lasting. There were many reports that the committee members often drank themselves into a stupor and pillaged the stocks of all peasants indiscriminately.[65] Often they seized grain for their own needs and failed to deliver any to the state.[66] Their activities provoked considerable resistance, including scattered uprisings—and not just by the kulaks, as Lenin held, but by the peasantry as a whole. And no wonder. Since Lenin's estimate of the size of the kulak class (about 13 per cent of the peasantry) was far overblown, it was inevitable that middle and even poorer peasants would become targets of the *kombedy*, and that necessities as well as surpluses would be requisitioned at gunpoint.

As a result, the peasants became increasingly alienated from the government: 'we were for the Bolsheviks but not the Communists' was a common peasant commentary on the two stages of the revolution. Many responded by cutting back on the area of land sown. Ignoring (and perhaps frightened of) the *kombedy* claim for all power in the rural areas, Lenin diplomatically declared their tasks accomplished after the autumn harvest, and urged their dissolution and assimilation into the local soviets dominated by the mass of middle peasants, with whom Lenin now realized more than ever the need for compromise and alliance. Those poor peasants who had been mobilized by the committees were, on the whole, reabsorbed into normal village life, though some took up leadership positions in the soviets.[67]

In late July 1918 Lenin had argued that 'there is not a village left where the class struggle is not raging between a miserable handful of kulaks on the one hand and the vast labouring majority ... on the other. The class struggle has penetrated every village.'[68] But despite such optimistic appraisals, the Russian peasantry had by and large failed to split. There were virtually no purely kulak uprisings against the government in these years, largely because the Bolshevik-inspired 'anti-kulak peasant revolution had failed to take place.'[69] Once again, as at the turn of the century, Lenin had overestimated the extent to which capitalist development and class differentiation had advanced in the countryside, and hence could only see polarization and class struggle taking root everywhere. The organization the poor peasants lacked would be generated from outside, by state and party initiative and with the aid of hungry urban workers and the most marginal elements among the peasantry. The poor peasants themselves took little initiative in the organization of the *kombedy*, as Zinoviev admitted at the Sixth Soviet Congress in November.[70] The model of class conflict had been simplistically projected onto the rural population. What was necessity for the cities (to avoid starvation) became for Lenin the necessary and inevitable development of class struggle and socialist organization in the countryside. Indigenous forms of peasant culture and social structure, other than those directly related to class domination, were ignored or treated as secondary or ephemeral. However, as

Teodor Shanin concludes:

'The revitalization of the communes, the levelling within the framework of the institutionalized traditional channels for mobility among peasant households, the reabsorption of the enclosed farms into the communes and the increase in the external pressures from the state would result in increased social and political cohesion within the peasant communities. This solidarity underlay both the tremendous spread of peasant revolts in 1920 and their disappearance, all at the same time, in 1921. It was to be reflected, moreover, in the remarkable unity which the peasantry was to show in its spontaneous attitudes and actions to come and which reached a new climax in the period of collectivization.'[71] But ten years later policy towards the peasantry was guided by the same ideologically induced blindness as in 1918.

In the area of collective agriculture the poor peasants also disappointed the great hopes the Bolsheviks had held for them. The Land Law of February 1918 placed a priority on the distribution of land and material and cultural assistance to those who wished to cultivate it collectively for the benefit of the community as a whole and to increase efficiency and productivity.[72] Although he had held that a transition to socialist forms of agriculture could occur only gradually and by force of example, Lenin was encouraged enough by late fall 1918 to state that 'the peasants themselves, the majority of the working peasants, are striving toward collective farming.'[73] The new law of February 1919 reflected this optimistic estimate. All forms of individual agriculture were to be regarded as 'having outlived their time,' and all land was to be placed in a single state fund under the direct control and supervision of the commissariats. According to Article 8, 'This land fund is to be used, in the first place, for the needs of Soviet farms and communes; in the second place, for labour artels, partnerships and collective farming; and, in the third place, for individual farmers desiring land as a means of subsistence.'[74] Priority in the supply of implements from sequestered estates was to be given to the state farm (*sovkhoz*), which was to be managed by a state appointee, who, it turned out, was frequently the former landowner. The workers committee, which was to supervise working conditions, was not to interfere with the latter's decisions.

Agricultural communes (*kommuni*—not to be confused with the *mir*) were the next favoured form of collective agriculture. The *kommuni* were egalitarian and utopian farms, members often sharing not only production activities but also living quarters, eating facilities, and the like. All property was held in common, and those who withdrew had the right to take with them only articles of immediate personal use. They were self-managed by a general assembly of all members and an elected administrative board, although some apparently reproduced the patriarchal relations of the village commune. 'From each according to his ability, to each according to his needs' was the rule for distribution wherever possible. Otherwise, egalitarian standards were used. Discipline was exercised by the work group, although the party tried to introduce individualistic material incentives as well. Most *kommuni* remained fairly small—twelve to thirty families on the average—although some exceeded several hundred, and a few went as high as 8,000. The use of hired labour was prohibited.

The more stable middle peasants do not seem to have been attracted to them, because of the potential loss of their property if they decided to leave. Most of their members were marginal elements: unemployed industrial workers, ex-Red Army soldiers, war wives and widows, some intellectuals, students, and teachers, returning immigrants, refugees from war zones, and the poorest of the peasants, often from the *kombedy*. Very few were set up on confiscated estates by their former labourers, as the Bolsheviks had first hoped in 1917, since local peasants wanted the estates divided up. The most productive and stable communes were often founded by members of religious sects, like the Old Believers and Sectarians, of whom there were at least fifteen million in 1917. But the party saw these as culturally reactionary, and often failed to give them a commensurate degree of support. The productivity of the *kommuni* was generally fairly low, partly because they often had the worst land and least experienced farmers. But they still usually produced a better yield than peasants working individually. The Bolshevik Kalinin claimed that they were more efficient than the state farms, where the workers were little more than wage labourers for the state. During the winter months the communes often organized small crafts production for their own needs, a form of self-reliance later developed extensively by the Chinese. They were to work within the regional plans established by the Commissariat of Agriculture, according to the February 1919 statute, and their surplus production was to be requisitioned according to general state regulations. Any profits received through exchange with state supply organs were to be used exclusively for the improvement of the farm.[75]

The 1919 law also made it fairly easy for peasants desiring less sweeping forms of voluntary collective agriculture to form such associations. A majority vote of any *mir* would suffice to transform it, and any minority had the right to an enclosed parcel of land from the *mir* for such purposes. The artel, which attracted a more prosperous group of peasants than the *kommuni*, permitted the retention of land and property above the entrance requirement, and a good part of this was returned if the individual peasants left. Labour was done in common, as prescribed by the general assembly, with common use of livestock and equipment, but above the established norm these remained for private use and profit. The *TOZ*, more loosely structured, was simply an association for collective cultivation and marketing, where individuals retained rights over their own inventory and a share of the total product in proportion to their share of the jointly cultivated land.[76]

The spread of such collective forms of agriculture proved disappointing, despite official encouragement and some scattered attempts at forcible collectivization. Given the condition of Russian industry, the needs of the Civil War and the blockade by the Western powers, the government could encourage the collectives only with increasingly valueless rubles. The tractors Lenin saw as crucial for convincing the peasants of the value of cooperative cultivation simply were not there. The vast majority of the peasants, including the poorer ones, still clung to the old forms of land tenure. By the end of the Civil War, no more than 3 to 5 per cent of agricultural land was held by collectives. The rest remained almost completely under traditional communal tenure, cultivated by individual households. But amidst the prevalence of the old forms of cultivation, there was a noticeable trend in the opposite direction, as the table below reveals.[77]

	Sovkhozy	Kommuni	Artels	TOZ	Total
1918	3,101	975	604	–	4,680
1919	4,063 (516)	1,961	3,605	622	9,251
1920	5,928 (1,636)	1,892	7,722	886	16,428
1921	6,527 (2,136)	3,313	10,185	2,514	22,539

Most auspicious was the increasing participation of the middle peasants through their village communes in the partial forms of collectivization. Perhaps under more favourable circumstances the communal and egalitarian aspects of the *mir* could be stimulated and used as a bridge to collective forms of agricultural production on a more general scale.

Left SR Alternatives

Such, indeed, had been the position of the Left SRs, the erstwhile partners of the Bolsheviks in the new socialist experiment in the early months of the Soviet regime. At times the Left SRs tended to romanticize the *mir* and the depth and extent of its democratic and communal traditions.[78] But their general position was based on a fairly realistic assessment that the profoundly egalitarian yet narrow by collectivist aspects of the village commune could develop towards socialist forms of agricultural production only over the course of time, as their benefits were freely demonstrated. But in order for this to happen, the progressive features of the *mir* would have to be nurtured carefully. The influence of the parties and the state had to be used to ensure that land distribution was as equitable as possible. According to the account of Spiridonova, a Left SR leader, the validity of which was publicly acknowledged by Lenin himself, 'The agrarian reform ... will require according to our calculations ... about a billion rubles. ... When I approached

Lenin and almost went down on my knees to ask for two hundred millions ... he replied in a brutal and cynical way: "They [the peasants] have grabbed the land—let them divide it by themselves." That's all the satisfaction I received.'[79]

Lenin not only believed that the land could not be equitably distributed, but also held that the encouragement of equitable distribution was positively harmful to the future development of socialism, since it would dampen the class struggle within the peasantry itself. Only on the basis of class formation and class struggle could he envisage the development of socialist agricultural production.

As they had rejected the mechanistic stage theories of the Mensheviks, who held that socialist revolution could occur only after mature capitalist economic development, so also did the Left SRs reject as mechanistic Lenin's belief that socialist transformation could occur in the countryside only after the proletarianization and class polarization of the peasantry. They argued that the seizure of power and the mobilization of the urban and rural working people had opened up new possibilities. The supposedly unalterable laws of social and economic development must no longer be seen as primary, as determining and strictly circumscribing revolutionary options. The subjective factor, class consciousness and revolutionary will, indeed the moral and spiritual resources of all the labouring classes, have provided an exit from that dismal necessity, and it is these that must be consciously cultivated and encouraged by the policies of the revolutionary state.

Lenin, however, who had done so much to introduce a non-deterministic perspective in regard to the urban revolution, failed to understand its relevance to the countryside. He ignored the relatively egalitarian and communal traditions and institutions of the peasants as a potential basis for the gradual development of collective and democratic forms of production. In a decidedly mechanistic formulation aimed at the Populists of an earlier decade, he had argued that progress was not a matter of 'plucking elements from various social formations'. In his writings on the peasants, he avoided any serious analysis of the *mir*, and as a typical Marxist of his day treated them as a veritable 'sack of potatoes'.[80] Even where he himself spoke of the gradual demonstration by force of example of the benefits of collective production, he concentrated almost solely on the use of technology and never on the social context provided by existing forms of peasant solidarity and cooperation.[81] The Left SRs held that to ignore these, or worse, to consciously attempt to disrupt and destroy them through such policies as the Committees of Poor Peasants, would irreparably erode the class base of what would undoubtedly be a long and protracted struggle for socialist transformation. This struggle had to proceed with an internationalist outlook, but could not rely, as the Bolsheviks did, on an international revolution in the very near future to compensate for its own material backwardness and its very meagre urban proletarian class base.[82]

The Left SRs and the Bolsheviks had had some very serious differences from the very outset of their brief coalition. The Left SRs favoured a broad socialist coalition government, and although they placed the major blame for the failure of the coalition talks on the Mensheviks and SRs, they felt that the Bolsheviks, particularly Lenin and Trotsky, had obstructed them as well.[83] They also strongly opposed the Bolsheviks' penchant for revolutionary terror, which they saw as both morally corrupting and largely unnecessary given the constellation of class forces, and acting from within the Commissariat of Justice and the Cheka, they succeeded in restraining it.[84] They also levelled constant criticism at the hypercentralist tendencies of the Bolsheviks, who from the beginning tended to concentrate real power not in the network of local soviets or even in the elected Soviet Central Executive Committee, but in the Council of People's Commissars and the Central Committee of the Bolshevik party itself.[85] They functioned as an opposition force within the government until the peace of Brest-Litovsk, when they resigned their commissarial posts but remained in the Soviet Central Executive Committee as a legal opposition. They had supported a separate peace with Germany until they saw the harsh terms, whereupon they concluded that it would be better to fight a revolutionary guerrilla war than cede such a large territory and abandon the people of the Ukraine to German domination. The final break came only after several months of further secret Bolshevik negotiations with the Germans, rumours of greater concessions, and rising unrest in the Baltic and Black Sea fleets, which many felt (and not without reason) were to be ceded to Germany. Thereupon the Left SRs resolved to attack the representatives of

German imperialism in the hope of sparking off renewed hostilities, and if threatened by the Bolshevik government for such actions, to defend themselves by force of arms. With their assassination of the German ambassador in July, the breach became final, as they were rounded up by the Cheka and expelled from the Fifth Soviet Congress, then in session.[86]

Although any of these differences alone might have pushed the Left SRs into irreconcilable opposition, it was the Bolsheviks' peasant policy that underlay the radical and final estrangement of the coalition partners. For the Left SRs were a political party whose support lay primarily in the great mass of the middle peasantry, although they had a considerable following among sectors of the urban working class, the poor peasantry, and the troops as well.[87] And it was the middle peasantry—in deed if not in theory—that was the object of the Bolsheviks' attempt to stimulate class war in the villages through the use of armed detachments of urban workers and village paupers. The Committees of Poor Peasants, the Left SRs argued, were not only ineffective, but positively counter-productive:

'In regard to the food question, we insist that only the local soviets are capable of getting the surplus from the kulaks. The food armies sent from the centre are not representative of the best workers, but consist of men whose ambition is to plunder the village. They get very little grain but bring about a united front of the kulaks and the hired hands and an open war between city and country. The peasants are beginning to look upon the soviets as nothing better than robber gangs. On hearing that the food armies are coming, the kulaks distribute the grain among the hired hands and arm them to fight the invaders. We know of battles where scores of workmen were killed. Of all your stupid and criminal measures, the food armies and the committees of the village poor are the worst.'[88]

Requisitioning was made necessary only by the peace of Brest, Steinberg later argued, which removed large grain-producing areas from Soviet control.[89] But if it had to be done, let the local soviets, which are elected by the peasantry and familiar with local conditions, assume the responsibility. In no circumstances would the Left SRs accept the dictatorship of the city over the countryside. The dictatorship of the proletariat in an agricultural country was an absurd and reactionary position, they held. And as Spiridonova said at the Fifth Soviet Congress, 'the peasant question is the one on which we are fundamentally divided, and on this question we will fight you to the end with all our might.'[90]

Inevitable Estrangement?

The estrangement of the two major revolutionary parties was a profound tragedy for the later development of the revolution in Russia, since the Left SRs were the only significant political force committed to socialist development that had any roots at all in the countryside, where the vast majority of the population lived. And—as the history of peasant revolutions in the twentieth century has since revealed—the transformation of rural social relations in a socialist direction depends fundamentally on the ability of conscious revolutionary forces to penetrate the village. This process had only just begun in Russia during the revolution of 1917. The villages had mobilized to seize the land, had begun to organize themselves into soviets on a broad scale, and had been opened to the political influence of nearby urban workers and returned servicemen who had imbibed the revolutionary ideology of the Left SRs and Bolsheviks. In fact, the traditionally introverted Russian villages had been quite receptive to outside influences in the early stages of the revolution.[91]

Disillusionment with the Provisional Government and the unfavourable terms of trade with the cities reversed this, and non-peasant elements, like teachers and local intellectuals, were expelled from *volost* committees as time went on. The deterioration of industry after October and the military requirements of civil war exacerbated the short-term problems, while the long-term tasks facing those committed to socialist transformation were enormous. Agricultural production would have to be progressively collectivized and technologically modernized. Power relations within the village would have to be democratized, patriarchal authority extirpated. Institutional and cultural foundations for the integration of the peasantry into national political life had to be laid. If these tasks could be accomplished at all, it could be only through the protracted struggle of conscious revolutionaries immersed in the daily life and work of the villages themselves. Any attempt to impose such changes from the outside, as the *kombedy* campaigns demonstrated, would meet with the unified opposition of the villages in ways that both drew upon and reinforced traditional forms of authority and solidarity. The Left SRs understood this, and although their own rural organizations were relatively weak,[92] they represented a significant potential resource (literacy, administrative skills) for staffing the lower and middle levels of the soviets and the supply apparatus that would provide the crucial link between town and country.

Without the organizational cadre, political experience, and ideological perspective of the Left SRs, the Bolsheviks proved themselves incapable over the next decade of penetrating the natural villages so as to transform them from within. In 1916 the party had had only four rural branches, leaving the political field to the SRs during the struggles of the following year. Even with its land programme and the revolutionary land law, its actual membership in the rural areas remained small, concentrated in the administrative centres at the district and provincial levels. At the Sixth Party Congress in 1917 there was not a single peasant delegate. After the *kombedy* campaign of the second half of 1918 and their infusion into the local soviets, the Bolsheviks still gathered only 3 per cent of the vote in local soviet elections. Only in 1919 did the party establish a department for rural work. However, as Shanin notes, '... the department only managed to enlist fifty-five party organizers in all, who were sent to thirty-five *guberniyas* with a combined population of not less than fifty million peasants. Small wonder that, at the end of a year, the report of the department concluded: "as may be deduced from our data, party work in the villages does not exist."'[93]

Indeed, once single-party rule was secured, active propaganda in the countryside virtually ceased. Most of those Bolsheviks listed as having peasant backgrounds in these years joined the party while in the Red Army, where there were political education programmes and where the peasants were subject to extra-village influences and interests. But peasant-in-arms membership was highly unstable, as the mass withdrawals at Kronstadt in late 1920 revealed.[94] In the absence of village-oriented party programmes and experience, most returning party servicemen were reintegrated into traditional village life. Those that remained members were concentrated in the Soviet administrative apparatus.[95] A study conducted in the early 1920s by Yakovlev, the future Commissar of Agriculture, concluded that 'there are no party branches in the villages—there are only supplementary Soviet organizations. There is no branch of the party which exercises working-class influence on the peasantry. There is only an office carrying out the orders of the authorities and tax collection.' In the eyes of the local population, the party branches were hostile outside agencies that 'just collect taxes and order people around.' When asked in a survey conducted in 1924–25 why they did not join the party, many peasants answered simply: 'How could the party find so many posts (*dolzhnosti*) for us?'[96]

In the absence of commitment to Bolshevik goals generated from within the village itself, and with no combination of organization from above and below, as in the Chinese Communist experience in Yenan, the party attempted to impose a system of centralized administrative control on the local rural soviets.[97] The local soviets were strictly subordinate to the next highest soviet organs, all the way up to the All-Russian Central Executive Committee and the Council of People's Commissars. They had virtually no input into the formulation of national policy or the selection of political leadership. Other parties were illegal *de facto*, if not always *de jure*, and oppositionists generally had to run for election as independent, unaffiliated candidates. Elections were tightly controlled, and the party often disbanded unfriendly congresses and assemblies or intimidated their members, sometimes with the aid of the Cheka. While such tactics did not always guarantee compliant soviets, the party was much more successful in concentrating the power of the local executive committees and their presidia in the hands of its local cells: the two were often completely fused and remarkably stable in membership. The further up from the village level, the more complete was this control. The model was considered democratic centralist, despite the extreme disproportion in the significance of the two components.[98]

The reality, however, was quite different. Except for the requisitioning of grain by outside authorities, which continued throughout the civil war, the party proved unable to strictly subordinate the local soviets to its centralized directives. Even in the case of grain requisitioning, force was often required and even then proved highly inefficient. But in the daily organization of village affairs, from land use to social services and taxation, the local authorities exercised a great degree of autonomy. The party had not yet evolved mechanisms of self-control, and hence could hardly bring the largely non-party soviets consistently to heel. The lack of an effective communication network likewise obstructed the exercise of strict bureaucratic authority. And the system of plenipotentiaries from the centre was too erratic to affect ongoing activities. The local soviets were not adequately financed by the central government and hence had to depend on the village commune for their funds. Indeed, the chairman of the local soviet was often the village elder himself. The affairs of the *mir* and the soviets were so intertwined that meetings of the latter were often not even called. Participation in soviet elections was very low, an average of 22.3 per cent according to one survey. And this situation persisted until forced collectivization. As a Soviet study published in 1929 concluded, 'the commune gathering made itself felt as the real master of the village and its economic life. The rural soviet was elbowed aside and made to ask for final authorization of all its decisions by the commune gathering.'[99] The commune, for its part, continued to function in much the same way as it had for decades. The more well-to-do peasants were not ousted, and indeed began to regain the disproportionate influence they had largely lost in the early stages of the revolution. The landless were excluded, as were women. And the poor generally remained passive. Only heads of households voted at meetings. Tradition continued to reign supreme. Soviet law imposed from above had done little to transform the daily lives of the average peasant.[100]

With the recognition of the politically dangerous effects of the *kombedy* and their abolition in late 1918, Lenin began increasingly to stress the need for a firm alliance with the middle peasantry. Indeed, he gradually came to realize that the redistribution of the land through the *mir* had considerably blunted class distinctions among the peasantry, and that the vast majority were now actually middle peasants: small farmers producing enough grain for themselves and sometimes a surplus, but without exploiting the labour of others. While he still maintained that 'in a country of small peasants, our chief and basic task is to be able to resort to state compulsion in order to raise the level of peasant farming,'[101]

Lenin now began to argue that the past abuses of requisitioning had to be eliminated. Blows aimed at the kulaks must not be allowed to fall on the middle peasant. Any requisitioning outside the strictly established guidelines must be severely punished. Coercive attempts to push the peasants into collectives must be abandoned. Above all, the alliance with the middle peasants can be forged by providing them goods in exchange for their grain. Unfortunately, however, the condition of industry and the needs of the Red Army made this impossible on any widespread and regular basis. Requisitioning, therefore, would have to continue, but once conditions improved, this 'loan' from the peasants would be repaid.[102]

Agricultural production during these years of civil war declined dramatically. In 1909–13, the annual average of sown area was 83 million *desyatins*. In 1916–17 this had fallen to about 79 million. By 1920 it was down to 63 million, and in 1921 stood at a low of 58 million. The decline in productivity on that land was even sharper. The average gross harvest in the pre-war years was about 3.8 thousand million *puds*. This had fallen to 3.4 and 3.3 thousand million in 1916 and 1917 respectively. In 1920 the figure stood at 2.1 thousand million, and by 1921 at a low of 1.7 thousand million. The causes of this precipitous decline were numerous. The destruction and wearing out of implements was a major factor. In 1919 a shortage of 1.4 million ploughs, five million scythes, and forty-two thousand seed machines was reported, causing millions of *desyatins* of land to go uncultivated. The loss of manpower during the First World War and then the Civil War further contributed to the general decline of agriculture, as did the frequent devastation of much crop land as a result of these conflicts. And more than one-fourth of all draft animals were lost between 1916 and 1921. The disruption of land distribution no doubt contributed to the crisis, as did the loss of economies of scale as a result of the breakup of many of the larger and more efficient estates. Scattered strip-holding predominated now more than ever. The voluntary curtailment of sown acreage in response to the government's requisitioning policies (which were further extended in 1919) also was a factor, although more recent studies question the pre-eminence accorded it by Popov's 1920 study, which influenced Lenin's own thinking. Indeed, the decline seems to have been greater in production for the peasants' own consumption than in that destined for the black market, which continued to play an important part in feeding the cities throughout the period, and which the regime periodically tolerated because of this.[103]

The material condition of the rural population, especially in the producing provinces, was considerably better than that of the town dwellers for the first two years of the civil war, although hardly enough to justify Lenin's assertion that the bulk of the peasants were eating better than before.[104] By the end of 1920 however, crop failure brought much of the peasantry to the brink of starvation, and masses roamed the countryside looking for food. As Dorothy Atkinson notes, 'by February 1921 grain consumption was reduced to two-thirds of the pre-revolutionary level in the areas that had traditionally provided the grain surplus for the rest of the country.'[105] Under these conditions, continued grain requisitioning became unbearable, especially as the threat of the landlords' restoration seemed finally to have been eliminated by the Red Army. The countryside flared up in open rebellion once again. In February 1921 alone the Cheka reported no less than 118 separate peasant revolts.[106] The New Economic Policy, with its replacement of requisitioning by a tax in kind and the allowance of free trade in grain, was soon introduced to stem these revolts and establish worker-peasant relations on a new basis.

Was the radical alienation from the new regime of the peasantry and the Left SRs—the only organized peasant political expression committed to the socialist transformation of Russia—inevitable under the conditions of civil war and the disorganization of industry? Given the inability of Russian industry to produce a sufficient quantity of goods to induce the peasants to exchange their produce with the cities freely, and given also the isolation of the revolutionary regime from sources of foreign aid, most commentators sympathetic to the Bolsheviks have assumed that the estrangement was a necessity, tragic but inevitable if the cities were to be fed and the urban social basis of the revolution and future industrial production secured.

The dangerously low level of food being delivered to the cities in the winter and spring of 1918 certainly lends weight to this argument. Somehow the peasants had to be induced or forced to deliver their surpluses, and perhaps even some of their own necessities, if the industrial working class was not to starve or completely disintegrate into the rural mass. But the *forms* taken by this largely one-way exchange of produce, while understandable in the light of the urgency of the situation, were perhaps not so predetermined or inevitable. The Committees of Poor Peasants were chosen as the primary instruments of grain extraction in 1918 for primarily ideological reasons. Lenin theoretically translated the fact of dire necessity into the need for the socialist stage of revolution in the village, though there was virtually no concrete evidence for such a position. The poor peasants' lack of the self-consciousness and self-organization required for such a task would be compensated by their urban comrades, under party direction.

The outcome of such a policy was completely predictable, and the Bolsheviks were duly warned by their erstwhile coalition partners. As the Left SRs foretold, the peasantry would be alienated from the regime and the common front of the villages against the cities solidified. This common front would make it that much more difficult to ferret out the concealed stores of grain of the more well-to-do peasants. The abandonment of the *kombedy* in late 1918 was a belated acknowledgement that this was true. But the subsequent requisition policies, which continued to depend primarily on the central administrative apparatus of the Commissariat of Food and its local branches, never overcame the basic problems of providing accurate assessments of land, implements, livestock and potential and actual food production. This resulted in great inefficiency, as well as the highly erratic application of standards for collection, some villages being assessed several times, for example. As early as 1918 many local Bolshevik committees condemned the requisitioning policies as worse than inefficient. In 'such abusive language [that] had hardly been known inside the party before the October Revolution,' they even referred to their own comrades in the food agencies as alien 'occupiers' of the countryside.[107] In 1920 local party conferences continued desperately to urge the centre to cede the initiative and responsibility for collecting grain to the local soviets. As Abrams argues, these were clearly the administrative organs best suited to the tasks of calculation, collection, and the distribution of food.[108]

This policy, belatedly recognized as necessary by the Bolshevik authorities in the summer of 1920, was similar to that proposed by the Left SRs in the spring of 1918. At that time, however, Lenin saw it as no more than a spineless fear to fight the kulaks.[109] The blinders of rural class-struggle ideology obstructed any realistic assessment of the relative administrative capacities of the different levels of state organization. Unfortunately, the disastrous harvest of 1920 makes it impossible to determine with any degree of certainty how effective this new policy might have been, and by the same token whether it would have been feasible in the spring of 1918. Several factors suggest that it might well have been, as the Left SRs and many local Bolsheviks argued. In 1920 there were instances of successful grain collection and distribution by local soviets. Had the regime taken the time and effort to actualize such possibilities earlier in more favourable circumstances—which could also have assured the support and participation of the Left SRs—a more effective system might have been established. Indeed, peasant resentment and resistance seem to have been a response to the arbitrary and haphazard methods of requisitioning (a result of the top-down administrative application of standards by people unfamiliar with and hostile to village life) more than to requisitioning as such.[110] And the early grain shortage probably had much more to do with the organizational difficulties of the new regime (not the least of which was the breakdown of transport) than the Bolsheviks, in their effort to blame everything on the hoarding kulaks and their domination of the local soviets, were prepared to admit.[111]

But there would have been formidable difficulties too, and some form of coercive pressure from the political authorities would have been requisite, even if combined with a greater degree of local initiative and responsibility. The condition of industry and the requirements of the Red Army meant that not enough was being produced in the cities to induce a free exchange of products. And because of the low level of agricultural production, not just kulak grain, and not just the surpluses, but some of the necessities as well would have had to be handed over to the state authorities. The mass of working peasants could never have been expected to impose such sacrifices on themselves freely for the sake of the ideals of the revolution, or for their distant urban comrades (whom they had traditionally distrusted deeply), while receiving nothing concrete in return. The Left SRs tended to underestimate the gravity of the objective conditions underlying the problem of food provisioning, perceiving the Bolsheviks as totally responsible for the disruption of industry, the early loss of the Ukraine and other grain-producing areas to the Germans, the organizational problems associated with constructing an efficient distribution apparatus, and the increasingly unfavourable exchange prices for agricultural products.[112] This attitude would perhaps have foreclosed the possibility of Left SR cooperation in food-requisitioning policies that did not accord *complete* responsibility to the local soviets. But if the Bolsheviks had formulated a policy toward the peasantry permitting significant initiative and responsibility at the local level, one that did not start from completely misguided premises about village structure that inevitably fuelled policies of urban-led warfare against and the indiscriminate pillaging of the countryside, then the Left SRs might have been more cooperative. They had compromised on many issues, and their commitment to the revolution was unquestionably profound. The split was indeed a tragedy—one whose effects would continue beyond the emergency of 1918. It seems quite possible that it could have been avoided.

6
State and Labour in Civil War

In late May 1918 the Czechoslovak Legion, which had been station-ed in the Urals until it could be transferred to the West European battle zone, revolted against Soviet authorities. Within days it mov-ed west, taking city after city, and the Soviet government was once again seriously threatened by military force.

The peace with Germany had scarcely been established; indeed, German troops still occupied the Baltic states and the Ukraine. Now counter-revolutionary governments were set up and the Allied powers began pouring in military aid. Civil war, which had previously remained largely confined to Cossack areas, was in full swing, and would not be completely resolved in the Bolsheviks' favour until late 1920. During that time, Russia was to become, in Lenin's words, a 'besieged fortress,' and much of Soviet life, especially the economy, was geared to meeting the immediate needs of the war.

This period, which was subsequently dubbed War Communism, was marked by a pervasive centralization in both politics and economics, with the growing use of authoritarian, even military methods to resolve the profound social crises caused by several more years of death and destruction. The meaning of the revolu-tion, as Stephen Cohen has expressed it, became almost inseparable from the defence of the revolution.[1] Policies occasioned, if not necessitated, by the almost constant state of emergency—in battle, in food, fuel, and raw materials supply, in transport, in health crises of epidemic proportions—often came to be viewed as the substance of socialism itself. The period of War Communism was also one of temporary emergency measures and grand ideological illusions whose effects would be felt long after the military battles had been won.

Soviet State Power: Post-Revolutionary Dynamics

By the end of the civil war the apparatuses of the revolutionary state had become generally, if not quite completely and effectively, subordinated to those of the Bolshevik party, and the relation of unconditional party dominance had been ratified by Leninist theory. The conditions of military struggle and economic collapse relentlessly fostered centralization in both state and economy. Yet the narrowing of the party composition of the revolutionary government had begun in October 1917 itself, even though the masses of people who lent active or passive support to the seizure of power overwhelmingly supported a multi-party socialist coalition. While these developments do not appear to have been inevitable, as my analysis of Left SR/Bolshevik relations on the peasant question has indicated, they do reflect profound contradictions at the heart of the project of the revolutionary transformation of Russia.

It is undoubtedly true that Lenin had never been particularly enthusiastic about sharing power or profoundly committed to the principle of party pluralism.[2] Of the major Bolshevik leaders, he was among the most uncompromising on the question of a coalition with the Mensheviks and SRs. Indeed, he had proposed such a coalition on several occasions before the seizure of power, but even in September, when the Bolsheviks won a majority of seats in the Petrograd Soviet, he opposed proportional representation in the Presidium for the moderate socialists.[3] Only a homogeneous soviet leadership could be effective, he argued. During the coalition negotiations after the revolution, Lenin was considerably less ardent in his attempt to reach an agreement than most others in both the left and right wings of the party. In his view, the negotiations 'were to serve as a diplomatic cover for military operations.'[4] He even went so far as to threaten the use of force against the majority of his party, when he said: 'As for an agreement, I cannot even speak about that seriously.... If you want a split, go ahead. If you get the majority, take power in the Central Executive Committee and carry on. We'll go to the sailors.... Our current slogan is: No compromise. A homogeneous Bolshevik government.'[5]

But intense negotiations did occur, because a majority of Bolshevik leaders were convinced of the need to broaden the government if they were to maintain democratic power, and few saw an impending European revolution as relieving them of this necessity. Even many on the left felt this way, and leaders from the right went so far as to resign from the Central Committee to press the point. In the military committees, trade unions, and factory committees, including the radical Central Council of Factory Committees, support for a coalition was overwhelming.[6] The Left SRs delayed joining the new government, hoping for an acceptable agreement with the other socialists. But none was to be had. Virtually all major pro-soviet revolutionary organizations that had supported coalition placed the onus on the Mensheviks and SRs, and lent their active support to the Bolsheviks and the decisions that had been taken at the Second Congress of Workers and Soldiers Deputies ratifying the seizure of power and a revolutionary programme. The Left SRs, though highly critical of Lenin and Trotsky during the negotiations, subsequently agreed to join the government. The Soviet Central Executive Committee was expanded to include delegates from the Extraordinary Congress of Peasant Deputies, which had also ratified the seizure of power later in November, and Left SRs assumed commissarial posts within a few weeks.[7]

The specific demands of the SRs in particular revealed their fundamental intransigence.[8] They ranged from the outright exclusion of all Bolsheviks from the coalition and the inclusion of bourgeois parties, to the exclusion only of the Bolsheviks' two major leaders, Lenin and Trotsky, and minority representation for the left. At one point they demanded that Kerensky's troops be allowed to march into the capital, and that the Red Guards be disarmed. They had taken up arms against the new government from the very start. Indeed, only military defeat had induced them to negotiate. The Mensheviks, on the other hand, were considerably more conciliatory in their demands, and Martov's wing was generally successful in restraining those who wished to join in armed resistance. But an agreement, which seemed quite possible at one time, never materialized. To point to the 'tactical error'[9] and 'political short-sightedness'[10] of the moderate socialists in the immediate post-revolutionary days, however, threatens to obscure the larger questions that were at the heart of pluralist political possibilities: the legitimacy of the revolution itself, the institutional form of state power, and the immediate programme for the problems of the hour.

The SRs rejected the legitimacy of the revolution as such, as well as the soviet form of state power itself. The Mensheviks were less uncompromising here too, but only a full year later did they make the defence of the soviet government an explicit point of policy. In effect, this doomed any possibility of a coalition, since although the Bolsheviks might have been willing to accept a Constituent Assembly as an institutional complement to the soviet system, they never would have allowed any such assembly to displace the soviets from their position of prominence, and certainly not an assembly that refused to ratify the revolutionary programme on land, workers control, and peace (especially the latter, which had been at the heart of government paralysis and social disintegration throughout 1917). On this question the SRs had made virtually no progress whatever.[11] However the evidence and conflicting claims about the coalition negotiations and the alleged democratic representativeness of the various soviet congresses and Constituent Assembly elections are sifted, the fundamental differences on the form of state power and the immediate programme of the revolution seem to have been unbridgeable. However much the failure to achieve a broader coalition and establish the basis for a pluralist political order may be regretted, there is little evidence that any coalition not led by the Bolsheviks could have dealt more effectively with the immediate problems of the day. The Constituent Assembly, with its SR majority, would 'have fallen of its own weight' had it not been disbanded by the Bolsheviks.[12] If any realistic possibilities for a more pluralist political order existed, they could have been realized only on terms more socially revolutionary and more compromising on the issue of a separate peace than the SRs and the Mensheviks were willing to entertain.

This early failure to work out an agreement between the left and the moderates did not definitively foreclose the advent of a pluralist political order in revolutionary Russia. Only with the grain crisis of 1918 was the fateful wedge driven between the two major parties committed to the revolutionary transformation of Russia, even though other serious political differences had threatened peaceful cooperation. As we have seen, this crisis brought to the fore ideological tendencies within Leninism that, in turn, legitimated agrarian policies that ruptured the town/country revolutionary alliance embodied in the Bolshevik/Left SR coalition. Here more than anywhere else lay the real tragedy of pluralist revolutionary politics. It was further compounded by the military and economic emergencies of the civil war.

Despite Bolshevik willingness to legalize the SRs on the condition that they desist from armed opposition, the latter continued to oppose the new regime with all the force at their disposal, and actively participated in counter-revolutionary governments in the outlying regions. The Mensheviks seldom engaged in such activities, and hence enjoyed greater, though far from extensive and principled, toleration by the Bolsheviks. Until the Czechoslovak Legion's uprising and the beginning of full-scale civil war and foreign intervention, both parties sat in the Soviet Central Executive Committee. After having been expelled from the soviets in the summer, the Mensheviks were again active in them in 1919 and 1920.

But the civil war had rigidified Lenin's approach to the question of multi-party participation. He persisted in lumping the Mensheviks with the SRs as *de facto* accomplices of the White Guards. The Mensheviks' support of economic liberalization (similar to the Bolsheviks' NEP of 1921) and the independence of the trade unions from party control, as well as their support of the economic demands of the workers in the last months of the civil war, heightened their influence in the working class, which could no longer endure the burdens and constraints of war communism. But this support spelled their doom, for by then Lenin could tolerate neither the independent action of the working class nor a serious contender for their allegiance. With the introduction of economic liberalization came the completion of political repression, as the lingering vestiges of legitimate extra-party opposition were eliminated and the contours of the homogeneous one-party state perfected and rationalized. To have allowed the Mensheviks full political participation during the crises of the civil war and immediate post-war period may, indeed, have undermined the very basis of the soviet regime. 'But to eliminate them completely from the public life of Soviet Russia and destroy them as a party was fatal to Soviet democracy.'[13] Lenin never gave any clear and explicit indication that such exclusion was anything less than permanent. His almost completely pragmatic attitude, which never confronted the question of multi-party freedom and participation in a principled fashion, was now finally being resolved in a denouement towards which it had tended all along.

The oligarchic tendencies of the soviet system through 1917 were exacerbated in the post-October period. Effective power in the local soviets relentlessly gravitated to the executive committees, and especially their presidia. Plenary sessions became increasingly symbolic and ineffectual, except for the period of intensive popular debate of the Brest peace.[14] Executive committees showed remarkable stability, although at the local rural levels this usually meant prolonged tenure for ordinary village leaders who could not be easily Bolshevized. The party was much more successful in gaining control of soviet executives in the cities and at *uezd* and *guberniya* levels. These executive bodies were usually able to control soviet congresses, though the party often disbanded congresses that opposed major aspects of current policy. On the whole, however, due to widespread popular support among workers and soldiers and superior organization, the Bolshevization of the urban soviets took place peacefully, though not without considerable manipulation in many places.[15] Delegates to the urban soviets most often came from other organizations, especially the trade unions. Those not organized in their workplaces or military units (and this would include many women) seem to have been largely unrepresented. White-collar workers, however, were disproportionately represented, especially in positions of authority, because of their administrative skills. There was considerable local variation in the procedures for determining voter eligibility, though according to one survey of village soviets at the end of the civil war, only 1.4 per cent of the population was effectively disenfranchised. Less than a quarter of the people actually voted, however. Local soviets had little input into the formation of national policy, though they often effectively resisted the implementation of central decrees.[16]

Even at the higher levels, institutional power shifted away from the soviets. The All-Russian Congress, which convened every three months or so during the first year of the revolution, met annually thereafter. Its elected Central Executive Committee, conceived by many as the supreme and permanent legislative organ, also began to meet less frequently, and at the height of the civil war in late 1918 and throughout 1919, it never once met in full session. But from the very outset, it was overshadowed by the Council of People's Commissars. Its functions were never clearly delineated, even in the constitution, despite vigorous attempts by the Left SRs. Rigby's conclusion, that Lenin never saw this highest soviet organ as the genuine equal of his cabinet and that the Bolsheviks deliberately obstructed efforts at clarification, is convincing.[17] In the first year, only 68 of 480 decrees issued by the Council of People's Commissars were actually submitted to the Soviet Central Executive Committee, and even fewer were actually drafted by it.[18] Administrative departments of the CEC, many of which predated the seizure of power, gave way to or were absorbed into the commissariats. Even relations with the local soviets were preempted by the Commissariat of Internal Affairs, the Cheka, and other extra-ordinary organs.[19] By the end of the civil war, the Soviet Executive Committee had become primarily a symbolic promulgator of decrees, not an actual legislative body.[20]

If state power was not democratically centralized through the soviets, neither was it effectively controlled by any other set of government institutions. As Rigby correctly notes, 'one could hardly claim that either order, discipline and harmony or clarity and unity of purpose prevailed among the Bolsheviks as they set about the task of building an administrative apparatus.'[21] Instead, confusion and bureaucratic contradiction prevailed. In the first weeks, the loosely structured and highly erratic Military Revolutionary Committee was the effective government, since the commissariats were established slowly and acquired staffs only as the passive and active resistance of the former civil servants was broken. This took weeks, sometimes months. Jurisdictional conflict was rife even after the commissariats were formed, and the highest officials were constantly shuffled from one bureau to another, and from one area of the country to another. The party's own executive machinery could not effectively compensate for the deficiencies.

With the onset of full-scale civil war later in 1918, the institutional structure of the state became even more bureaucratically snarled. As provisioning of the army became even more important than actual production, administrative confusion in the supply apparatuses led to military debacles. At one time late in 1918 at least three separate commissions competed for authority over arms production itself. Extraordinary organs were established with dizzying speed, each with broad powers encroaching on other bodies with often similarly broad areas of jurisdiction. After a series of such institutional improvisations, the Council for Workers and Peasants Defence was established on 30 November 1918. And though it had the formal powers to issue binding orders to all persons and institutions for the mobilization of national resources for victory, and though it did operate more effectively than the previous array of organs, it fell far short of eliminating some of the basic confusion and jurisdictional conflicts that traversed the new state system. With the temporary easing of the war emergency in late 1919, the Defence Council was trimmed of its powers and the Council for Labour and Defence was created to prepare for post-war reconstruction. But no overall coordination had been achieved even in 1920, and local soviet administrative departments and various extraordinary organs and commissarial bureaux were mired in constant conflicts. Through it all, the interference of the Cheka, which no other state or even party organ seemed able to control,[22] was pervasive.

This bureaucratic confusion among state institutions, however, became the occasion for the enhancement of actual party authority, and eventually for its effective organizational control of state institutions at all levels. The continual reshuffling and jurisdictional uncertainty made it difficult for state organs to take root and stabilize themselves. When the conflicts did not produce mere confusion and administrative chaos, they led to appeals to party organs to settle disputes. The Central Committee acted as the ultimate arbiter in important matters, but its own administrative resources were inadequate to the tasks brought to it, and competing organs would often appeal to local party committees. Party membership became an important criterion of loyalty to the regime at a time when state mechanisms for accountability were not very strong.[23] The steady influx of middle-class elements motivated by opportunistic careerism, and the steady outflow of workers who had joined in the heady days of 1917, however, often rendered such loyalty of questionable value from a popular democratic standpoint.[24] The prolonged state of emergency necessitated the continual reassignment of some of the most competent personnel, and nomadism of functionaries became a way of life. Careers thus came to depend increasingly on the party, rather than on performance of any particular state role. Given the general insecurity of the period, functionaries naturally looked to the most stable organization.

It has been argued that such institutional conflicts and reorganizations represented a deliberate attempt by the Bolsheviks to enhance the role of the party.[25] While Bolshevik leaders did at times reassign party dissidents to make their opposition less effective, this claim is surely an exaggeration, and ignores the enormous difficulties of institution-building that any party would have faced under conditions of revolution and civil war. Rigby's judgement on the role of the party as the sole directing and integrating element in the state system is much more judicious: 'In the first year or so after the Revolution there was no evidence that leading Bolsheviks believed the Party should perform such a role, there was no attempt to equip it to do so, and it did not in fact do so.'[26] Indeed, the party largely neglected its own organizational consolidation in favour of building up state institutions, even if its conceptions of the latter were often unclear and its initiatives improvised. By 1919 this relative inattention to party administration had caused much consternation, particularly as it became clear how much organizational affairs had come to depend on a single person, Party Secretary Sverdlov, who died in March. It was only then that deliberate efforts were made to strengthen the party organization and to make it the effective directing instrument within the state system, without actually merging it with state institutions. The Central Committee was expanded, and the Politburo and Orgburo—which quickly became the two most powerful organs in the entire system—were created at the Eighth Party Congress. It is interesting to note, however, that some of the most democratic elements in the party were most vocal about the need for such changes. Osinsky and Sapronov, both former Left Communists and later leaders of the Democratic Centralist opposition, saw the strengthening of (democratic) party organization as a way to counteract the often unchecked and arbitrary power of the commissariats, the extraordinary organs, and particularly the Cheka. The supremacy of the party itself was not questioned, but the greatest danger was seen in the elaborate and convoluted bureaucratic state structure, staffed with many functionaries from the old regime.[27]

This consolidation of the party, however, did not lead to greater democratization of the state structure. There were many reasons for this, and for the erosion of democratic possibilities in general. One, however, was that many of the Bolshevik leaders, including Lenin, saw little need for an organizational clarification in the state system similar to the one in the party. At the very same party congress, Osinsky presented a series of proposals to eliminate some of the overlap and confusion, and in particular to transform the commissariats into departments of the Soviet Central Executive Committee. Later in 1919, when the military situation eased temporarily, support for a revival of the soviets and their CEC received widespread support at the Seventh Soviet Congress, among both Bolsheviks and oppositionists such as Martov, who played a vocal role in the congress. Resolutions were passed along these lines, and the CEC was revived after a long hiatus. But the resolve was more evident on paper than in practice. Even after the civil-war emergency had finally passed, Lenin never considered proposals to transform the CEC into a genuine legislative body, and the Council of People's Commissars into its executive arm, as anything more than bankrupt parliamentarism.[28] This attitude to institutional clarity and democratic accountability was strikingly similar to that expressed in the debates around the regulatory organs of the economy in early 1918.

The peculiarities of state development in this period, however, clearly have deeper causes than the attitudes of the Bolshevik leaders. The socio-economic crisis of early 1918 and the civil war exacerbated all the problems of effective democratic participation that had been evident in 1917. Daily life became ever more arduous, the struggle for survival increasingly tenuous, popular constituencies less and less stable. The most competent and politically reliable workers were siphoned off into the various administrative apparatuses and the Red Army. Indeed, not only material resources, but relatively scarce organizational resources as well were concentrated on the war effort—to the detriment of soviet and other state institutions.[29] The proliferation of extraordinary state organs was due largely to the nearly constant state of emergency. Attempts to revive the soviets in late 1919 were soon followed by an intensification of the war and by Polish intervention. By the time of its conclusion, the civil war had gutted the social base of soviet democracy and warped many of its most effective cadre. The industrial proletariat, the foundation for soviet democracy, had been decimated, reduced from 4 million in 1917 to little more than a million by January 1921.[30] The demobilized soldiers and officers that took up civilian posts at all levels of the state and economic system had been profoundly influenced by military styles of discipline and command.[31]

But the development of a highly bureaucratic state system, whose coherence came increasingly to be based on the directives and organizational controls of a single party, was in definite ways determined by the specific form of political transition itself. The delay, confusion, incompetence, and institutional contradictions that provided the context and rationale for the effective pre-eminence of the Bolshevik party throughout the new state system were to no small extent due to the fact that the revolutionary political crises took the form of dual power. Because of the lack of a democratic parliamentary heritage at both national and local levels, popular rebellion had expressed itself through a historically venerable but largely improvised system of soviets. These bodies possessed overwhelming legitimacy among the popular classes, but despite significant achievements under unfavourable conditions, the system was not able to develop the administrative capacity to govern effectively.

Soviet institutions continally looked to the organizational resources of the parties, and increasingly to the Bolshevik party. And although the Bolsheviks' resources were superior to those of their rivals, they were not immediately adequate to the tasks of state administration. Long years of political exclusion under the tsarist autocracy had fostered certain kinds of political-organizational skills, but had simultaneously hindered the acquisition of the higher administrative skills required to manage a complex state and economic system. Many leading Bolsheviks had virtually no work experience at all before the revolution, and some even resisted accepting important posts in the new regime—at times with near-comic fanfare—for fear of their own incompetence.[32]

The Menshevik and SR refusal to grant revolutionary legitimacy to the soviets was due at least in part to the recognition of political-administrative underdevelopment in the revolutionary camp. And their unwillingness to support the revolution further reduced the administrative capacities of the democratic forces. Local soviet administration seems to have been more effective where the old *zemstvo* and *duma* personnel were absorbed into the new institutions—in other words, where the two poles of dual power were merged at the level of personnel. In fact, the old officials eventually seem to have carried the burden of administrative work.[33] But not before an intervening period when political and institutional conflict led to the fragmentation of potential administrative resources, and hence provided the rationale and opportunity for further intrusion by even less democratically accountable state organs, or by party fractions.

The new regime also had to depend on the old government ministries at the higher levels of state administration, and both structural and staff continuities in the newly created commissariats were quite marked. Bureaucratic hangovers were thus considerable, as Lenin and other leading Bolsheviks were only too aware. Yet the form of political transition did not merely reproduce old bureaucratic tendencies, but compounded them in specific ways, even if soviet democratization clearly reduced them in other ways. It was the muddle of state-building and administration with multiple organs of power that led, under conditions of crisis, to even more convoluted institutional arrangements, to the decline of democratic and even regular bureaucratic accountability through state mechanisms, and to the eventual ascendancy of the party as not merely the political leader but the very organizational fabric of the entire state system. And it was in the new apparatuses (including the party), which were less directly built on the foundations of the old, that the most abusive *chinovnik* behaviour emerged.[34] The ironies of democratic state-building had been cruel indeed.

The Management of Industry

The June 1918 nationalization decree, it will be recalled, legally transformed all large-scale industry and many medium-sized firms into state property, although the former owners were to remain in their management positions until they received specific orders from the Supreme Economic Council. The actual pace of nationalization, however, continued to be determined by local and regional economic councils and the factory committees more than by the SEC. The June decree, like the decree on workers control in November 1917, provoked a wave of spontaneous nationalizations, as workers found it hard to understand how industrial property could be formally nationalized but still operate within the old structures of authority, and even with a continued private-profit incentive. In October 1918 the government passed yet another decree forbidding any organ but the SEC from sequestering industrial property, but as before, this apparently had little effect. By the end of 1918, an estimated 3,338 firms had been nationalized, only 1,125 of which were under the control of the SEC. The most important factories in the country had been nationalized by then, and the number of seized firms rose only gradually until the wholesale nationalization of small-scale industry in November 1920. Within the People's Economic Councils struggle continued between Leftists and Leninists or moderates. The latter argued for relatively slow-paced nationalization resting on the existing management structures. The former—based largely on the factory committees and some trade unions—pressed for the decisive implementation of the June decree and the greater democratization of management.[35]

Although collegial forms of control persisted in many plants, and worker-elected management boards even continued to function in some, the trend was clearly toward individual management. Lenin was unequivocally in favour of it, arguing that the proletariat had to *imitate the bourgeoisie* in its administration of the state and the economy. On one occasion he stated: 'The shrewdest and richest bourgeoisies are the British and the American; the British are in many respects more experienced, and they know how to rule better than the Americans. And do they not furnish us with examples of maximum individual dictatorship, of maximum speed in administration, and yet they keep power fully and entirely in the hands of their own class? There you have a lesson, comrades.'[36]

Collegial management, he maintained, may have been necessary in the early stages of the revolution, but efficient, practical work required a transition to individual management. Collegial management, even with strict individual accountability for the execution of tasks, almost always squandered resources or failed to get the tasks accomplished.[37] Concerning the concept of 'industrial democracy', which was revived by a number of groups in 1920, Lenin held that 'industry is indispensable. Democracy is a category proper *only* to the political sphere.... Industry is indispensable, democracy is not.'[38] Besides he continued, it is a concept that has not been fully tested, and the masses may misinterpret it. Exactly how such a concept would be tested in practice and what role it might play in the future, if not in the present, was never clarified.[39]

Lenin further argued that the number of members on management boards was irrelevant, since the essence of democratic centralism was the election and recall by the workers in the localities, not the number of those elected.[40] But since few individual managers were elected by the workers, and few were recalled by anyone but higher administrative bodies, it is not surprising that many saw individual management as the epitome of an authoritarian, anti-proletarian industrial policy. Opposition was greatest in the factory committees, the trade unions, and the local People's Economic Councils. Tomsky, a leading Bolshevik trade-union leader, considered collegial management 'the fundamental principle in the construction of the organs regulating and administering the economy, which alone can guarantee the participation of broad non-party masses through the trade union.'[41] The Central Council of Trade Unions resisted ratification of individual management until 1920, and both the Second and Third All-Russian Congresses of Councils of National Economy rejected it as well, the latter making an exception in special cases if the union's approval was previously obtained.

But the Ninth Party Congress in March 1920 decided the issue in favour of individual management, despite the opposition of the Democratic Centralists Osinsky, Sapronov, and others. Collegiality, the approved resolution stated, should continue at the higher levels (in the SEC, the *glavki*), but management at lower levels should be individual. Exceptions could be made in the case of already existing collegia functioning efficiently and under a strong president, and various intermediary arrangements could be tried in the process of developing full-fledged individual management (a trade-unionist manager with a technical assistant, a bourgeois specialist manager with one or two trade unionists as assistants or commissars).[42] Intense party pressure was henceforth brought to bear on the unions, and their resistance was soon broken. Whereas at the end of 1918 only 3.4 per cent of the nationalized firms were under individual management, and only 10.9 per cent in 1919, in 1920 and 1921 the percentages rose dramatically to 71.2 and 90.7 per cent respectively.[43]

With extensive nationalization, the functions of the factory committees had to be redefined, since the original law on workers control was enacted during a situation of dual power and assumed that it was necessary to oversee the activity of potentially hostile capitalist owners. The SEC thus issued a new set of regulations on the administration of nationalized enterprises, modelled on instructions issued by the Saratov PEC in April 1918 for its nationalized glass factories. A director was to be appointed by the PEC with full administrative responsibility. He was to be assisted, solely in an advisory capacity, by a representative Economic-Administrative Council, and could be supervened only by a factory commissar sent by the PEC. The factory committee was to regulate working conditions and the general affairs of the workers, and it had representation on the advisory council. But management decisions were to remain the sole prerogative of the director. The factory committee could issue complaints, but had no legal right to veto, delay, or change any decisions.[44]

While such schemas may have been the ideal of the SEC, the actual functions of the factory committees varied considerably. In October 1918, for instance, a Metalworkers Conference resolved that the Central Administration of the State Combine of Metallurgical Works (Gomza) should consist of two-thirds elected workers representatives and one-third SEC appointees, the former to be confirmed by the SEC, and the combine as a whole to work within the guidelines set by the SEC's Metallurgical Section. In the factories and shops themselves, the Central Administration should appoint a managing board at least one-third of whose members would be workers and one-third technical and commercial personnel. The factory committees should be abolished, since 'The organization of the administrative bodies of these enterprises guarantees that the representatives of the trade unions of the proletariat and the regulative organs of the state will have a decisive influence in the management of the amalgamated shops; the need for the previously existing special organs of workers control is thereby removed.'[45] The All-Russian Conference of Tanners, after demanding an absolute majority of seats for their trade union in the central administrative organs of the industry, passed a similar resolution, and in the resin industry the functions of control were transferred to the regional PEC.[46]

However, in factories in which the committees were officially abolished or virtually disempowered, complaints against authoritarian management continued to be voiced, and many committees refused to be dissolved. Even the SEC had second thoughts about the committees when the Commissariat of State Control began to demand that all control functions be centralized under *its* direction and that all trade unionists participating in control be ratified by the Commissariat alone. The SEC, either out of fear for its own bureaucratic privileges or genuine concern that the Commissariat, resting mainly on bourgeois elements, was a threat to proletarian power, called for the revival of factory-committee control functions. The committees would have the right to block decisions they considered hostile to the working class, but they were not to participate at the higher levels of adjudication. Their activities would be overseen by the unions and their All-Russian Central Council, but final decisions would be reserved for the SEC itself. The Central Council of Trade Unions, however, objected to two major aspects of this proposal: 1) the factory committees must not have the right to veto decisions, since this would be too disruptive of plant operations; and 2) not the SEC but the Central Council itself should have overall direction of workers control, since unionists working through the SEC as a state institution might become typical state bureaucrats with little or no vital contact with the workers themselves.[47]

The Second All-Russian Congress of Councils of National Economy, meeting in December 1918, took this trade-union position as its starting point, with the amendment made by the author (Glebov-Avilov) himself that in special circumstances the control commission could temporarily block management decisions. Taking note of the new situation, with trade-union participation in the administration of the nationalized enterprises at the higher levels, the approved resolution stated: 'In these circumstances the task of workers control must be limited to monitoring factory production and to inspecting the activity of individual plant administrations, as well as to the activity of the administration of whole branches of industry. Workers control is to be carried out in the following order of priority: it should follow rather than precede the work of administration.'[48]

In other words, the workers-control commission was not to participate in management deliberations and decisions, but to check on these decisions *ex post facto*. With the goal of 'gradually training the broad masses of the working class for direct participation in the management and organization of production,' the Congress approved a scheme whereby the control commissions would be based on a more or less permanent core of workers delegated by the union and a rapidly rotated group of workers to serve for 'the shortest possible time' and to be elected by the general council of workers. The rationale was that rotation would acquaint the greatest possible number of workers with factory administration. This arrangement, however, would seem to have allowed in-plant workers very little knowledge of production, while safely leaving the power of control (meagre as it was) in the hands of the permanent core of union appointees.[49]

Even this feeble role for the control commissions soon proved unacceptable. Within three weeks Glebov-Avilov had amended the resolution overwhelmingly approved at the Second All-Russian Congress of Councils of National Economy. Under intense pressure in party ranks, not a single other Bolshevik trade unionist mentioned it at the Second All-Russian Congress of Trade Unions in January 1919. The resolution approved at the latter congress again limited control to *ex post facto* supervision, and strictly subordinated the control commissions to the unions, with a rapid turnover of in-plant members. But the *main* function of workers control was now seen as educational, and the control commission was not to have the right to block management decisions in *any* circumstances. Likewise, the union control commissions were to work closely with the Commissariat of State Control, a decision that foreshadowed the government decree of 9 April merging the control commissions with the state control apparatus, under the authority of the latter. Glebov-Avilov's original fear, expressed when he spoke for the Central Trade Union Council, that union members would become detached from their constituencies if they worked primarily through state institutions, now seemed even more apposite as the Commissariat of State Control became the primary vehicle of 'workers control.'[50]

Lenin, who supported these moves to disempower the factory committees and establish one-man management throughout industry, clarified his views on the first anniversary of the revolution. Speaking to the Extraordinary Sixth Soviet Congress, he noted: 'At first our slogan was workers control.... We did not decree socialism immediately throughout industry, because socialism can only take shape and be consolidated when the working class has learnt how to run the economy and when the authority of the working people has been firmly established. Socialism is mere wishful thinking without that. That is why we introduced workers control, appreciating that it was a contradictory and incomplete measure, but an essential one so that the workers themselves might tackle the momentous tasks of building up industry in a vast country without and opposed to exploiters.

'Everyone who took a direct, or even indirect, part in this work, everyone who lived through all the oppression and brutality of the old capitalist regime, learned a great deal. We know that little has been accomplished. We know that in this extremely backward and impoverished country where innumerable obstacles and barriers were put in the workers way, it will take them a long time to learn to run industry. But we consider it most important and valuable that the workers have themselves tackled the job, and that we have passed from workers control, which in all the main branches of industry was bound to be chaotic, disorganized, primitive and incomplete, to workers industrial administration on a national scale.'[51]

By the latter he meant the centralized administration of industry through the SEC and similar bodies, to which the trade unions sent their representatives. While he correctly recognized the inability of the working class to administer industry completely on its own, he failed to clarify what exactly constituted the transition to *workers* administration, a transition that, he noted a year later, 'has, by and large, already been accomplished.'[52] Essentially, Lenin seems to have believed that because the trade unions sent representatives to central and local management boards (although these were subject to state and party controls at all levels), such a designation was warranted.[53] During the debate over individual management at the Ninth Party Congress, he argued that collegial management was irrelevant to the question 'how a class governs and what class domination actually is.' For, he continued, 'the victorious proletariat has abolished property, has completely annulled it—and *therein* lies its domination as a class. The prime thing is the question of property. As soon as the question of property was settled practically, the domination of the class was assured.'[54]

If the prime issue is property and not who *controls* and *manages* the means of production (and whether that management is democratically constituted), then factory-committee control becomes just as irrelevant as collegial management. And in the years after 1918 this is exactly what happened. In many instances, it was no doubt inevitable. The worsening scarcity of competent organizers in the factory put a premium on the consolidation of directing functions. This necessity was greatest in plants with very large contingents of unskilled workers, although the siphoning off of the most skilled into the army and state administration was a general phenomenon. The permanent state of war made speedy decisions requisite, so it was increasingly impractical to explain everything to the work-force, or even to have lengthy discussions among smaller groups of elected representatives.[55]

At least in certain cases, however, the extreme concentration of authority was counterproductive. As Rosenberg notes, 'the result of replacing workers committees with one-man rule (*edinonachal'stvo*) on the railroads, for instance, was not directiveness but distance, and increasing inability to make decisions appropriate to local conditions. Despite coercion, orders on the railroads were often ignored as unworkable.'[56] And one wonders whether some of the difficulties of industrial production in these years might themselves have been turned into advantages of a sort. The frequent interruption of production due to organizational and supply problems, for instance, provided occasion for discussion and education that was not immediately detrimental to efficiency. In fact, systematically utilizing these interruptions would seem ultimately to be less demoralizing than simply letting workers hang around, wander off, or get drunk. But some organized mechanism for influencing plant operations would have to exist to motivate workers to participate. While little is known of the creativity that was actually exercised in these areas, the ideological positions that were developed in response to the chronic crisis clearly dampened such creativity. The decline in effective participation was undoubtedly inevitable. The emerging hegemonic ideology made it increasingly irreversible.

The higher levels of economic management and regulation were also marked by mounting bureaucratization. The conflict between vertical centralization and horizontal federalism had been implicit since the establishment of local and regional People's Economic Councils alongside the *glavki* and *tsentry* of the SEC, and the First All-Russian Congress of Councils of National Economy had left it unresolved. The Congress had given the regional PECs the right to name up to two-thirds of the management of nationalized enterprises, subject to SEC approval, and the regional councils had begun to play an energetic role in this with the creation of special Departments for the Administration of Nationalized Enterprises. But the Congress had simultaneously vested in the SEC and its various departments broad powers that supervened those of the regional councils. The SEC was to determine all plans for production, finance, and so on, and was to approve all nominations to factory management boards. But it also had the right to reorganize existing boards and to directly appoint its own managers—a right it began to use with greater frequency from June 1918 onwards. All the decrees establishing the *glavki* explicitly prohibited interference by local organs in the management of nationalized enterprises, and this provision was confirmed by the Commissariat of Internal Affairs. By nominating a majority to the various management boards, the SEC was attempting to secure nothing short of direct control of the nationalized firms, without the interference of regional and local authorities. On 31 October 1918, the Moscow Regional PEC was dissolved, and the Second Congress of Councils of National Economy in December decided to eliminate all similar regional councils except those of the Northern region and Turkestan. Regional councils, the approved resolution stated, are simply 'redundant institutions, which complicate the general system of economic relations, thus making it more difficult to further the progress of planned centralization.' The SEC would now have the right to appoint two-thirds of the members of the management boards of the nationalized firms, with the remaining one-third still reserved to the workers and employees of the plant itself.[57]

The dissolution of almost all the regional councils met with considerable resistance from the affected bodies and from partisans of regional federalism generally. This resistance was strongest in the Urals, and in the Northern region, which was for the time being unaffected by the decision and assumed the role of general critic of top-down centralization. Antipov, a member of the Presidium of the Northern PEC and a former member of the Central Council of Factory Committees, had earlier called for the dissolution of the *glavki* rather than of the regional councils. He thought exclusive rights of management should rest with the regional councils, the SEC having only the right of veto and, in special cases, the right to name a commissar. Molotov, another member of the Presidium, supported this position, as did Kaktyn, who went so far as to propose severing all ties to the SEC and working more closely with the soviets instead. The elimination of the regional councils, it was argued, removed the levers of power farther from working-class control—a position shared by the Left Communists. Some local councils actually resisted the decisions of the Second Congress by hoarding raw materials and finished products. Opposition, which was aired in the press and lasted for several months, was so great that the SEC may have felt it was too dangerous to convene a national congress in 1919. Opposition was still vocal at the Seventh Soviet Congress in December 1919, as the Democratic Centralists attacked the regime's decisions as bureaucratic. And one speaker noted that if the population was asked 'what should be destroyed on the day after the destruction of Denikin and Kolchak,' ninety percent would answer 'the *glavki* and the centres.'[58]

Some small concessions to local control were finally made at the Third All-Russian Congress of Councils of National Economy in

January 1920. All industry was divided into three categories of size and importance. Large-scale factories of national significance were to be directly managed by the *glavki*. Approximately one-third of all nationalized firms fell into this category. Medium-sized firms that produced for a national market (approximately one-half the total) were to be run by the local PECs, but under the general supervision of the *glavki*. In practice, this often meant little more local initiative than for the first category. Small-scale industry with purely local significance was to be managed entirely by the local PECs. This last category, which comprised only about 15 per cent of the affected firms, dramatically increased in size and importance with the November 1920 decree nationalizing all small-scale industry.[59]

Although the fear of bureaucratic centralization was real and the ideological motivations for some form of federalist decentralization were compelling, the conditions of the civil war overwhelmingly favoured centralization. At the September 1918 meeting of the SEC Plenum, Rykov noted that the People's Economic Councils often hoarded resources for distribution to firms in their own locality. Chubar, a former member of the Central Council of Factory Committees and now in the SEC's Metal Department, criticized the localities for not sending adequate information to the centre.

Attempts to maximize local interests, of course, are perfectly understandable under conditions of scarcity and general disorganization. No local organ could be expected willingly to sacrifice today's goods and materials when it could not be reasonably sure that recompense for such sacrifices would be forthcoming tomorrow, or even that there would be a tomorrow if what little it had was lost. But while such a localist and parochial response is understandable, it was nevertheless intolerable under war conditions, when all efforts had to be concentrated on the single goal of defence and victory if anything at all was to be salvaged of this new social experiment. As E.H. Carr has noted, 'as early as October 1918 the shortage of raw materials made it imperative to close the less efficient factories in many branches of industry and concentrate production in the most efficient; such decisions could only be taken by a strong central authority.'[60]

The regions and localities were not self-contained economic units—even less so with the military invasions and the economic destruction left in their wake. Sources of raw materials and fuel, for instance, often lay hundreds, even thousands, of miles from the industries that consumed them. The linkages of the national economy, already strained as a result of the breakdown of the transportation network, might have been tragically shattered without some form of centralized maximization of the use of resources, indeed, without the centre's extensive encroachment on the prerogatives of the localities.

The civil war also brought greater concentration of power within the SEC itself. The 8 August 1918 decree had provided for a policy-making Plenum of sixty-nine members, ten appointed by the Soviet Central Executive Committee, twenty by the regional economic councils, and thirty by the Central Council of Trade Unions. There was also to be a Presidium of nine, the president appointed by the Soviet Executive and the remaining eight by the Plenum, with the approval of the Council of People's Commissars. The Presidium, however, soon began to gather all power in its own hands, and the Plenum finally ceased even to meet. The *glavki* and *tsentry*, which administered the particular branches of industry, had a fairly high percentage of workers, many (if not most) elected at trade-union conferences. In December 1918, for instance, according to a report by Molotov, the composition of the twenty most important *glavki* was: 43 per cent workers, 10 per cent former owners, 9 per cent technicians, and 38 per cent officials of various departments. Lenin cites a 1920 report claiming that the representation of workers was 51.4 per cent. In some *glavki* it was considerably higher, as a result of constant pressure from the unions. In Tsentrotekstil, for instance, fully two-thirds of the central board were elected by the Textile Workers Congress, as was the case in tanning and water transport. But even in those *glavki* where elected workers constituted a majority, the power of the SEC Presidium over the respective unions was not greatly diminished. The SEC chairman had to sign all decisions of the individual *glavki*, and all trade-union representatives had to be confirmed by the SEC Presidium. The latter, in violation of the elective principle approved at the First Congress of Councils of National Economy, began to appoint the entire membership of the *glavki* presidia, a practice that was endorsed at the Second Congress later in the year. Trade-union participation in the various branches of the SEC, seen by many as an antidote to bureaucracy, gave the state administration a definite proletarian character, but without directly enhancing the actual power of the workers.[61]

While the SEC steadily tightened its control over industry at the expense of the local and regional PECs, the trade unions, and the factory committees, its control over the economy as a whole was eroded. The founding decree had promised to make the SEC the centre of the entire economy, with power over distribution and finance as well as industry, although its relation to the economic commissariats was not clarified. At the First Congress of People's Economic Councils in May 1918, Lenin had spoken of the economic councils, including the SEC, as those 'which alone of all the state institutions are destined to endure.' The closer Russia came to a truly socialist society, the more the old state administrative apparatus would disappear, 'while the apparatus of the type of the Supreme Economic Council is destined to grow, to develop and become strong, performing all the main activities of organized society.'[62] But such hopes were soon to be dashed. The 8 August 1918 decree effectively limited the SEC's powers to the management of nationalized industry, although distribution was perfunctorily included in its duties as well. The economic commissariats were not subordinated to the SEC. Specifically, all decrees of the Commissariats of Food and of Agriculture were to remain in effect, and finance was to be overseen in conjunction with the Commissariats of Finance and of State Control. In November 1918 the power of the Food Commissariat, so crucial in view of the dangerous state of food production and distribution and the urgent needs of the army, was enhanced at the expense of the SEC, when the former was assigned control of the distribution of all household and personal goods. As Leftist Lev Kritsman noted, 'From 1919, the exclusive role of the Supreme Economic Council in the system of economic authorities was more an idea; in reality it was increasingly transformed into one authority among many, into a people's commissariat of industry.'[63]

But even within industry the SEC's orders were more and more often countermanded by those of the emergency organs established to prosecute the war more effectively: first the Extraordinary Commission for the Supply of the Red Army and then the Council for

Workers and Peasants Defence. Bureaucratic confusion prevailed. Attempts to bring about a more efficient use of resources through the 'shock system' of designating particular factories and branches of production as especially important showed few results, as the number of such designated firms steadily grew and the category itself became progressively meaningless. The particular plans of the *glavki* and other departments and commissariats remained almost completely uncoordinated. As Kritsman remarked, capitalist anarchy of production had merely been replaced by proletarian anarchy.[64] Even in planning for post-war reconstruction, and in particular Lenin's prized electrification project, which was to bring Enlightenment through Light to the whole country, the SEC lost out to the department of the Council for Labour and Defence. Lenin himself rebuffed the SEC's attempts to subordinate the economic commissariats to its own overall direction.[65] The civil war had rendered the ideal of coordinating the national economy through a system of popularly elected councils irrelevant as far as the leading Bolsheviks were concerned. It withered away long before any of the more traditional state economic institutions showed any signs of erosion.

Disciplining Labour

As the civil war occasioned a stricter top-down administration of the economy, so also did it lead to the rising use of direct compulsion in the organization and distribution of labour. The primary reason for this was the dramatic fall in labour productivity, which threatened not only the war effort but also the very existence of the urban population. An estimate by Prokopovicz puts average labour productivity in 1920 at 30 to 35 per cent of its pre-war level, and the total productivity of industry at 14.5 per cent.[66] Of the many causes of this decline, malnutrition and exhaustion of the workers themselves continued to be central. In early 1920 the average daily calorie intake was only 2,980 (compared to 3,820 before the war), which may have been enough for survival, but certainly was not adequate for the regeneration of labour-power.[67] This poor nutrition largely accounts for the increasing number of days lost per year by the average worker. As of early 1920 in Petrograd, for example, the average worker lost nineteen days a year due to sickness and fifty-two days due to non-illness-related causes (simple exhaustion, drunkenness, and so on)—an increase of 157 per cent and 214 per cent respectively compared with the period 1913–16.[68] In one Petrograd textile plant observed over a three-day period in 1920, some 15 to 18 per cent of the workers were absent each day, another 5 to 9 per cent were late, 3 to 5 per cent had temporarily quit, and 4 to 15 per cent had quit permanently.[69] When food rations rose, as they did temporarily in late 1920, so also did productivity.[70] But this was the exception throughout this period. Days lost on account of plant idleness were also significant: fifty-three per year on the average in Petrograd up to early 1920. The use of hourly wages in some places also apparently affected productivity adversely. In the Petrograd metal industry, for instance, piece wages were temporarily suspended in October 1918 as a result of rank-and-file protest, and production soon declined. The People's Economic Council of the Northern region, on whose presidium sat a number of radicals from the defunct Central Council of Factory Committees, soon decided to re-introduce them; this, it was argued, raised productivity two to three times.[71]

With results like these, it is no wonder that piece wages were used ever more extensively wherever possible. The Second All-Russian Trade Union Congress in January 1919 approved of them, as had many individual unions and the Central Council of Trade Unions in the previous year. The Congress also attempted to establish a uniform wage policy for all of Russian industry. All workers (except specialists) were to be classified into four categories with a total of twelve gradations; the ratio of the lowest-paid rates to the highest was to be 1:1.75. This was a significant levelling compared with pre-revolutionary days, though it is unclear what the actual ratios were by 1919.[72] Wages were to be set by the government in consultation with the unions. But such uniformity represented more the wish than the reality, as factories and industries competed with each other for scarce skilled labour. Bonuses in kind (mainly food) became one way of getting around these rates, and they became significant as wages themselves were increasingly paid in kind because of the enormous devaluation of the currency. In 1921, for instance, Preobrazhensky estimated that the ruble had fallen to one-twenty-thousandth of its former value. Payment in kind, although prompted primarily by necessity, came to be seen by some as the first step toward the abolition of money. At about the same time, a number of goods and services were provided free: hot lunches for school children and workers, some consumer goods to employees of state firms and institutions and to families of army personnel, rent, gas, electricity, and water for those in state-owned and municipal housing. But devaluation also meant that money was relatively useless as a work incentive.[73]

As workers became physically exhausted and often weakened by illness and disease, the disciplinary measures to keep them at their work benches became more severe and authoritarian. The trade unions and factory committees, while they favoured fairly harsh measures for lateness, absences, unauthorized departures, and work stoppages, had insisted in the spring of 1918 that discipline be left up to them. But discipline imposed by the workers organizations does not seem to have stemmed the tide. Workers may have been unwilling to impose strict measures against fellow workers whose miserable plight they understood themselves only too well. Undoubtedly, there was also resentment that they had virtually no control over the establishment of the ever-rising production norms. As Falk Döring notes, even the hopes of the Northern PEC for workers self-discipline soon gave way to the resigned acknowledgement that control from below was unable to prevent further decreases in productivity.[74] But the Eighth Party Congress declared itself in favour of comradely discipline, and on 14 November 1919, the regime issued a decree calling for the establishment of comradely courts to adjudicate infringements of work rules. These courts were to impose the following penalties:

'(1) public reprimand, (2) temporary suspension—up to six months—from participation in trade-union elections or from being elected, (3) demotion with reduced pay for a period not to exceed one month, (4) assignment to hard, socially useful labour with corresponding rates of pay. Particularly obstructive workers who repeatedly refuse to submit to disciplinary measures will be subject, as non-workers, to discharge and confinement in concentration camps.'[75]

But the newly established 'comradely courts' had little in common with their predecessors, the comradely element being quite limited. At the lowest level, only one of the three judges was actually from the workplace. One was appointed by the local union hierarchy, the other by the relevant state industrial administration. At the next highest level, all were state appointees. Actual deliberations took place within the factory if it employed more than 500 workers. Otherwise, they were convened at union offices. The courts were financially dependent on the Commissariat of Labour, which could disband them and create new ones. And only the unions and management could initiate proceedings. Workers were not permitted to bring managerial personnel before the court for any abuse or infraction of established rules. Nor is it likely that the failure to delimit the term that might be served in a concentration camp was mere oversight. Because of the scarcity of skilled workers, the harshest penalties probably seldom imposed on them, regardless of work infractions (though they were often fiercely used against the bourgeoisie).[76]

But many unions, because of the divisions developing within them over the power of the unions vis-à-vis the state, failed to empanel such courts. Because of their distance from the workers in the plant, those that were established do not seem to have been particularly effective.[77] Lenin admitted in late 1920, more than a year after the decree, that he had no idea how effective they were, and that no one in the party had actually studied the matter.[78] By that time, however, state Commissions on Compulsory Labour had been established to enforce penalties for lateness and absence. In April 1921, after the war had ended, the court statute was revised slightly to the workers' advantage, but with the NEP the idea of comradely courts was eventually shelved.

Before the end of the civil war the free labour market was itself virtually eliminated. In September 1918 unemployed workers were forbidden to refuse jobs in other towns under penalty of loss of benefits for three months and relegation to the bottom of the list. The Labour Code of December promulgated a general obligation to work for all able-bodied citizens between fifteen and fifty years of age, but workers retained the right to refuse jobs not in their own trade. But this was soon modified. Labour exchanges, transferred from the trade unions to the Commissariat of Labour, were to become the primary medium for the hiring of labour. In industry after industry, beginning with the rails in November 1918, the workers were either conscripted (legally treated as mobilized soldiers subject to military discipline) or frozen in their places until further notice. In 1920, all people (except those employed in the food industry) who had previously worked in metals, electrical, fisheries, woolens, coal mining, and the fleet were ordered to return to these jobs. In January of that year, a decree was passed requiring all citizens to perform compulsory labour in addition to their regular occupations wherever such work was required. A Central Committee on Universal Compulsory Labour (Glavkomtrud) and a network of local committees were established under the Council of Defence to administer such additional labour, most of which consisted of unskilled emergency work like fuel procurement, rail repair, and clearing snow off roads and rails. The stringency of the measure was symbolized by the appointment as chairman of Felix Dzerzhinsky, the head of the Cheka.[79]

Compulsion became the norm even in the area heralded by Lenin as 'the *actual* beginning of *communism*,' the prefiguration of that future society of completely voluntary association and work for the common good without concern for the quantity of goods received in return, namely the 'subbotnik' movement.[80] 'Subbotniks' meant voluntary, unpaid labour on Saturdays. They were begun with great enthusiasm at the spontaneous initiative of party workers on the Moscow-Kazan railway in May 1919, and were soon followed by voluntary Sunday labour (*voskresniks*) and were spoken of as not only a higher form of class-conscious labour, but also as far more productive than ordinary labour. However, the party began to set strict regulations for their organization and even to make them mandatory for party members, as Lenin recommended, to help purge the party of opportunistic elements. Soon they were used as a general yardstick of political consciousness and, in some cases, made mandatory for entire trade-union organizations. Eventually, as Sorenson notes, 'the campaign took on the undesirable feature of a drive for unpaid overtime,' and shortly thereafter fell apart.[81] In its thirst for increased production and political control, the party was unwilling to leave unsullied even the one area of labour policy that prefigured a freer future.

In the circumstances, it seems undeniable that some forms of compulsory labour, if not militarization, were inevitable if Russian industry, transport, and military defence were not to collapse, and with them the bases of soviet power, which, however distorted and undemocratic it had become, still represented hope for the future transition to socialist production and democracy once conditions became more favourable. Labour was in very short supply, and that which was available was unproductive, indeed, dangerously so. Large segments of the skilled labour force, the bulwark of Bolshevik support and membership, had been recruited into the state administration and the army. Others had gone back to the countryside, where at least, they thought, they would be able to eat. Still others made a living on the black market. According to Trotsky, of the 1,150,000 registered trade-union members in 1920—itself a much reduced figure compared with the 1917 level—some 300,000 fell into the latter two categories. Thus, in order to 'reassemble the disrupted ranks of skilled and trained workers' under the specific conditions of 'sharp economic decline of the country, resulting from the imperialist war and the counter-revolutionary attacks on the soviet state,' the Central Committee of the Communist Party adopted on 22 January 1920 a broad set of theses on the necessity for compulsory labour.[82]

Trotsky, however, who drafted these theses, did not confine himself to listing the reasons for specific forms of compulsion in a particular emergency, but proceeded to develop an elaborate theoretical justification for state compulsion over labour and even the complete militarization of the workforce during the transition to socialism. From the basic assumptions that all labour, including the juridically 'free' labour of bourgeois society, has always been compulsory, that all societies must work to reproduce themselves, and that, during the transition to the abundance and all-round development of full communism, the principle must hold that 'he who works not, neither shall he eat,' Trotsky concluded that the workers state has the right to send workers wherever they are needed to fulfil economic tasks. This is essential to the very nature of an economic plan capable of overcoming the anarchy of capitalist production. And 'the introduction of compulsory labour service is unthinkable without the application, to a greater or less degree, of the methods of militarization of labour.' This 'represents the *inevitable* method of organization and disciplining of labour-power during the period of transition from capitalism to socialism' (emphasis added).

Accused by the Mensheviks of trying to build socialism with the methods of the Pharaohs (a phrase he would later himself use against Stalin), Trotsky replied that direct forms of compulsion did not necessarily have harmful effects on labour or its productivity. Even serf labour had been productive in its own time, and so also would militarized labour. Indeed, this was the only way to educate and prepare the peasant recruits for industrial work. The central question was not compulsion as such, but 'who applied the principle of compulsion, over whom and for what purpose? What state, what class, in what condition, by what methods?' In present-day Russia there need be no fear, since control 'remains in the hands of the working class, in the person of its Communist Party.'[83]

Along with compulsion and militarization, however, Trotsky insisted that the workers must be educated to the tasks at hand. The economic plan must be explained to them in full, and the sacrifices they are called upon to make must not be disguised in hypocrisy and lies. Specifically, they must be told that the personal payoff in consumer goods would occur only in the last stage of the plan—a plan that, clearly, the masses would in no way participate in formulating, even through indirect pressure by the trade unions for a rise in their standard of living. The party, at the head of the 'workers state', would decide these questions, but would not mystify the workers about the meaning of their sacrifices as did the bourgeoisie, for example, through religion. Moral persuasion and education would eventually make compulsion superfluous. How long this would take remained undefined, although Lenin told the Third Trade Union Congress in April 1920 that 'the creation of new forms of social discipline requires decades.'[84] To what extent these forms of compulsion might be eased and worker participation increased prior to their full enlightenment also remained unspecified. Trotsky's plan represented nothing short of the full application of military methods to the peaceful construction of socialism for the indefinite future.[85]

Such were some of the grand illusions of War Communism: that socialism could be built with the methods of the Pharaohs; that the forms of labour compulsion during the transition were irrelevant as long as state power remained with the proletariat 'in the person of its Communist Party'; that statist methods of organization could stimulate enlightened popular initiative in the creation of a free society. Nor were these illusions confined to the commissar of war, from whom advocacy of the application to peace-time economic tasks of methods used to secure military victory was perhaps understandable. Bukharin, one of the party's leading theorists and formerly in its left wing, wrote what was essentially a paean to war communism in his *Economics of the Transition Period*, attempting to derive from it the universal laws of proletarian revolution. Arguing that under a proletarian dictatorship in which the capitalist form of property has been abolished 'any kind of exploitation whatsoever [is] inconceivable,' Bukharin rationalized all forms of state compulsion, from execution to labour conscription, as 'nothing other than the self-organization of labour by the masses.'[86] And Lenin, who had never gone as far as Trotsky in theoretically justifying the militarization of labour as a general principle, had only the greatest praise for those sections of Bukharin's book dealing with the role of coercion. Alongside many of the most significant passages Lenin scribbled 'very good,' often in three different languages, and described the important tenth chapter on 'extra-economic' compulsion during the transition period as nothing short of excellent.[87] It was only in 1921 that Lenin began to recognize some of the illusions of war communism for what they were.[88] But at the time he was convinced that statist forms of organization and direct coercion were completely consistent with socialist construction. Indeed, in November 1919 he went so far as to say that 'the organization of the communist activity of the proletariat and the entire policy of the Communists have now acquired a final, lasting form.'[89]

Opposition and Resistance

This 'final, lasting form' would be shattered only after peasant, worker, and sailor revolts in the winter of 1920–21 had convinced the party that some relaxation of the measures of war communism, especially in regard to peasant policy, was in order. Trotsky's original theses on the militarization of labour, despite a supporting speech by Lenin, had been overwhelmingly rejected by the Central Council of Trade Unions as early as 12 January 1920, not least because they implied the militarization of the unions themselves. Trotsky spelled this out at the Ninth Party Congress in March, where the militarization policy received full party endorsement. With unknowing prescience, however, Trotsky wrote at the time: 'If compulsory labour came up against the opposition of the majority of the workers it would turn out a broken reed, and with it the whole of the Soviet order. The militarization of labour, when the workers are opposed to it, is the State slavery of Arakeheyev.'[90] In early 1920, however, the chief party leaders were in no doubt of the workers' support. As Bukharin so confidently expressed it at the time, between the vanguard party and the class there 'is not a grain.'[91]

This could not be maintained for long, however, in face of the seething discontent among the workers and at all levels of the trade unions. Dissatisfaction in the trade-union hierarchy over the issues of militarization and individual management was expressed in the form of two proposals. The first, supported by a broad coalition of trade-union leaders, including Tomsky and other moderates, called for the subordination of all Communist trade-union members to the party fraction within the Central Council of Trade Unions. This would have given the Council considerable power and independence from the party's Central Committee, and in effect would have created a party within the party. Shlyapnikov, former metal worker, Commissar of Labour, and currently chairman of the Central Committee of the All-Russian Metalworkers Union, went even further, proposing a separation of power and functions between the party, the soviets, and the trade unions. The latter would be given control over the economy. The soviets would control all political administration. The party, finally, would be in charge of fostering the proper ideology, but would not have the power to interfere in the other two areas directly. The attempt to lodge economic control in the hands of the trade unions without direct party and state interference was the kernel of the emerging position of the Workers Opposition. Lutovinov expressed a similar view at the Ninth Party Congress in March 1920. Both proposals were rejected by the Central Committee.[92]

The storm, however, broke around Trotsky. In March he had been authorized by the party to reorganize the transport system to resolve the chronic crisis there. An all-embracing new administration (Glavpolitput) was established over the rails, which completely bypassed the railworkers union. In August the union's central committee was unilaterally disbanded and replaced by a new committee, known as Tsektran. At the party fraction meeting of the Fifth All-Russian Trade Union Conference in November, Trotsky threatened the unions with further 'shake-ups.' In response to vitriolic criticisms by the unionists, Trotsky prepared a full-blown programme calling for the complete statization of the unions, their total absorption into the party-dominated state.[93]

Lenin, who had supported Trotsky's policies until then, and for whom the principle of the party's right to appoint trade-union leaders was never in doubt,[94] now came out against Trotsky, partly as a matter of theoretical conviction and partly because a scapegoat was needed to soothe the rising anger and hostility of the trade-union leaders. On 9 November the Central Committee accepted Lenin's proposal condemning 'the degeneration of centralism and militarized forms of work into bureaucratic practices, petty tyranny, red tape,' while advocating 'sound forms of the militarization of labour'.[95] In December he supported Zinoviev's call for the abolition of Glavpolitput and Tsektran, and began to present a general theoretical critique of Trotsky's positions. The trade unions, Lenin argued, must continue to maintain an independent organizational existence because their primary role of educating the workers in economic administration and management was still required, and they could not perform this role as state organs, as organs of coercion. Further, while the party exercises the dictatorship of the proletariat, it still needs non-party organizations like the trade unions to serve as 'links' between the vanguard and the masses. Trotsky, Lenin continued, '... has lost sight of the fact that we have here a complex arrangement of cogwheels which cannot be a simple one: for the dictatorship of the proletariat cannot be exercised by a mass proletarian organization. It cannot work without a number of transmission belts running from the vanguard to the mass of the advanced class, and from the latter to the mass of the working people.'[96]

But the motor force in this complex system of transmission belts—the party—must not operate too heavy-handedly. What Trotsky failed to recognize was that the trade unions may have had a legitimate gripe, that perhaps party policies were excessively bureaucratic. The root of this error, Lenin argued, was Trotsky's belief that in a workers state there is no need for trade unions to defend the material and spiritual interests of the workers. But this is wrong, for what exists in Russia is not an abstract workers state, but rather a workers and peasants state, and one 'with a bureaucratic twist to it' at that. The proletariat therefore needs its own organizations to protect itself from this state.[97]

Lenin's retreat on the party's heavy-handed and excessively bureaucratic control of the trade unions came too late, however, to prevent the formation of a left-wing opposition demanding the further democratization of the economy through the trade unions and a revived system of factory committees. Alexandra Kollontai, one of the leaders of the new left tendency known as the Workers Opposition, posed the central question of the economic construction of socialism thus: 'Is it to be bureaucracy or the self-activity of the masses?'[98] She considered Lenin's views on the unions as simply another variant, along with Trotsky's, of the bureaucratic approach that had been practised for the past three years and, in the words of Shlyapnikov, another opposition leader, had 'debased [the unions] to an information and recommendation bureau.'[99]

Lenin wanted to postpone union and proletarian control over the economy indefinitely. As Kollontai characterized his position, 'when the trade unions have brought up obedient and industrious Peters and Johns, we will "inject" them into the Soviet economic institutions. Thus, the unions will gradually disappear, dissolve.' The major fault of this approach, which sees the unions simply as 'schools of Communism' training workers to manage the economy in some distant future, is that '... all these systems of "education" lack provisions for freedom of experiment, for training and for the expression of creative abilities by those who are to be taught. In this respect also, all our pedagogues are behind the times ... *the unions are not only schools for communism, but they are its creators as well.*'[100]

In calling for a shift to economic management by the unions, the Workers Opposition referred to the resolutions of all three previous national trade-union congresses, which called for the statization of the unions but left the schedule and exact methods unclear. As a matter of fact, many Bolsheviks interpreted these resolutions to mean state control and absorption of the unions rather than, as the oppositionists saw it, the unionization of the state. But the resolution the opposition most often cited was Point 5 of the party programme passed at the Eighth Party Congress in March 1919, which declared that '... the trade unions must achieve a *de facto* concentration in their own hands of the entire administration of the whole national economy considered as a single economic unit.'[101] This is what the Workers Opposition was demanding, not for the distant future but in the coming period 'through a series of preliminary measures aimed at an orderly and gradual realization of this aim.'[102]

The goal was to democratize the economy by vesting overall power in an elected All-Russian Congress of Producers, which would in turn elect a central management organ. Similarly elected bodies were to exist at regional and local levels, and industrial trade-union congresses would elect organs to manage their particular branches of industry. All existing economic administrative institutions were to be subordinate to these, as were all specialists. Although Kollontai expressed much hostility toward bourgeois specialists, she made it quite clear that their employment was as absolutely essential technically as it was inadequate to create new forms of work and new incentives. Elected workers' committees, as the basic cells of the unions, were to assume management functions in the individual plants. The intention, similar to that of the Left Communists in 1918, was to create an elected and revocable economic centre able to formulate a unified plan and mitigate institutional dualism, while at the same time preserving a high degree of local and regional initiative. Only thus would new work incentives evolve and the productivity of labour rise immensely. Only thus could the emancipation of the working class be the act of the workers themselves.[103]

The Workers Opposition, however, seems to have envisaged the democratization of the economy within the overall framework of continued party direction and control—albeit of a thoroughly democratized party. Indeed, much of Kollontai's pamphlet is devoted to measures of party reform, from the expulsion of non-proletarian elements and mandatory periodic manual labour for all party members to full return to the elective principle and freedom of thought and opinion. 'There can be no self-activity without freedom of thought and opinion,' she argued in regard to the party's inner life, without ever invoking a similar principle in regard to the non-party masses. She saw restrictions on their activity as reasonable during a civil war, but never indicated when and if such restrictions might be lifted once the country returned to peace. In a number of places she spoke of the party as controlling the policy of the soviets, without confronting the question of whether this control would be achieved in the free competition of political programmes with other parties.[104]

Shlyapnikov, at the Tenth Party Congress, explained that the trade-union congresses that would elect organs to manage the economy would 'of course' be composed of delegates nominated and elected 'through the party cells, as we always do it.'[105] Clearly, the democratization proposed by the Workers Opposition was to be carefully managed, developing only within the bounds of continued political and ideological control, and primarily as an offshoot of the democratization of the party itself. The evolving fusion of party and state, however, had to be reversed, and overlapping posts at the higher levels should be restricted.

The oppositionists' programme contained other serious deficiencies. No attempt was made to clarify the relation of industry-wide authority and competence to that of geographical units, a problem that had plagued earlier attempts at decentralization. The issue of work discipline was avoided by arguing simply that the new system of workers control, along with the payment of wages in kind, would somehow automatically increase incentives and productivity. This naîvety was linked to an idealization of past experience in this area. And while proposals to start communal gardens at factory sites represented an imaginative (if limited) response to the food shortage, as well as an attempt to foster collective activity among the workers themselves, Kollontai's efforts to extend some of the more distasteful necessities of war communism, such as communal kitchens and laundries, revealed her own distance from the realities of working-class life.[106]

The programme of the Workers Opposition also contained quite unrealistic demands for the immediate improvement of the material lot of the workers, including the preferential treatment of workers in the distribution of consumer goods. This reflected what was probably their greatest programmatic failing: complete inability to come to terms with the problem of the peasantry, and general unwillingness to placate the peasants' demands for an end to forced requisitioning and the introduction of a freer exchange of their products for industrial goods. In this area, the policies of war communism were to continue. But this would have threatened the cities with starvation and dashed the opposition's hopes of raising labour productivity. The already diminishing chances for establishing the alliance between the urban and rural labouring population, essential to the construction of a democratic socialist order, would have been further undermined. To cement this alliance was an affirmed aim of the Workers Opposition, but more would be needed than mere pious calls for workers committees in agricultural enterprises.

Lenin met the proposals of the Workers Opposition with unmitigated hostility. By this time he had completely lost patience with all opposition and did not stop short of personal invective and even sexist innuendo to put an end to it.[107] This deviation, he claimed, this complete break with the principles of Marxism, is the result of the influence of the petty-bourgeois element on the proletariat. It is syndicalism at its worst, for it makes the party as vanguard superfluous. Why have a party at all, if the trade unions, nine-tenths of whose members are non-party workers, are to administer industry? For, 'Communism says: The Communist Party, the vanguard of the proletariat, leads the non-party worker masses, educating, preparing, teaching and training the masses—first the workers and then the peasants—to enable them eventually to concentrate in their hands the administration of the whole national economy.'[108]

Only the dominance of the party could guard against inevitable petty-bourgeois vacillations and narrow craft unionism among the workers. The trade unions would be able to control the economy only after many years, after the country had been completely electrified and illiteracy completely abolished, after they had rid themselves of all the 'filth' and habits of the old world and were no longer vulnerable to petty-bourgeois influences. Indeed, only after the petty-bourgeois peasantry had been mainly abolished could there be talk of concentrating the whole national economy in the hands of the trade unions, for agriculture was nowhere near the stage where it could be managed by trade unions. At one point Lenin argued that a Congress of Producers could exist only at the stage of full communism, when all class distinctions between workers and peasants had been completely abolished. Economic self-management, in other words, was to be postponed to the distant future as a matter of principle, not as a result of temporary exigency.[109]

Lenin had certainly hit upon a number of genuine weaknesses in the programme of the Workers Opposition, particularly in regard to peasant policy and the possibility of narrow workerism in the proposed Congress of Producers, though it should be noted that proposals to abandon war-communist requisitioning measures had received widespread support among rank-and-file urban workers before the party was forced to abandon them.[110] But he used these arguments to shirk the major challenge of the Workers Opposition to further democratize the economy by vesting powers in the workers organizations as such, as opposed to merely utilizing and coopting trade-union members in a way that cut them off from their working-class base and from any accountability and control from below. Inimical to his conception of the transition to socialism was even the opposition's project of controlled and gradual democratization, under which a (reformed) party would continue to maintain political dominance and exercise the major influence within the factory committees and trade unions that were to form the base of the economic regulating organs. Such a project, it would seem, did not presuppose the complete disappearance of classes, but rather was required if the working class was to maintain and develop its power in the process of that transition. Nor did such a project suggest that every worker had first to know how to administer the economy, but only that their organizations maintain ultimate control over those who, by virtue of the inherited division of labour, currently possess the knowledge requisite for economic management, and that these organizations have the decisive role in the formulation of economic policy. The Workers Opposition held that the trade unions could not effectively operate as 'schools of communism' unless they also had power to make decisions—unless learning was linked to a process of creative self-activity, and initiative was lodged in workers economic organizations as such. For Lenin, it seems, this power of initiative and overall control would come only after the learning process had been completed.[111]

The Workers Opposition was decisively defeated at the Tenth Party Congress. In the final voting, their platform received only 18 votes, against 50 for the combined Trotsky-Bukharin platform, and 336 for the 'Platform of the Ten' (Lenin *et al.*).[112] Although the extent of their support is difficult to gauge exactly, it was certainly much greater than these figures suggest. The virulence of Lenin's attack, his initiation of moves to have the oppositionists formally censured as a syndicalist deviation and to have all organized factions in the party banned henceforth, would indicate that they posed a significant threat. Lenin was apparently aware of the mass support for the opposition.[113] That support was particularly strong in the metalworkers union, and there were opposition concentrations among workers in Samara, the Urals, the Ukraine, Vladimir, Moscow, and to a lesser extent Petrograd. But however widespread potential sympathy for such ideas may have been, the organizational basis for mobilization around them was quite feeble. By late 1920 a vibrant institutional network of factory committees with resources to mobilize behind such a leftist ideological programme no longer existed. The workers themselves were physically exhausted and demoralized.

The disjunction between the rank and file base and party leaders espousing economic democracy had widened even further since the last major challenge to Lenin in early 1918. Nor had the continuity of that ideological challenge survived the years of civil war. Osinsky and other former Left Communists, while continuing to press for democratic reforms in the party and state, refused to make common cause with the Workers Opposition. And the latter, in turn, did not even mention Osinsky's ideological interventions of 1918. The reasons for this are not completely clear, though apparently the Democratic Centralists saw the Workers Opposition as going too far too fast in regard to workers power. In any case, the Democratic Centralists had been greatly weakened by the 'administrative onslaught' against them in the spring of 1920.[114] Kollontai, though a Leftist in 1918, was very much the belated and not particularly well developed theorist of economic democracy in 1921. But she was the most dynamic leader the opposition had. No one in the party Central Committee lent support. The major organizational base was in the unions. But the opposition had no leaders in the All-Russian Central Council of Trade Unions, and despite support in relatively important positions below this level, the party had solidified its organizational control after 1919. Important opposition leaders like Shlyapnikov had been sent on diplomatic missions to undercut their organizing efforts. And despite an openness of debate unheard of during the previous two years, the party machinery was used to obstruct a fair representation of the opposition's views before the Tenth Party Congress in March 1921.[115]

The civil war, in short, had undermined the organizational basis of factory democracy, tightened the party's control over the unions at all levels, and further rigidified the dominant Bolshevik ideology on workers control and political democracy. The major opposition group was neither well organized at the base nor well situated in the party hierarchy. Nor did its workerist ideological bent make it receptive to the needs of the peasantry, even when some of its staunchest supporters, such as the metalworkers, were themselves demanding an end to requisitioning. As a result, the protests that broke out first in Moscow and then in Petrograd and Kronstadt in February 1921 triggered further repression instead of occasioning genuine reforms. The gulf between the party hierarchy and rank-and-file workers and sailors had become enormous, and even the Workers Opposition could see only counter-revolution when there was much room for negotiation and compromise.[116] These protests, which had followed a crescendo of peasant revolts in late 1920, did force the party leaders to revise their peasant policies. But the Kronstadt demands for genuine soviet democracy and workers control found no similar resonance across the icy gulf of Finland. The brutal suppression of Kronstadt on 17 March 1921 marked the symbolic death of those ideals—the ideals of October itself—although the party unabashedly celebrated the fiftieth anniversary of the Paris Commune with parades through the streets of Petrograd on the very next day.

Part Two

Discourses of Democracy

It is indubitable that Bolshevik policies in the post-revolutionary period were determined to a very considerable extent by the objective conditions of economic devastation, civil war, foreign intervention, international isolation, and the narrow and contradictory social basis for revolutionary transformation. The overwhelmingly hostile circumstances in which the new regime found itself narrowly circumscribed the options for socialist development and strongly influenced the decisions taken.

Yet the course of the revolution cannot be understood without recognizing some of the basic theoretical orientations underlying the practical choices of Bolshevik leaders, Lenin in particular. The perception of the options available, the anticipation of possible problems, and the calculation of the relative costs and benefits of alternative policies exhibit a coherence that points to deep theoretic structures. As the following chapters will attempt to demonstrate, a profound productivist and evolutionist problematic lies at the heart of Leninist theory, and has a substantial resonance in the works of Marx and Engels as well. This productivist problematic provided orientation and rationalization for a number of issues that were central to revolutionary transformation: workers control over production and the division of labour, the state and the party, bureaucracy and cultural revolution.

To be sure, productivism is not the only discourse in Lenin or Marx, and it is certainly not the dominant one in Marx. Lenin's case is less clear, since his thinking often seemed caught in a productivist problematic even as he vigorously challenged it, perceiving some of the problems and shifting emphasis to mass action and emancipatory critique. A number of recent analyses have failed to recognize just how profound this productivism was and how many problems are defined by it, while others have taken their critique beyond what seems theoretically justifiable or historically useful. In any case, it is clear enough that the productivist logic of Leninist theory not only affected policies in the immediate post-revolutionary years, but also in many ways established the frame of reference and terms of discourse for later debates on social and economic development—with momentous consequences for the possibility of democracy and the emancipation of labour in the Soviet Union.

Productivist Evolutionism and the Dialectics of Labour

The work of Marx has been reinterpreted by Jürgen Habermas and Albrecht Wellmer in a manner that uncovers the theoretical roots of the productivist tendency within Marxism and facilitates an understanding of its development towards a kind of technological evolutionism justifying a revolutionary-elitist technocratism: a theory whose primary *telos* is the extension of the productive forces in a society managed by a party-elite. There is, argues Habermas, a fundamental ambiguity in the work of Marx. In terms of categories, Marx often conceptualizes the self-constitution of the human species through *labour* alone, through the instrumental action by which the species controls and harnesses nature to meet its material needs. Human self-objectification and reflection are thus conceived within the problematic of the control and transformation of matter. On the level of his actual investigations, however (if not always in his philosophical frame of reference), Marx includes a second element: the self-constitution of the species through systems of symbolic interaction such as institutions, cultural traditions, and ideologies. Relations of authority and inter-subjectively compelling norms are constituted at this level, but so also is the capacity for reflection, since the irreducible core of ideological and cultural formations is the utopian anticipation of the good life. These two frameworks were never fully reconciled in the work of Marx, and their theoretical elaboration leads to two fundamentally opposed conceptions of Marxism as a science, the one positivist and reductionist, the other critical and emancipatory.[1]

Emancipatory Critique and Positivist Science in Marx

The major aspiration of Marx's work is towards a critical theory of society that comprehends systematically the historical constraints on human development with the practical goal of their elimination and the full realization of human freedom in politics, labour, and culture.[2] His early critique of the Hegelian conception of the state, for instance, took the form of an immanent critique of ideology, which unmasked the pretentious claims of the state to overcome the divisions and particularistic interests of bourgeois civil society. The hypostatization of the division between state and civil society could be transcended, however, not by simply abolishing the polarity, or reducing one sphere to the other, but by realizing in practice the utopian elements embedded within the ideological pretence of the state as universal polity. The bourgeois-democratic state had established the 'fictitious' ideal of a discursive formation of the will that dissolves political domination, and the goal of socialism was to realize that ideal by destroying the capitalist system, whose (hidden) domination negated the possibility of true democracy. [3]

In Marx's own words: 'Reason has always existed, but not always in rational form. Hence the critic can begin with any form of theoretical and practical consciousness and develop the true actuality from the forms *peculiar* to existing reality as that which it ought to be and its ultimate goal. As far as actual life is concerned, it is precisely the *political state* in all its modern forms that contains the demands of reason, even where that state is not yet consciously aware of socialist demands. And it does not stop at that. Everywhere the political state represents reason as realized. But at the same time it falls into the contradiction between its ideal nature and its actual presuppositions. Therefore social truth can be developed everywhere from this conflict of the political state with itself.'[4]

Marx's critical scientific method depends fundamentally on a non-reductionist conception of ideology. The symbolic productions of the human species, even those that thoroughly distort and mystify social reality, have an irreducible core of social truth that points to the 'good life' beyond the existing forms of domination. This rational core, this 'utopian excess,' provides the ground and the *telos* of any critique of existing reality with emancipatory intentions.

Marx's critique of religion and the later critique of the ideology of equivalence exchange follow the same dialectical logic. Religion is the 'fantastic realization of the human essence,' it is the 'protest against real suffering,' simultaneously as it pacifies people to accept this suffering (it is the 'opium of the people').[5] Equivalence-exchange ideology represents a distorted expression of justice that becomes the basis for the reflective recognition of injustice—which Marx, by introducing the distinction between living labour and labour-power, and hence the concepts of surplus-value and exploitation, is able to demonstrate theoretically. Indeed, the critique of the commodity-form that determines the entire logic of *Capital* ultimately derives its theoretical impetus only by reference, however weakly articulated, to certain normative conceptions critically appropriated from the Western philosophical tradition. In the first chapter of the first volume, Marx lays the basis for a critique of the commodity-form of economic interaction (in which 'a definite social relation between men ... assumes, in their eyes, the fantastic form of a relation between things'), by uncovering the particular historical set of social relations underlying what appears as simply natural, as second nature. He historicizes and 'denatures' the capitalist mode of production by comparing it with feudalism and a hypothetical Robinson Crusoe. But his critique derives its force not simply from this historicization and denaturation, but also—and crucially—from a particular normative conception of de-alienation or non-alienated social production.

The critique of the commodity form, and of the social relations of alienated labour underlying it, requires the anticipation of a condition of non-alienated production. In the same chapter of *Capital*, Marx refers to this as 'a community of free individuals, carrying on their work with the means of production in common, in which the labour-power of all the different individuals is consciously applied as the combined labour-power of the community.' This is a normative conception, an anticipation of the good society in which the 'practical relations of everyday life offer to man none but intelligible and reasonable relations with regard to his fellowmen and nature,' and in which there is no class domination either directly through political controls (as in feudalism) or indirectly through commodity relations. As a normative ideal, this is essentially the same as those concepts that grounded his earlier critique of alienation and the state, namely, 'free human production,' 'species being,' 'commonwealth' (*Gemeinwesen*), and 'communist essence' (*das kommunistische Wesen*). The ideal of a free association of producers runs throughout his monumental critique.[6]

It is this version of Marx's project as emancipatory critique that provides the basis for politics conceived as active revolutionary struggle and democratic determination of all the conditions of existence, from labour to culture. The positivist and productivist interpretation of his project, however, is derived from the version of historical materialism in which labour is the sole fundamental constitutive activity of the human species, and the dialectics of symbolic interaction are traced back and reduced to the dialectics of production. According to the theory elaborated in *The German Ideology* but never completely abandoned subsequently, the category of ideology assumes an entirely different meaning. It is now one-dimensionally conceived as a mental product whose sole function is to maintain domination. Ideology is reduced to a mere (objective) illusion perpetuating class rule. 'The ruling ideas are *nothing more than* the ideal expression of the dominant material relationships, the dominant material relationships grasped as ideas; hence of the relationships which make the one class the ruling one, therefore, the ideas of its dominance.'[7] The concept of ideology has been flattened out here; the rational core, the utopian moment of truth within it, has been eliminated. Now, for Marx, 'the illusion of rationality is, so to speak, [merely] a formal desideratum which every inauthentic form of social intercourse must satisfy in order to be a *dominant* consciousness.'[8]

The history of consciousness, of course, can never be seen as independent of the history of real people, of concrete historical subjects transforming the material world (and themselves) under conditions of scarcity and the organization of social power. Here lies one of the basic insights of Marx's critique of idealism. But with the functional conception of ideology articulated above, the history of consciousness becomes *merely* the reflex of this 'real' history. The self-constitution of the species through language, culture, ideology—in those spheres in which the ideals of freedom and the good life have been historically projected, albeit in an inverted and distorted form, and through which alone these ideals can be reflectively comprehended and acted upon—has vanished from the categorical framework. Material production becomes the sole and autonomous motor force of history. Consciousness becomes mere 'reflex' and 'echo.'

In this framework, relations of authority and the ideational forms of social intercourse can be analysed solely in terms of whether they foster or fetter the development of the forces of production. They have meaning only in relation to the progressive technological self-objectification of the species. As Marx says in *The German Ideology*: 'These various conditions, which appear first as conditions of self-activity, later as fetters upon it, form in the whole evolution of history a coherent series of forms of intercourse, *the coherence of which consists in this*: in the place of an earlier form of intercourse, which has become a fetter, a new one is put, corresponding to the more developed productive forces and, hence, to the advanced mode of the self-activity of individuals—a form which in turn becomes a fetter and is replaced by another. Since these conditions *correspond at every stage* to the simultaneous development of the productive forces, their history is at the same time the history of the evolving productive forces taken over by each new generation, and is, therefore, the history of the development of the forces of the individuals themselves.'[9]

With this reduction of the self-constitution of the human species to productive labour, the concept of revolution assumes a peculiar meaning. Revolution is now seen as the outcome of the contradiction between the forces of production and the existing forms of social intercourse (later defined more narrowly as the relations of production).[10] Only the forces of production have an autonomous development. At certain points they tend to 'outgrow' the prevailing relations of production and forms of social interaction, which previously fostered the development of these very same forces. Revolution occurs only as all the productive forces that can no longer be contained within the existing social relations, which have become fetters, burst through them. Such revolutionary contradictions also take on 'subsidiary forms, such as all-embracing collisions, collisions of various classes, contradiction of consciousness, battle of ideas, etc., political conflict, etc.'[11] However, to reduce the latter to subsidiary forms implies the reduction of social contradictions to the 'dysfunctionality of a form of domination in regard ... to the systematic goal of the development of the productive forces.'[12] This view is at variance with the predominant one in Marx's work that sees history as first of all the progressive development of humanity's freedom from domination through class struggle, which presupposes and is given impetus by the development of the productive forces, but is at no time inevitably determined by or reducible to the latter. But Marx's historical materialist framework often belies this view, and substitutes for it a kind of technological evolutionism, where socialism becomes the enforced result of the irresistible advance of the capitalist productive forces themselves, and revolution becomes simply the moment of transition (mediated by class struggle and made inevitable by the objective position of the proletariat in the production process)[13] to the unfettered development of the productive capacities of the species. Marxism becomes the science, positivistically conceived after the model of the exact natural sciences, of determining such material transformations.[14]

These evolutionist-determinist aspects of Marx's thought derive from the reduction of the concept of ideology to mere legitimation of domination. Enlightenment of the proletariat is no longer the result of the critical appropriation of the rational-utopian core of truth within its own internalized forms of thought and culture. Rather, enlightenment of the class now means the abolition of 'everything that still clings to it from its previous position in society', the stripping away of all illusions so that the proletariat can see the world 'with sober eyes', so that it can view without ideological bias, and in a manner 'open to confirmation in purely empirical fashion', the newly evolving relations of production, which are the enforced result of the productive forces' breaking through their old (and final) fetters.[15] The goal of the revolution is also determined with this ineluctable advance: the universal appropriation which implies that self-activity now 'coincides with material life, which corresponds to the development of individuals into complete individuals and the casting off of all natural limitations.'[16] Collective humanity's perfected control of nature—coincident with and identical to the full development of individuality—appears as the *telos* of history.

This inevitabilist logic is manifested yet again in sections of the *Grundrisse*, as capital is projected to rationalize itself out of existence. Capital (accumulated labour) develops to the point at which science and technology, and no longer direct labour and labour-power, become the major source of wealth, and eventually the system of capitalism based on exchange-value collapses of its own meagreness. Simultaneously, labour develops into the external regulator of the production process—which is equivalent to the development of the 'general intellect' of the species and the true 'social individual.'[17] Traces of this kind of analysis appear even in *Capital*, a work so fundamentally alien to it in most respects. In general, there is no technological evolutionism in *Capital*, and the forces of production are not seen to develop according to a dynamic of their own. Rather, their development is profoundly shaped by capitalist relations of production, and the imperatives of profit and control are incorporated within the very technologies themselves. Capitalist class relations are responsible for the fragmentation of factory work, for the concentration of knowledge and control in the directors of the labour process, for the separation of science and labour, and for the conversion of the worker into a 'crippled monstrosity.' The worker, *formally* subsumed under the control of capital through capitalist property relations, becomes increasingly subsumed in a *real* sense as a result of the transformation of the labour process itself. Capitalist social relations become inscribed within the very organization of the productive process, and active revolutionary transformation is necessary to reverse this.

And yet in the chapter 'Machinery and Large-Scale Industry' in volume one, Marx shifts from speaking of their development under capitalist relations to the development of modern industry *as such*, and its *inevitably* liberatory impact on labour: 'But if, at present, variation of labour imposes itself after the manner of an *overpowering natural law*, and with the blindly destructive action of a natural law that meets with obstacles everywhere, large-scale industry, through its very catastrophes, makes the recognition of variation of labour and hence of the fitness of the worker for the maximum number of different kinds of labour into a question of life and death. This possibility of varying labour must become a *general law of social production*, and the *existing relations must be adapted to permit its realization in practice*. That monstrosity, the disposable working population held in reserve, in misery, for the changing requirements of capitalist exploitation, must be replaced by the individual man who is absolutely available for the different kinds of labour required of him; the partially developed individual, who is merely the bearer of one specialized social function, must be replaced by the totally developed individual, for whom the different social functions are different modes of activity he takes up in turn.'[18]

The complete rationalization of the production process and the perfection of collective technical mastery of nature, however, are really only the penultimate goal of this inevitable historical dynamic, the means for consolidating the material basis of the realm of freedom, which lies *beyond* the realm of necessary labour. They permit the reduction of the necessary labour time of society to a minimum, and augment the amount of time available for the all-round development of every individual (artistic, scientific, and so on). This conception, however, which is present in *Capital* as well as the *Grundrisse*,[19] is open to a revolutionary-technocratic interpretation, as long as the political conditions of economic rationalization remain unstated. The relations of power and authority at the relevant levels of the social system within which the perfected technical mastery of nature takes place tend to remain unarticulated in the productivist version of historical materialism, because they are subordinate to and implicitly a spin-off from technical-economic control systems *beyond which alone* lies real freedom. But if the realm of freedom does not lie *within* the realm of necessary labour itself, within the social organization of the technical control systems, then it becomes possible to justify purely administrative and authoritarian measures to perfect and manage the mastery of nature in order to expand the realm of freedom of the producers outside the labour process.

Labour, Technique and Transition in Lenin

This is, to be sure, only one possible interpretation of Marx. But it is a reading that is suggested by an analytic logic that runs throughout his work, sometimes more baldly stated, sometimes modified in a critical and emancipatory direction. And it exerted a profound influence on the Marxism of the Second International, even though some of the earlier texts were unknown at the time.[20]

In the work of some of its major thinkers (Kautsky, Plekhanov), deterministic philosophical premises were fused with the general technological optimism of the nineteenth century to produce a thoroughly productivist version of the historical dynamic between the forces and relations of production. The complete material basis for socialism was being formed within capitalist society and would be appropriated as it is by a socialist regime. The revolutionary seizure of power would eliminate the last institutional barrier to the further extension of these neutral and objectively emancipatory productive forces. Revolutionary rupture served the continuity of the development of human control of nature as embodied in the latest capitalist technique and forms of labour organization.

Lenin, who learned his Marxism from these same Second International theorists, never fully freed himself from their conception of the interaction between forces and relations of production, as he did on the issues of imperialism, state power, and revolutionary struggle. At the level of economic organization, he held, socialism represented an essential continuity with the highest stage of capitalism. In a typical formulation, he argued in 1917 that state-monopoly capitalism represented the 'complete material preparation for socialism.' It is 'a rung on the ladder of history between which and the rung called socialism *there are no intermediate rungs*.'[21] Indeed, socialism was 'nothing but state capitalism made to benefit the whole people.'[22] The capitalist infrastructure would remain intact as the socialist regime unfettered its tremendous productive capacity to serve the material needs of the people. With the full development of state-monopoly capitalism, it would be necessary only to transform the political superstructure by seizing state power, 'to remove the top and to transfer what remained to the proletariat.'[23]

Lenin thus had nothing but praise for the productive organization of German capitalism, which represented the highest development of emancipatory technique, and he urged the adaptation of whatever barbarous methods were necessary to mimic it. The productive infrastructure of German state capitalism represented one half of socialism, which had only to be connected to that other half, revolutionary state power. Indeed, the *'sum total* of the conditions necessary for socialism' were large-scale capitalist technique based on the last word of modern science and proletarian state power. If such conditions were met, the further development of socialism would be inexorable.[24]

Central to this conception of social development and revolutionary transformation is the primacy attributed to the development of the productive forces and productivity of labour *above all else*. In a passage already quoted above,[25] Lenin sees this as the foremost task of the revolution, that which defines the superiority of the new social system and provides the imperatives of its institutional organization. In 1919 he argued in the same vein: 'In the last analysis, productivity of labour is the most important, the principal thing for the victory of the new social system. Capitalism created a productivity of labour unknown under serfdom. Capitalism can be utterly vanquished by socialism creating a new and much higher productivity of labour.'[26]

The practical result of such premises was a policy striving for the *'increase in production* at all costs.'[27] The mastery of nature through enhanced technological development and labour productivity serves as the defining characteristic of superior social organization and the motor force of history and human emancipation. In Trotsky's thinking this logic is even more pronounced: 'The creation of socialist society means the organization of the workers on new foundations, their adaptation to those foundations, and their labour re-education, with the one unchanging end of the increase in the productivity of labour.'[28] And in 1925 he argued further that the transition from socialism to a classless communist society 'wholly depends upon the technical progress of a society.'[29] These formulations of the original Bolshevik leaders are but a short step from Stalin's maxim that 'technique decides everything.'

Given these general premises, it is not surprising that Lenin sought to appropriate the principles of scientific management developed by Frederick Taylor and to apply them to the task of socialist economic construction. For Lenin the introduction and extension of Taylorism, unlike the payment of higher wages for bourgeois specialists, was not an unavoidable compromise warranted by specific historical conditions. Rather, he saw it as the last word of modern science in the organization of the labour process, and particularly in the scientific study of work motions. However, although Lenin argued on many occasions that bourgeois science and technology were to be taken over in their entirety,[30] he was not completely uncritical of Taylorism. He warned of the possible negative effects on the health of the workers that the intensification of work might have. Nor, as Robert Linhart points out,[31] did Lenin ever sing the praises of de-qualification, or of the establishment of a bureau of methods separate from the workers. And on a number of occasions he spoke of just the opposite: the involvement of the mass of workers in the study and application of scientific work methods. In his very first analysis of Taylorism (1914), he had linked it to the possibility of the distribution and rationalization of labour by workers committees.[32] And he consistently stood for the popularization of scientific knowledge and the principles of work organization.[33] All this distinguishes his position from that of Taylor himself, and from the application of scientific management in capitalist industry too.

But the critical dimension of Lenin's approach never became dominant, and his enthusiasm for Taylorism helped legitimate a Soviet scientific-management movement whose effects clearly enhanced managerial control over labour. At the extreme end of the spectrum were those like Gastev, director of the Central Labour Institute in Moscow, who sought to extend the principles of scientific management to every sphere of life, and who consciously and unabashedly compared the human being to a machine. For him the army, the prison, and the monastery were the ideal forms of human organization, and completely routinized and standardized work was the future of socialist production. Lenin, who seems to have sympathized with some of Gastev's critics, nonetheless lent enthusiastic support to his Institute. And the party threw its support to him in the early twenties, thus paving the way for his prominent role in the forced industrialization and Stakhanovism of the thirties.[34]

Most critics, such as Yermansky, whose book Lenin singled out for special praise, focused on the health dangers posed by work intensification, and made elaborate attempts to distinguish this from genuine productivity factors. But only a few criticized the movement's 'fetish of production' purchased at the price of transforming people into 'dull and unthinking producers without qualification and all-round development.'[35] And on the question of de-qualification, Taylorism and Fordism received explicit support from party leaders. In 1926, for instance, responding to the question 'But what about the monotony of labour, depersonalized and despiritualized by the conveyor?' Trotsky replied that such concerns were reactionary and 'directed against the division of labour and against machinery in general. ... It is necessary that human labour shall produce the maximum possible quantity of goods.'[36]

Neither Lenin in his support for mass involvement in scientific work organization nor the critics of extreme fragmentation proposed linking the study and application of work methods to workers control. Whatever was scientifically neutral in work research thus tended to be subsumed under the interests of authoritarian managerial control. Indeed, the latter had received strong ideological articulation in Lenin's writings from 1918 onwards. Modern technology was seen as an objectively neutral force whose very essence required the social form of dictatorship in the workplace, the concentration of authority in the hands of management, the 'unquestioning subordination' of the will of the workers to a single order-giver.[37] In this area as well, the new socialist regime had to 'imitate the bourgeoisie', for the fundamental task was to raise the productivity of labour, and that warranted no unnecessary interference by the workers themselves. Democracy in the workplace was seen as quite dispensable without at all undermining the basic dynamic of socialist transition.[38]

In the trade-union debate of 1920–21, Lenin criticized the expression 'industrial democracy' in terms that reveal several aspects of a productivist problematic: 'In the final analysis, every kind of democracy, as political superstructure in general (which must exist until classes have been abolished and a classless society established), serves production and is ultimately determined by the relations of production in a given society.'[39] In other words, the primary rationale of democracy is to increase production; and the democratic control of the means of production by the workers is separable from and a mere superstructural derivative of the more basic socialist relations of production, conceived as juridical property relations and not real power relations. These propositions help explain Lenin's ambivalence about workers control and the factory-committee movement throughout 1917, his tendency to view workers control as essentially a matter of accounting and checking on the fulfilment of decisions made by others, and his decisive resolution of that ambivalence in favour of top-down control both in the individual workplace and in the regulatory organs of the economy as a whole. Once again, socialism was seen as the result of the continuous and logical development of the productive forces spawned by capitalism. The social forms of economic organization had to be adapted to these hypostatized forces if the latter were to accomplish their world-historical emancipatory task.

In view of the many critiques that have been made of Lenin in recent years, it is important to delineate the limits of his theoretical approach to technology and the division of labour. It is not the case, for instance, that Lenin lost sight of the ultimate aim of the revolution: a classless society. In 1920 he referred to the need 'to eliminate the division of labour among the people, to educate and school people, give them *all-round development and all-round training* so that they *are able to do everything*.'[40] While that was certainly impossible, the general intent is clear enough. And in the course of the trade-union debates, he repeatedly referred to the ultimate goal of workers management of industry through their own organization.[41]

Nor was Lenin wrong to recognize that the starting point for a transition to classless society was the existing division of labour and technology inherited from capitalism. As Harry Braverman has put it, 'the same productive forces that are characteristic of the *close of one epoch* of social relations are also characteristic of the *opening of the succeeding epoch*; indeed, how could it be otherwise....'[42] Indeed—it is that simple. Those critics who claim that once the political rule of the working class is established, the utilization of capitalism's economic base is precluded make it impossible to comprehend the concrete forms a historically possible transition could take. A rapid and total transformation of the inherited technologies and division of labour is hardly feasible.[43]

Many recent Marxist studies of the labour process, while they have contributed a great deal to our understanding of the concrete ways technologies and organizational forms have been developed to enhance managerial control of labour, have gone to the other extreme in correcting the earlier neglect of this problem. In the process, they have tended to articulate a different form of productivism, in which the struggle to thoroughly transform the labour process becomes the foremost struggle a priori. But if the struggle for socialism entails the transformation of all the conditions that impede democratization and equality among the working class, and between the working class and peasantry, and if not all those conditions can be transformed simultaneously, then the assignment of such priority becomes a form of dogmatism. The struggle for production and against poverty on the basis of available technologies is not necessarily economism or productivism, if it allows for the reconstruction and stabilization of personal, familial, and community lives, mitigates the everyday struggle for existence, and permits a reduction of the working day, all of which are conditions for the possible democratization of public life in general. Clearly, after seven years of war, suffering, and profound disruption of the fabric of everyday life, democratization in Russia could not have proceeded without using the technologies available for increasing industrial production. Nor does the use of such technologies automatically doom the larger socialist project of breaking down the class division of labour. Such a project is inevitably a long one, filled with compromise and contradiction, in which the various forms of technology, organization, participation, remuneration, and so on must be viewed in their relatively autonomous relationship to each other and to the larger forms for social transformation. Relations of domination do not necessarily 'totalize' themselves from inherited forms of technology and divisions of labour to all areas of society and politics. Nor does the use of particular forms inherited from capitalism preclude all genuine control from below and all conscious mass activity.[44]

In place of such an absolutist either-or approach, we must recognize that there is a range of compatibility (as well as limits of compatibility) between specific technologies, forms of organization, and relations of authority. Alternative technologies are generally possible on the basis of a given ensemble of techniques, and alternative organizational forms are possible for the utilization of given technologies.[45] It is quite possible, for instance, to import technology from capitalist countries and modify certain aspects to mitigate the fragmentation of work and strict hierarchical controls. Likewise, a range of compatibility exists between time-motion studies or remuneration through piece rates and various forms of worker participation, as Lenin at one time held. The utilization of the former does not rule out a strategy of progressive democratization. This does not mean that compatibility is perfect or that the utilization of capitalist technology or piece-rates does not involve contradictions. But a historically relevant political judgement could be made only by investigating the range of possible forms and degrees of compatibility that might sustain a dynamic of participation and control within the context of the constraints and contradictions of the revolutionary process that transcend the labour process itself. Such a judgement cannot be made on the basis of theoretical premises that essentialize and totalize relations of domination embedded in particular technologies and work methods. If capitalist relations of production are not merely extrinsic to the forces of production, as Lenin generally thought, nor are they totally intrinsic. Hence the strategies for their effective disentanglement cannot be theoretically predetermined.[46]

The major theoretical flaw in Lenin's approach was to view the goal of a democratic and classless division of labour as more or less an automatic result of the development of the capitalist productive forces pushed to their limit and the concomitant education of the entire population in economic management.[47] By this view, there was little danger in introducing and perfecting capitalist forms of labour organization, or adopting all the latest techniques of advanced capitalist industry. The subjective factor in this process, namely the socio-cultural formation of the working class within this productive apparatus, was almost completely ignored. Lenin could therefore dismiss as unserious the Left Communist arguments that the introduction of Taylorism, the fragmentation of work tasks, the emphasis on material incentives in the form of piece rates, would tend to undermine the solidarity of the working class, reduce its social initiative, and narrow its horizon to the favourable sale of individual labour-power, thus perpetuating on the subjective side the basic premises of the commodity form. And he could brand as an objectively reactionary syndicalist deviation the argument of the Workers Opposition that education for economic management had to be combined with the power to make decisions, scope for initiative, and an institutional framework for the exercise of workers economic power.

Lenin postponed the question of self-management to the distant future, when the entire population would be fully educated to the tasks of economic administration. This goal was not to inform the practical tasks of the transition period. Indeed, any attempt to achieve it in the interim, even in the limited ways proposed by the opposition, would interfere with the full extension and rationalization of the productive forces, which often appeared as the major criterion and the only guarantee of progress toward that goal. Lenin's approach, while aware of the ultimate intention and at times of some of the contradictions in the process, tended to efface the necessity for *conscious struggle* in the intervening period against the strictly hierarchical division of labour in the factory and against the forms of authority that undermine the creative initiative of the working class. His view of the factory was narrowed, as he saw it as a place where *things* alone are produced, ignoring that relations between people are also produced and reproduced there, and extend their influence beyond the factory gates.[48] He had little fear that the division of labour and relations of authority could crystallize into a new form of class society during the transition because the party was in control of the state apparatus that would guide the development of the productive forces so as to eliminate the material basis for social domination. Social emancipation would be a more or less direct and automatic offshoot of technical progress.[49]

Political Power and
Socialist Transformation

'The dictatorship of the proletariat is impossible except through the Communist Party.'[1] At the Tenth Party Congress in 1921, Lenin thus reiterated what had become the cornerstone of Bolshevik thought on the issue of political power during the transition to socialism. The tenet was seen as unique to neither the Russian revolution nor the specific conditions under which the new regime was labouring. Rather, it had become the basic political principle of Leninist theory, and as such was mandated for all other communist parties throughout the world.

It went completely unchallenged even during Lenin's later struggle against bureaucratic degeneration. Indeed: the very distinction 'dictatorship of the party *or* dictatorship of the class ... testifies to the most incredibly and hopelessly muddled thinking.'[2] The emancipation from class domination could take only one form: revolutionary state power dominated by a single party with the right to determine all important matters of policy. All other political forms of mediation were secondary, since 'the Party is the leader, the vanguard of the proletariat, which *rules directly*.'[3] Of course, the functions of government must be 'performed through the medium of special institutions which are also of a new type, namely, the Soviets.'[4] Here Lenin saw no contradiction, even though the soviets were supposed to be unique institutions for popular democracy enabling the masses themselves to govern directly with complete control over those they elect to represent them. Yet Lenin spoke of party dictatorship and soviet power as though they were complementary. How was it possible that a commitment to mass initiative in the struggle for human liberation and an articulated theory of the institutions of mass democracy modelled on Marx's analysis of the Paris Commune could come to be seen as thoroughly consistent with such a constrictive form of political rule as the single-party dictatorship?

Party and Soviets

Before 1905 the party was the only revolutionary institutional organ incorporated into Lenin's theory. It was envisaged as a tightly knit body of professional revolutionaries organized in a small central committee. Its discipline consciously aped that of the capitalist factory. In *One Step Forward, Two Steps Backward* he outlined its principles of organization thus: 'Bureaucracy *versus* democracy is in fact *centralism* versus autonomism; it is the organizational principle of revolutionary Social Democracy as opposed to the organizational principle of opportunist Social Democracy. The latter strives to proceed from the bottom upward, and, therefore, wherever possible and as far as possible, upholds autonomism and "democracy", carried (by the over-zealous) to the point of anarchism. The former strives to proceed from the top downward, and upholds an extension of the rights and powers of the centre in relation to the parts.'[5]

While this conception of the party was strongly influenced by the prevailing conditions of autocracy, Lenin nonetheless attributed a more general relevance to this structure.[6] His earlier *What Is To Be Done?*[7] outlined the function of the party: to introduce revolutionary consciousness into the ranks of the proletariat *from the outside*. Revolutionary Marxism had arisen independently of the working-class movement. It was the product of the (ex-bourgeois) socialist intelligentsia. The working class could not achieve revolutionary consciousness itself, for its spontaneous struggles against capitalism could lead at best to trade-union consciousness. Its self-activity remained trapped within bourgeois ideology.

As Louis Menasche has correctly noted, *What Is To Be Done?* is a polemic against economism in the working-class movement, and this accounts for some of the starkness of its formulations.[8] In fact, some of these are neutralized by other statements in the same text and elsewhere, which suggest that Lenin did not maintain that there was a chasm between consciousness and spontaneity. The party's role was to make fully conscious, and thereby effective, what was present only implicitly and confusedly in the spontaneous struggles of the working class against its oppressive conditions, and to help situate particular struggles in the context of the total movement to transform capitalist society. Nor was Lenin a Blanquist in any traditional sense, since he always stressed the necessity of linking the work of the party with the masses, the aim being to make the latter fully class conscious. He repeatedly criticized the terrorist activity of the SRs because of their neglect of mass work.[9]

Nevertheless, in this early period the independent action of the workers remained anathema to him, as did the idea of their revolutionary self-organization beyond the confines of the party that held a monopoly on fully developed revolutionary consciousness. Even in the early part of 1905, as the strike wave and the new soviet movement was sweeping the country, he urged the party to 'dominate [the] ... spontaneous movement of the masses', and strongly opposed the slogan of 'workers initiative'.[10] Clearly, despite more subtlety of formulation than he is usually given credit for, Lenin still held that the party should completely direct and control the workers movement and, if only implicitly at this point, institutionally embody the power of that class in any revolutionary regime that might result from that movement.

It is therefore not surprising that the Bolshevik faction of the party educated by Lenin over the past few years should greet the soviets of St Petersburg and elsewhere with distrust and hostility. The consensus among the Bolshevik majority was that the parallel existence of the two institutions in the long run was impossible, especially if the soviets laid claim to any political role. Thus it was proposed that:

'1) The Bolsheviks should attempt to induce the soviet to limit itself to trade-union functions;

'2) should this fail, the soviet was to issue a declaration *on principle* accepting its subordination to the leadership of the RSDWP;

'3) the soviet was then to be dissolved forthwith, since its continued existence as a Social Democratic organization alongside the party would be superfluous.'[11]

No mass representative organization could compete with or even exist alongside the party in the political arena. Subordination to the party through acceptance of its programme was a matter of *a priori* principle, since it was a matter of principle that the party held a monopoly on correct political consciousness, and anything outside it was inevitably tinged with bourgeois ideology. Indeed, one Bolshevik leader in St Petersburg argued for a boycott of the soviet because 'the elective principle cannot guarantee its class consciousness and Social Democratic character.'[12] And if it could not be used as 'a technical instrument of the party',[13] perhaps 'exploding the Soviet from within'[14] was the only option. Dissenting Bolshevik voices were few and far between.

Lenin himself initially viewed the political role of the soviets with hesitation and suspicion. In late September 1905 he was still arguing against the Menshevik slogan calling upon workers to elect committees in the factories, committees that soon were to form the basis of the St Petersburg Soviet.[15] But the apparent success of this and other soviets modified his attitude and encouraged those aspects of his thinking more oriented to mass political action. In an article written in Stockholm in early November, 'Our Tasks and the Soviet of Workers Deputies', he argued that the dichotomy of party *or* soviets was wrong and that the workers movement required both forms, since the base of the movement had to be widened as much as possible. Thus, people should not be artificially excluded by prematurely demanding that the soviet accept the party's programme or disband. 'We do not shut ourselves off from the revolutionary people but submit to their judgement every step and every decision we take. We rely fully and solely on the free initiative of the working masses themselves.' Therefore, the soviet should be expanded to include delegates from the sailors, soldiers, and peasants. As such, it would form the 'embryo of a *provisional revolutionary government.*' Here for the first time the soviets were identified as the institutional form of the revolutionary democratic dictatorship of the proletariat and peasantry.[16]

Although he repeated this position on a number of occasions during the next year and a half, Lenin never completely overcome his hesitancy and ambivalence. His prefatory paragraph to the article expressed doubts about the opinion expressed therein, for he had not seen the Petersburg Soviet first hand. It was not clear whether his doubts concerned the factual information available to him or the principles on which his analysis seemed to be based. He left it up to the editorial board of *Novaya Zhizn* to publish it or not, and it went unpublished and unknown for the next thirty-five years. But Lenin himself returned to the Russian capital several days later, and the fact that the article still went unpublished, Solomon Schwarz concludes, 'suggests that it met with violent opposition from the Bolshevik leaders in Petersburg and that Lenin agreed not to publish it. It is inconceivable that *Novaya Zhizn* would have refused to print Lenin's "Letter to the Editors" had he insisted.'[17]

Lenin's other writings confirm this rather rapid backsliding. Only a few weeks later, in a piece written to justify the exclusion of the anarchists from the Soviet Executive Committee, he argued that 'the Soviet of Workers Deputies is not a labour parliament and not an organ of proletarian self-government, nor an organ of self-government at all, but a fighting organization for the achievement of definite aims.'[18] Several days later he went even further: "socialists may participate in non-party organizations only by way of exception ... only on strictly defined, restrictive conditions.'[19] The article did not completely exclude party participation, nor was the precondition of party discipline antithetical in itself to democratic control within unions and soviets. But the shift from his previous openness was clear. This represented a virtual return to the Bolsheviks' earlier position.

As the upswing of the largely spontaneous mass soviet movement of 1905 temporarily fostered the more open and democratic side of Leninism, so the political reaction that followed gave impetus to its narrow and authoritarian aspects. Once again the party became a small sect with all the characteristics of extreme dogmatism and monolithism.[20] Its attitude to the soviets and other open, mass non-party organizations further rigidified. In his draft of resolutions prepared in February 1907 for the Fifth Party Congress, Lenin proposed that organizations like the soviets be utilized only 'for the purpose of developing and strengthening the Social-Democratic Labour Party', and argued that if party activities were properly organized, 'such institutions may actually become superfluous.'[21] In other words, the revolutionary movement and revolutionary state power could dispense with open organizations in which different political programmes freely competed for the allegiance of the people.

The soviets were increasingly conceived as tactical instruments in the struggle for power, and as organs of insurrection. In April 1907, in a polemic against the Menshevik proposal for an open,non-party labour congress, Lenin concluded: 'Soviets of Workers Deputies and their unification are essential for the victory of the insurrection. A victorious insurrection will inevitably create *other* kinds of organs.'[22]

In the years after 1907, the soviets disappeared almost completely from Lenin's writings, except for a passing reference now and then. He certainly made no attempt to systematically develop the ideas he had tentatively held during the height of soviet activity. Compared with the enormous time and energy he put into sectarian squabbles, including the long philosophical diatribe against Bogdanov on the nature of materialism, the question of the possible institutional forms of revolutionary state power capable of fostering the democratic socialist transformation of society received scarce attention indeed. Even in his long interpretation of Hegel (1914), in which he re-evaluates the dialectical concepts of activity, self-movement, subjectivity, practice, and so on, not once, even in passing, does he mention the highest form of revolutionary self-activity thus far attained by the Russian workers movement, the soviets of 1905.[23] Nor is this surprising, since as Liebman has correctly observed, even in his more favourable analyses of the soviets at that time Lenin employed a method that was almost totally pragmatic and empiricist.[24]

The need for rigorous thinking about such matters, the need for a theory of soviets or other forms of revolutionary state power, went unrecognized. It was only in late 1916 and early 1917, under the challenge of Bukharin's writings on the state (as well as the views expressed earlier by Pannekoek), that Lenin began to question his own statist assumptions (and even then with difficulty) and to consciously link the soviets to the entirely new form of state envisaged by Marx in his writings on the Paris Commune.[25] Before then, the idea of the soviets played virtually no role in Bolshevik programmes or propaganda, strategy or tactics. The party educated by Lenin over the decade preceding the revolution remained almost completely oblivious to them, so that in early 1917 its leaders in Russia were again befuddled by their appearance. When the soviets were finally given official encouragement in mid-March, *Pravda* had to go back to a 1906 resolution and even amend the text![26]

These attitudes changed drastically with Lenin's return to Russia. In his April Theses he issued the call for the socialist revolution and demanded that all power be transferred to the soviets as 'the *only possible* form of revolutionary government'.[27] He began the process of defining more clearly the specific characteristics of such a revolutionary state, a process that culminated with *State and Revolution*.[28] The basic premiss of his new position was taken primarily from Marx's writings on the Commune:[29] the proletariat cannot simply lay hold of the existing state apparatus and use it for its own purposes. Rather, this apparatus has to be smashed (*zerbrechen*), and an entirely new one created, fully responsive to the control of the people. The political instrument for the oppression of labour by capital cannot be the instrument for emancipation from this oppression. The main characteristics of such a state—which immediately begins to wither away since it no longer stands as an independent force above the people—are: full election and instant recall of all officials, the right to vote to working people only, [30] full publicity of all governmental affairs, the unity of executive and legislative functions, the suppression of a standing army and civil bureaucracy (though not of the technically trained experts within them), the payment of workers' wages to all officials, and the enlistment of all working people in the business of state administration.[31] Such a state would be dictatorial in relation to the old ruling classes and any counter-revolutionary resistance. But it would be democratic in a new way in that it would truly represent the majority of the population.

These ideas represented a great advance over Lenin's previous thinking, and reveal the profoundly popular and participatory character of his conception of the transition to socialism. Yet a number of important problems remained. He remained vague and evasive about many questions concerning the nature of such a state, its institutions, the mediation of political differences, the formation of consensus, the relation of different levels. For instance, nothing is said about how different political programmes and parties would operate within such a system. Indeed, it is quite amazing, if not somewhat suspicious, that the Bolshevik party, cornerstone of all Lenin's thinking, receives only passing reference in *State and Revolution*. 'By educating a workers party', he notes at one point, 'Marxism educates the vanguard of the proletariat, capable of assuming power and of *leading the whole people* to Socialism, of directing and organizing the new order.'[32]

This seems to imply an identification of the party with the state—the *one* party embodying the correct path to socialism. This position would be consistent with the major thrust of both his earlier and later thinking on the subject. But it is unclear from this passage, and *that* such a question could remain unclear in such an important theoretical work is itself significant. The relative absence of the party from *State and Revolution* may be due to Lenin's heightened estimation of the role of the masses themselves, and the increasing osmosis between the Bolshevik party and the industrial proletariat of the major cities.[33] Or the absence may have been deliberate, as Daniel Tarschys suggests, since Lenin was under pressure to answer his critics, who argued that the Bolshevik party was too small and incompetent to govern all of Russia. By shifting attention to the role and competence of the masses themselves, Lenin largely avoided the question of the party.[34] In any case, in his other writings he certainly did not lose sight of the role of the party and its essential distinctiveness from the working class as such (not to mention the rest of the working population). His failure to deal with the relation of the party (or parties) to the state in a systematic and principled fashion thus remains quite significant.

In *State and Revolution* Lenin speaks more often than not in terms that imply that the revolutionary masses will govern without any institutional mediation at all. The 'masses themselves' carry out the tasks of state administration directly.[35] Even the soviets are hardly mentioned. Although the course of events and Lenin's involvement in the *practice* of revolutionary struggle prevented him from finishing the work in 1917, the outlines for the unfinished chapter indicate that his projected treatment of the soviets would have focused primarily on strategic questions like the subordination of the soviets to the policies of the Mensheviks and SRs. There is no hint that he intended (or felt it necessary) to concretize his conceptions of the institutional mediations of revolutionary state power any further.[36] As a matter of fact, *State and Revolution* was written at a time when the Bolsheviks, at Lenin's urging, had withdrawn the slogan 'all power to the soviets'. Power had actually passed, he argued, to the military dictatorship, supported by the Mensheviks and SRs. Dual power had vanished, since the soviets were completely impotent. Within the soviet structure the proletariat was incapable of rejecting the SR-Menshevik leadership and could not transform the policies of its own soviets, despite its full powers of recall. Indeed, Lenin went so far as to argue that in the existing soviet framework 'the proletariat will always support not only the vacillating petty bourgeoisie but even the big bourgeoisie.'[37] The party, with the support of the most revolutionary masses, therefore had to seize power in the streets, outside the present soviets and in opposition to them. It would be a great revolutionary sin to substitute the abstract for the concrete, to place concern for the principle of 'all power to the soviets' ahead of the recognition of their bankruptcy. New, purified soviets would be established later.

Lenin's position in this period raises the question whether in his mind *any* form of democratic institutional mediation of popular will, even one with full powers of election and recall, was adequate to the requirements of the revolution and the expression of the revolutionary interest. Implicit in his actions was the notion that such institutions only hindered the revolution and that the interests of the working class could be served only by acting outside them, at the initiative of the party and with the support of the most revolutionary section of the population. Mass support guaranteed the popular character of such actions without the test of full discussion and representation of the organized people themselves.

Lenin's arguments were strongly contested within the party. Some maintained that 'all power to the soviets' represented a broader conception of revolutionary dictatorship, one that included the peasants and soldiers as well as the workers, and that the revocation of such a slogan would irreparably narrow the social basis of the revolution. Bukharin, along with others, argued that 'we must not denounce the form of the soviets because their composition has proved unsuitable', and urged a campaign to transform the soviets through new elections—a line of action that, although not approved at the Sixth Party Congress, became

Bolshevik policy in the late summer. Lenin's analysis had proven completely wrong; the soviets were not hopelessly tied to the Mensheviks and SRs. The masses were capable of transforming the policies of their representatives through the democratic processes of the soviets. And Lenin was forced to reintroduce the old slogan as the Bolsheviks began to win soviet majorities.

But the arguments of Bukharin and others had not persuaded him. In the spring he had argued against Bukharin's position, writing: 'For us the soviets have *no importance as a form*; what we care about is which classes the soviets represent.' Form and content were thus completely separable, the former being mere abstraction. The interests of the revolutionary class(es) could be represented other than through institutions in which their representatives were democratically chosen. The party, as the only true representative of the revolutionary class(es), had the right to assert its will against such institutions. Stalin, who represented Lenin's position at the congress, argued the same point when he said that the party 'is, of course[!], in favour of those soviets in which it commands a majority. The heart of the matter is not the institutions, but which class will prevail in the institutions.'[38] Otherwise translated: the institutional forms were more or less irrelevant; what mattered was whether the party was able to use them to exercise power and implement its programme.

With the re-introduction in September of the slogan 'all power to the soviets' and the decision, taken in spite of Lenin's outspoken opinion to the contrary, to seize power in conjunction with the convening of the Second Congress of Workers and Soldiers Soviets, the soviet form became fully inscribed on the banner of the socialist revolution. Its designation as the most fitting form of socialist democracy was never again officially challenged. As Bukharin noted several years later, 'The soviets are the perfect form of proletarian dictatorship discovered by the Russian revolution.'[39] But many of the contradictions and ambiguities in Lenin's theory of the soviets persisted. Indeed, under the pressure of counter-revolution and foreign intervention, they were aggravated and gradually came to be resolved in favour of an explicit conception of the soviets as subject to single-party control and domination. To be sure, Lenin never abandoned the principle enunciated at the Seventh Party

Congress in 1918, when he said: 'But socialism cannot be implemented by a minority, by the party. It can be implemented only by tens of millions when they have learned to do it themselves.'[40] But this self-activity and popular initiative was increasingly viewed as necessarily mediated by the party and subject to complete party control and guidance.

The working people were encouraged to involve themselves in constructing the new socialist order, but the content of their activity was to be determined by, or at least subject to the veto of, the party, which alone would decide what was in the 'revolutionary interest'. Democracy was a mere form, an abstraction. And 'formal democracy must be subordinate to the revolutionary interest.'[41]

Trotsky, in fundamental agreement with Lenin on such questions, criticized the Workers Opposition in these terms at the Tenth Party Congress: 'They have come out with dangerous slogans. They have made a fetish of democratic principles. They have placed the workers right to elect representatives above the party, as it were, as if the party were not entitled to assert its dictatorship even if that dictatorship temporarily clashed with the passing moods of the workers democracy ....It is necessary to create among us the awareness of the revolutionary historical birthright of the party. The party is obliged to maintain its dictatorship regardless of the temporary wavering in the spontaneous moods of the masses, regardless of the temporary vacillations even in the working class.'[42]

Eventually, the very distinction between party and soviet institutions was eroded, as the former came to dominate the latter, and Lenin himself remarked, 'why, indeed, should the two not be united if this is what the interests of business demand?'[43] The requirements of revolutionary *administration* determined the institutional forms of revolutionary politics.

Class, Politics, and Administration

How is it possible to account for Lenin's pre-1917 reticence to discuss the forms of revolutionary state power that might be most appropriate to the democratic socialist transformation of society?

And his tendency, now latent, now quite manifest, to resolve the ambivalences of his own thinking in an unabashed and principled affirmation of the universal form of party dictatorship during that transition? The answers are not obvious, for Lenin was well aware of the need for rigorous and systematic theory in relation to all important aspects of revolutionary transformation and often expressed appreciation—sometimes much greater than others, to be sure—of the role of spontaneous mass initiative and even respect for the specific forms of struggle and power generated by the people themselves.

True, the party was always the most important element of Lenin's theory, but it was not the only one. Nor was it a foregone conclusion that the ambiguities of his thought would be resolved as they eventually were. Lenin was not a classic Jacobin or a cynical opportunist, nor a mere tactician unconcerned about the kind of society created by the revolution. His gnawing concern with the bureaucratic degeneration of the revolution toward the end of his life gives the lie to such notions. But how, then, can his theoretical resolution in favour of one-party rule be explained, a position that went unquestioned even through these last anguished reflections on the problems of bureaucracy?

The course of the revolution itself certainly lent great impetus in this direction. The problems of revolutionary administration under conditions of civil war and severe economic dislocation favoured political as well as economic centralization. The intransigence of the Mensheviks and the SRs in regard to participation in a revolutionary coalition did little to convince Lenin that pluralist political rule was practical. And Bolshevik agrarian policies—themselves deeply rooted in Leninist theory even if precipitated by dire emergency—foreclosed the possibility of an enduring coalition with the Left SRs. Yet beneath Lenin's practical responses, behind his theoretical pragmatism, his vagueness, his ambivalence, and his tendency to resolve the latter in the way he ultimately did, lay certain theoretical presuppositions about the nature of the state and politics both during the transition and in the society that stood as the end, the *telos* of social development, namely, pure communism. That Lenin never took seriously the possibility of the long-term perpetuation of mass political domination in a post-revolutionary regime that had eliminated capital, that he never took seriously the possibility of the formation and solidification of new class relationships based on the control of the nationalized means of production by a political bureaucracy dominated by a single party, can be explained only on the basis of certain theoretical precepts of the work of Marx and Engels, which Lenin followed quite carefully in his own attempt to adumbrate the problems of post-revolutionary politics.

Marx and Engels tended to define the state solely in terms of class domination. Its origin lay with the rise of classes and the division of society into irreconcilable contradictions. Its function was to moderate that conflict in favour of the class controlling the means of production, to create an 'order' conducive to its continued domination.[44] Political power 'properly so called', Marx repeated on a number of occasions, 'is merely the organized power of one class for oppressing another.'[45] As Engels noted in his introduction to *The Civil War in France*, 'the state is nothing but a machine for the oppression of one class by another.'[46] The proletarian state during the transition would also be simply a means of maintaining class power. As Engels puts it, '... the "state" is only a transitory institution which is used in the struggle, in the revolution, in order to hold down [*niederzuhalten*] one's adversaries by force, thus it is pure nonsense to talk of a "free people's state": so long as the proletariat still *uses* the state, it does not use it in the interests of freedom but in order to hold down its adversaries, and as soon as it becomes possible to speak of freedom, the state as such ceases to exist.'[47] Lenin repeated this formulation time and again: the revolutionary state was equivalent to the armed organization of the population for the sole purpose of repressing its class enemies.[48]

But there is another aspect of the proletarian state implicit though largely unarticulated in the work of Marx and Engels. In the period of transition, when the division of labour has not yet been overcome, when necessary labour has not yet been greatly reduced and work transformed from a burden to one of the prime necessities of life, when that overflowing abundance that will allow distribution according to individual needs has not yet been created, and when the anti-social culture of capitalist society has not been completely overcome, the proletarian state must exist to enforce norms of work, consumption, and general social legality among members of the working class itself. As Marx noted, the equality of labour and consumption that becomes possible in a transitional socialist society is still a 'bourgeois right', in the sense that individual and unequal needs and capacities for work are not fully recognized and cannot become the sole criteria of social responsibility and reward.[49]

Lenin was thus quite consistent with this line of thinking when he argued in *State and Revolution* that the state that takes upon itself the enforcement of such norms, however democratically constituted, is in this sense a kind of 'bourgeois state ... without the bourgeoisie'.[50] More explicitly than Marx and Engels he recognized that the force of the proletarian state would be directed against those members of the working class who violated its norms. He stated, for example, that the revolutionary masses who control the state establish control over the old ruling classes and 'the workers thoroughly demoralized by capitalism', and that not all subordination can be done away with immediately.[51] Here he distinguished himself, as Marx and Engels often did, from the pure anarchist position, which would permit no use or threat of coercion whatever against members of the exploited classes themselves who might violate agreed-upon social norms (continual absence from work, for instance). And Lenin's position here is essentially correct, if it is added that resort to coercive measures should occur only after all reasonable attempts at discussion and persuasion have failed, that such measures must be commensurate with the violation, and that some form of due process must be maintained.

But Lenin often distorted these principles when he lost sight of the necessarily democratic formulation of the social norms to be enforced—in theory, as well as in the inevitably more compromised practice. This was the case, for instance, when severe disciplinary measures were taken against workers who had virtually no say in work intensity and output norms, or when Lenin rather glibly characterized the workers involved in the independent factory-committee movement as 'demoralized by capitalism', or when he excluded from the ranks of the true proletariat all those who opposed the party's position on the statization of the trade unions.[52] In other words, Lenin often tended to pervert the essential truth of his conception of the necessarily coercive aspects of the socialist state *vis-à-vis* not only members of the counter-revolutionary classes but also members of the proletariat itself, when he identified the party as the exclusive determinant of this state's norms and policies and when he used essentially politico-authoritarian criteria to determine who was 'demoralized' and 'backward' and who was a member of the true proletariat.

The basic theoretical position that recognizes the moment of coercion in the relation of the socialist state to the working class itself, however, tends to be submerged by the more prominent formulations that stress only its role *vis-à-vis* the old ruling classes. And together with Marx's premiss that the origins of the state lay solely in the existence of material scarcity and the consequent division into classes, such formulations sometimes lead to a naive conception that the disappearance of political domination is inevitable. The elimination of political domination becomes the *automatic* result of the defeat of the old ruling classes and the abolition of capital. The elimination of scarcity—made possible by the abolition of the last mode of production that fetters the productive forces—makes the existence of classes, and hence of the state, no longer necessary. And that which is no longer necessary *necessarily* disappears. With the abolition of classes the need for the state 'will automatically disappear.'[53] As Engels says on another occasion, 'Do away with capital, the concentration of all means of production in the hands of a few, and the state will fall of itself.'[54] And in *Socialism: Utopian and Scientific*, we find the classic statement:

'When at last it [the state] becomes the real representative of the whole of society, it renders itself unnecessary. As soon as there is no longer any social class to be held in subjection; as soon as class rule, and the individual struggle for existence based upon our present anarchy in production, with the collisions and excesses arising from these, are removed, nothing more remains to be repressed, and a special repressive force, a state, is no longer necessary. The first act by virtue of which the state really constitutes itself the representative of the whole of society—the taking possession of the means of production in the name of society—that is, at the same time, its last independent act as a state. State interference in social relations becomes, in one domain after another, superfluous, and then dies out of itself; the government of persons is replaced by the administration of things, and by the conduct of processes of production. The state is not "abolished". It dies out.... The proletariat seizes the public power, and by means of this transforms the socialized means of production, slipping from the hands of the bourgeoisie, into public property. By this act, the proletariat frees the means of production from the character of capital they have thus far borne, and gives their socialized character complete freedom to work itself out. Socialized production upon a predetermined plan becomes henceforth possible. The development of production makes the existence of different classes of society thenceforth an anachronism. In proportion as anarchy in social production vanishes, the political authority of the state dies out.'[55]

Once again the growth of the productive forces becomes the motor of social transformation. Political domination is rooted solely in the material scarcity that gives rise to class division. With the abolition of capital, the productive forces can be fully planned and rationalized, and political domination will inevitably and automatically disappear as a direct result. The *practical need* to struggle against the perpetuation of political domination in a society in which the means of production have been nationalized by a revolutionary government subtly disappears as the elimination of such domination becomes the automatic offshoot of the elimination of scarcity.

The full potential impact of this logic is avoided as long as Lenin insists on the democratic control of the people over their representatives. But as this comes to be seen as unrealistic or potentially threatening in the immediate sense, or as theoretically inconsistent with the role of the party as the sole true representative of the objective interests of the working class, then the force of this productivist logic re-emerges. Because the goal of the elimination of political domination is determined primarily by the development of the productive forces, the *conscious struggle against such domination in the transitional period* becomes that much less necessary, especially since political coercion in the proper sense of the term is limited in theory to the old ruling classes, or, when it is recognized as existing within the proletariat itself, is unilaterally defined by the party in a way that masks its political character in supposedly neutral and unambiguous determinations of 'demoralization' or 'backwardness'.[56] The necessity for systematic struggle against political domination becomes increasingly obscure in Lenin's writings, partly because of the naive formulas on the inevitable withering away of the state which he inherits from Engels, and, to a lesser extent, Marx. Indeed, Lenin could be so complacent about the threat of the crystallization of new class relationships in a society dominated by a single party uncontrolled from below because he was convinced that all domination would automatically disappear with the full flowering of the productive forces.

But there is another reason as well. As Karl Wittfogel has shown,[57] Lenin largely accepted a mechanistic and unilinear scheme of social development that left no theoretical room for the possibility of any class society after that based on private capital had been destroyed. Marx's analysis of the Asiatic mode of production, under which the state was, in effect, the landlord, and the social surplus was appropriated by the ruling bureaucracy, suggested that private control of the means of production was not the sole model of class society, and that such a bureaucracy could legitimately be called a ruling class.[58] But Marx avoided this conclusion, at least explicitly, and although elements of such an analysis are present in Engels as well,[59] his best-known works on these questions (*Origin of the Family, Private Property and the State*, and the later sections of *Anti-Dühring*) retreat to a single model of state and class rule based exclusively on the relations of private property. Slavery, serfdom, and capitalism become the three successive forms of class society, which would be followed by socialism and, finally, communism. Political domination was seen solely as the result of economic or class domination based on the private ownership of the means of production, and would thus disappear with the latter.

Lenin, despite certain earlier analyses of 'asiaticism' and some oblique references accompanying his later struggle against bureaucracy, followed Engels, especially his *Origin*, very closely, both in *State and Revolution* and in his 1919 lecture on the state.[60] In these works, only the private-property-based states are mentioned. There is absolutely no discussion of Oriental despotism and its theoretical implications for the class-state model. Although it is somewhat suspicious that Lenin makes no reference to any of the works of Marx and Engels that discuss the concept of Oriental despotism, some of which were known to him, one need not accept Wittfogel's claim of conscious deception and opportunism. The evolutionist aspects of the work of all three men are strong enough to account for the omissions.[61]

Lenin's tendency to leave the institutions of revolutionary political power ill-defined and to resolve his ambiguities and contradictions in favour of a principled theory of party dictatorship derives as well from the distinction between politics proper and administration, which runs through his thinking. Closely following Marx and Engels, he narrowly delimits the category of 'politics' to the struggle between hostile classes.[62] Politics and political power in the transition are thus defined solely in terms of the suppression of the class enemies of the proletariat. As Daniel Tarschys has noted, Lenin operated on 'the premiss that the political drama was enacted between not within classes.'[63] In his major pieces of 1917 on the subject, namely, 'Can the Bolsheviks Retain State Power?' and *State and Revolution*, the dominant imagery is that of us versus them—a very large and powerful 'us' versus an insignificantly small 'them'—where the decisive elements in struggle will be physical force and the technical-administrative abilities of the masses.[64] Vague characterizations of the state as no more than the armed organization of the people usually suffice, since the decisive political question is the application of revolutionary force. Since divisions and differences among the workers (and other revolutionary strata) are usually not recognized as properly political, it becomes less necessary to develop a theory of the political-institutional mediation of such differences.

As 'politics proper' tends to be collapsed into the exercise of force against the class enemy, all other questions become simply matters for revolutionary *administration*. As Lenin puts it in *State and Revolution*, 'accounting and control—these are the *chief* things necessary for the organizing and correct functioning of the *first phase* of Communist society.'[65] This theme is repeated time and again: it is all a matter of proper organization and technical-administrative competence. Indeed, the entire argument of this work rests on the assumption that only because capitalism has generalized the basic skills necessary for efficient administration (literacy, arithmetic) can the old state apparatus be smashed within twenty-four hours and the old rulers (administrators) replaced by the people themselves. What normally had been considered political functions have become so simplified that they 'can be reduced to such simple operations of registration, filing and checking', of 'watching, recording and issuing receipts.'[66] The post office stands as the model institution of the new revolutionary state.[67]

Virtually every exhortation on the need for mass participation during the transition, in *State and Revolution* and in Lenin's other works, speaks primarily in terms of participation in the technical tasks of administration.[68] To my knowledge, no theoretical statement—in fact, no statement whatever except those relating to the questions of revolutionary strategy and the seizure of power in 1917, before the Bolsheviks had established political hegemony—speaks of mass political participation in the formation and revision of policy. The soviets are seen as ideal because they involve the masses of people in administration, not because they provide the forum for the democratic mediation of popular differences the formation of consensus, and the continued revision of policy in accordance with the development of the views of the people. Indeed, Lenin later argues that the existence of divisions and differences precisely disqualifies mass organizations embracing the entire proletariat from deciding policy and ruling directly, and necessitates the imposition of a unifying line by the party.[69] The political role of the soviets is similar to that assigned the trade unions in the economic realm: to train the masses in the skills required for administration, while simultaneously involving them in it. But in the soviets as in the trade unions, full participation in the formulation of policy is out of the question until full competence and political reliability have been achieved. Since the goal is the abolition of political functions as such and their transformation into 'the simple administrative functions of watching over the true interests of society',[70] the major tasks of the transition are increasingly defined in these terms as the resistance of the former ruling classes is overcome. The party and the soviets should be merged if this serves the interests of efficient administration. Political and theoretical discussion and debate should be suspended if it inter-feres with efficient administration.[71]

Efficient administration, of course, is an important task for any revolutionary regime, and it is testimony to the fundamentally popular character of Lenin's thought that he so emphasized the de-monopolization of such functions and the training and involvement of all the people in their fulfilment. But no matter how extensively it draws in the broad masses of people, such administration re-mains basically authoritarian if it is not preceded by the full ar-ticulation of needs and interests in public discourse and the forma-tion of consensus and compromise through processes of democratic decision-making. And in Lenin's theory it is not, or at least never consistently so. One reason for this is Lenin's theory of the party itself, which as Miliband correctly perceives, postulates a 'sym-biotic organic relationship' between the class and its party, so that the party becomes the natural expression of an undivided revolu-tionary proletarian will,[72] or at least of that section of the pro-letariat which is not demoralized, corrupted, and thoroughly degraded by capitalism.[73] Thus Lenin can make the claim—border-ing on complete rhetorical self-delusion if it is not simply tautological—that the Bolshevik party 'since 1905 or earlier has been united with the whole revolutionary proletariat'; its dictator-ship thus fully expresses the rule of the working class itself.[74] In January 1921, at the very nadir of party influence among the peasantry, Lenin made a similar assertion: the party has won the support of the peasants after decades of hard work, and 'everybody believes the word of the Bolsheviks who have had twenty years of party training.'[75]

Since the party correctly expresses the undivided revolutionary will of the workers, since it is a 'vanguard that has absorbed the revolutionary energy of the class,'[76] there is no need for democratic policy-making institutions to forge consensus out of division and difference. Indeed, differences are never recognized as even possibly legitimate, but are automatically branded an insidious threat to revolutionary unity, an expression of demoralization and degradation revealing the persistence of capitalist ideology and culture. The revolutionary interest is one, and so must be the revolutionary will. Only the party can guarantee this.[77]

Politics in the Classless Society

Lenin's tendency to suppress issues concerning the political mediation of popular interests and will in favour of those of technical administration is ultimately related to his conception of the pure communist classless society that stands as the goal of all revolutionary
activity. The utopian *telos* informs the tasks of the transition.
Although Marx and Engels often decried attempts to speculate on
the nature of the future society, they nonetheless bequeathed to
future generations of Marxists a set of texts that, while they do not
attempt to outline the institutional contours of full communism,
certainly define some of the basic principles according to which
such a society would be organized. Lenin was not only fully aware
of these basic principles, but saw himself as consciously ap-
propriating them and integrating them into his revolutionary
strategy for the transition period. As he said at the Seventh Party
Congress in 1918, 'as we begin socialist reforms we must have a
clear conception of the goal towards which these reforms are in the
final analysis directed, that is, the creation of a communist
society.'[78] Unfortunately, his conception was neither clearer nor
more adequate than that of his mentors, and their common shortcomings had a significant influence on Lenin's attempt to theorize
the political forms of the socialist transition.

In a fully developed communist society, the Marxian wisdom has
it, all political power will disappear. With the elimination of
classes, the abolition of the division between mental and manual
labour, and the full development of the productive forces by the
associated producers, there will no longer be any need for the
systematic application of social coercion, nor for institutional
arrangements that enforce social norms. No special coercive apparatus will be required because there will be no class to be held in
subordination; 'people will *grow accustomed* to observing the
elementary conditions of social existence *without force and without
subjection*.' Observance of the everyday rules of social life will
become habitual. If there are individual excesses and violations,
they will be rectified by the armed people themselves 'as simply and
as readily as any crowd of civilized people, even in modern society,

parts a pair of combatants or does not allow a woman to be out-raged.'[79]

The responsibilities of work and the rewards of distribution will be spontaneously and harmoniously shared, so that no calculation according to standards of justice and equality will be needed. 'From each according to his ability, to each according to his needs' will be the sole criterion of social contribution and individual reward.[80] 'No fixation of social activity' will be necessary. All individuals will be free to develop talents and skills in any area of activity they wish, and perform them whenever they wish. (It becomes 'possible for me to do one thing today and another tomorrow, to hunt in the morning, fish in the afternoon, rear cattle in the evening, criticize after dinner, *just as I have a mind*, without ever becoming hunter, fisherman, shepherd, or critic.'[81]) The social division of labour will thus be completely voluntary, and no continuous individual commitment to any necessary social task need be mandated. As control over nature is perfected, the government of persons will be replaced by the 'administration of things' and the 'watching over of the true interests of society'. The latter are unambiguous and served voluntarily, because they converge with the interests of every individual. The rules of social interaction become those of everyday civility. Democracy, which is nothing but the last and highest form of the state for the subjugation of the minority by the working majority, itself becomes unnecessary and withers away.[82]

Lenin's tendency to conceive of mass participation in the construction of socialism largely in terms of technical administration is theoretically continuous with this conception of communist society as an administrative utopia where the need for democracy itself vanishes and all individual and social interests are harmonized more or less automatically. But this conception is untenable. It is a form of utopianism that oversteps the boundary of what is theoretically conceivable under conditions of material social existence as such. It is utopia as the myth of total reconciliation and harmony, rather than as the normative dimension of critical social theory. While the latter is requisite for any systematic critique that informs the struggle to overcome conditions of domination, the former tends to mystify the criteria according to which that struggle must be waged if a truly free and human society is to result. Such is the case with Lenin: the mythical goal of pure communism distorts the politics of socialist transition and helps justify essentially authoritarian means.

The Marxist argument for an administrative utopia rests primarily on an objectivist concept of scarcity. Scarcity refers to the (absolute) insufficiency of material goods and services, of free time and humanly fulfilling work. The full expansion of the productive forces and the concomitant all-round development of the entire population eliminates scarcity in all these areas, so that no relative choice must be made among them, need or desire in any particular area never conflicting with that in another. The possibility of conflict between one individual's and another's preferred use of social resources (including, of course, society's human resources), or between a minority and a majority, is automatically ruled out. Control of nature is so perfect and communist society so productive that every individual need can be accommodated without sacrifice in any other area or by any other individual or group. There is no reason to prioritize individual and group needs or to mediate them through public discourse, through democratic processes to arrive at consensus or equitable compromise concerning the allocation of collective resources. Equally unnecessary, therefore, is any standard of right to influence such decisions or to enforce the decisions of majorities. The use of social resources by individuals and groups, however broad, will never impose sacrifices on others that cannot be completely offset by the remaining resources. Just as the origins of the state lie in the scarcity that gives rise to classes, so the full development of the productive forces eliminates the objective basis of political power. Democracy itself withers because the abolition of scarcity eliminates any possible divergence of legitimate desires and needs.

'Economy of time, to this all economy ultimately reduces itself.'[83] Here Marx succinctly summarized what should be regarded as a fundamental tenet of any materialist social theory, whose relevance extends not only to capitalism, where economy of time takes the particular form of the law of value, but to any society, even a classless communist society. As Marx notes, 'Thus, economy of time, along with the planned distribution of labour time among the various branches of production, remains the first economic law on the basis of communal production. It becomes law, there, even to a higher degree.'[84] The utopian administrative conception of communism precisely fails to recognize this: economy of time will always be necessary because time is *always relatively scarce*. This fact is impressed on every individual with great existential force, and on every society facing the task of organizing labour for the needs of its members, present and future. The relative scarcity of time is a universal feature of individual and social life. For social theory this implies that every commitment of socially necessary labour always has its costs, in the sense of the possible alternative uses of relatively scarce labour time. It could never be a matter of general indifference, therefore, how that time is spent, how it is organized, how much of it is socially committed or how much freely disposable by the individual.

Every decision to allocate resources involves a very specific use of relatively scarce time, or at least of its socially committed component. Whether it be to create more free time in the present or future by increasing productivity or decreasing consumption, to make routine work more tolerable by organizing it in a more pleasant (perhaps slower, more casual) fashion, to organize more production in a craftlike manner, to create more opportunities for individual development by providing greater learning and training opportunities, to provide more and better goods and services by increasing production—every such decision implies allocation of socially necessary time, as well as a certain distribution between this and completely free, personally disposable time. Any relative priority of needs implies the relative sacrifice of other needs. The complete elimination of scarcity is thus inconceivable, and so also is the complete dissolution of social power premised on it, and on the elimination of classes that is seen as a condition for it. The priorities of some may not be fully satisfied and conflict may thus remain a basic feature of social life. Indeed, only on the basis of completely unwarranted assumptions about human psychology and communication networks in a complex and pluralist society could it be assumed that this possibility will not become inevitable.[85] Every allocation of social resources is therefore an expression of social power. The 'administration of things' can never be a completely neutral, apolitical, power-less, and conflict-free process, since 'things' in the broadest sense are ultimately reducible to human time and labour. The problem of social and political power, and hence of conflict, cannot be reduced to the problem of class.[86]

Since, under conditions of relative scarcity and the great variety of individual life possibilities, we can never *assume* the automatic harmonization of all individuals' needs and priorities for the use of their time, the set of principles according to which social inter-action, and particularly the organization of socially necessary labour and socially available rewards are organized, must be ar-ticulated. There must be a system of norms governing access to work options, the minimum acceptable fulfilment of work tasks and the maximum consumption of socially produced goods and services—even in a society in which the means of production are collectively owned and democratically managed, in which labour is highly productive, and in which the class division of labour has been overcome. And in such a communist society—if I may use Marx's nomenclature while amending certain aspects of its substance—the only consistent standards are those of equal right and equal responsibility, which Marx and Lenin, from their perspective of a purely administrative, non-political utopia, designate as 'the narrow horizon of bourgeois right [to] be fully left behind.'[87] A fundamentally egalitarian communist society must recognize the equal right of all of its citizens to free time beyond the socially required commitment; the equal right to influence the deci-sions that determine the partition of socially necessary and in-dividually free time, and of necessary work that can be creative and interesting and that which tends to be less so; the equal responsibili-ty to share in that work which is less inherently rewarding; the equal responsibility to perform these and the socially necessary but more creative tasks in a manner that is at least roughly equivalent in terms of time and/or productivity to that of the rest of society, as this is democratically determined; the equal responsibility to re-main within the standard of consumption of goods and services im-plicit in the collective decisions about the level of production for present use, except as that consumption results from production during one's own or others' free time and from social resources designated for this. From a fully communist point of view, the determinate negation of the capitalist principle of the allocation of labour responsibilities and consumption rights, namely the law of value, can only be a principle of conscious social planning whose basic calculus is derived from the full recognition of such equal rights and responsibilities.[88]

The *systematic application* of egalitarian *norms* for the organization of social labour will thus be indispensable in any communist society, no matter how highly developed, *even if* the various levels of decentralized decision-making (networks of family, friends, workmates, local community) permit a considerable degree of flexibility in the application of such standards; even if the voluntary 'subsidization' (through the assumption of extra work responsibilities, for example) of individuals and groups by others is possible, and the struggle for existence pacific, so that no meticulous calculation of the fulfilment of responsibilities is necessary. It is obvious that such possibilities for institutional and informal flexibility and deviation are highly desirable in a society devoted to the full development of each person's individuality. Indeed, here is the truth at the core of Marx's dicta 'from each according to his ability, to each according to his needs', and 'the free development of each is the condition for the free development of all.'[89] But the converse of this latter principle is equally important: equal opportunities for the free development of all are the condition for the free development of each. Options for individual flexibility and deviation in the area of social labour must thus proceed from the recognition of the prior right of every individual to have equal access to the social resources that are the condition for such individual development, and hence the prior responsibility to fulfill the tasks allocated according to democratic decision-making processes and egalitarian norms of distribution and performance. In other words, legitimate deviation must still be seen as deviation from an egalitarian norm, and unless purely a matter of voluntary subsidization from the free time and personal resources of others, must occur according to rules consistent with such egalitarian norms. Other norms of deviation, or the completely haphazard application of such norms, would implicitly deprive others of their equal rights to the socially available 'goods', work and life opportunities, as well as the security of knowing where their social responsibility ended and their freely disposable personal time began.[90]

The determination and systematic application of social norms for the fulfilment of collectively made decisions on the use of social resources—decisions that inevitably express social power to the extent that they do not completely converge with every individual's personal priorities—imply the delegation of legitimate authority for monitoring and enforcing such norms, and for regulating possible conflict. Even a classless communist society, then, will require institutionalized focal points for the exercise of social *power*. The institutions through which such social decisions are made, alternative norms debated, competing needs mediated, and the decisions enforced are political and legal institutions in the full sense of those terms. They need not be considered a 'state' in the sense in which Marx, Engels, and Lenin used the term. They need not stand above and independent of the people, mystifying their activities in secrecy and incomprehensible rules, unable to be held accountable for their activities, systematically suppressing the interests of a particular class. If the associated individuals have well internalized the norms for the fulfilment of their responsibilities, then such political and legal institutions would not have to operate oppressively and obstructively. Nor does the existence of such institutions presume any particular form of enforcement or sanction, or completely preclude informal moral pressure and communication-education as the more desirable forms for the expression of such sanctions. But such institutions must exist if social interaction under conditions of relative scarcity is to be regulated at all.

Lenin's conception of pure communism, derived completely from Marx and Engels, denies the inevitability of socio-political power and conflict, and thus the problem of their organization. The origin of classes, and hence of political power, is explained by an objectivist concept of scarcity, which assumes the complete disappearance of power with the extension of the productive forces and the abolition of the division between mental and manual labour (which itself is seen as a more or less automatic offshoot of technological development). The common interest in such a project is assumed to be undivided, since the perfected rational control of nature will allow the complete fulfilment of all individual needs and desires. Social and individual interests will be wholly congruent. There will be no need to mediate divergent individual needs institutionally, since the abolition of scarcity will permit all individual needs to be satisfied fully. Democracy itself will wither away, and social life will be regulated by the habitual observance of the everyday rules of civility.

While it would be wrong to overestimate the effect of this concept of pure communism on Lenin's theory of the transition or on his actual revolutionary practice, it is nevertheless an essential moment of the theoretical problematic he drew upon in his efforts to answer the major questions of revolution and socialist transition. This utopian moment of his thought encouraged the suppression and authoritarian resolution of the problems of the political and institutional mediation of revolutionary popular will. Since the utopian goal was the dissolution of all political institutions, the question of the most suitable institutions for the transition became that much less important. They were mere form anyway, class tools to hold down the old ruling classes, and to be progressively discarded as they fulfilled this purpose. Since all social power would eventually wither away with the full development of the productive forces, the question of its form of organization became subordinate to the question of the most immediately effective forms for organizing such development. Since all politics would ultimately dissolve into mere administration, the question of mass participation during the transition was conceived primarily in administrative terms. Since the ultimate revolutionary interest was unambiguous and undivided, it did not require democratic mediation but could be represented by a single political party not subject to popular control.

The problem of power in social interaction could be ultimately and permanently resolved by the growth of the productive forces and the concomitant abolition of the division between mental and manual labour. Indeed, one of the reasons why Marx took the problems of association for collective production for granted,[91] and why his critique of the capitalist mode of production remained at the level of abstract negation and avoided concrete articulation of the organizing principles of a communist mode of production, was that he tended to reduce social interaction to labour, the problems of social power to the problem of technological development and the control of nature. But this theoretical reduction completely disregards scarcity, misconstrues some of the basic questions of social and political organization, and becomes readily available as a rationalization for an authoritarian politics of socialist transition.

Bureaucracy and Cultural Revolution

'We must learn to admit an evil fearlessly in order to combat it more firmly, in order to start from scratch again and again: we shall have to do this many a time in every sphere of our activity, finish what was left undone and choose different approaches to the problem.'[1]

When Lenin wrote these words in late 1921 he was referring above all to the evil of bureaucracy, which would become one of the central concerns of the few remaining years of his life. The naive hopes of *State and Revolution* that the old state machinery would rapidly be shattered, replaced by the active and competent revolutionary masses, had themselves been dashed. The soviets, Lenin was forced to admit as early as March 1919, had become not organs run by the working people themselves, but organs *for* the working people directed by the vanguard party.[2] And even that vanguard did not know how to run the new state.[3]

Bureaucratic abuses against the workers and peasants were rampant, and red tape strangled constructive activity everywhere. 'The departments are shit,'[4] he boldly admitted, and the new regime was mired in lethargy. Something had to be done, but what? The problem had not previously received serious study, he conceded. He himself did not fully understand it.[5] With the breathing space provided by the NEP, and the illusions of war communism disintegrating rapidly, he set himself the theoretical task of analysing the roots of the new soviet bureaucracy and the political task of extirpating it thoroughly.

Roots of Bureaucracy

One of the major causes of bureaucracy, Lenin came to realize, was the largely self-enclosed Russian village in which the great mass of the people lived. In more developed capitalist countries, the ruling class requires a bureaucratic, military and judiciary apparatus to suppress the revolutionary workers movement. But 'in our country bureaucratic practices have different economic roots, namely the atomized and scattered state of the small producer with his poverty, illiteracy, lack of culture, the absence of roads and *exchange* between agriculture and industry, the absence of connection and interaction between them.'[6] The causes of this disruption Lenin attributed to the civil war. But he himself recognized that although there was truth in this, the roots of the problem went much deeper. 'The wider the dispersal of the peasantry, the more inevitable are bureaucratic practices at the centre.'[7]

This atomization was the heritage of Russian development upon which the tsarist state had been built. Here Lenin was reiterating a familiar theme, one that was repeatedly struck in Marx and Engels's treatment of Oriental despotism. As Engels argued, 'such a complete isolation of the individual communities from one another, which creates throughout the country similar, but the very opposite of common interests, is the natural basis for *Oriental* despotism, and from India to Russia this form of society, wherever it prevailed, has always produced it and always found its complement in it.'[8] And as Lenin now recognized, the social basis upon which the tsarist state had arisen could not be revolutionized as easily as it had been overthrown.

Even the extent to which the old tsarist apparatus could be smashed had been grossly overestimated. Lenin noted in 1923 that with the exception of the Commissariat of Foreign Affairs, the old apparatus had been taken over almost in its entirety. At the summit, of course, stood thousands of committed revolutionaries, but at the base of the new state administration were hundreds of thousands of former functionaries who, by and large, were hostile to the revolution and jealous of their bureaucratic privilege. Lenin recognized the typical tsarist bureaucrats for what they were: Great Russian chauvinists and petty tyrants. But their services, like those of the specialists in private industry and agriculture, the army, education, and so on, could not be dispensed with immediately.

The revolutionary population was ill-equipped to perform all the complex tasks of a modern industrial society. The regime could not afford the time and disruption that would be required to train all of its own functionaries from scratch, even if the task were feasible. The old bureaucrats and specialists would have to be used, and the people would have to learn from them. There simply was no other way. But they must work under the vigilant eye of the commissars, and no political concessions must be made to them. Economic concessions were inevitable, and these, along with a proletarian atmosphere of fraternal collaboration and lack of direct coercion, might induce them to work for the revolutionary state. At times Lenin even hoped that many of the experts would be re-educated and would come to serve the socialist cause enthusiastically: 'As they see the working class promoting organized and advanced sections, which not only value culture but also help to convey it to the people, they are changing their attitude towards us. When a doctor sees that the proletariat is arousing the working people to independent activity in fighting epidemics, his attitude towards us completely changes. We have a large section of such bourgeois doctors, engineers, agronomists and co-operators, and when they see in practice that the proletariat is enlisting more and more people to the cause, they will be conquered *morally*, and not merely be cut off from the bourgeoisie politically.'[9]

But the great danger was that the opposite could also happen, that the style of work of the old bureaucrats and administrators could corrupt the relatively few Communists and non-party workers and peasants whose job it was to learn from them while keeping a watchful eye over the politics of their activities. Indeed, according to Lenin, this is exactly what was occurring: the former tsarist functionaries were establishing their hegemony over the daily operations of government. The party itself was being infected by 'communist conceit', the tendency to solve all problems by issuing decrees and orders.[10]

At the Eleventh Party Congress in 1922 Lenin employed a striking analogy to illustrate the process taking place: 'If we take Moscow with its 4,700 Communists in responsible positions, and if we take that huge bureaucratic machine, that gigantic heap, we must ask: who is directing whom? I doubt very much whether it can truthfully be said that the Communists are directing that heap. To tell the truth, they are not directing, they are being directed. Something analogous happened here to what we were told in our history lessons when we were children: sometimes one nation conquers another, the nation that conquers is the conqueror and the nation that is vanquished is the conquered nation. This is simple and intelligible to all. But what happens to the culture of these nations? Here things are not so simple. If the conquering nation is more cultured than the vanquished nation, the former imposes its culture upon the latter; but if the opposite is the case, the vanquished nation imposes its culture upon the conqueror. Has not something like this happened in the capital of the RSFSR.? Have the 4,700 Communists (nearly a whole army division, and all of them the very best) come under the influence of an alien culture? True, there may be the impression that the vanquished have a higher level of culture. But that is not the case at all. Their culture is miserable, insignificant, but it is still at a higher level than ours. Miserable and low as it is, it is higher than that of our responsible Communist administrators, for the latter lack administrative ability.'[11]

If the cultural level of the party administrators, many of whom had been skilled and literate workers before the revolution, was low, that of the masses of unskilled workers and peasants was far lower. In the most advanced regions of the country, Lenin noted in 1923, not more than 330 of every 1,000 persons were literate.[12] How could politically self-conscious mass participation in government be a reality in such conditions? How could bureaucracy be avoided when so many people lacked the basic skills for administration and articulate political discourse? 'An illiterate person stands outside politics, he must first learn his ABC. Without that there can be no politics; without that there are rumours, gossip, fairy-tales and prejudices, but not politics.'[13] This low cultural level was perhaps the most important reason for the perpetuation of bureaucracy.[14] While in some ways it made the task of overthrowing the old regime easier than it would have been in the more advanced capitalist countries, it also made the construction of a new socialist order, one without tremendous bureaucratic deformations, that much more difficult.[15] With the declassing of the already narrow proletarian social base of the revolution as a result of the civil war, with the disruption of industry and food provisioning and the absorption of the most politically active elements into the Red Army and the new state apparatus, the difficulties would be even greater.[16]

Finally, in addition to their low technical and cultural level, the masses of workers and peasants retained many ideological and cultural aspects of the old society. Lenin complained again and again that the masses were still too timid to take matters into their own hands. The old society had instilled in them a sense of diffidence and lack of confidence. They had become accustomed to waiting for orders from above, and the revolution of 1917 had not completely dispelled this attitude. Too few, for instance, spoke up at meetings.[17] Many were still imbued with petty-bourgeois attitudes, and some of those involved in the Committees of Poor Peasants were prone to sprees of drunken looting. As Lenin noted in early 1919: 'The workers were never separated by a Great Wall of China from the old society. And they have preserved a good deal of the traditional mentality of capitalist society. The workers are building a new society without themselves having become new people, or cleansed of the filth of the old world; they are still standing up to their knees in that filth.'[18]

When the old society perishes, he had written elsewhere, its corpse cannot be neatly buried. 'It disintegrates in our midst; the corpse rots and infects us.'[19] The construction of socialism would not be so difficult if it did not have to be done with people inherited from and corrupted by capitalism. But if we waited to construct socialism until all people were ready for it, until all people had purged themselves of the filth of the old society, we would wait forever.[20] No, we must build socialism with people who grew up under capitalism. But this means that one of the foremost tasks of the period of socialist transition is to transform the people themselves. The proletariat, Lenin argued, is 'fighting for socialism, but at the same time is fighting against its own shortcomings.'[21]

Cultural Revolution

The persistence and growth of bureaucracy in the new soviet regime had deep roots, Lenin held. The struggle against it would therefore be long and arduous. It could not be eliminated simply by passing new laws and 'paper resolutions.' 'You can throw out the Tsar, throw out the landowners, throw out the capitalists. We have done this. But you cannot "throw out" bureaucracy in a peasant country, you cannot "wipe it off the face of the earth". You can only *reduce* it by slow and stubborn effort ... you have to try, not 2–3 times, but 20–30 times—repeat your attempts, start over again.'[22] The elimination of bureaucracy would require nothing less than a cultural revolution, and the transformation of the culture of the people would require many years.[23]

One of the central aspects of this cultural revolution, Lenin wrote in January 1923, was the organization of the peasants into cooperatives. In 1921 he had argued vehemently against them: 'freedom and rights for cooperation mean freedom and rights for capitalism.'[24] The NEP, he now believed, placed too little importance on peasant cooperatives. As long as the land belonged to the state, and the state, in turn, was dominated by the proletariat, there was little to fear from peasant cooperatives. They represented the simplest and most acceptable way of drawing the peasants into the tasks of collective socialist construction, and the state should grant them special material privileges (like favourable loan terms) to encourage the broadest participation, which must in all cases be voluntary. Indeed, 'the mere growth of co-operation ... is identical with the growth of socialism.' But this required a 'cultural revolution': 'Strictly speaking, there is "*only*" one thing we have left to do and this is to make our people so "enlightened" that they understand all the advantages' of everybody participating in the work of the cooperatives, and organize this participation. "*Only*" that. There are no other devices needed to advance socialism. But to achieve this "only," there must be a veritable revolution—the entire people must go through a period of cultural development.'[25] Such a revolution in the peasant way of life would require an entire historical epoch. At best it could be achieved in one or two decades.

On another level, the threat of bureaucracy could be fought by reforming the ruling party and bringing it into closer contact with the masses. Non-party conferences were to be held so that the party could get a better idea of what the masses were actually thinking and feeling, and so that new people could be brought into the party itself.[26] Party members were urged to live among the masses as well, for unless they remained in touch with the real aspirations of the people, the party would be in danger of running too far ahead, thus becoming isolated. The party must be able to 'straighten out the line' in response to creative input from the masses.[27]

At present, Lenin admitted in 1922, the proletarian character of its policy was determined not by the social composition of its membership but by its still prestigious Old Guard. Probation periods for membership should be increased to discourage the entry of opportunists.[28] The Central Committee should be enlarged to include workers and peasants who have not had extensive service in soviet administration and who are therefore closer to the rank and file and still relatively uncorrupted by the ways of the typical Soviet bureaucrat.[29] The 'bureaucrats' and 'puffed-up commissars' should be purged on the basis of suggestions of the non-party masses, although the latter must not have the final say in such matters, since (especially in times of exceptional weariness and suffering) they 'yield to sentiments that are in no way advanced.'[30] The trade unions' quasi-autonomy of the party and state must be guarded, since they are able to protect the people's material and spiritual interests against the bureaucratic distortions of the state in ways that are impossible for the apparatuses of the state itself.[31] At the Eleventh Party Congress he went so far as to propose an organizational separation of the party and state.[32] But bureaucracy would be defeated only as more and more people were drawn into the actual business of administration, as more trade unionists were drawn into the management of industry, as more non-party people were promoted to government and economic posts. Socialism without bureaucracy could be built only with the active participation of the people, and not by the vanguard alone.[33]

Lenin placed great hopes on one institution in particular: the Workers and Peasants Inspectorate (*Rabkrin*). Created in February 1920 on the basis of reorganized state control departments, *Rabkrin* was to oversee the accounting and reporting methods of all state offices, have the power of a commissariat to issue orders rectifying mistakes, and inspect for possible cases of fraud. All working people, especially women, were to be gradually drawn into its work in stages, depending on their level of basic literacy and competence. Non-party people would thus be reciprocally controlling party and state officials who exercised general control over the population. In this way, the state machinery would be made to function more honestly and less bureaucratically, while ordinary workers and peasants learned the art of administration themselves.[34]

The most important aspect of Lenin's conception of cultural revolution, to which he returned time and again, was the full appropriation of bourgeois culture itself. Already in 1919 he had articulated the principle that had dominated most of his earlier work on this question. 'We must take the *entire* culture that capitalism left behind and build socialism with it. We must take *all* its science, technology, knowledge and art.'[35] The basic question is 'how to unite the victorious proletarian revolution with bourgeois culture, with bourgeois science and technology, which up to now has been the property of the few.'[36] Bourgeois culture had to be completely appropriated and simultaneously democratized. The cornerstone of this policy was to make the entire population fully literate. 'Our primary and most important task is to attain universal literacy.'[37] Education must be free, poly-technical, and compulsory up to age sixteen, and must also remain closely tied to production. The state should vigorously aid all forms of self-education as well: libraries, studios, cinemas, adult schools, public lectures, people's universities. Learning by rote must be abolished. The prestige of teachers should be enhanced, but the entire community should be mobilized to run the schools collectively and to determine curricula.[38] The training of all workers in the latest technological and organizational skills of capitalism should begin as soon as possible.[39]

Art must also be democratized, removed from the exclusive domain of the small elite who have produced and consumed it in the past, for 'art belongs to the people. Its roots must be deeply implanted in the very thick of the labouring masses.'[40] Contrary to prescribed theory, the political and social revolution in Russia preceded the cultural revolution, preceded the normal development of bourgeois civilization. But this should not deter us from the task of socialist construction, for we can now achieve 'the prerequisites for that definite level of culture in a revolutionary way.'[41]

The Limits of Critique

Lenin's commitment to the democratization of all culture as a pre-condition for full self-government again reveals his profoundly libertarian aspirations. His emphasis on the acquisition of the basics is likewise apposite, for how could the people participate actively in the construction of socialism if the great majority of them remained illiterate? But one of the problems with Lenin's formulation of the question of cultural revolution is that the *critical* moment in the appropriation of bourgeois culture almost always remains vague and understated. As Carmen Claudín-Urondo has argued, Lenin tends to see the problem as one of a linear acquisition of culture rather than a simultaneous *transformation* of that culture.[42] The ideological elements of bourgeois culture are played down in favour of the neutral or historically progressive ones. It is simply a matter of combining proletarian state power with bourgeois culture. Lenin's post-1917 writings seem to suggest that he would have seen no need for a cultural revolution if socialist transformation had begun in the more developed Western capitalist countries, or had Russia itself advanced further along the capitalist road.

It is not as if the transformative moment of cultural acquisition is ignored, however. In a 1913 article on the national question, for instance, Lenin had articulated what was perhaps his most forthright critical position. Arguing that democratic and socialist elements arise in every national culture where there are exploited people, he asserts that it is nonetheless true that the dominant culture, which organizes and gives general form to the experience of the masses, is bourgeois culture. The general national culture is that of the landlords, the clergy, and the bourgeoisie. Hence, 'in advancing the slogan of "the international culture of democracy and of the world working-class movement," we take *from each* national culture *only* its democratic and socialist elements; we take them *only* and *absolutely* in opposition to the bourgeois culture and the bourgeois nationalism of *each* nation.'[43] And in his dispute with the movement for proletarian culture—Prolecult—in 1920, his position was again essentially critical: the best elements of the existing culture must be developed '*from the point of view* of the Marxist world outlook and the conditions of life and struggle of the proletariat in the period of its dictatorship.'[44]

But this critical position was never well developed, and after 1917 it tended to become almost completely submerged beneath the dominant conception of cultural revolution as the mere appropriation of bourgeois culture by the backward Russian masses. The two components of socialism—proletarian state power and bourgeois knowledge and technique—must simply be brought together into the happy union for which they were destined. Talk of constructing a new proletarian culture was quite premature. 'For a start,' Lenin noted in 1923, 'we should be satisfied with real bourgeois culture; for a start, we should be glad to dispense with the cruder types of pre-bourgeois culture, i.e., bureaucratic culture or serf culture, etc.'[45] He spoke as if there were a set of neatly predetermined stages through which the people must go in their cultural liberation, first at the school of the bourgeoisie. Whatever new socialist culture was to arise 'must be the *logical* development of the store of knowledge mankind has accumulated under the yoke of capitalist, landowner, and bureaucratic society.'[46] As Claudín-Urondo notes, it is remarkable that Lenin characterizes this development as logical. The connotation of the Russian phrase is that of a normal, regular, law-like process, rather than a dialectical or contradictory one. The element of change or revolutionary rupture is overwhelmed by the continuity of natural progression.[47]

This kind of conception precluded a specific revolutionary struggle on the terrain of ideology, as was propounded by the Prolecult movement. On the basis of a theory that the political, economic, and cultural spheres were relatively autonomous, Prolecult argued for a distinct movement of conscious intervention and transformation in culture in order to foster socialist consciousness in every area of daily life, including those in which elements of bourgeois ideology coexisted with a high degree of conscious political militancy (authoritarianism in the party, for example). By no means did Prolecult advocates reject all previous culture, as some critics have wrongly held.[48] But they did give pride of place to the critical aspects of any cultural appropriation, with a view to forging a new and distinct socialist consciousness. The elements of general human value must be clearly and vigorously separated from the ideological components of bourgeois culture. Only a new culture and consciousness, it was argued, could stabilize and solidify the gains of the political and economic revolution. And such consciousness would not arise from the mere acquisition of bourgeois culture or as the automatic by-product of technological and economic development. The class struggle remained to be won on the level of ideology.[49]

The Prolecult movement had many shortcomings, of some of which Lenin was acutely aware. Many of the artists trained in Prolecult studios were, to the dismay of its leaders and theoreticians, prone to every passing modernist fad (futurism, for example). Some developed an imagery and mythology of the collective activity of the working class that was closer to the automatism of robots than to the conscious association of autonomous individuals.

Here again, Gastev stood at the extreme, though his work was sharply criticized by others in the movement. All cultural cooperation with bourgeois specialists who had not adopted the Marxist world view was rejected out of hand and the peasantry was ignored both as an object of educational/cultural activity and as a source of progressive values. Prolecult activity was often highly sectarian and exclusivist, as adherents claimed for themselves alone the right to certify authentic proletarian culture. Like Lenin himself, they failed to link the development of new forms of solidarity and new incentives for work to the extension of democratic forms of self-management in the state and the economy, as the Workers Opposition and the Left Communists before them had proposed.

The party, however, at the urging of Lenin, intervened against the movement—which until 1920 had enjoyed considerable support from and independence of the Commissariat of Education—only when it demanded full power for itself in the cultural field, independent of all state and party organs. Thereafter it was to be strictly subordinate to the Commissariat. But the real theoretical difference lay in Lenin's rejection of the need for a specific struggle in the domain of ideology to create a new socialist culture.

Capitalism, he held, had already provided the elements required for socialist construction: discipline and organization. And the proletarian state had laid the basis for a discipline that would be comradely, no longer motivated by the fear of starvation. Thus, against 'all these intellectual fads and "proletarian cultures" ... I advocate the ABC of organization. Distribute grain and coal insuch a way as to take care of every good pood—this is the object of proletarian discipline.... If you solve this elementary and extremely simple problem of organization, we shall win.'[50] Once again the questions of socialist consciousness and cultural transformation were subsumed under those of administrative organization and technical control.[51]

The administrative-technical approach became predominant even in Lenin's direct attempts to stem the tide of bureaucracy in state institutions. The Workers and Peasants Inspectorate, originally intended as a means of involving the mass of the people in controlling the activities of state officials, itself degenerated into a hopelessly bureaucratic agency. Very few of its staff were ordinary workers and peasants, and those who did participate, lacking any basic and regularized power to effect policy, were often manipulated by those whose activities they were supposed to oversee, or were simply absorbed into one or another bureaucracy themselves.[52]

It was naively thought, as in the recommendations for expanding the party Central Committee, that the infusion into positions of authority of people of working class or peasant origin would significantly curtail bureaucratic practices and bring the apparatuses closer to the rank and file. For the most part, however, these administrators of plebeian origin soon became full-fledged bureaucrats in their own right. Without the constraints of genuine popular control by the constituencies from which they came, they often exhibited abusiveness befitting the more tyrannical of the old *chinovniki*.[53]

Lenin, however, while recognizing the failure of the Inspectorate, did not seek to devise new methods of struggle or new ways to involve the masses, but further limited his approach to seeking more effective means of executive control. In March 1922 he forcefully argued: 'We do not need new decrees, new institutions or new methods of struggle. *What we need is the testing of the fitness of our officials; we need executive control....* *To test men and verify what actually has been done*—this, this again, this alone is now the main feature of all our activities, of our whole policy.'[54]

On bureaucracy, he noted on another occasion, '*we still have a great deal to learn from the capitalist.*'[55] And in his last reflection on the problem in March 1923, he spoke not of broadening but of narrowing mass participation. The Workers and Peasants Inspectorate was to be reduced to three or four hundred people, and these were not to be enlisted from the general population, but had to be 'irreproachable Communists.' No longer were people to learn the skills of administration while participating in the control functions of the Inspectorate. Now they were to be screened beforehand for their special knowledge of the state apparatus, and were to be sent to Taylorist labour research institutes for further training in the principles of the scientific organization of labour—a point he reiterated more than any other. Special delegations were to be sent to Germany, the United States, Britain, and Canada to study how the capitalists organized labour and administration.[56]

Lenin's other recommendations for fighting bureaucracy were likewise strictly circumscribed by a system of tight party controls. The relative trade-union independence, for instance, that was seen as necessary if the unions were to protect the workers from the bureaucratic distortions of the state (as well as from the newly revived capitalist firms during the NEP), was undermined by the persistent subordination of the unions to the party. The primary functions of the unions were to *mediate* disputes between workers and management, to promote and train factory managers recruited from the working class, to draw up wage scales, and to operate disciplinary courts. They were to help in the staffing of various state economic organs, but were to have no direct control over the operation of individual enterprises or the economy as a whole. Even limited forms of workers control were no longer to interfere in the complete freedom of the individual managers. The proposals of the Workers Opposition for the devolution of management functions to the trade unions within an overall framework of control by a democratized Communist Party were still proscribed as syndicalist heresy. Granted, Lenin recognized that there were contradictions between methods of persuasion and methods of coercion. But party dictatorship was not acknowledged as one of them. Rather, the party was seen as standing above these contradictions, settling the disputes and conflicts they might generate. Except for the use of 'special tact', no other method was proposed for overcoming them.[57]

Throughout Lenin's last considerations on the problem of bureaucracy he never questioned the principle of party dictatorship, nor even, it seems, the prohibition of organized factions within the ruling party. Soviet democracy could hardly become an antidote to bureaucracy unless the people had the ability to choose between alternative social policies and development strategies. Lenin's weakly articulated version of what was later to become the 'mass line' theory of leadership in China was hardly an effective substitute. Although the theory and practice of the mass line has proven capable of mobilizing the people for the construction of socialism and of checking the consolidation and rigidification of bureaucracy, even at its best it contains fundamentally authoritarian elements and has yet to prove itself adequate to the tasks of building a socialist democracy.[58] And the role of mass initiative as a direct check upon the activities of state and party officials has a considerably more muffled resonance in Lenin's theory than in Mao's. Even the (powerless) non-party conferences are to be abandoned if they provide a platform for socialist opposition.[59] No new institutions, no new methods of struggle are necessary, only better executive control. As Moshe Lewin has argued, Lenin 'approached the problems of government more like a chief executive of a strictly "elitist" turn of mind,' than as a Marxist.[60] Because the problem of bureaucracy was too often seen as merely a holdover from tsarist times, Lenin's primary focus remained fixed on organizational realignments that would allow the party leadership to exert effective executive control over the old bureaucrats in a way that emulated rational capitalist administration. New commissions were to be set up, old ones expanded or contracted, existing ones merged in the never-ending search to perfect elite control of an unwieldy apparatus. Trotsky reports that shortly before his death Lenin was about to propose yet another special commission of the Central Committee to fight bureaucratism.[61] Nor was it ever clear how the merged Workers and Peasants Inspectorate and Central Control

Commission of the party was to be subordinate to the party as a whole, since the Congress had lost its authority; nor how its members, appointed by the Orgburo, were to control the very authorities (most notably the General Secretary, Stalin) who appointed them.[62]

Lenin seems never to have considered reviving some form of genuine soviet democracy as an antidote to bureaucratization. Even the party-dominated soviets were not to be allowed to interfere with the decisions of the State Planning Commission, to which Lenin proposed to grant legislative powers.[63] The separation of legislative and executive powers that had been proposed by oppositionists like Osinsky continued to be seen as bourgeois parliamentarism, whereas in fact the so-called revolutionary fusion of powers served as a rationalization for the nearly complete preoccupation of soviet bodies with administration and propaganda. Nor was the Soviet Central Executive Committee, which had the greatest potential as a revolutionary democratic legislature, allowed to function as a genuinely deliberative parliamentary body. As Erik Olin Wright has argued, Weber's astute insights on the potential role of parliaments in organizing bureaucratic accountability and generating dynamic and responsive political leadership had no place in Lenin's thinking. 'Nowhere ... does Lenin emphasize the specifically *political* dynamic at work in the reproduction and extension of bureaucratic structures in the post-revolutionary state apparatus.'[64] If popular participation was primarily a matter of administration, and politics the prerogative of the party, then administrative adjustments, along with cultural and economic development, would eventually solve the problem of bureaucracy. It was only with the excrescence of the Stalinist bureaucracy in the thirties that these premises were seriously challenged by a major Bolshevik theorist. Only then did Trotsky, one of the original critics of Lenin's theory of the party, propose that the freedom of Soviet parties, free elections, and rights of criticism were essential conditions for undermining the bureaucratic autocracy.[65]

Lenin's analysis of bureaucracy does have the merit of having posed some of the basic questions concerning its social roots and possible transformation. If Russian society was not to be administered in a strictly top-down fashion from its urban centres, then the peasants would have to be drawn into national life. Illiteracy would first of all have to be eliminated, and the networks of communication and exchange with the cities developed. If the peasants were to be progressively drawn into the work of socialist construction, various forms of cooperatives would require vigorous inducements. Only the firm alliance of the working class and peasantry could guarantee the mass basis necessary for socialist construction. Nor was Lenin wrong to stress the benefits of rational bureaucratic organization and executive control. Otherwise an efficient and responsive administrative apparatus could not have been achieved on the scale necessary, especially given the persistent obstruction and lack of commitment to revolutionary goals by the old tsarist officials. Radical democratic methods could never have secured regularized supervision of bureaucratic procedures. And rational bureaucratic administration was preferable to, and possibly could even have acted as a bulwark against, the personalized domination and intimidation of a Stalin.[66] More strongly than most Marxists before him, Lenin emphasized that socialist construction requires not only the transformation of objective social structures but also the transformation of the people themselves. After the political revolution, a prolonged process of cultural revolution would lie ahead, for socialism must inevitably be built of the human material inherited from capitalist and (in the case of Russia) pre-capitalist social formations. In *State and Revolution* he had already recognized that socialism would have to be constructed 'with human nature as it is now, with human nature that cannot do without subordination, control, and "managers".'[67]

His theory of the party, however, and his more general productivist and evolutionist attitudes towards socialist development, narrowly constricted his approach to the resolution of the fundamental dilemma of how to begin socialist construction with the 'human material' inherited from capitalism while at the same time opening up the greatest possibilities for self-transformation. The popular initiative required for such creative self-transformation was all too often restricted by the well defined political and bureaucratic prerogatives of the party. No mass mobilization of the people without close party direction was conceivable, for the party alone commanded correct political consciousness. Any form of mass participation and control that threatened to interfere with the model of strict capitalist efficiency was excluded. Such an approach made it increasingly impossible to distinguish between the timidity inherited from the old order and the apathy and cynicism induced by the continued application of unnecessary authoritarian and administrative controls. Although the line between the unnecessary and the inevitable is often difficult to draw, the only way to determine it in practice is to allow sufficient scope for mass initiative, for trial and error, for a learning process based on the feedback of relatively free self-activity.

But Lenin, who tirelessly reiterated the principle that socialist construction could not be achieved by the vanguard alone, continued to retreat from the implied conclusions. No new institutions, nor even the revival of old ones like the factory committees, were necessary to counter the trends towards bureaucracy. No new methods of struggle and mass mobilization. Organizational tampering, bureaucratic reshuffling, executive control, the cooptation of individual rank-and-file workers and peasants into the apparatus, and the rationalization of this apparatus according to the latest techniques of capitalist labour and management research—these would suffice. Power would devolve to the workers' own organizations only after the workers were fully trained and competent, only after they had fully appropriated the culture of the bourgeoisie. As Claudín-Urondo has so neatly noted, in this approach the proletariat is locked into a 'sort of nursery school of history where, whichever way it turns, it is always the student "who does not know" of one educator or another.'[68]

How long such a situation could last before the powerless students completely retreated from active participation in socialist construction and the bureaucratic teachers fully consolidated their own privileged positions, Lenin did not say. But there seemed little reason for serious concern, as long as the state controlled the major means of production. As Lenin had argued in 1920: 'The victorious proletariat has abolished property, has completely annulled it—and therein lies its domination as a class. *The prime thing is the question of property.* As soon as the question of property was settled practically, the domination of the class was *assured*.'[69] Later developments were to prove otherwise.

Part Three

The Russian Experience in Comparative Perspective

Workers control and council democracy were inextricably linked to the first socialist revolution. But they were hardly unique to Russia. Movements for workers control emerged on a broad scale in the wake of the First World War, and revolutionary situations of dual power arose in several countries. Coherent lines of theoretical demarcation arose in response to the new movements and the new forms of state crisis. And even as the terms of debate and organizational allegiances have shifted over time, the issues raised have remained crucial for socialist movements.

In the following chapters these issues will be analysed from a comparative historical perspective. The experience of workers control in the period of the First World War, as well as its emergence and institutionalization in a variety of contexts throughout the century, permit a broader understanding of Russian developments and their long-term potential. This, of course, can be assessed only in relation to the Stalinist alternative that triumphed little more than a decade after the radical democratic experiments of 1917.

Comparative analysis of the first post-war period will also serve as the basis for a partial evaluation of some of the theoretical debates to which they have been intimately connected. The councilist perspective of Gramsci and Pannekoek, in particular, will be critically analysed in terms of trade-union and factory-committee forms of organization.

Labour, Control, and Ideology

Workers Control and the First World War

The struggle of workers to control their own productive activities has been perennial, encompassing various stratagems—formal and informal, deliberate and spontaneous—to set their own pace and style of work and to resist the routine of the clock and the discipline of the boss. As David Montgomery has noted, workers control of production has been 'a chronic battle in industrial life which assumed a variety of forms.'[1]

The more deliberate attempts to regulate production by workers with highly developed skills and craft traditions have received the most attention from historians, but resistance to hierarchical authority at work has scarcely been limited to such workers. During the First World War and the immediate post-war period this struggle assumed new forms for sectors of the European working classes. For the first time, the efforts of skilled workers to control their own jobs grew into mass struggles to wrest control of production from the capitalist class and to lodge it in organs democratically constituted by the workers themselves. Those skilled workers who had previously been in the forefront of job-control struggles began to create organizational forms that promised to transcend craft boundaries and to include the mass of less skilled workers in the general project of democratic management. Truly mass struggles were waged to give specific institutional form to the socialist project of reappropriating the means of production and transforming the relations of production. The historic battles for labour dignity received innovative institutional expression, and significant aspects of the class division of labour were challenged.

Although rudimentary conceptions of workers control could be found in the socialist, anarchist, and syndicalist writings of previous decades, it was only with the rise of mass movements for control that the vocabulary of the socialist left began to incorporate the idea of industrial democracy. That theoretical shift, of course, has hardly been even or unilinear. Indeed, it is one of the great ironies of the period that the country in which workers control had advanced furthest in practice was the one in which it was most thoroughly expunged from theory.

The First World War generated peculiar conditions for workers protest and organization, and accelerated certain underlying trends that shaped the contours of struggle. The industrial working classes experienced a noticeable (though differential) decline in their living and working conditions in all the belligerent countries of Europe—a decline that contrasted sharply with the general drift of previous decades. Galloping inflation reduced the real wages of most workers, though increased employment opportunities for women and children compensated for this among certain families. Only a thin stratum of the most highly skilled workers in the war industries were able to score wage gains that kept pace with the constant price rises.

General working conditions deteriorated as hours were lengthened and protective legislation (where it existed) often suspended or ignored. Workplace discipline intensified severely, especially for those draft-age males affected by the various forms of labour mobilization and special exemption. Labour mobility was itself curtailed, though never completely or effectively. Shortages of food, housing, fuel, and other necessities became increasingly severe as the war dragged on. They not only aggravated the tribulations of the working classes, among whom the incidence of undernourishment and sickness rose considerably, but also starkly revealed the differential capacities of the various classes, especially wherever the black market served as a necessary supplement and alternative to official rationing policies. Awareness of the immense profits being made on the war also contributed to the mounting sense of unequal sacrifice and reward, and fuelled the anti-war sentiments that continued to swell as the initial patriotic enthusiasm slackened and the war came to be seen as endless and senseless.

While the war brought about a relatively abrupt and dramatic reversal of pre-war trends towards a general (though not uninterrupted) improvement of conditions, it simultaneously led to rising expectations about the role of the working classes in the national polity, and also created labour-market conditions favourable to enhanced working-class power. The very nationalism used to mobilize the workers behind the state became a two-edged sword that cut in the direction of greater popular participation and social reform as well as labour integration. Indeed, labour's cooperation in the war effort had been achieved only with explicit or implicit promises of reform, some of which were not to be postponed even until the war's end. And the war-induced labour shortage provided the leverage—particularly in war-related industries—for workers to press their demands in the face of the two major restrictive factors: state repression (including dispatch to the front) and trade-union opposition or lack of support. The threat wildcat strikes posed to the war efforts of the respective governments and to the swollen wartime profits of the owners was responsible for the relatively high proportion of settlements favourable to the workers.[2]

The war also accelerated trends towards more rationalized production: serial techniques, the use of chronometry, piece-rates, and bonuses. In fact, a major structural transformation in industry had been under way since at least 1890, and provided the basis for the worldwide economic growth that had followed the long depression. The 'second industrial revolution' in steel, electricity, and chemicals was transforming production processes, and scientific management ideologies and techniques spread throughout Europe. But the peculiar suitability of such methods to the wartime bulk production required especially in munitions, the direct and indirect state support in the form of guaranteed markets and profits and preference for uniform standards, and the sudden and severe shortage of skilled labour as a result of the call-ups, provided the impetus for a real take-off in this regard. The metal and machine industries were most directly affected, but they were not alone. The industries producing for the war experienced not only a hugh growth in their work forces, but a disproportionate increase in the number of semi- and unskilled workers, mainly women, peasants, and youth.

The introduction and extension of rationalized production methods and scientific managerial techniques, of course, was a direct threat to the power and position of most of the more highly skilled workers, those excluded from the limited opportunities for advancement (into the supervisory hierarchy, the tool rooms, and so on) created by the new methods. The relative monopoly on productive knowledge and technique the skilled workers possessed had allowed them a degree of informal control over the process of production, the pace of work, the amount of output, and the training of new workers. This informal control was sometimes formalized in union work rules imposed on the owners unilaterally and not subject to bargaining. The extent of such job control, however, varied considerably from industry to industry, country to country. Even in the British engineering works most directly affected by the war, the dilution of skill had progressed considerably in previous decades under the impact of new machinery. A long craft tradition and strong craft-union muscle had been relatively effective in maintaining the old rates for de-skilled work. But the objective basis for this kind of response was rapidly being undermined by wartime transformations, which received ideological and political impetus from the presence of a foreign threat.

In the war industries on the continent craft control had never been as strong as in Britain, and there was even less possibility of successfully resisting the introduction of new methods. The expansion of the number of dilutees during the war tended to strengthen management's hand against the skilled workers on questions of discipline, and intensified the workers' fears of becoming expendable and hence subject to duty at the front.

But most conflicts seem to have centred on wages: the differential between skilled and less-skilled rates, the wages of the hordes of new recruits, and the establishment of piece-rates for those who had been shifted off hourly scales. Hourly wage scales and piece-rates were a constant issue of contention under conditions of steep inflation (which continued into the post-war years in Germany, Italy, and France). The actual process of establishing wages seems to have remained as sharply contested as it had been, for instance, when chronometry was first introduced in the Renault factories in 1912 and the workers insisted that their own delegates participate in its application (the famous *grève du chronométrage*). Piece-work itself was a focus of some struggle. A prominent slogan of the Free Trade Unions in Hamburg, for instance, captured the widespread feeling: *Akkord ist Mord*—piece-work is murder.[3]

The burgeoning of demands for direct representation and inter-vention by workers at the workshop and factory level was the result of these· changes. The war, however, not only produced peculiar conditions of struggle and accelerated long-term changes in the labour process, but also bred major political transforma-tions that, in turn, gave further impetus to the fight to democratize production. In the victorious parliamentary democracies, par-ticularly Britain and France, political crisis was least pronounced. In Italy, where the social and economic costs of victory were far higher, political crisis erupted within a parliamentary system that only recently had extended the mass base of representation. This crisis, compounded by the uncertain reliability of the coercive ap-paratuses in the wake of the war, encouraged popular challenges in the factories and on the land.

But the dynamic relation between political and economic demo-cratization in a period of crisis was clearest in the defeated auto-cratic states. The overthrow of the Kaiser and the establishment of Workers and Soldiers Councils in Germany afforded the process of democratization of the workplace some degree of political en-couragement and protection. Demands for participation by the workers spread to a great variety of sectors (including state workers and clerks), at least partly as a natural extension of poli-tical democratization. The resolution of dual power in favour of a parliamentary state that was largely hostile to socialism and workers control finally curbed this process.[4]

In Russia the overthrow of the tsar and the establishment of organs of soviet power enormously facilitated the extension of workers power at the point of production. Unlike in Germany, however, this power spread constantly as the administrative and coercive capacities of the soviets themselves were progressively enhanced. But this dual movement of political and economic democratization was rooted in the wartime economic dislocation that had been far more severe than in any other country. The most extensive and intensive development of workers control in this period thus occurred in the country with the least democratic national state and the economic structure least capable of total war mobilization. Both these factors, under conditions of continued struggle against counter-revolution, circumscribed the possibilities for institutionalizing the forms of economic democracy they had so greatly fostered. Revolutionary state-building required the transfer of large numbers of the most qualified workers from the factories and their committees to the new apparatuses of political and military power. Prolonged economic disruption further transformed the urban working class and imposed tasks of economic reconstruction that strictly limited the democratization of production. The war had been the great facilitator—but also the great debilitator.

Divisions of Labour and Democratic Forms

A central feature of all the movements for workers control in this period is that they were dominated by skilled workers. This reflected both the favourable labour-market conditions that encouraged protest, particularly among the skilled in the war industries, and the peculiar threats posed by the phase of accelerated rationalization. But it also mirrored broader aspects of the inherited divisions of labour and the concomitant distributions of cultural and political skills. Indeed, these movements drew upon and in some ways reproduced inequalities that were, in other fundamental ways, challenged by the very forms of representation forged in the struggle against capitalist management.

The skilled workers dominated the movements because they were the most competent of the workers technically and administratively—attributes that became more important as the movements spread beyond particular workshops and as actual control of production was attempted (in Russia and, to a lesser extent, Germany, and in Italy with the factory occupations). Skill and sex distinctions usually coincided in industry. Patriarchal cultural patterns reinforced divisions between leaders and led along sexual lines, however, and wartime shortages and long rationing lines exacerbated the problems of the participation of women in the affairs of the workplace. Skilled male workers also tended to have the most developed political cultures, including experience in the political and economic organizations of working-class struggle. Even in Russia, where the gap between previous trade-union organization and factory committees was much greater than in other countries, the committees were able to draw upon the resources of the parties, particularly the Bolshevik party, whose cadre were primarily skilled workers. Finally, although the intellectuals like Gramsci, Korsch, and G.D.H. Cole helped articulate ideologies of workers control, it was the historical experience of skilled workers in determining their own work patterns and rhythms that provided the material basis for the development of thoroughly democratic and universalist conceptions of liberated labour.

The less skilled workers tended to be more instrumental in their attitudes towards work, their demands focusing not on control, but on wages, conditions, and treatment by supervisors.[5] But skilled workers, even where craft control had been quite limited (as in Russia compared with Britain and the United States), were able to translate their own productive practices into more general ideological conceptions that promised to provide the institutional framework for the participation of the less skilled in the inevitably long and contradictory process of overcoming unnecessary hierarchies in production.

The skills of the more privileged workers were thus an organizational and ideological asset in the movements for workers control. There has yet to be a struggle for workers control or institutionalized participation in the management of production that has not been dominated by the more skilled (and male) workers.[6] Yet skill was hardly an unambiguous asset, since the relative privilege and narrow exclusiveness of the skilled workers were often quite manifest, reflecting basic contradictions rooted in the division of labour. It was not the case, as Gramsci held, that solidarity was incarnate in production itself. His view conformed to some of the peculiar characteristics of the Turin proletariat, among whom craft traditions and corporatist consciousness were much weaker than in most other labour movements. But it also exhibits the limits of Gramsci's critique of the capitalist division of labour, which did not find wide gradations in expertise problematic, but considered them as functionally necessary and hence the basis for a solidarity rooted in the mutual recognition of indispensability.[7] This idealization of unitary interests rooted in productive functions ignores the contradictory and conflictual dynamic involved. So, however, does the antipodal position of those German and Italian historians who interpret the council movement as merely the corporatist struggle of skilled workers threatened by rationalization and striving to ensconce themselves at the summit of the hierarchical organization of production.[8]

The dynamic of struggle was determined not by privileges of skill or the interdependencies of productive functions, but by a range of political, organizational, and ideological factors that interacted with these. Such factors included the previous extent of rationalization, the form of union organization, the degree of mobilization of the less skilled workers, cultural and ideological formations in the working-class movements, the extent to which alternative forms of production and power appeared as possible solutions to crisis, and the forms of council democracy themselves.

In British engineering, for instance, various syndicalist, industrial unionist, and guild socialist ideologies helped 'to transform this narrow demand (for craft control) into a wider movement for workers control.'[9] Under conditions of wartime dilution, skilled engineers were able partly to transcend their former exclusiveness through periodic solidarity with the less skilled on questions of wages, food, and the war, and through demands for all-grades organization. But in the absence of a general political crisis at the war's end and more vigorous pressure from the less skilled, the 'ambiguous inheritance'[10] of the craft tradition was resolved towards the pole of exclusiveness.

In the German and Italian metal industry, where dilution had proceeded further and the unions were more industrialized in structure, solidarity between skilled and unskilled workers was more pronounced. And wherever factory-council organizations had influence, wage differentials were narrowed. In Russia, skilled workers dominated the factory committees, and the less skilled workers seem to have accepted this on practical grounds. Yet struggles occurred within the general assemblies over wages, discipline, and layoffs. Unskilled and women workers were highly mobilized, and were thus able to use the organizational forms of factory democracy to assert their interests. Oppressive supervisors were often removed, working conditions improved, and wages preferentially increased for the lowest categories. Skilled workers, among whom egalitarian values were pronounced, often displayed noteworthy solidarity on the latter issue.[11] The opportunities for expanding workers power economically and politically created more favourable terrain for bridging the divisions between the skilled and unskilled.

In all these council organizations, however, the form of democratic participation played a relatively autonomous role. Even though all the movements drew upon (and hence in some ways reinforced) the inequalities of existing divisions of labour, democratic and universalist forms tended to foster an egalitarian dynamic of their own. This is true of almost all subsequent workers control projects as well. In Spain during the civil war, in Chile under Allende, and in Yugoslavia, democratic forms of participation have generally narrowed wage differentials and have sometimes had egalitarian educative effects as well. Only in post-liberation Algeria, where unskilled workers tended not to be mobilized, and often clung to highly traditional forms of deference to authority, were the forms of *autogestion* frequently used to foster the narrow interests of the skilled workers.[12] Factory councils, while they have generally not launched frontal assaults on the capitalist division of labour, and could conceivably be stabilized alongside it,[13] have tended to challenge important aspects of inequality and to provide significant opportunities for participation by and education of the less skilled. Much more than the earlier forms of craft control, which kept unskilled workers in a strictly subordinate and often quite arbitrary position in the productive hierarchy, the forms of workers control that arose in Europe during the First World War and have taken root in other countries since, have challenged the hierarchical division of labour in significant ways. Formal workplace democracy, while not sufficient to break down the unnecessary hierarchies, has historically appeared as the initial crucial step.

In Russia, where control and exercise of actual managerial functions developed furthest in this period, formal democracy was important in at least two other ways that were relevant to the division of labour: supervision of the experts and responsibility for self-discipline. In both cases, the committees established by the workers challenged traditional relationships and yet pursued strategies that generally recognized the practical limitations imposed by these relationships. In regard to the experts, workers used their committees to affirm their own dignity in the face of a long history of abuse, and to limit technical sabotage. Some rudimentary efforts were made to get the experts to share in manual labour. But on the whole, the committees were pragmatic in recognizing the limits of dispensing with technical and administration experts, or of levelling their material privileges. Skilled workers in particular seem to have been most cognizant of the technical requirements of industrial production, and were in the forefront of committee attempts to establish relations of mutual trust and clear lines of authority.

The leadership of the committee movement fully recognized the need to retain specialists, but sought to limit their powers to the execution of policies democratically determined by the workers. The committees, in short, did not indulge in mindless attacks on the role of experts in the division of labour, but they were concerned about checking their power. Anarcho-syndicalists and Left Communists, who generally agreed with this approach, articulated more coherently the danger of new forms of domination unless democratic controls were established. This combination of democratic challenge to the powers of the experts and pragmatic recognition of the constraints imposed by the historical weight of the division of labour was a universal feature of workers-control proposals in this period. Since then, workers involved in control have paid prime attention to the practical tasks of maintaining production. Success has been registered even when executive hierarchies were maintained more or less intact.[14]

In regard to work discipline as well, the factory committees took up the challenge of creating new forms that were more consistent with the workers' struggle for dignity, and yet would not impede the requisites of industrial production in very difficult circumstances. In the early months, the owners continued to sabotage production, workers were often not paid, the supply of fuel and raw materials was constantly disrupted by the breakdown in transport, a double reconversion was imposed on many plants in military production, and the provisioning of food was substandard—sometimes critically so—for several years. Before the civil war, when conditions worsened dramatically, the factory committees produced some noteworthy successes in the area of self-discipline. The initial decline in productivity after October was reversed within a few months. Even in areas such as the Urals, which were characterized by persistent peasant traditions, workers control was quite successful until disrupted by the civil war. The committees seem to have been the most effective organization in regard to work discipline, and did not shrink from imposing severe penalties when they thought it necessary.[15] The civil war undermined these positive achievements, and indeed transformed the working class itself. Its absolute numbers declined by half, and many of the skilled workers who had formed the core of the committees were lost to the Red Army, the party, and the state administration. As Peter Sedgwick has noted, this represented 'a literal hemorrhage of the revolution's social basis'.[16]

Technology and Workplace Organization

The constraints on development imposed by the civil war were severe. Yet the promises were no less real. Industry had to be revived quickly and productivity steadily increased if exchange with the peasantry was to be soundly established and the international vulnerability of the revolutionary state reduced. The only option was to build on the industrial infrastructure bequeathed by tsarism (which the civil war left largely intact, though in great disrepair) and simultaneously to import capital and technological assistance.

A rapid reintegration into the world market was requisite, since the proximate possibilities for indigenous technological development were close to nil. Russia had traditionally been an exporter of farm products, fuel, and raw materials, and an importer of capital goods. The revolution hardly changed its dependent position or its specific forms of leverage in the world economy. It would again be necessary to sell gold, lumber, furs, manganese, oil, sugar, wheat, butter on the world market in order to finance imports of the latest industrial technology. An extended period of autarky in the early stages of industrial reconstruction and expansion was inconceivable. In view of this, and the virtual de-skilling of the industrial working class brought about by civil war and revolutionary state-building, there was little choice but to borrow and copy the most advanced Western technologies and rationalized production methods. Only these promised to raise industrial productivity quickly.[17]

Viewed from a broader perspective, the Russian situation was hardly unique. Production methods had been undergoing steady rationalization before the war, and the war itself marked their irreversible triumph internationally. The industry and currencies of the European belligerents had lost considerable ground to the United States, whose leading industries continued to set the pace in rationalization. In the absence of an effective international strategy, for which European labour movements never had the organizational capacity, some form of accommodation to Taylorism and Fordism became necessary if the national gains of labour were to be protected and extended, even in countries in which the skilled workers constituted the organizational core of the labour movement.

In Germany the unions embraced rationalization, partly in response to the war-induced problems of hyper-inflation and the reparations imposed by the victors. Leaders of the Confédération du Travail in France, vigorous opponents of Taylorism before the war, came to regard it as sensible and necessary if the position of French industry in the world market was to be maintained so as to secure wage increases and the eight-hour day, both central goals of the French working class. Their ambitious reform programme, which included extensive union participation in economic management, was specifically linked to the need for enhanced rationalization.[18] Leaders of the metal unions in Italy had a similar attitude. The response of the Amalgamated Society of Engineers in Britain was but a partial and temporary exception. And the technical and organizational assistance provided to the Soviet state by foreign unions, such as the Amalgamated Clothing Workers of America, was generally based on the assumed necessity for accommodating to the latest and most productive techniques.[19]

In Russia, the constraints were even more severe than elsewhere. The currency had become virtually valueless during the civil war. Industrial productivity was much lower than in any other industrial nation, and was not compensated for by other sectors of the economy. Exchange between agricultural and industrial sectors had been disrupted. Wages were much lower than in pre-war years, and skilled and unskilled alike pressed for both steady increases and reductions in the working day, which only continual rises in productivity could provide. In fact, for the unskilled peasant workers who poured into the factories in the 1920s, the struggle for wages, hours, housing, and secure employment seems to have taken precedence over struggles against the fragmentation of work or piecerates as a form of payment. As in other European labour movements, rationalized production methods often brought a relative improvement in some conditions of employment.[20]

But if accommodation to the latest Western techniques was necessary, the nearly complete and uncritical imitation of them was not. Certain limits were imposed by the technologies themselves, the contractual conditions for their transfer, and the preferred modes of operation of the foreign specialists who advised and often managed, even when formal power rested with Russian authorities. But various forms of modification and workers' participation were possible. And greater efforts could have been made to engage the help of Western unions committed to moderate forms of participation and trade-union control, as was the Amalgamated, whose assistance fostered workers' participation in the setting of norms and rates of pay. As it was, few overtures seem to have been made to potentially sympathetic Western unions, perhaps partly because of the threat this might have posed to the patterns of party domination of the Russian unions.[21]

Given the positive achievements of the factory committees in the initial months of revolution, workers control of production would seem to have held great promise once the emergency of civil war had abated. The core of skilled workers that had staffed the committees had been reduced, but not eliminated. And while the tradition of factory democracy had been seriously weakened, it did at least exist in the twenties, in contrast to 1917, and at least moderate support for participation was manifested among the rank and file. Some factory committees were vibrant organizations closely involved in the daily lives of workers. Opposition circles of workers demanding control, such as the Workers Group, continued to emerge. Even productionist campaigns like the 'socialist emulation' movement that began in 1926 and drew upon a degree of genuine enthusiasm among the workers challenged the authority of managers and specialists. And peasant workers unused to the rigours and rhythms of industrial discipline could be mobilized periodically for greater voluntary output.[22]

The factory committees had proven themselves capable of disciplining workers in the past, and had been willing to take severe measures where necessary. With the stabilization of the food supply in the twenties, however, the problems of absenteeism declined and committees could have been aided by the unfortunate though probably unavoidable levels of unemployment. Resentment of specialists, rooted in long years of abuse, continued to be a major concern that warranted some form of workers control, particularly when labour-market conditions placed the less skilled in a highly vulnerable position.[23] And most studies have shown that reduction of close supervision tends also to reduce absenteeism and turnover and to increase productivity.[24] Job rotation to mitigate boredom and broaden workers' knowledge was also a real possibility that might not have lowered productivity appreciably and perhaps could have even enhanced it in the short run. Simple forms of rotation, especially when linked to in-plant forms of collective education, could have provided the basis for genuine job enlargement. The reduction of the working day by an average of 1.5 hours between 1917 and 1928 (when it stood at 7.4 hours) made such forms of education a real possibility.[25]

Workers control would have had to remain quite limited in the conditions prevailing in Russia in the 1920s. Technical, administrative, and organizational experience in the factory was scarcer than in 1917. Material incentives (whether collective or individual) were meagre, and productivity requirements would inevitably have outstripped freely determined production norms. Most new technologies did not readily lend themselves to direct control by work groups. And the disciplines of factory labour would have remained arduous for those relatively unused to them and for those mired in certain pre-war craft traditions. Perhaps the biggest challenge was to instil industrial skills and work habits in the new peasant workers without reproducing the harshness and brutality of capitalist industrialization, while encouraging commitment, participation, and learning.

The Yugoslav and Cuban experiences have since demonstrated that the formal institution of workers control, although far from a panacea, has real potential in this regard. In Yugoslavia forms of self-management have been relatively successful in inculcating the alien norms of factory life among the many peasants who have taken up industrial work since the Second World War, when the percentage of peasants in the population was roughly similar to Russia in 1917. And although unemployment serves as a whip, it has been modified by disciplinary bodies constituted by workers themselves. Workers councils have nourished the egalitarian values brought by many peasants from the villages, and wage differentials have narrowed. Participation has been positively linked to productivity increases, technological progress, and relatively high growth rates. And at least to some extent, technologies have been selectively generated and borrowed in ways that reinforce egalitarian values and democratic forms of power in the workplace.[26]

In Cuba, where the population had been less broadly mobilized at the time of the revolution, workplaces had severe problems with absenteeism, discipline, and productivity throughout the 1960s. Typical Soviet-style methods, followed first by Guevarist stress on moral incentives and ideological mobilization and later by even stricter regimentation (military supervisors, labour identity cards, imposition of new work norms from above) failed to resolve the problems. It was only when the absolute power of the managers was challenged and participation by workers introduced that productivity began to rise and absenteeism was brought under control.[27]

These experiences demonstrate that it does matter how alien work routines are introduced and that formally democratic methods can be quite consistent with increased productivity even when large segments of the work-force are of recent rural or semi-rural origin. Workplace democracy is relevant not only where industrial cultures are well developed, a view often expressed by Bolsheviks who upheld industrial democracy as a long-term goal. In fact, the chronic inability of Russian Marxism to understand the culture of the peasantry influenced the forms of industrial development that were seen as possible in the 1920s. No sympathetic analysis of village culture and peasant traditions was expressed in the industrialization debates, even in those programmes that would have been less harsh on the villages. In contrast to the hereditary proletariat, the newly proletarianized peasants were viewed simply as backward, ignorant, and petty-bourgeois masses whose indigenous culture was to be extirpated. No attempts were made to tap the positive aspects of village solidarity and peasant egalitarianism, or to construct social forms in the workplace to nurture these in the interests of socialist development. Conscious aid for the traditional *zemlyaki* support networks in the factories and neighbourhoods, for instance, might have been used to cultivate solidaristic commitments and democratic participation in the factories in order to mitigate the alien quality of urban industrial life and mobilize the peasants' deep-seated anti-hierarchical and anti-bureaucratic attitudes in the service of socialist construction, instead of permitting them to evolve into passive resistance to the state and its industrial *chinovniki*. For peasants who were traditionally non-political and suspicious of the state, forms of factory participation that had some continuity with village life might have offered the most promising basis for stimulating a broad democratic political culture.[28]

Because of the Bolsheviks' views of the peasantry, and the dominant productivist discourse on workers control and technological development, very little imagination was brought to bear on the problems of popular participation in the difficult tasks of industrialization that faced the Soviet regime. Production conferences and factory committees were not allowed to interfere in actual production, and were used primarily as mechanisms for imposing more stringent work norms. Workers' suggestions were seldom heeded.[29] Job rotation schemes were dismissed as a waste of time, and in-plant education for collegial management functions neglected in favour of highly personalized opportunities for individual worker managers. Voluntary efforts to raise productivity, such as *subbotniks*, were manipulated, and the party inexorably tightened its control over all levels of workers organizations. The party, in turn, was often so out of touch with rank-and-file workers, that when the seven-hour day was selectively introduced in 1928, for instance, it was in split three-and-a-half-hour shifts that disrupted people's lives.

Even the most minimal forms of participation would have averted such problems. And limited forms of genuine participation tend to lead to greater demands for participation.[30] Even formal democratic participation limiting effective control of production to the more highly skilled and opening technical hierarchies to very slow modification could at least have involved the less skilled in decisions on wages, discipline, and working conditions without undermining productivity and accumulation. This could have encouraged an egalitarian dynamic that might progressively have asserted itself in the course of cultural and economic development. The exact forms and scope of such experiments could have been determined only in practice. Yet the previous results of workers control, and persistent shop-floor struggles against authoritarian and heavy-handed management, indicated some of the limits and possibilities set by the workers themselves. The experiment that was tried instead—forced-march industrialization with more rigid regimentation and neglect of the labour force—quickly encountered those very limits.

The Role of Ideology

While it is certainly true that ideologies do not 'provide *the key* to the nature of revolutionary outcomes', it seems less arguable that they do not 'in any sense'[31] provide some important indications of why revolutions developed in a certain manner, and why some options seemed more practical or morally and politically justifiable than others. Revolutionary outcomes cannot be understood simply by an analysis of the forms of political and structural crises and the organizational capacities available for their resolution, since ideological formations and the modes of their implantation in active historical subjects can determine in significant ways both the nature of crisis and the utilization of potential organizational and administrative resources.

In the Russian revolution, Bolshevik ideology reacted and contributed to crises, and selectively influenced immediate choices in ways that had both short-run consequences and cumulative effects on social development. For instance, the Leninist ideology of class polarization, combined with views that linked communist distribution with state requisitioning of grain, largely determined the specific institutional forms employed to solve the critical problem of feeding the cities. The ideologically induced option to create Committees of Poor Peasants was adopted despite the very accurate warnings of the Left SRs about their political impact and administrative effectiveness. And Bolshevik choices failed to utilize and build upon the potential administrative capacities of the local soviets, which Left SRs and later many local Bolsheviks familiar with the everyday operations of the supply apparatus claimed would be more efficient and less disastrous politically. The ideological illusions of war communism persisted beyond the point that administrative effectiveness or political pragmatism could reasonably be invoked by the central authorities. They were shattered only by popular rebellion in the countryside and the cities. The effects of this lag of ideology behind reality continued to have a cumulative impact into the twenties, even as specific policies were altered. Likewise, the considerable political and administrative resources commanded by the Left SRs, who had been profoundly committed to revolutionary transformation, were dissipated in no small measure because of the ideological blinders of the Bolshevik approach to the peasantry. The ideological practices of the past became part of the material and institutional constraints of the future. In short, crises that were not of the Bolsheviks' own making were often exacerbated, and political and administrative capacities for managing those crises were often rejected as a result of the cognitive content of Leninist ideology.

That administrative and organizational capacities were not predetermined independently of the ideological inclinations of the leadership and cadre is evident in the development of industrial forms as well. The confusion, ambiguity, and contradictions of Bolshevik ideology on workers control before October had a significant impact on the organization and coordination of the factory-committee movement. Efforts by local militants to construct a democratic and administratively effective economic centre failed to receive adequate assistance, partly because Bolshevik ideological conceptions of the apparatuses of the revolutionary state held no place for such a centre. At first this was due to omission as much as bias, though the latter became more prominent in Leninist economic ideology as the revolution moved into its phase of emergency reconstruction. After October, the persistent ideological commitment to state capitalism and dual power in the factories, and the sustained neglect of the practical and principled arguments of the factory-committee leadership, obstructed the struggle against capitalist sabotage and the efforts at rapid economic coordination, thus contributing to disorganization. Only struggle by rank-and-file workers and their committees contained the sabotage and forced *de facto* nationalization. The administrative capacities of both local committees and their coordination organs were not used or developed as they might have been.

At a time when organizational and institutional boundaries were still relatively fluid, ideological preconceptions helped shift the weight of institution-building activity both to unions that had much less experience in administering production and less legitimacy among rank-and-file workers and to state organs whose bureaucratic competencies were so confused and conflictual as to further disorganize what they were intended to control. The failure of the calls for institutional clarity by various oppositions ever to find any sympathetic resonance in the dominant Leninist ideology reveals the extent to which that ideology presumed that the party would afford the system its basic organizational coherence. And the initial failures of institutional coherence only exacerbated the party's tendency to cast itself as the organizational cement of the system at all levels.

The degree to which Leninist ideology on workers control operated according to a relatively autonomous dynamic of its own is revealed by the fact that *none* of the major criticism of the Left Communists or the Workers Opposition was *ever* given serious, principled, and extended consideration, despite the recurrent articulation of these positions, the real support they enjoyed, and the negative consequences of the dominant approach. These consequences were filtered through a discourse that became increasingly incapable of articulating them as anything but the by-product of backwardness or betrayal. It was as a matter of theoretical principle, not as a practical response or temporary compromise warranted by historical conditions, that any link to issues of genuine power over productive activities was systematically filtered out. Thus, in the early and middle twenties, when emergency conditions eased and the most critical choices on the tempo and forms of industrial and agricultural development had yet to be faced, workers control, even in limited forms, was not taken seriously by party leaders. Shlyapnikov continued to voice the programme of the Workers Opposition for several years, and the Workers Group called for workers control and productive trade unions. But despite widespread knowledge of these views in the party, no serious response to them was forthcoming, not even tentative experiments that might have interfered least with the uncontested power of management in production. The ideological reaction formation of 1918, buttressed by the deep structures of productivist logic in Lenin's Marxism, continued to fetter practical imagination and institutional renovation into the twenties and beyond.

Although Leninist ideology contained a relatively autonomous dynamic of its own that blocked recognition of workers control as a constructive form for industrial and social development, and hence left untapped an institutional potential that had proven its considerable value in difficult circumstances, we must not lose sight of the historical context of practical struggles in which this ideology was formed and legitimated among the leaders and cadre who shaped the revolutionary process most decisively. Shop-floor struggles for control of production do not seem to have been prominent in the pre-war Russian labour movement. Traditions of craft control had not been well developed for a number of reasons, among them the weakness of traditional artisan guilds, the late and rapid industrialization, which employed the latest techniques, and the political conditions, which foreclosed the possibilities of the organization of legal craft unions. Because of the autocratic political structures, the struggle for basic trade-union and political freedoms remained predominant, even though the subterranean struggle for dignity and respect in daily relations with supervisory personnel became a constitutive element of working-class culture. The goals of political revolution and democracy preoccupied the leaders of the workers movement. Even as shop-floor struggles for dignity and against the intensified pressures of rationalization became more prominent in the eyes of the rank and file during the war, wartime repression further widened the gap between leading theorists and the ranks, a characteristic effect of autocratic structures. Russian Marxist thought was therefore even less influenced by the practical struggles that developed before and during the war than European Marxism was. Ironically, the labour movement that would face the most challenging tasks of workers control was the one least prepared to do so ideologically. And Russian economic backwardness accentuated the productivist aspects of Marxism, which were themselves in no small measure an ideological response to the material tasks of industrialization in a world where poverty and insecurity were the most pervasive characteristics of working-class life.

The practical struggle for workers control did receive ideological support and articulation from two sources in particular: anarcho-syndicalism and Left Communism. Anarcho-syndicalist activism, however, though a significant influence in some places during 1917, was able to draw upon only a vague ideology that evaded many of the crucial issues of coordination and systemic institution building. Its own organizations had suffered severely from tsarist repression, and did not develop after the February revolution sufficiently to present a serious challenge to the other parties, to some extent because of its own ideological proscriptions against centralism. Its diffuse influence is difficult to gauge, though it was certainly real and may even have contributed pivotal ideas to the leaders of the Petrograd Central Council of Factory Committees.

The Left Communists, on the other hand, developed the critical conceptions of Marxism itself on the issues of labour organization and economic democracy. In their formulation of a wide-ranging programme—perhaps the most elaborate and carefully argued of any group at the time—they developed an analysis that drew directly on Marx's *Capital* and other writings. Yet Left Communist theorizing about workers control was primarily a *response* to the movement, not a source of guidance. The ideological lag was not particularly great in absolute terms. Only a few months after the October revolution, relatively coherent conceptions were worked out, and a poignant critique of the dominant Leninist approach formulated. Yet in 'revolutionary time', when tasks were urgent and institutional structures could not long afford to remain protean, the delay was significant. Immediately after October, when Left Communists were politically and institutionally in a position to have a major impact on the new economic structures, their own economic ideology was largely unformed. By the time they became more coherent, other institutions inimical to their conceptions were entrenched, and the factory-committee movement was very much on the defensive. The theory of economic democracy and the organizational basis of practical struggle were diverging rather than converging, and the onset of the civil war made their unification far more difficult.

During the early period, when the factory-committee movement was most vibrant, its ideological resources, potentially a guide to its future tasks in revolutionary economic reconstruction, were at their most meagre. This movement was essentially defensive and pragmatic in its orientation to local factory problems; the relation between leaders and supporters was constituted primarily in the instrumental calculation of possible benefits.[32] But in the process of attempting to satisfy the largely rational-pragmatic claims of rank-and-file workers in the committee movement, the leading activists were prompted to improvise and selectively borrow ideological conceptions that would guide, inspire, and justify. This improvisation proceeded at a rapid clip alongside the practical efforts to coordinate the movement and respond to problems that could be solved only through systemic organization. In fact, it was probably only the breadth of systemic crisis that motivated such swift program-matic-ideological progress, since the influence of anarcho-syndicalist ideology was not very great, and the Marxism of shop-floor militants was rudimentary at best. As Georges Haupt has argued, 'it is the dynamic of mass mobilization in a period of social tension that renders the workers movement, or more precisely the workers in motion, more susceptible to ideological considerations.'[33]

Nevertheless, without a tradition to build on, the noteworthy ideological achievements of 1917 proved insufficient either to penetrate broad masses of committee activists (not to mention the workers less directly involved), or to impress enough of the party's leaders, whose policies, though also largely motivated by practical concerns, sought much more consistent ideological justification in terms of Marxist theory. As a result, the ideological challenge of economic democracy was pressed exactly when the conditions for denial and repression by the leading theorists were greatest. And not enough of an articulate mass base arose to mount an *independently* effective campaign, particularly in view of the subse-quent dispersal of the critical core of leading committee activists throughout the various apparatuses of the economy and state, where their own relatively privileged positions in the division of labour as skilled and organizationally experienced workers could no longer be held in check by democratic controls, but were instead reproduced and compounded by other mechanisms. In the twen-ties, workers control could have been revived only with the vigorous support of party and union leaders. But the ideological legacy of Leninism made this possibility unlikely.

The problem of ideology in the workers control movements of this period was not unique to Russia. Most pre-war labour move-ments had been concerned primarily with the problems of poverty and unemployment, wages and hours, trade-union organization and, in the more authoritarian states, political freedoms. Second International Marxism had remained predominantly productivist, in no small measure because many of the most pressing problems appeared soluble through political power coupled with rational planning, the efficient use of productive resources, and the pro-gressive development of the latest technologies in the interests of job security, augmented consumption, and the reduction of the burden and duration of toil. In Germany, where the most influential Marxist theorists wrote, there was no strong anarcho-syndicalist movement before the war. The struggles for control on the shop floor had found virtually no resonance in theory, even on the left of the movement, where concern was focused on the mass political strike more than on productive reorganization and workers control.

Anton Pannekoek, the Dutch theorist who was actively involved in the German debates as a critic of Kautsky and who later became a leading theorist of workers councils, began to develop rudimentary conceptions of the councils only in 1919, after both the Russian and German movements had burst onto the historical stage. And it was only much later that more elaborate ideas were developed.[34] Karl Korsch, also a leading council theorist later, had come into contact with British Guild Socialism and French syndicalism before the war. But the emphasis of his own writings had remained cultural. In his case as well, theoretical elaboration came only after the actual movements had developed.[35] In November 1918, then, when political power in Germany was still in flux and the Workers and Soldiers Councils might still have attempted to seize the initiative economically as well as politically, no clearly articulated ideology existed that might have guided and legitimated a struggle for the rapid extension of workers control as the real basis for the socialization being demanded in the higher council organs. The leadership of the new mass movements was too recently formed and theoretically undeveloped to be able simultaneously to lead the struggle on the shop floor around questions of control and the fight in the political council organs around basic issues of programme and power. Leadership and ideology developed further in the course of the mass struggles themselves, and an economic council programme was elaborated and widely propagated in the winter and spring of 1919. But the rise of a leadership with even a minimally coherent ideology articulating the needs of the new movements came too late. The effect of council thinking on the mass of workers was thus very irregular, even in the areas of most intense struggle. Not only was the council leadership unable to coordinate the movement to produce the maximum effect, it was also unable to educate the movement enough to ensure that it would not be derailed by skilful yet meagre concessions and vague promises by the government and the Social Democratic Party. In November ideological coherence around questions of workers control and socialization had been lacking; at the height of the mass movement in early 1919 it had only begun to take shape.[36]

In other European countries, where the opportunities were never as great as in Russia and Germany, the late development of ideologies of workers control was also evident. In Italy, the pre-war syndicalist movement had failed to produce a coherent theory that might guide the post-war upsurge around issues of control, although active syndicalists did have a practical impact outside their traditional strongholds in small industry.[37] It was only with the actual development of the workshop struggles that a group of young Marxists in their twenties, led by Antonio Gramsci, developed theoretical conceptions that placed the factory councils at the centre of political strategy and socialist transformation. The older leaders and theorists had not anticipated such problems. According to the young *ordinovisti*, the councils were to become the material and organizational basis for the creation of a new culture and consciousness, and would prepare the workers both technically and spiritually to run society without the bourgeoisie.

The active propagation of these ideas, with their emphasis on universalist criteria of representation in the councils, facilitated the rapid rise of the movement, particularly in Turin in late 1919 and early 1920. Yet even the mass movement in Turin, where theoretical councilism was most directly linked to practical activity, did not accept many of Gramsci's basic premises. His failure to elaborate a more radical critique of the division of labour, and his explicit appropriation of Taylorist principles of labour organization, left him out of touch with some of the most urgent shop-floor concerns.[38] And on the role of the unions and the tactic of factory occupation, workers in Turin and elsewhere continued to act in ways that violated the spirit of the new councilist strategy.[39]

In Britain the immediate pre-war upsurge in labour militancy and the disillusionment with parliamentary socialism had opened the labour movement to various syndicalist, industrial unionist, and Guild Socialist theories. These, in turn, provided the basis for the ideological translation of craft control into revolutionary workers control. But the latter remained extremely vague as a systemic goal, and was never accepted by the mass of skilled workers, or even the engineers. As a result, it was unable to survive post-war political stabilization and the officialization of stop stewards within the unions.[40]

Despite the significant national and local variation due to trade union, industrial, and political structures and traditions, the overriding characteristic of this period was that relatively coherent and elaborate ideologies of workers control arose only in conjunction with, and predominantly as a response to, actual struggles. The period of dramatic reorganization of production, which in some countries was coupled with severe political crisis brought on by the war, had given rise to mass struggles that pointed beyond craft control and simple economic demands. Marxist and labour theory had been largely unprepared for this, and wherever real opportunities for democratization of production opened up, the practical effects of this ideological underdevelopment were revealed. Even less developed than analysis of the role of democratic forms in production was a more general critique of the class division of labour. Workers raised particular dimensions of this problem in their struggles against Taylorism, and democratic forms contained the dynamic potential for a more fundamental challenge. But it seems to have been only with the consolidation and generalization of Taylorism and Fordism in both capitalist societies *and* the Soviet Union that more coherent theoretical critiques have developed. Korsch is one of the few early exceptions here.[41] In view of Gramsci's theoretical fusion of productivism and council democracy, and even later that of Diego Abad de Santillan, the leading Spanish anarcho-syndicalist theorist, who urged his comrades in the most vibrant revolutionary anarcho-syndicalist union federation in history to model the automobile factories of Barcelona on those of Detroit, Lenin's productivist prescriptions for revolutionary development in backward and beleaguered Russia do not appear exceptional.[42]

11

Factory Committees
and Trade Unions

Gramsci and Pannekoek

New organizational forms emerged from the control struggles during the period of the First World War. Though called by various names at the time, they have since come to be known as factory councils or workers councils. Their distinctive characteristic was that they directly represented workers at the level of the workshop and factory. Despite their variety, their relations with the trade-union organizations were tense, often hostile. In the context of revolutionary crisis in Europe, this antagonism gave rise to a theoretical re-evaluation of the role of various workers organizations in the struggle for socialism. A distinctly 'councilist' perspective emerged, and the trade unions were subjected to the most radical critique to date in the Marxist tradition. In the writings of Gramsci, and later Pannekoek, the Russian experience served as a benchmark, though their knowledge of it was extremely limited. Nor were they aware, it seems, of the theoretical writings and programmatic positions of the Left Communists and the Workers Opposition. For the most part, their inspiration came from Western and Central Europe. An analysis of these experiences, however, as well as that in Russia, reveals serious flaws in councilist thinking, and places its relevance for contemporary movements in question.

In Gramsci's view, the trade unions were organs suited to the struggle for more favourable terms for the sale of labour-power as a commodity, but not to the abolition of the commodity form itself. Industrial legality was a great achievement for the defence of the workers' interests *within* capitalism, but hardly suited to the movement of revolutionary offensive *against* capital. Because the unions were divided by trade, and because one of their functions was to enforce discipline and the collective bargain, they inevitably grew away from the rank and file. They became bureaucratic organs rather than organs of proletarian democracy striving to institute full working-class control over all aspects of production. This could be achieved only by factory committees, which built upon the solidarity incarnate in the production process itself and were the very antithesis of industrial legality, because they refused to trade off control against better wages and conditions. Factory councils would be the material and organizational basis for the creation of a new consciousness, and would prepare workers technically and spiritually to run society without the bourgeoisie. 'All power to the workshop committees,' the *ordinovisti* demanded. These were to be the basis of the new proletarian state. Though they were to cooperate with the unions to make sure that the movement away from industrial legality occurred at the most opportune moment, cooperation was to be achieved through overlapping membership and voluntary association, not formal organizational ties. The radically distinct functions of the factory committees and the trade unions required strict organizational separation.[1]

Pannekoek's pre-war critique of the unions anticipated Gramsci's conception of them as 'vendors of labour-power' that 'operate on the same territory' as capitalism. Their functionality in reproducing capitalist relations was limited only by the fact that capitalism was not a balanced, crisis-free system. Union demands thus remained essentially antagonistic, and union structures were an indispensable element of socialist transformation. The French syndicalist model, which sought to institute workers control over production through direct action and the general strike, could not be the basis of strong and stable union organizations that included the mass of workers, who were interested primarily in moderate improvements in their conditions.[2]

In the post-war period, however, this critique of the unions was radicalized. They were now seen as appropriate *only* to the earlier phase of expanding capitalism, which has irretrievably passed. In the current struggles, their bureaucratization and legalization have made them 'organs of domination of monopolist capital over the working class.' Thus new organs—the workers councils—arise spontaneously and irresistibly. They are completely unlike unions in structure and function. They are neither bureaucratic, nor do they seek an accommodation with capitalism, but strive to secure complete domination by the working class. Unlike the unions, the councils are rooted in organic production groups, where the 'collective will' naturally expresses itself. And in the mass strikes, which are the fertile soil in which the councils grow, all previous and partial forms of workers organization wither. 'Workers Councils are *the* form of organization during the transition period in which the working class is fighting for dominance, is destroying capitalism and is organizing social production.' They are, as they were for Gramsci, the basis for the new proletarian state.[3]

Patterns of Organization

The Italian council movement disappointed Gramsci's hopes and expectations, and a general analysis of the movements in this period suggests very serious flaws in councilist thought, particularly in regard to the relationship between factory councils and trade unions. The resilience of the unions in the face of serious organizational strains was as noteworthy as the weakness of the council structures striving for autonomy. The unions never really lost their dominant role, and the factory committees did more to revitalize than to displace them. In fact, the distinct tendency that finally prevailed everywhere favoured the (re)incorporation of the committees into the unions. A closer examination of the development of these respective forms of organization suggests why this occurred, and why councilism in its most radical form is of limited relevance today.

Pressure for workshop representation had arisen primarily in response to the tightening of labour discipline, the acceleration of rationalization, and the steep inflation that resulted from the war. Favourable labour-market conditions enabled workers to mobilize around these issues, but political and structural factors limited their ability to utilize the unions, particularly their central offices, for this. In those countries with legal and well-established trade unions, such as Britain, Germany, Italy, and France, the political factors were roughly similar. The major union federations had renounced class-struggle tactics that might disrupt the war effort. Their decisions had been conditioned by four factors: the very real possibility of state repression, which threatened to smash their organizations; pressure from the workers themselves, whose nationalistic sentiments often ran deep, and whose anti-militarism was extremely vulnerable in the absence of an effective internationalist strategy for preventing the outbreak of war; the union leaders' reformist politics, which had evolved in the pre-war years in the context of a general, though not uninterrupted or evenly distributed, economic improvement for the working classes; and the possibilities of significant concessions in exchange for official participation and collaboration in the war effort. By the second half of the war, all of the major union federations in these countries had begun to expand considerably. But to maintain favourable government treatment and to seize upon possibilities of further growth and reform at the war's end, they renounced militant tactics and withheld organizational resources from those engaging in them.

The political basis for the unions' lack of response to rank-and-file protest beyond the limited legal channels was complemented by certain structural features of the unions. In the pre-war years they had became relatively stable, bureaucratic, and centralized organizations based primarily on craft associations, with geographical membership jurisdictions. This organizational structure was seen as the only real alternative to the high degree of instability (in terms of membership and concrete gains) that characterized the low-dues, anti-bureaucratic, anti-centralist and class-warfare practices of the syndicalist form of organization. Syndicalist organization had presented a significant challenge to the CGL in Italy, and had characterized many unions in the French CGT before the latter began to adopt more 'traditional' forms of organization in response to the increasing centralization of capital and the demands of the workers themselves for more stable and secure achievements. Craft associations formed the core of the major union federations in these countries, with the exception of the CGT in France, which had made considerable progress towards industrial forms of organization by the time of the war, and further progress during it. But even in France the actual organization of the unskilled and semi-skilled workers proved extremely difficult before the war's end. In Germany, Italy, and Britain a multiplicity of craft associations in each workplace was the rule. And the craft unions exercised hegemony in the labour movement as a whole, and even in many unions with a significant number of unskilled members.

Given the collaborationist, centralized, bureaucratic, and craft character of the trade unions, the rising protest warranted alternative forms of organization. These would have to be able to respond to the immediate problems arising in the workplace, instead of mediating these problems through sections based in geographical units outside the factory. They would have to be able to respond quickly to the ever-changing structure of wage rates, averting cumbersome bureaucratic processes. And they would have to cut across craft distinctions, which changes in the production process were making increasingly outmoded and dangerously divisive.

The relative degree of autonomy of shop-floor forms of representation, however, depended on the structure and policies of the pre-existing union organizations. Where unions were rigidly craft structured and geographically based, or where they were weak or did not exist, shop-floor organizations tended to develop outside the unions. Glasgow and Sheffield in Britain were cases in point. Militant independent shop-stewards movements emerged there partly because the Amalgamated Society of Engineers was so rigidly craft structured, and because its response to the crisis of dilution of skills was essentially conservative, largely ignoring the organization of the less skilled and an all-grades strategy.[4]

In Russia, it was the weakness of the unions at the time of the February revolution that permitted the factory committees, which had some roots in the state-sponsored war-industry committees, to develop so extensively. And even though unions developed quickly thereafter, their growth was loose, disorderly, top heavy, and ridden with jurisdictional disputes and craft divisions. Factory committees thus served as more easily established and immediately responsive surrogates. A distinct tendency towards unification of committees and unions accompanied the ascendancy of industrial over craft forms of organization, and of Bolsheviks over Mensheviks in union leadership positions. Yet organizational merger was impeded by the disintegration of the economy, which increasingly brought the committees' control functions to the fore and rendered the collective bargaining functions of the unions quite secondary. But with the practical resolution of dual power in state institutions and in the factories, the trend towards organizational unification finally triumphed.

The autonomous tendencies of shop-floor representation were limited by the extent to which industrial forms of union organization prevailed. The British munition centres of Coventry and Birmingham offer a striking contrast to Glasgow and Sheffield. In the former cities, dilution had proceeded further in the pre-war period, and the wartime crisis was therefore less acute. The industrially organized Workers Union had a much stronger presence there, and was capable of structurally accommodating shop stewards. Revolutionaries among the stewards were thus deprived of leadership in the struggle for recognition of the stewards' functions.

In the French CGT, and particularly in the metal unions, this pattern was much more general. The unions themselves proposed a system of workshop delegates (*délégués d'ateliers*) to deal with questions of wage adjustments, manner of payment, and working conditions, in the hope that their power would spread and that their organizations, which were structurally congruent with the delegate innovation, would be buttressed. The system that was introduced, while not officially endorsing the unions' proposals, permitted many of the delegate groups to serve in effect as directly elected factory cells of the union. Very few radical councils claiming independence of the unions emerged, despite widespread revolutionary sentiments in the immediate post-war period, especially in the Parisian metal industry. The CGT's vigorous post-war programme calling for nationalization and democratic forms of management, which bore the stamp of its syndicalist heritage even as the unions themselves became more centralized and bargain-oriented, helped contain the aspirations for workers control within the union framework. Autonomism developed least in the country with the most profound ideological consciousness of workers control.[5]

Germany and Italy present situations somewhere between these two poles of autonomization and integration. Many local sections of the Deutsche Metallarbeiter Verband (DMV), the major union in the metal works engaged in war production, had moved towards an all-grades organization. Craft control had never been very strong, and craft organization was further weakened by the massive influx of previously unorganized and often unskilled recruits in the last half of the war. A new mass base arose with little tradition of trade-union discipline and stable organizational work. But the normal channels of protest and leadership challenge within the unions were blocked for the duration of the war. A new stratum of rank-and-file organizers thus came forward to fill the leadership gap. In the larger factories and cities (especially Berlin) this stratum of trade-union functionaries rose to responsible and influential positions without getting quickly coopted into the union bureaucracy, as was usually the case in the smaller factories and cities. Revolutionary *Obleute*, or shop stewards, thus emerged from *within* and drew upon the resources of the various metalworkers' locals that had moved towards an all-grades organization. While the tensions were considerable, the mutual benefits of cooperation were real enough to check the autonomization process.[6]

The factory-committee movement that arose in Italy at the war's end was centred mainly in Turin, the major Italian industrial city producing for the war. As in Germany, the dominant metal-union federation (FIOM) was formally structured in craft sections, with a fairly high degree of sectional consciousness among founders, coppersmiths, and so on. But as in Germany, the actual extent of craft control was not very great—not nearly so much as in Britain before the war. This was especially true in Turin, a city whose fairly recent and breakneck development as an industrial centre was based on a more extensive use of the latest production methods. There was thus little hope of preventing or reversing the trend towards increased rationalization of production. But the issues thus raised required an all-grades approach and a shop-based organization that could not be provided directly by the union. In the interstices of the union organizations internal commissions (*commissioni interne*) thus arose. These were usually elected on the shop floor by all union members irrespective of craft distinctions (though they were sometimes appointed from above); they acted essentially as grievance committees overseeing the application of wage agreements. Their functions were at first quite limited, and their official existence tenuous, for the union was suspicious of the increase in local initiative they represented.

But there was considerable pressure from below for their official recognition, and rather than risk a breakaway movement or the loss of locals to the syndicalists, the unions moved to incorporate them into their structure near the end of 1918. The February 1919 national FIOM agreement recognized the internal commissions as organs competent to negotiate directly with management on all collective and individual grievances arising out of the application of the agreement. Some in the union hierarchy seem to have honestly viewed the commissions as preparatory organs for workers self-management. But until the revolution, which few saw on the immediate agenda, they were to strive to raise productivity, ensure the smooth application of new methods, and maintain overall industrial peace. Indeed, FIOM had come around to the monopolies' programme for industrial reconstruction and development, which was predicated on the unions' renouncing all claims of control of the labour process and discipline, and of the right to strike for the duration of the contract. In return for a free hand to press forward with rationalization, the owners conceded the eight-hour day and substantial pay increases. (A similar agreement in 1911 had been disrupted by rank-and-file rejection and syndicalist-led strikes whose defeat resulted in the loss of all concessions. FIOM leaders were determined not to let this happen again.) Thus, the 1919 agreement also established a cumbersome apparatus for the mediation of conflicts in order to avoid spontaneous strikes, and stringent penalties for the failure to pursue grievances through the proper channels. But under immediate post-war conditions, with inflation continuing apace, working conditions deteriorating, and a steady influx of unskilled factory recruits creating pressure for industrial unions, the integration of the internal commissions came under severe strain. In the second half of 1919, with the union chiefs leading strikes in other parts of the country, radical councilist conceptions spread throughout Turin.[7]

Limits of Challenge

In no country, however, did the autonomous councilist tendency prevail. Trade-union structures were often severely strained, but ultimately councilist structures did not offer a successful challenge. Even in Russia, which in many ways represents a limit case, integrated union organizations eventually won out. The reasons for this reflect certain peculiarities of the period, and some basic features of labour organization and organizational change as well.

In Britain as well as France (where autonomist tendencies had not been strong in any case, as a result of union structures and policies), the basic stability of the post-war parliamentary state set the limits of any organizational shift in the labour movement towards rejecting the ground rules of collective bargaining. In Britain, however, the limits of the independent stewards' movement itself were clearly revealed. No broad national organization developed to contest for power within the unions or to forge political links with other opposition groups. Leadership and organization remained localized. As a result, the movement was condemned to rebellious isolation, and the militant actions in the various centres were defeated in turn. To some extent this was motivated, and generously rationalized, by an anti-bureaucratic and anti-statist ideology that foresaw the radical construction of an industrial republic within the increasingly hollow and fragile shell of the political state, which would soon crumble on its own. But organizational deficiencies had a much more basic dynamic, and the tendency towards integration and officialization, which already existed in a number of centres during the war, was generalized by the Shop Stewards Agreement of 1919. Subsequently, even the most radical stewards decided to work within union structures.[8]

In Italy, where political conditions were far less stable and a more direct challenge was mounted, the limits of the factory councils were exposed in the two major confrontations of 1920. In April the owners, supported by a massive deployment of troops, declared a lockout in response to the growing tendency of workers and factory councils to bypass the arbitration machinery set up the previous year. The council leadership and their *ordinovisti* supporters helped organize a massive strike of some half a million workers in Turin and the surrounding province. But national support was not forthcoming from the Socialist Party (PSI) or the CGL. The councilists never had control of the situation, and responsibility for local negotiations quickly passed to D'Aragona, reformist secretary-general of the CGL. The settlement was a shattering defeat for the councils. The internal commissions were stripped of most of their recently claimed powers, and the provisions of the old FIOM agreement were reaffirmed. The workers were embittered, not least by the deficiencies of the council leadership. Gramsci and *L'Ordine Nuovo* were thoroughly discredited locally as well as nationally, and the movement that revived around other questions was never again in their hands. In fact, it was Gramsci's former collaborator Tasca who now led the PSI Maximalist effort in Turin to unify the factory councils and trade unions, while utilizing the former to democratize and industrialize the latter. Control functions were not to be abandoned, but neither were specific demands made in this domain. Tasca's scheme, similar to that proposed by Schiavello in Milan (where the autonomist tendency on the shop floor was much weaker), was approved in the Turin Chamber of Labour, though little was done to implement it. The scheme was opposed only by a handful of anarcho-syndicalist delegates, and it was they, not the former *ordinovisti*, who now led the struggle to revive the councils and to push the revolutionary movement forward both in Turin and elsewhere.

But it was the movement for higher wages led by FIOM against employer intransigence that brought about the major confrontation the anarcho-syndicalists had been seeking all along. FIOM's tactic of a slow-down provoked lockouts in the metal industry nationwide, and a half-million metal workers responded by occupying their factories. Factory councils were revived to manage the various aspects of the occupation, not the least of which was maintaining production. In Turin, where factory councils were again most vigorous, an entire local economic network was soon established, managed by the workers and sympathetic technicians and clerks. Overall cooordination, however, was in the hands of FIOM and the Chamber of Labour. The CGL itself now pressed for workers control (through the union) and the restoration of the pre-April powers of the internal commissions. But its National Council rejected the idea of a revolutionary political solution put forward (probably not seriously) by the PSI Directorate, and the latter was unwilling to act without the support of the union leaders. As Terracini, a former *ordinovisto* and founding member of the Italian Communist Party, was to say at the Third Comintern Congress in 1921, 'when the comrades who led the CGL submitted their resignations [in response to the PSI's proposal for a national movement to seize power], the party leadership could neither replace them nor hope to replace them. It was Dugoni, D'Aragona, Buozzi who led the CGL; they were at all times representative of the mass.'[9]

Though it underestimated the revolutionary impulses that guided a certain proportion of the workers, particularly in Turin, Terracini's statement underlines a basic fact of this period, namely that the unions had weathered the onslaught of the factory councils and had maintained the leadership and allegiance of the majority of organized workers. Their structures and policies had been severely strained by the massive influx of new members after the war (bringing about a ninefold growth in two years), but they effectively resisted the challenge of the factory councils. The relatively youthful workshop-based leadership of the council movement proved incapable of dislodging the veteran union functionaries from overall control, even as their activity helped democratize and industrialize some union structures. To the great mass of organized workers, especially those not as directly affected by the employers' drive for increased rationalization and productivity, the traditional union leadership seemed capable of renewing and sustaining the generally favourable secular trend that had been interrupted by the war.

The negative example of Russia and the constellation of international forces further reinforced the union's reformist tendencies. Trade union leaders, including Colombino of FIOM and D'Aragona himself, had been in Russia with PSI chief Serrati just that summer and were quite shocked at the harsh dictatorship and economic devastation they witnessed. A revolution in Italy at that time, they felt, given the minority support for socialism even among the industrial workers and the inevitable blockade by other capitalist powers (to which Italy, with its geographical position and dependence on fuel, raw materials, and food imports, was particularly vulnerable), would lead to conditions similar to those in Russia. The overwhelming vote to return to work on 24 September, though by no means unambiguous evidence of what workers might have been willing to do two weeks earlier, testifies to the hold of the unions. Only in Turin was the vote even close. And the metal-workers were the *vanguard* of the Italian revolutionary movement. Towards the end of the strike, most workers were concerned primarily with getting paid for the time they had worked during the factory occupation. This, along with the reestablishment of the old functions of the internal commissions and promise of limited trade-union control in industry, finally brought them back to work. The issue of control over production had not died, but neither had it decisively overstepped the framework of trade-union legality. The momentum of workers control stopped short of the revolutionary tasks set for it by its theorists. As the *ordinovisti* had been discredited by the April strike, so now were the syndicalists, whose 'favourite weapon—factory seizure—had been shown up as ineffective.'[10]

In Germany too the deficiencies of factory-council leadership and the inability to break decisively from union organizational structures were evident. In the early months of 1919, factory councils were established on a wide basis, and district and regional councils were set up to coordinate the movement for socialization and workers control. But the massive strikes in the three major areas of council activity—Berlin, the Ruhr, and Central Germany—were never adequately coordinated, and each was defeated in turn. Cadre from the Independent Socialists (USPD), formed during the wartime split of the SPD, provided leadership. But the young party was deeply divided, and decentralist in philosophy and structure. Though its growth had been impressive, it remained an expression of the mass movement itself more than an organizational base for coordinated activity.[11] Only the unions effectively provided this. For most of them, the gains achieved through wartime collaboration had further cemented their reformist strategy. And the post-war *Arbeitsgemeinschaft* under the leadership of capital provided the basis for an eight-hour day, full recognition of collective bargaining, industry-wide contracts, more uniform wages and conditions, labour exchanges, and the end of employer support for yellow unions. These concessions helped promote the phenomenal growth of the unions to an extent unimaginable before the war. Neither these specific gains nor general organizational growth were to be sacrificed for what the unions perceived as premature and quixotic attempts to usher in socialism.

Moreover, the unions saw the factory committees' attempts to displace them—which was a tendency in the practice, though not in the theory or policy of council leaders—as dangerous, since unions would have to persist under socialism. The unions, to be sure, did not remain completely untouched. Organizational growth itself, from two million members before the war to eight million by 1919, shook them profoundly. Councilist ideas exercised a broad appeal in some of the most expansive unions (metals, mining), as well as in sectors that had been previously unorganized (chemicals, state workers, clerks). New recruits had little tradition of union discipline, and council forms thus competed more effectively. Likewise, in those unions that had already been structured along industrial lines (metals, mines, rails), councilist factory organization found a natural base. And by mid–1919 many workers had become disillusioned with trade-union and SPD moderation. But after the defeat of the winter and spring strikes, opposition manifested itself primarily within the unions, and not in separate council organs. In the end, that opposition was able to win control of just a single union, albeit the largest and most important: the metalworkers union (DMV). But by then the more radical councilist movement had been defeated, and councils with very little power were written into the Weimar Constitution. They were to be strictly subordinated to the unions, and barred from interfering with production in any way. The unions and not the councils thereafter remained the major organizational base for mass labour struggles, except during the inflationary crisis of 1923.[12]

Both the autonomist tendencies and the relative organizational weakness of councilist movements can be partly explained by their emergence during a phase of sudden wartime and post-war crisis coming just after a period of economic expansion generally conducive to cautious labour reformism and bureaucratic craft-structured organization. Despite some fierce strikes by the unorganized and the limited but noteworthy development of revolutionary industrial unionism, the preceding growth of 'organized capitalism' had brought unknown prosperity, the end of chronic mass unemployment, and unprecedented expansion of the rights and organizations of labour. This contrasted starkly with the Long Depression of 1873–96, which had been marked by high levels of unemployment, violent fluctuations in the labour market, and conditions generally unfavourable to trade-union growth and consolidation.

The contrast of these two periods, and the difficult transition from one to the other, had deeply imprinted itself in the collective memory of the older workers, particularly those who had risen to leadership positions in labour organizations. Karl Mannheim's idea (borrowed from Pinder) of the non-contemporaneity of contemporaries had a very definite organizational translation here.[13]

The heritage of moderation by union officialdom was reinforced by the kinds of concessions that were or appeared achievable during the immediate post-war period. The factory committees, on the other hand, had for the most part emerged quite suddenly in the heat of local factory struggles during the war. As a result, they often lacked the organizational and agitational experience gained through years of struggle and constructive activity. Their factory constituencies were often quite unstable during the time of their ascendancy. Their ideological conceptions of both the means of struggle and the institutional goals towards which they were striving were only semi-coherent at best, and this often reinforced organizational deficiencies. During the war they were constantly constrained by state repression, which limited their abilities to organize beyond the plant level. Under these conditions, factory-committee movements found it difficult to provide the kind of broader organization and coordination required to make an effective challenge during the relatively brief periods of political crisis when it was most possible. Those that had developed partly within the unions, and were thus able to draw upon union resources, evinced an overriding tendency to be fully reintegrated into union structures, albeit reformed ones. In some ways, these new movements were the growing pains of industrial unionism more than a viable alternative to trade unionism as such.

Even in Russia, where conditions did not favour the rise of stable bargain-oriented unions and where the February revolution found the union movement in great disarray, the tendency that finally prevailed was not the autonomization of the factory committees, but the organizational integration of committees and unions. Despite the enormous achievements of the committees, and their noteworthy extension beyond the gates of their particular factories, the largely improvisational character of their activity in a period of abrupt crisis left them far short of a firm institutional base from which to cope with the urgencies of revolution. The very disorganization of the unions that had permitted the committees to develop so far and so fast in the first place, combined with the unions' hostility toward workers control, left the committees without an organizational base from which to effect coordination. And the splintering and waste of valuable resources in organizational competition were scourges that virtually all segments of the workers movement strove to banish. The Bolshevik party provided much-needed, though not always consistent, assistance to the committees. But even here the heritage of practical struggles under tsarist autocracy reasserted itself quite strongly. The seasoned organizers of the earlier period were union militants, not leaders of factory committees. It was they who had the most direct access to party leaders, thus providing a distinct organizational bias to the production of the knowledge required to formulate economic strategies. And the conditions of political autocracy had bred relations of dependence of the unions on the Social Democratic party. As a result, even though the committees had demonstrated their relative merit in matters pertaining to the organization of production, institutional support emphatically leaned toward the unions.

Terrain of Struggle

Organization and leadership are scarce and tenuous resources.[14] The conditions of working-class life make this a particularly poignant fact. The scarcity of time and resources, the overtaxing commitments, the demands of daily struggle, the uneven distribution of crucial skills, and the disruptive and cooptive efforts of hostile authorities and employers—all these factors constantly threaten to undermine the hard-won organizational achievements of the working classes. This was repeatedly shown in the Russian Revolution. The Bolshevik party had to ration its own limited organizational resources in the struggle for power, and neglected to aid the factory-committee movement as much as it might have. Compromises had to be made with moderate trade-union leaders to ensure their support for the revolution. Factory committees had to recognize how limited their power was apart from the unions and the new state apparatuses established by the Bolsheviks. Organizational competition at the workplace was seen as a very real deficit by workers and activists alike. Even in the country that experienced an abrupt revolutionary break, the relatively weak party and union organizational networks asserted themselves over the vibrant and mass-based, yet hastily improvised factory committees that had arisen in the heat of crisis.

If the deficiencies of councilist theory were manifest in the limit case of Russia—which nevertheless served as a paradigm of sorts for Gramsci and Pannekoek—they were even more glaring in countries with better-established trade-union movements. The dearth of organizational resources and the relative historical weight of previously existing structures would seem to make it highly unlikely that new forms generated in the heat of crisis could decisively displace the old ones. The challenge of the factory councils was ultimately very limited in the countries of Western and Central Europe. A further advance towards revolution and more extensive forms of workers control could have been achieved only with the support of the trade unions. And this was a time when unions were not nearly as well-established or fortified by participation in state apparatuses as they are today, when the sudden and massive influx of new recruits put great strains on the unions' organizational capacities, and when the specific struggles of highly skilled workers against accelerated wartime rationalization were most intense. During and immediately after the Second World War, the autonomist tendencies of council organizations were far less pronounced than they were in the First World War.[15] And the experience of prolonged mobilization for total warfare, which created peculiar conditions for quasi-autonomous factory organization, is unlikely to be repeated in the core industrial states.

Since the First World War, the relative weight of trade unions in struggles over control of production has been quite evident in core and peripheral states alike. Even the most militant shop-floor struggles in Europe after the Second World War did not lead to autonomous factory councils. In Italy, for instance, the struggles of 1968–69, despite initial union hesitancy, led rather quickly not to independent councils, but to councils integrated into union structures. And these, in turn, have been revitalized as they have begun to bargain on control issues at the national level, while becoming much more open to decentralized negotiations on the details of everyday work practices.[16] In Sweden in the late sixties, militant wildcat strikes, which raised control issues and challenged the overly centralized trade unions, led to a major reorientation of the labour movement around issues of industrial democracy. Within a few years the unions had won extensive powers over health and safety issues, changes in the production process, and hiring and firing.[17]

Such bargaining over control, which has become a feature of many European trade-union movements, has been complemented by national legislation, such as the Swedish Democracy of Work Act of 1976 and the 1970 Italian Law on Workers Rights. (Even in Britain, with its decidedly voluntarist collective-bargaining traditions, a strong tendency for legislation emerged in the seventies before the Conservative government cut it short.) Such favourable treatment by the state, which has permitted workplace democratization to spread more evenly to sectors of the workplace that might not have had the power to win it on their own, could only have been achieved in conjunction with official union organs, and not unofficial autonomous councils. Vibrant shop-steward organizations, such as those in Britain, remain dependent on the resources of the larger union movement, and are often more effective in protecting the 'frontier of control' when they act according to the rules established through conflict and bargaining in the larger arena of trade-union action.[18]

Under the Allende government in Chile, trade unions were given responsibility for the implementation of workers control. Whenever they hesitated, autonomous factory councils did not arise to fill the gap. The reforms were eventually carried through only with the support of the unions. Actual worker participation tended to be positively correlated with sympathetic attitudes and ideologies among union leaders.[19]

In the Peruvian reforms of the early seventies it was the established unions that provided the organizational basis for popular mobilization around workers participation, and obstructed the utilization of the newly created *Comunidades Industriales* for purely integrative purposes. (In fact, from the workshop delegates in France during the First World War to participation schemes in West Germany today, employers have often argued for the separate election of delegates outside union channels as a way to weaken the power of workers and unions alike.) The older organizations in Peru proved so much more effective not only because of their accumulated resources and experience, but also because they could continue to defend the workers as wage-earners while they struggled to extend their role in decision making.[20]

In Algeria, though *comités de gestion* formed spontaneously with the desertion of French managerial *colons* in 1962, it was the major trade-union federation (UGTA) that played the chief organizational role in their consolidation and diffusion on a democratic basis.[21] And, finally, the factory committees born in the midst of revolution and civil war in Spain (particularly in Catalonia) in 1936 spread rapidly and were partially coordinated only through the mediation of the anarcho-syndicalist union federation, the Confederación Nacional del Trabajo (CNT).[22]

The radical councilist conceptions of Gramsci and Pannekoek fail to recognize that, because of the scarcity of organizational resources, it is extremely difficult, if not impossible, to sustain autonomous councils born in periods of crisis; and that long-established trade unions invariably tend to prevail, even if they are modified in structure and function. A revolutionary break in state power could change this, and create conditions for relative institutional autonomy of the control structures and for the defence of the material interests of the workers. The separation of workers councils and trade unions in Yugoslavia is a case in point. But the conditions of struggle prior to the seizure of state power warrant the concentration and coordination of resources to a degree that is unlikely to be achieved by the voluntary cooperation and overlapping membership proposed by Gramsci. In time, formal linkages tend to develop, and to be consolidated within the structures of the stronger and more established organization. A major reason for this is the need for lasting coordination above the plant level, which autonomous councils have not been very successful in achieving. Nor does the history of labour movements reveal a radical separation of functions parallel to that of organizational structures. Unions of various types, from revolutionary syndicalist to centralized industrial, from recently formed to long-established, have struggled at various times for workers control. Syndicalist and revolutionary forms of organization that reject collective bargaining for short-term gains, however, have been unable to sustain themselves as mass-based organizations, or have been compelled to adopt more centralized structures and bargaining procedures.[23] The progressive decommodification of labour-power that was central to the critiques of Gramsci and Pannekoek has occurred both within and outside the sphere of production. State actions that loosen the bonds between the market and subsistence (unemployment insurance, transfer payments for children, the handicapped and the aged), and legislation and collective bargaining that reduce the portion of the life-cycle spent in wage labour, represent a partial decommodification.[24] But progressive decommodification *within* the production process through workers control and the democratic determination of the conditions of employment has hardly been a function peculiar to autonomous or spontaneously generated factory councils, even if they have frequently imparted a most important impetus to that struggle.

Because of the bargaining and hence disciplinary functions of trade unions, they are '*necessarily* an ambiguous ally for the cause of workers control.'[25] But it is undeniable that they are a necessary ally. A dual strategy for working within established unions while constructing independent rank-and-file organizations for control from without can only lead to splits that weaken both control and economic bargaining.[26] And while informal controls exercised by rank-and-file groups and autonomous council-type organizations may be more effective in some workplaces where the conditions of struggle are particularly favourable, it is formalization through control bargains and legislation that enables the power of control to be extended over time and over sectors of the work-force less favourably situated for struggle or less conscious of control issues.

The formalization of gains is essential if workers' claims are to be legitimated in the larger society, if industrial democracy is to appear as a real alternative, and if a base for the further extension of control is to be secured. The more uniform and balanced spread of workers' control made possible by formalization is a prerequisite for an egalitarian and solidaristic movement. The dangers of officialization and bureaucratic encapsulation make the democratization of the unions absolutely essential.[27] But this remains a problem for any labour movement of great size, strength, and durability under conditions of antagonistic struggle. No effective and lasting workers organization can fully escape the contradictory effects of struggle under conditions of capitalist power. Nor have autonomous council movements been particularly able to solve these problems. Trade unions may indeed be a difficult and dangerous terrain on which to wage the battle for the control of production, but history has afforded us no more effective arena.

Epilogue

Stalinism and the
Russian Revolution

The Russian Revolution never presented a genuine choice between a strategy of dual power based on popular councils and one based on the seizure of power through existing state structures. There was never much question among the workers and soldiers who determined the course of events after February that democratic revolutionary legitimacy lay with the soviets. The Provisional Government, itself hastily assembled and continually reshuffled in the wake of the overthrow of the tsar, never possessed the administrative capacity to compensate for its conditional legitimacy—at least not as long as no expeditious exit from the war was forthcoming. The Mensheviks and SRs let slip whatever chances may have existed for the advent of a liberal-democratic order by not taking power, signing a separate peace, and calling an early election for a Constituent Assembly. By the time the Assembly convened, it was already unviable and would have undermined itself before long had it not been disbanded. The October revolution only ratified what had become evident to broad sectors of the most strategically located political actors: the possibilities of democracy, which required peace and effective economic controls to stem disintegration, rested with the soviets.

But what happened to these possibilities? How could a state theoretically inspired by the principles of the Paris Commune be transformed in little more than a decade into the hypertrophied Stalinist Leviathan, a state that exhibited more continuity with the political culture of the tsarist autocracy than any revolutionaries would have dreamed? How could the unprecedented democratization of relations in the factory of 1917 be transformed by the 1930s into even more arbitrary, abusive, and authoritarian arrangements than existed under Witte and Stolypin? How could the peasantry that dealt a swift and final blow to the power and privilege of the landed nobility be subjected to a second serfdom of collectivization more brutal than any they had known in the past?

These questions have haunted those who have identified with the Russian revolution, and there has been no lack of simple and ready answers from supporters and detractors alike. Any long view of the revolution and its significance for the twentieth century and beyond must confront them anew. My aim has been to reconsider the significance of the events of the early revolutionary years for these longer-term questions by examining the objective possibilities of popular democracy and the options of institutional formation. Yet when the war and civil-war conditions that created and constrained such possibilities are viewed in combination with deep-rooted features of Russian socio-political history, it becomes quite clear that the momentum overwhelmingly favoured the rise of a top-heavy bureaucratic regime.

The fundamental basis for autocratic rule was the dispersed and scattered character of Russian villages, a structural feature the revolution had done little to alter. No bourgeois-democratic reforms had ever provided the political infrastructure for peasant participation above the village level. And no peasant-based opposition movement in this period ever had the autonomous capacity for state-building. The urban-based, proletarian revolution thus inevitably implied that a political superstructure would be imposed on the villages, even though this might have been done in less oppressive forms.

The proletariat itself was numerically weak, its general cultural level low; these factors were exacerbated by the social disintegration, bloodletting, and state-building of the civil war. The bureaucratization of the soviets, already evident in early 1917, could only have been exaggerated by 1921. Former tsarist functionaries, whose bureaucratic habits were deservedly notorious, were needed for state administration. Yet under the conditions of economic disintegration, neither the old administrative apparatuses nor the new organs of dual power provided the basis for an institutional transformation that could sustain widespread democratic control. The resulting institutional inconstancy, irregularity, and immateriality produced its own peculiar forms of authoritarian control and despotic abuse. The confusion of state-building and the erosion of the social basis of the revolution led increasingly to reliance on the Bolshevik party as the substitute subject of historical transformation. By the end of the civil war, military styles of behaviour had become ever more predominant within the party, while its democratic heritage of free discussion and debate was in retreat. At the next critical juncture, militarized modes of coercive mobilization seemed venerable and workable solutions.

If rapid and forced industrialization was eventually necessary to transform the Soviet Union into a major power able to sustain growth and defend itself from foreign military attack, then any attempt to evaluate short-term democratic possibilities in the state and the workplace must be largely beside the point. Such possibilities might reveal interesting dynamics of revolutionary participation that may be relevant for understanding other movements. Or they may uncover the roots of heroic revolutionary myths that inspire future ones. But any view that accepts the necessity of forced industrialization can only find these possibilities fundamentally irrelevant to long-term development prospects. Factory committees and trade unions with even very modest rights of participation and autonomous bases of power would never have freely accepted the harsh regimentation, considerable decline in consumption, and general upheaval of urban living conditions entailed in the Stalinist industrialization drive. Political institutions with even modest representation mechanisms would never have endorsed that drive, or would have quickly recoiled from its evidently disastrous effects on the lives of the great majority of the population. And why investigate the developmental possibilities of the village commune if no conceivable conditions could have stimulated them or persuaded the peasants to voluntarily deliver enough grain to sustain industrial growth?

Rudolf Bahro, a major proponent of a contemporary alternative in the Soviet bloc, has argued that forced industrialization and collectivization were necessary to overcome peasant backwardness and prevent a return to capitalism. The party struggles of the 1920s were 'nothing but the birthpangs of a new depotism', and Stalin won because he 'fit' the tasks that history imposed on the Soviet state.[1] Theda Skocpol, presenting a more careful comparative argumentation about revolutionary state-building processes, and shunning any appeal to the historical imperatives of industrialization, nevertheless arrives at a similar conclusion. Once the NEP had promoted recovery based on pre-war industrial potential, 'extraordinary infusions of capital and manpower' were required. But given the productive capacity of Soviet industry and the pricing policies that favoured state-controlled industry over agriculture, the peasants would not market enough grain to permit this. Since the party-state lacked the political-organizational means to persuade the peasants to deliver more grain voluntarily, or to facilitate more productive agricultural techniques, the choice was either to attack them, or allow them to continue to exercise effective veto power over national economic development. Stalin's solution was the most feasible because it promised quick enough results to satisfy the needs of military preparedness and built upon the party's heritage of civil-war-style activism. 'Bukharin's strategy would have been more promising if Soviet Russia had inherited well-developed consumer industries and a rural sector sufficiently prosperous and commercially oriented to provide strong demand for light industries. The fact that neither of these conditions was present suggests that Bukharin's approach was inherently unworkable.'[2]

The judgement that Stalinist forms of forced industrialization and collectivization were historically necessary (or were most workable in the circumstances) is emphatically challenged by much recent Western research, and by a number of important Soviet studies as well. The NEP had not exhausted its possibilities, despite the grain crises of the late twenties. Compared with the predictably disastrous results of the Stalinist alternative for agriculture and industry, continuation of the NEP framework was eminently feasible and preferable, even if it might not have fulfilled all Bukharin's expectations. As Robert Tucker has argued, 'the insistently emerging conclusion from scholarly researches based on the more abundant data now available from Soviet sources is that "a continuation of the New Economic Policy of the 1920s would have permitted at least as rapid a rate of industrialization with less cost to the urban as well as to the rural population of the Soviet Union".'[3] In fact, Bukharin foresaw so many of the short and long-term costs of Stalinist policy, and presented sufficiently practicable alternatives, that his approach can now be regarded as having been generally vindicated.[4]

The Bukharinist strategy as it evolved in the later years of the NEP did not suggest that the peasants passively be allowed to determine the course of national economic development, nor did it play down the active role of the state. This was more characteristic of his earlier views. But by 1927 all parties to the debate agreed that a steep increase in investment was required, and Bukharin fully accepted that the capital-goods sector had to grow faster than the consumer-goods sector. The question was how much faster, and what rate of growth Soviet industry and agriculture could sustain. A high and steady growth rate in the region of the 20 per cent achieved in 1928 seemed optimal, while a much greater rate would have quickly been marred by diminishing returns, as in fact happened. The state, Bukharin argued, should not sit idly by and let the market take its course. It should take an active role in planning, but should avoid the kind of over-planning that would stifle the initiative of smaller producers, and for which organizational capacities were insufficient in any case. Bukharin likewise agreed that the state had to seize some of the peasants' resources and promote a partial but voluntary collectivization. Nor is it true that Stalin appropriated the programme of the defeated left, since Trotsky and Preobrazhensky did not reject the fundamental framework of the NEP. In fact, despite the left's underestimation of the danger of Stalin, the programmes of Bukharin and Trotsky revealed a basic convergence from the fall of 1928 onwards. Trotsky was highly critical of Stalin's super-growth tempos, and called for an end to forced collectivization and de-kulakization. By 1932 he was offering what was, in effect, a complete restatement of the Bukharin platform of 1928–29. The highest programmatic thinking and the range of serious Bolshevik economic analysis occurred *within* the parameters of the NEP. And when Stalin abandoned the plan of the Fifteenth Party Congress of December 1927, which was an amalgam of left and right elements, 'he abandoned the mainstream of Bolshevik thinking about economic and social change.'[5]

The military rationale for Stalin's forced industrialization and collectivization is also open to serious question. There seems never to have been any real possibility of invasion in this period, and top Soviet leaders recognized this. Rather, 'the war scare was in fact grossly and crudely manipulated by Soviet politicians in 1927,'[6] and continued to be invoked to justify Stalinist policies and the tremendous sacrifices they entailed. If Stalin's fears were real, then the policies pursued would have been suicidal in view of the obvious risks. The change in the Comintern line, which now identified the Social Democrats as the main enemy, facilitated Hitler's rise to power. Moreover, if the Soviet Union had been attacked in the early years of the five-year plans, it would have suffered the enormous disadvantages of breakneck and chaotic growth coupled with unprecedented social disruption, and would have enjoyed virtually none of the advantages. A sizeable increase in military production was quite feasible under a different economic strategy. The country might then have faced the German invasion with a much greater degree of social cohesion, a broader and more vigorous demographic base, greater overall economic efficiency, and an agricultural sector that was not such a serious drag on the war effort.[7] In 1936, when the Soviet Union was officially proclaimed socialist, more children died in the cities than were born. Nor does the rationality of Stalin's defence efforts gain much credence from his purges of the most capable officers in the Red Army. No development strategy was without its risks. But Stalin's was hardly the bearer of an unambiguous rationality of military defence.

From the standpoint of agricultural and industrial development as well, the 'mass collectivization of Soviet agriculture must be reckoned an unmitigated economic policy disaster.'[8] To argue that at least it entailed a rapid expansion of state-controlled activities in both sectors is to allow the monologic of Stalinist state-building to get the better of an analysis of the relative practicability of alternative policies.[9] Grain collections did increase sharply in these years, but as a result of the breakdown of the market only slightly more went to industry, which compelled the state to provide grain to the smaller towns and timber areas.[10] Total marketed agricultural product actually decreased. The increase in industrial investment was scarcely, if at all, financed by a rise in the agricultural surplus, but rather by the super-exploitation of the urban working class made possible only by coercive measures. Collectivization actually resulted in a net transfer of resources from industry to agriculture, simultaneously leading to a decline in agricultural productivity and the worst famine in Russian history. Quite predictably, the peasants reacted to collectivization with passive resistance and the massive slaughter of livestock, more of which was lost in the first year of collectivization than during the entire civil war, and the regime was compelled to divert precious investment into the production of tractors, although without being able to achieve the level of tractive power that existed prior to the Big Drive. Millions of lives were lost in this process, and Soviet agriculture has suffered chronic stagnation ever since.[11]

In contrast, Bukharin's policy recommendations seem far more soundly based. Small-scale industry and handicrafts constituted 35 per cent of gross industrial output before the First World War, and could have been relatively easily mobilized with small capital outlays. The number of workers in industrial cooperatives alone was already quite substantial by 1925. As even many local kolkhoz organizers realized, agricultural output could have been raised even without modern machinery. The proposals of Bukharin and other economists for the production of hoes, ploughs, and fertilizers, and for the improvement of seeds and various other simple agricultural techniques, were eminently sensible and could have been achieved without great cost. Moreover, such labour-intensive techniques in both industry and agriculture would have helped absorb the rural population surplus. This sound policy of 'walking on two legs' was practicable in the late twenties,[12] even if a Chinese-style collective reorganization of peasant production was not.

The relative feasibility of this policy is even more apparent in the light of the monumental waste of capital that resulted from Stalin's super-tempos and the lack of technological diversification, which so fully confirmed Bukharin's maxim that 'it is not possible to build today's factories with tomorrow's bricks.' Because of the forced industrialization drive, construction projects were over-extended, and many were bogged down for years. Bottlenecks caused by the unplanned and chaotic lurch forward left much existing capacity idle. The early purges of bourgeois adminstrators created serious difficulties, and the increasingly over-inflated apparatuses siphoned off needed resources from other sectors. The industrialpurges and system of controls entailed by the mobilization had a very negative effect on technical progress, as engineers fled industry, managers devised elaborate ways to pass the buck and resist innovation, and results on paper came to be prized over actual ones.[13] With the neglect of the production of consumer goods, the increase in grain exports, and the breakdown of the distribution network and resulting spread of speculation, urban living standards fell, and labour productivity along with them. The morale of the working class plunged to an all-time low, and mass thefts were as commonplace as they were seemingly uncontrollable. As Moshe Lewin has put it, 'the nation, disrespectful towards state property, seemed to have been transformed into a nation of thieves.' [14]

There can be little doubt that while Stalin's policies enormously enhanced the size of the working class, they simultaneously brutalized and atomized it as a class. At a time when skilled labour was scarce, the most talented and experienced workers were often unnecessarily drawn away from production and dispersed throughout the administrative machinery as a result of politically motivated and socially manipulative purges. Avenues for achievement and advancement became highly individualized even as they were ensconced in a terroristic bureaucratic environment. For the massive number of new arrivals in cities that could not house them, the factories became like railway stations and 'nomadic gypsy camps.'[15] Yet at the beginning of this period, the Russian working class still evinced considerable capacities for mobilization. The 'high degree of conflict over workers control and the rights of technical specialists, which characterized the Russian revolution and continued throughout the 1920s,' did not greatly diminish until 1931.[16] The 'cultural revolutionary' campaigns of the turn of the decade revealed a profound basis for anti-authoritarian and utopian/idealistic mobilization among workers and youth, a great many of whom looked back to the heroic days of the revolution but had not been steeled in militaristic styles of activism through participation in the civil war.[17] This was no doubt particularly true of Soviet women, for whom the suffering and loss of the civil war years did not retain the mythical quality it had acquired for many men. With other alternatives closed off and the economic insecurities of working-class life exacerbated, much of this anti-authoritarian potential was channelled exclusively into individual upward mobility, or, for the less fortunately situated, into desperate and often anti-social strategies of survival.

But Stalinist industrialization was not simply imposed on a passive and apathetic mass of workers. And it is undoubtedly true that the alternative economic strategies available would have permitted far greater opportunities for working-class mobilization. Much more social historical research would be required to determine the exact forms this might have taken. Trade unions with at least quasi-autonomous status certainly would have been possible under a continuation and progressive transformation of the NEP. And although Bukharin had not remained a proponent of workers control, various forms of workers participation would seem to have been consistent with his overall approach.

Such participation could have tapped the profound anti-authoritarian sentiment among Russian workers, and their no less profound capacities for learning through productive labour, revealed in the extent to which so many of them were promoted to responsible posts even without a formal framework of collective support from their fellow workers. American engineers working on Soviet projects themselves testified to the not uncommon disruption caused when new university-trained engineers did not heed the advice of skilled workers and the 'practicals' who had become engineers through experience in the shop.[18] Collective learning and participation opportunities were made more possible by the shortening of the working day, and Bukharin's programme called for yet a further reduction in order to increase the number of multiple shifts and enable more efficient use of industrial capacity.

Reduced hours, along with greater opportunities for participation and learning, could have partially compensated for wage demands, though the latter would have inevitably exerted strong upward pressure. Yet workers' participation schemes, under a variety of conditions, have not been fundamentally inimical to relatively high levels of investment and wage restraint. Nor would state controls regulating the overall rhythms of accumulation have been completely inconsistent with a range of participatory forms that would have not simply unleashed the kinds of corporatist demands that would undermine an effective economic alliance with the peasantry—the cornerstone of Bukharin's programme. The tensions of such a system would have been considerable, to say the least. And militant struggle against the workerist tendencies of the most democratic factions on the socialist left would have been an absolute necessity. Yet the options available within a Bukharinist strategy were far from maximalist. If the experience of the revolution is any indication, factory committees with responsibility and sanctioning power would have been more effective in controlling industrial theft, particularly under less exploitative and chaotic conditions than those entailed in Stalin's super-tempos, than were factory managers, party cadre, or the secret police. And in conditions in which workers' suspicion of the specialists was not cynically manipulated to divert attention from economic problems,[19] factory committees might have been able to work out more stable relationships and clear lines of authority than those entailed in Stalin's policies. Factory committee behaviour in this regard had not been irrational and mindless during the revolution, but was motivated by a profound desire both to curb abusive *spetsy* attitudes and to cooperate with them in maintaining production.

Many tensions and abuses would no doubt have persisted on both sides, given the role of specialists in everyday productive activities, the privileges they enjoyed, and the fact that workers themselves were starved for opportunities. Yet it is difficult to imagine that various collective, public, and accountable controls exercised by elected workers' organs could have produced as much insecurity, risk, fear, confusion, and lack of innovative incentive among specialists as existed during the 1930s. As one engineer put it, 'in production the engineer trembles all the time.'[20] This was also a result of the tempos and forms of industrialization, and not simply of the local abuse of power.

Under conditions in which the possibilities of genuine political democratization on a national scale remained limited, factory committees with relative institutional autonomy and participatory power in significant areas of productive life would have represented the best hopes for a democratic socialist order in the long run. Newly urbanized peasants could have been acculturated to the disciplines of industrial production in a way that built upon traditions of egalitarianism and cooperation. Factory committees responsible for defending and modifying the conditions of labour and providing important cultural services could have helped stabilize workplace constituencies and make them less vulnerable to totalitarian manipulation and control. They could have provided an important mechanism for recruitment and for the renewal of democratic practices within local party cells—a development that would have reverberated throughout the system. Perhaps they could even have revived the traditions of multi-party competition within the working class in a way that least threatened the overall socialist project. And given the concentration of the urban proletariat and the centrality of the workplace in its daily life, a relatively small number of committed militants would have been able to foster progressive democratization through such institutions. The ideological obstacles were quite strong among leading Bolshevik thinkers, and workers control was banned as an anarcho-syndicalist heresy. But despite disciplinary measures, the promise of workers control continually reappeared both within and around the party, and the organizational capacities at least for initiating a process of workplace democratization were not lacking.

The causes of the triumph of Stalinism will no doubt continue to be debated for many years to come. The question has lost neither its scholarly significance nor its political relevance. The current state of our knowledge, however, does not make it romantic or voluntarist to assert that 'there was enough in the historical environment, tradition, and social relations to sustain different roads.'[21] That a different road was not taken can be explained only by reference to the considerable impact of factors that were realistically open to modification. If it is true that the momentum of development was overwhelmingly in favour of top-heavy and urban-centered bureaucratic rule, it is nonetheless true that not all forms of bureaucracy are equally oppressive or inconsistent with progressive democratization. The Communist Party became the dominant organizational force in building the Soviet state. The impact of civil-war-style methods had been deep, its implantation in the countryside was minimal, and careerism was widespread. And yet the party-state bureaucracy was hardly the animating force of the great transformation that took place after 1929. It was much more a conservative and recalcitrant stratum that had to be whipped and spurred on by the Stalin clique to measures far more radical and dangerous than it would otherwise have taken.[22] Many, including numerous senior party officials and perhaps even a majority in the Politburo, wanted nothing to do with a return to the methods of war communism.[23] This outright antipathy or passive reticence reached deep into the party-state apparatuses. And high Bolshevik programmatic thinking remained fundamentally within the parameters of the NEP.

In view of the basic convergence of left and right over economic development strategies in the late 1920s, the banning of factions at the Tenth Party Congress turned out to be a measure of momentous historical consequence. Had a more rational exchange of differences been able to occur without the risk of punitive sanctions, that basic convergence might well have been recognized before the Stalinist option had been forced. The latter would almost certainly have been reversed once the consequences became apparent. But as long as formal factions were outlawed, Stalin could utilize his peculiar position as General Secretary, and the only member of the Politburo with a seat on the Orgburo, to manipulate factional differences to destroy his opponents and maximize his own personal power. Both left and right paid dearly for not having challenged organizational mechanisms that needlessly undermined the very substantial pluralistic tendencies within the party, and that were in no way inevitable, or necessary for the preservation of power and the tasks of state-building in the 1920s.[24] Nor for the construction of socialism in the first revolutionary state of the twentieth century.

Notes

Introduction

[1]Moshe Lewin, *Russian Peasants and Soviet Power*, trans. Irene Nove, New York 1975, pp. 15–16.

[2]Some of the basic premisses of such historical investigation are outlined in Dieter Groh, *Kritische Geschichtswissenschaft in emanzipatorischer Absicht*, Stuttgart 1973.

[3]A good critique of the earlier theories is presented in Rod Aya, 'Theories of Revolution Reconsidered: Contrasting Models of Collective Violence', *Theory and Society*, 8 (1979), pp. 39–99. As Michael Schwartz has so nicely put it, 'people who join protest organizations are at least as rational as those who study them'. *Radical Protest and Social Structure*, New York 1976, p. 135.

[4]E. J. Hobsbawm, 'From Social History to the History of Society', in *Historical Studies Today*, ed. Felix Gilbert and Stephen Graubard, New York 1975, p. 20.

[5]On the issues of technology and economic forms, this is true for the following recent analyses, though in different ways: Charles Bettelheim, *Class Struggles in the USSR, First Period: 1917–1923*, New York 1975; Carmen Claudín-Urondo, *Lénine et la révolution culturelle*, Paris 1975; Phil Slater, ed., *Outlines of a Critique of Technology*, Atlantic Highlands 1980.

[6]A monograph-length study of these phenomena in the period of the First World War was prepared several years ago, and an abbreviated version of it appeared as 'Workers' Control in the Era of World War I: A Comparative Analysis of the European Experience', *Theory and Society*, 9:1 (1980), pp. 29–88.

[7]The problems of dual power and parliamentary versus councilist forms of democracy also derive both theoretically and practically from the events of this period, but a lengthy discussion of these is not possible in this volume. For an analysis of these issues in the West today, see my 'Councils and Parliaments: The Problem of Dual Power in Comparative Perspective', *Politics and Society*, forthcoming 1983.

[8]Some of the problems of theorizing about the possible forms of an egalitarian and democratic society are analysed in my essay 'Production and Power in a Classless Society: A Critical Analysis of the Utopian Dimensions of Marxist Theory', *Socialist Review*, no. 59 (Sept.-Oct. 1981), pp. 33–82.

[9]Jürgen Habermas, *Knowledge and Human Interests*, trans. Jeremy Shapiro, Boston 1971, p. 285.

Chapter 1

[1]See Marc Ferro, *The Russian Revolution of February 1917*, trans. J.L Richards,

Englewood Cliffs 1972; and Anne Bobroff, 'The Bolsheviks and Working Women, 1905–20', *Soviet Studies*, 24:4(1974), 557.

[2]Tsuyoshi Hasegawa, 'The Problem of Power in the February Revolution of 1917 in Russia', *Canadian Slavonic Papers*, vol. 14 (1972), 613ff.

[3]Quoted in Robert Browder and Alexander Kerensky, eds., *The Russian Provisional Government of 1917*, Stanford 1961, vol. II, p. 710.

[4]Benjamin Ward, 'Wild Socialism In Russia: The Origins', *California Slavic Studies*, vol. 3 (1964), 136; Paul Avrich, 'Russian Factory Committees in 1917', *Jahrbücher für Geschichte Osteuropas*, vol. 11 (1963), 162ff.; Falk Döring, *Organizationsprobleme der russischen Wirtschaft in Revolution und Bürgerkrieg* (1918–1920), Hanover 1970, pp. 46–47; Robert Devlin, 'Petrograd Workers And Workers Factory Committees in 1917: An Aspect Of The Social History Of The Russian Revolution', unpublished Ph.D. dissertation, State University of New York at Binghamton, 1976, pp. 111–112.

[5]On the pre-1905 factory-based workers organizations, see Oscar Anweiler, *The Soviets: The Russian Workers, Peasants and Soldiers Councils, 1905–1921*, trans. Ruth Hein, New York 1974, 23ff.; Solomon M. Schwarz, *The Russian Revolution of 1905*, trans. Gertrude Vakar, Chicago 1967, especially pp. 267–300, 75–128; Dimitry Pospielovsky, *Russian Police Trade Unionism*, London 1971; Richard Pipes, *Social Democracy and the St Petersburg Labor Movement*, Cambridge, Mass. 1962, pp. 103–108; Jeremiah Schneiderman, *Sergei Zubatov and Revolutionary Marxism: The Struggle for the Working Class in Tsarist Russia*, Ithaca, New York 1976; Walter Sablinsky, *The Road to Bloody Sunday*, Princeton 1976.

[6]On 1905, see Sidney Harcave, *First Blood*, New York 1964; Anweiler, *The Soviets*; and Solomon Schwartz. Trade-union developments before the revolution will be analysed in chapter 2.

[7]For a detailed analysis of the pre-war strike wave, see Leopold Haimson, 'The Russian Workers' Movement On The Eve Of The First World War', paper delivered at the annual meeting of the American Historical Association, New York, December 1971; see also Victoria Bonnell, 'Trade Unions, Parties and the State in Tsarist Russia: A Study of Labor Politics in St Petersburg and Moscow', *Politics and Society*, 9:3(1980), pp. 299–322; and Bonnell, 'Radical Politics and Organized Labor in Pre-Revolutionary Moscow, 1905–1914', *Journal of Social History*, 12:2 (March 1979), pp. 282–300.

[8]See Anweiler, *The Soviets*, pp. 97–101; and S.O. Zagorsky, *State Control Of Industry In Russia During The War*, New Haven 1928, pp. 86–94; John Keep, *The Russian Revolution*, New York 1976, p. 42ff.

[9]William Chamberlain, *The Russian Revolution*, vol. 1, New York 1965, p. 73.

[10]On this general aspect of social movements, see Charles Tilly, *From Mobilization to Revolution*, Reading, MA. 1978, p. 141.

[11]See Paul Avrich, 'The Russian Revolution and The Factory Committees', unpublished Ph.D. dissertation, Columbia University, 1961, p. 12; Frederick Kaplan, *Bolshevik Ideology and The Ethics of Soviet Labor*, New York 1968, p. 127.

[12]John Keep, *The Russian Revolution*, p. 68.

[13]Marc Ferro, *The Russian Revolution of February 1917*, p. 112; see also Keep, p. 42ff.

[14]See Browder and Kerensky, II, p. 709ff.; Uwe Brügmann, *Die russischen Gewerkschaften in Revolution und Bürgerkrieg 1917–1919*, Frankfurt 1972, p. 47ff. In order to mitigate divisiveness, workers often invited soldiers into the factories to observe their conditions of work, and some claimed that shorter hours increased

productivity, since workers were less tired. Given the war exhaustion and nutritional conditions, this is not only plausible, but empirically corroborated for quite a number of firms. See Devlin, pp. 222-23, n.56; also Diane Koenker, 'Moscow Workers in 1917', Ph.D. dissertation, University of Michigan, 1976, p. 169.

[15]In addition to works already cited, see V. Ia. Selitskii, *Massy v bor'be za rabochii kontrol'* (*mart—iyul' 1917 g.*) Moscow 1971.

[16]See Haimson, 'The Russian Workers' Movement on the Eve of the First World War', p. 34ff.; Mark David Mandel, 'The Development of Revolutionary Consciousness Among the Industrial Workers of Petrograd Between February and November 1917', unpublished Ph.D. dissertation, Columbia University, 1978, pp. 188ff., 492; Devlin, p. 51ff.; Avrich, 'The Russian Revolution and the Factory Committees', p. 31ff.; and John Keep, *The Russian Revolution*, pp. 75,79. Keep, who tends to see the workers' actions as primarily irrational, does present a few cases where a rather large number of higher staff were expelled. But he examines none of the procedures, loosely terms such dismissals 'violent', and can admit no possible justice in the actions. In fact, some of the numbers he cites are not large at all. The 145 dismissals over a four-month period in the Urals, after all, represents less than four per factory in the survey, or less than one per month per factory. Hardly a mindless and violent industrial jacquerie. In a similar vein, Keep makes light of the suspicion of the workers that plant closures were deliberately designed to counter wage demands and discipline workers, referring to a survey conducted by the Ministry of Commerce and Industry, which simply asked the *owners* to list their reasons for shutting down. In less official statements the owners were considerably less disingenuous. See, for instance, Ferro, *The Russian Revolution of February 1917*, pp. 272-73.

[17]Koenker, 'Moscow Workers in 1917', pp. 330ff., 420; David Mandel, pp. 201ff., 230.

[18]Richard Lorenz, *Anfänge der bolschewistischen Industriepolitik*, Cologne 1965, p. 26; Anna Mikhailovna Pankratova, 'Les comités d'usines en Russie à l'époque de la Révolution 1917-1918', *Autogestion*, no. 4 (Dec. 1967), pp. 52-53; Brügmann, pp. 33-34; Devlin, pp. 63-64.

[19]Ferro, *The Russian Revolution of February 1917*, p. 121; Paul Avrich, 'The Bolshevik Revolution and Workers' Control in Russian Industry', *Slavic Review*, vol. 22 (1963), pp. 54-55.

[20]Quoted in Brügmann, p. 39. As David Mandel (p. 206) notes, factory committees generally did not want responsibility for technical and administrative aspects of production until full socialization of the economy could be achieved.

[21]See chapter 2 below. On developments at Putilov, see Heather Hogan, 'The Putilovtsy: A Case Study of Workers' Attitudes during the Russian Revolution', unpublished paper, University of Michigan, August 1974.

[22]Koenker notes that in Moscow, for instance, the percentage of economic strikes peaked in July and declined thereafter, while control-related strikes peaked in August and remained fairly high for the rest of the year. Koenker, 'Moscow Workers in 1917', pp. 410ff.

[23]William Rosenberg, 'Workers Control on the Railroads and Some Suggestions Concerning Social Aspects of Labor Politics in the Russian Revolution', *Journal of Modern History*, supplement, 49:2 (June 1977), D1187; Ronald Grigor Suny, *The Baku Commune 1917-1918*, Princeton 1972, p. 121.

[24]For the text of the agreement, see Browder and Kerensky, vol. II, pp. 712-13.

[25]Ibid., pp. 718-20; Avrich, 'The Russian Revolution and the Factory Commit-

tees', p. 38ff.; Marc Ferro, *La Révolution de 1917*: *Octobre, Naissance d'une société*, Paris 1976, pp. 238–39.

[26]Kaplan, p. 67ff.; Brügmann, p. 87. The Central Council was elected in early June. See below.

[27]Devlin, pp. 37–38; Kaplan, pp. 72–73.

[28]Quoted in Chris Goodey, 'Factory Committees and the Dictatorship of the Proletariat (1918)', *Critique*, no.3 (Autumn 1974), p. 32.

[29]Emile Vandervelde, *Three Aspects of the Russian Revolution*, trans. Jean Findlay, London 1918, pp. 74–75; Goodey, p. 34.

[30]Devlin, p. iii.

[31]Keep, *The Russian Revolution*, p. 82.

[32]Chris Goodey, 'Factory Committees', pp. 30–31; Vandervelde, p. 71.

[33]Reginald Zelnik, 'Russian Workers and the Revolutionary Movement', *Journal of Social History*, vol. 6 (winter 1971/72), pp. 218–19. See also Haimson, 'The Russian Workers' Movement on the Eve of the First World War'; and 'The Problem of Social Stability in Urban Russia, 1905–1917', Part One in *Slavic Review*, vol. 23 (1964), pp. 619–642, Part Two in vol. 24 (1965), pp. 1–22; Devlin, p. 9ff. Relatively close ties among *zemlyaki* (fellow villagers or countrymen) in both the factories and residential areas facilitated mobilization of the more recently proletarianized. See Robert Eugene Johnson, 'The Nature of the Russian Working Class: Social Characteristics of the Moscow Industrial Region, 1880–1900', Ph.D. dissertation, Cornell University, 1975, chapter 4.

[34]See Keep, *The Russian Revolution*, pp. 71ff., 258; David Mandel, pp. 178–9; and Benjamin Ward, 'Wild Socialism in Russia', p. 139ff. In one factory where women were dominant, the ratio of male to female wages was reduced from 5.72: 2.95 to 10:7. The unions and the soviets, it should be noted, also had an impact on the reduction of differentials.

[35]On this see Bobroff.

[36]As Zelnik notes: 'A scholarly analysis of the labour aristocracy phenomenon in Russia would have to include, inter alia, an investigation of: the absence in Russia proper of a strong legacy of traditional artisan guilds; the closing off of the craft union option to highly skilled workers because of the general illegality of trade unions (before 1906); the absence (before 1906) of legal political parties; the continued dispersal of skilled crafts in the countryside during years of industrial upsurge; the important role of foreigners and educated professionals in supervisory positions in Russian industry, thereby hindering the upward mobility of skilled Russian workers and their social identification with their immediate superiors; the possibility that wage differentials between skilled and semi-skilled workers were particularly low due to a combination of the shortage of capital in industry and the instability of the labour market.' 'Russian Bebels: An Introduction to the Memoirs of Semen Kanatchikov and Matvei Fisher', *The Russian Review*, vol. 35, no.3 (July 1976), pp. 262–63, n.12.

[37]David Mandel, pp. 37,50.

[38]Occuptional parochialism seems to have been more widespread on the rails, due to the more complex coordination problems, the deep political divisions among different categories of workers, and the fact that the Central Line Committees were dominated by very highly skilled engineers and technical personnel. See William Rosenberg, 'Workers' Control on the Railroads', D1186ff.

[39]Devlin, p. 77ff.

[40]Avrich, 'The Russian Factory Committees', p. 175; see also Avrich, 'The Rus-

sian Revolution and the Factory Committees', p. 38ff.; Brügmann, p. 36.

[41]Avrich, 'The Russian Revolution and the Factory Committees', p. 43; Pankratova, "Les comités d'usines", pp. 14–15; Keep, *The Russian Revolution*, pp. 84, 182.

[42]Avrich, 'The Russian Revolution and the Factory Committees', p. 57ff.; Devlin, p. 125ff.; Kaplan, p. 51ff.

[43]Roger Pethybridge, *The Spread of the Russian Revolution*, London 1972, p. 104. In this section on factory-committee coordination, I draw heavily on the data compiled in M.L. Itkin, 'Tsentry fabrichno-zavodskikh komitetov Rossii v 1917 godu', *Voprosy Istorii* (1974), no. 2, pp. 21–31. Itkin concludes from a still very incomplete survey that the factory committee centres were remarkably effective and that their role was incomparably greater than heretofore thought.

[44]Ferro, *La Révolution de 1917: Octobre*, p. 248.

[45]Selitskii, p. 172.

[46]Ferro, in *La Révolution de 1917: Octobre* (p. 313), notes an increase in the percentage of delegates who were 'appointed bureaucratically' from the first Petrograd conference in early June to the fourth in October. Neither the percentage increase (from 4% to 12%), nor the absolute numbers (16 to 20) are all that striking, especially since it is not clear what prerogatives these delegates had or whether they were allowed to vote. More ominous, however, is the significant decline in the absolute number of committee delegates who attended the conferences.

[47]See Falk Döring, p. 56ff.; Devlin, p. 199ff.; Kaplan, p. 67; Rosenberg, 'Workers' Control on the Railroads'. For a short period in June, a rival centre was set up that drew away a significant number of committees from the Bolshevik-dominated Central Council, including some rank-and-file party members from the militant Vyborg district. But this does not seem to have lasted. Its primary purpose was to push the *political* movement forward, not to coordinate workers control in a different manner. And the former goal was accomplished as the new centre helped instigate the July revolt, pushing the Bolshevik party further to the left and initiating a new phase of the revolution. See Goodey, 'Factory Committees', p. 42; Devlin, pp. 162–163.

[48]This conclusion is shared by various commentators, though to different degrees. John Keep (in *The Russian Revolution*, p. 158), for instance, concludes that ' "workers' control" was bound to create anarchy.' Avrich (in 'The Bolshevik Revolution and Workers' Control', p. 63) speaks of 'the elemental drive of the Russian masses towards a chaotic utopia'. See also Pankratova, 'Les comités d'usines', pp. 53–54; Jean-Marie Chauvier, 'Contrôle Ouvrier et "Autogestion Sauvage" en Russie (1917–1921)', *Revue des Pays de l'Est*, 14:1 (1973), p. 82; Charles Bettelheim, *Class Struggles in the USSR, First Period: 1917–1923*, trans. Brian Pearce, New York 1976, p. 146.

[49]Kaplan, p. 67.

Chapter 2

[1]See Bonnell, 'Trade Unions, Parties and the State', and 'Radical Politics and Organized Labor'; also Anna Pankratova, *Geschichte der Gewerkschaftsbewegung in der UdSSR*, Berlin 1956.

[2]Sandra Milligan, 'The Petrograd Bolsheviks and Social Insurance, 1914–1917', *Soviet Studies*, vol. 20 (1968–69), pp. 369–74.

[3]Isaac Deutscher, *Soviet Trade Unions*, London 1950, p. 1.

[4]There are no precise statistics about the size of the Russian working class, or universally accepted criteria of inclusion. Workers in heavy industry, including the railroad shops, are usually referred to as the proletariat proper, and numbered perhaps 3.4 million. This figure does not include the more than 800,000 other railroad workers, one million construction workers, and several million more in other forms of transportation, small industry, and commerce. These are estimates of Soviet historian P.V. Volobuev, cited in Michael Boll, *The Petrograd Armed Workers Movement in the February Revolution*, Washington, D.C. 1979, p. 1.

[5]Quoted in Keep, *The Russian Revolution*, p. 108.

[6]Ferro, *La Révolution de 1917: Octobre*, p. 275; see also Brügmann, p. 26ff.

[7]Quoted in Keep, *The Russian Revolution*, p. 100.

[8]Diane Koenker, 'Moscow Workers in 1917', chapter 6; Devlin, chapter 6.

[9]Koenker, chapters 6 and 7.

[10]Itkin (pp. 23–4), drawing upon studies by A.G. Yegorova and B.M. Freidlin, concludes that the failure to develop an independent centre of factory committees in Moscow is partly explained by the close integration of committees and district soviets, as well as the cooperation of the Bolshevik-dominated central bureau of trade unions and the committees. Perhaps the committees felt little need for further coordination, or were unwilling to drain scarce resources from those centres already functioning, especially since the more militant committee activities shared common political ties with many of them. This example underscores the fact that clear boundaries between different types of organizations (factory committees, soviets, unions) did not always exist; pragmatic goals could be achieved in various ways, depending on the peculiar constellation of local conditions.

[11]Avrich, 'The Russian Revolution and the Factory Committees', p. 75ff.; Koenker, 'Moscow Workers in 1917', p. 345ff.; Devlin, pp. 170–71; Anatolii Venediktov, *Organizatsiya gosudarstvennoi promyshlennosti v SSSR, Tom I (1917–1920)*, Leningrad 1957, pp. 98–99.

[12]Brügmann, p. 59ff.

[13]Richard Lorenz, 'Zur Industriepolitik der provisorischen Regierung', *Jahrbücher für Geschichte Osteuropas*, vol. 14 (1966), pp. 367–87; Simon Zagorsky, *State Control of Industry in Russia during the War*, p. 175ff.

[14]Quoted in Kaplan, p. 54.

[15]Ibid., p. 55.

[16]See Avrich, 'The Russian Revolution and the Factory Committees', p. 83ff.; the Right and Centre SRs, although they devoted most of their attention to general political questions and problems affecting the peasantry and soldiers, took a position similar to the Mensheviks on workers control. The Left SRs, on the other hand, sided with the Bolsheviks on these questions.

[17]Quoted in Avrich, 'The Russian Revolution and the Factory Committees', p. 36.

[18]Paul Avrich, *The Russian Anarchists*, Princeton 1967, p. 148.

[19]Paul Avrich, ed., *The Anarchists in the Russian Revolution*, Ithaca, New York 1973, pp. 64–66.

[20]Quoted in Alexander Rabinowitch, *Prelude to Revolution: The Petrograd Bolsheviks and the July 1917 Uprising*, Bloomington, Indiana 1968, p. 102; see also Kaplan, p. 170.

[21]Ferro, in *La Révolution de 1917: Octobre*, p. 234, claims that the anarchists were disproportionately represented in the semi-artisanal crafts and small firms, but

the evidence on this does not seem consistent.

[22]Lenin, *Collected Works*, fourth edition, London 1964, vol. 24, p. 24. There is a contradiction here that was to persist in Lenin's characterization of the revolution throughout most of 1917. At times he calls for a dictatorship of the proletariat and peasantry, at times simply for the dictatorship of the proletariat, or the proletariat and poor peasants. At other times, he characterizes the revolutionary government as a people's republic or a democratic republic. Some of the issues involved in these different characterizations will be analysed in other chapters. See Marcel Liebman, *Leninism under Lenin*, trans. Brian Pearce, London 1975, especially pp. 184–186.

[23]Lenin, vol. 23, pp. 240–41, 371–72; vol. 24, pp. 73–4, 241–43; vol. 25, pp. 43–5, 319–65. See also Herbert Ray Buchanan, 'Soviet Economic Policy for the Transition Period: The Supreme Council of the National Economy, 1917–20', unpublished Ph.D. thesis, Indiana University, 1972, chapter 1; Lorenz, *Anfänge*, pp. 40–58.

[24]A few exceptional references can be found in *Collected Works*, vol. 20, p. 154 and vol. 23, p. 24.

[25]Even the Petrograd Committee of the party called for workers control only on May 19. See David Mandel, p. 323.

[26]*Collected Works*, vol. 24, pp. 426–28.

[27]Ibid., pp. 513–14.

[28]Quoted in Avrich, 'The Russian Revolution and the Factory Committees,' pp. 69–70.

[29]Kaplan, p. 58.

[30]*Collected Works*, vol. 25, pp. 43–45.

[31]Avrich, 'The Russian Revolution and the Factory Committees', p. 85ff.; Kaplan, p. 63ff.

[32]Döring, p. 58; Ferro, *The Russian Revolution of February 1917*, p. 277; and Solomon Schwarz, in Browder and Kerensky, vol. II, p. 726.

[33]Kaplan, pp. 90–91.

[34]Ibid., p. 79; Keep, *The Russian Revolution*, p. 89; Lenin, *Collected Works*, vol. 25, p. 329; vol. 26, p. 105. Nationalization of the major syndicates became part of the party programme in August.

[35]One of another variant of this explanation can be found in Keep, *The Russian Revolution*, pp. 87–88; Avrich, 'The Russian Revolution and the Factory Committees', p. 69; Brügmann, pp. 65,90; Maurice Brinton, *The Bolsheviks and Workers' Control,* London 1970, pp. 5–6.

[36]See Avrich, 'The Russian Revolution and the Factory Committees', p. 164ff.

[37]Buchanan, 'Soviet Economic Policy for the Transition Period', pp. 81–82.

[38]Robert Service, *The Bolshevik Party In Revolution*: *A Study in Organizational Change*, New York 1979, pp. 61–62; see also Alexander Rabinowitch *The Bolsheviks Come to Power*, New York 1976, London 1979.

[39]Quoted in Rabinowitch, *Prelude to Revolution*, p. 93.

Chapter 3

[1]William Rosenberg, *Liberals in the Russian Revolution*, Princeton 1974, pp. 18,70.

[2]Anweiler, *The Soviets*, p. 104ff.; A. Andreev, *The Soviets of Workers' and Soldiers' Deputies on the Eve of the October Revolution*, trans. J. Langstone, Moscow 1971, p. 20ff. The Soviet was later reorganized to include only 1,200 dele-

gates, half soldiers and half workers, who generally met in separate sections.

³David Mandel, p. 133.

⁴Quoted in Anweiler, *The Soviets*, p. 131.

⁵The details of the agreement between the Petrograd Soviet and the Provisional Government are in Browder and Kerensky, vol. I, pp. 135–36. Also see Tsuyoshi Hasegawa, 'The Problem of Power in the February Revolution of 1917 in Russia', *Canadian Slavonic Papers*, vol. 14 (1972), p. 620ff.; on the Menshevik position, see especially Boris Sapir, 'The Conception of the Bourgeois Revolution', in Leopold Haimson, ed., *The Mensheviks*, Chicago 1974, p. 364ff.; and John Duryea Basil, 'Political Decisions Made By the Menshevik Leaders During the Revolution of 1917', unpublished Ph.D. dissertation, University of Washington, 1966, chapter 1.

⁶Ferro, *La Révolution de 1917*: *Octobre*, pp. 300–304, 311–12; Anweiler, *The Soviets*, pp. 113–14.

⁷Keep, *The Russian Revolution*, p. 131; Koenker, 'Moscow Workers in 1917'.

⁸Rex Wade, 'The Rajonnye Sovety of Petrograd: The Role of Local Political Bodies in the Russian Revolution', *Jahrbücher für Geschichte Osteuropas*, vol. 20 (1972), p. 226ff.; Koenker, 'Moscow Workers in 1917', pp. 322–23, 333–338.

⁹Wade, p. 236ff.; Andreev, pp. 58–59.

¹⁰Keep, p. 122ff.; Anweiler, *The Soviets*, p. 108ff.; Koenker, pp. 352–53. The actual recall of delegates, for which there were regular procedures ensuring adequate notice and opportunity to campaign, occurred quite frequently in practice—much more so than in the factory committees, it seems. The reason for this, no doubt, is that political differences were much more prominent in the soviets than in the committees.

¹¹Ferro, *La Révolution de 1917*: *Octobre*, pp. 309–10.

¹²Keep, *The Russian Revolution*, p. 125.

¹³Koenker, 'Moscow Workers in 1917', p. 313.

¹⁴Wade, 'The Rajonnye Sovety of Petrograd', p. 239.

¹⁵Keep, *The Russian Revolution*, pp. 122–23.

¹⁶Ferro, *La Révolution de 1917*: *Octobre*, p. 310.

¹⁷Gregory Guroff and S. Frederick Starr, 'A Note on Urban Literacy in Russia, 1890–1914', *Jahrbücher für Geschichte Osteuropas*, vol. 19 (1971), pp. 520–531; David Mandel, p. 20.

¹⁸Wade, 'The Rajonnye Sovety of Petrograd', p. 229; Koenker, 'Moscow Workers in 1917', p. 318.

¹⁹Robert Michels, *Political Parties*, trans. Eden and Cedar Paul, New York 1962.

²⁰Ferro, in *La Révolution de 1917*: *Octobre*, p. 314ff., tends to draw this conclusion from the decline in the frequency of general assembly meetings since March, and the rise in bureau meetings. Though his analysis is revealing on many points, he tends to collapse everything under the general rubric of 'bureaucratization', as if there could be no rational basis for limited participation that was consistent with democratic control. Likewise, simple things like the fact that workers stood around their delegated representatives in a photograph become unambiguous signs of bureaucracy. On the general relation between participation and democracy, see Robert Dahl, *After the Revolution*, New Haven, Connecticut, 1970, p. 40ff.

²¹David Mandel, p. 430ff.; and Deane Koenker, 'Moscow Workers in 1917', p. 351ff.

²²Oliver Radkey, *The Agrarian Foes of Bolshevism*, New York 1958, p. 233ff.; Keep, *The Russian Revolution*, pp. 128–29, 229.

²³Detailed accounts of these developments can be found in Rabinowitch's *Prelude*

to Revolution, and *The Bolsheviks Come To Power*. David Mandel's work is particularly useful in tracing the changes in working-class consciousness throughout these developments.

[24]The SRs, on the other hand, were considerably more nationalistic than the Mensheviks, and had a stronger attachment to the Allied cause. Their party was even financed to a considerable extent by loans from Allied banks. They did, however, follow the lead of the Mensheviks on most questions not directly related to the peasantry and the land problem.

[25]On developments around the issue of peace, see especially Rex Wade, *The Russian Search For Peace, February-October 1917*, Stanford 1969; and L.P. Morris, 'The Russians, the Allies and the War, February-July 1917', *Slavonic and East European Review*, 50:118 (January 1972), pp. 29–48. Russia's political links to the Allies were, of course, conditioned by its legacy of economic dependence, which involved a very heavy reliance on the West, and particularly France and Britain, for industrial investments (in some sectors more than 50% of total capital), for technology, and for government loans (especially during the war, when military expenditure and the disruption of its traditional export of agricultural products and raw materials had brought the government to the edge of bankruptcy). The Provisional Government's unwillingness to seek peace seriously was clearly related to this economic dependency. In the case of the Mensheviks, however, political and ideological factors played an autonomous, if not decisive role, in the formulation of their policies on war and peace. On the extent of Russian economic dependence, see Zagorsky, *State Control of Industry*, p. 14ff. Also see Theda Skočpol, *States and Social Revolutions*, New York 1979, pp. 92–93, 208–209.

[26]Wade, *The Russian Search For Peace*, p. 147.

[27]Ibid., passim, especially pp. 115–16; Morris, p. 41ff.

[28]Wade, pp. 70ff., 88ff.; Morris, pp. 45–56. See also Israel Getzler, 'The Mensheviks', *Problems of Communism*, vol. 16 (Nov.–Dec. 1967), pp. 26–27; and Herbert Ellison, 'The Socialist Revolutionaries', *Problems of Communism*, vol. 16 (Nov.–Dec. 1967), p. 5.

[29]Israel Getzler, *Martov*, Cambridge 1967, p. 152ff.; Radkey, *The Agrarian Foes of Bolshevism*, passim.

[30]Getzler, *Martov*, p. 157ff.; Radkey, p. 403; Leo Lande, 'The Mensheviks in 1917', in Haimson, ed., *The Mensheviks*, p. 18ff.

[31]See especially Getzler, *Martov*, p. 159ff.; Basil, p. 216ff.

[32]Radkey, *The Agrarian Foes of Bolshevism*, pp. 466–67.

[33]Rabinowitch, *The Bolsheviks Come To Power*, p. 174ff.; David Mandel, pp. 411ff., 430ff.

[34]Lenin, *Collected Works*, vol. 25, pp. 309–314; vol. 26, pp. 36, 67–68.

[35]Tsuyoshi Hasegawa, 'The Formation of the Militia in the February Revolution: an Aspect of the Origins of Dual Power', *Slavic Review*, vol. 32 (1973), pp. 303–322; D.N. Collins, 'A Note on the Numerical Strength of the Red Guard in October 1917', *Soviet Studies*, vol. 24 (1972), pp. 270–280.

[36]Quoted in Rabinowitch, *Prelude to Revolution*, p. 50.

[37]Leon Trotsky, *The History of the Russian Revolution*, trans. Max Eastman, Ann Arbor, Michigan 1962, p. 276. For the text of Order nos. 1 and 2, see Browder and Kerensky, vol. II pp. 848–49, 841–42. See also John Boyd, 'The Origins of Order No. 1', *Soviet Studies*, 19:3 (Jan. 1968), pp. 359–72.

[38]Marc Ferro, 'The Russian Soldier in 1917: Undisciplined, Patriotic and Revolutionary', *Slavic Review*, vol. 30 (1971), pp. 483–512; Marcel Liebman, *The Russian*

Revolution, trans. Arnold Pomerans, New York 1970, p. 154ff.

[39]Ferro; Catherine Chorley, *Armies and the Art of Revolution*, Boston 1972, chapter 6.

[40]Haimson notes that the high percentage of defeats had no parallel in other Western countries, and that these occurred under circumstances usually favourable to labour advances, namely, an industrial upsurge with a growing demand for labour and with increasing profits. See 'The Russian Workers' Movement on the Eve of the First World War', p. 63ff.

[41]Brügmann, pp. 51–52.

[42]Lorenz, *Anfänge der bolschewistischen Industriepolitik*, p. 26ff.; Brügmann, p. 79; Devlin, p. 32ff.

[43]Lorenz, p. 28ff.; Ferro, *La Révolution de 1917: Octobre*, chapter 6; David Mandel, pp. 473ff., 482ff.; Devlin, p. 242ff.

[44]Browder and Kerensky, vol. II, p. 721ff.; Ferro, p. 254ff.; David Mandel, pp. 292-93, 467-68; Devlin, p. 231ff. In some areas, the state, supported by the Menshevik minister, attempted to apply direct armed coercion against the committees. Nor was the Provisional Government particularly energetic in its attempts to prevent owner sabotage, through fines, inspections or sequestration—though perhaps it had even less capacity than willingness in such matters.

[45]David Mandel, pp. 467-513; Koenker, 'Moscow Workers in 1917', pp. 175ff., 412ff. Statistics on the number of factory committees in October are not completely clear or consistent. Brügmann (pp. 92-93) cites a fairly small percentage of firms with committees that assumed control functions, but fails to define what constitutes control, and, more importantly, fails to indicate the size of the plants involved and hence the relative proportion of the work-force organized in such committees. Much higher numbers are cited in Keep (*The Russian Revolution*, p. 487, n. 32), but he likewise ignores the problem of plant size. Evidence from Petrograd, Moscow, the Urals, Baku, the railroads, and other areas indicate that a very high percentage of industrial and transport workers were organized in committees by October, including nearly all those in the more sizeable plants. How extensive their control functions were, however, must remain an open question.

[46]Devlin, p. 261ff.; Ferro, *La Révolution de 1917: Octobre*, p. 288ff.; Selitskii, p. 193ff.

[47]Brügmann, p. 94ff.

[48]Service, p. 43; also see Diane Koenker, 'The Evolution of Party Consciousness in 1917: The Case of the Moscow Workers', *Soviet Studies*, 30:1 (Jan. 1978), pp. 38-62.

[49]Rabinowitch, *The Bolsheviks Come To Power*, is the best detailed account. See also Dietrich Geyer, 'The Bolshevik Insurrection in Petrograd', in Richard Pipes, ed., *Revolutionary Russia*, Garden City, New York 1969, pp. 227-28.

Chapter 4

[1]Quoted in Rabinowitch, *The Bolsheviks Come To Power*, p. 303.

[2]Lenin, *Collected Works*, vol. 26, pp. 264-65.

[3]E.H. Carr, *The Bolshevik Revolution, 1917-1923*, vol. 2, Baltimore 1966, pp. 73-75; Avrich, 'The Bolshevik Revolution and Workers' Control', pp. 49-50.

[4]See James Bunyan and H.H. Fisher, ed., *The Bolshevik Revolution, 1917-1918. Documents and Materials*, Stanford 1934, pp. 308-10, for the text of the law.

[5]Brügmann, p. 130.

[6]Didier Limon, 'Lénine et le contrôle ouvrier', *Autogestion*, no. 4 (December, 1967), pp. 73-74.

[7]Lozovsky, quoted in Kaplan, p. 119. At the First Trade Union Congress in January 1918, there were approximately nineteen All-Russian unions, at least five of which (metals, textiles, leathers, chemicals, and food) had more than 100,000 members. On the basis of the representational schema set forth in the 14 November law, the trade unions would have had at least thirty-one seats on the All-Russian Council of Workers Control, compared to five for the factory committees. See *Geschichte der Gewerkschaftsbewegung in der UdSSR*, N.P. Antropow, I.L. Borschtchenko, and I.P. Markow, trans. from the Russian, Berlin 1962, p. 226. These figures are, if anything, on the conservative side, since they do not include the large rail union or the ten or so other All-Russian unions not present at the Congress.

[8]See below.

[9]Venediktov, p. 92, who notes that the reason given for the lack of discussion and debate was that the Instructions were seen as tentative, pending correction and amendment by other organizations. However, criticism from the factory committees was ignored, while approval by the trade unions—essentially the same organizations that drafted them—was welcomed.

[10]Brügmann, p. 134; Limon, pp. 89-94.

[11]Quoted in Limon, p. 74.

[12]For the most important parts of the Manusl, see I. Gladkov, *Nataionalizatsiya promyshlennosti v SSSR* (Sbornik dokumentov i materialov, 1917-1920 gg.), Moscow 1954, pp. 77-82. This translation is from Goodey, 'Factory Committees', pp. 37-38.

[13]Gladkov, pp. 103-107; Brügmann, p. 131ff.

[14]Brügmann, pp. 136, 139; Venediktov, pp. 94-95; Lorenz, *Anfänge*, p. 99.

[15]Lorenz, *Anfänge*, pp. 101-102; Döring, p. 125.

[16]Quoted in Lorenz, *Anfänge*, p. 137. Though there is conflicting evidence on exactly how widespread nationalization was before the 18 June decree, most scholars agree that it was primarily the result of actions from below. In Pankratova's estimate, most important private firms had already been taken over by then. See 'Les comités d'usines', p. 61.

[17]Döring, p. 120ff.

[18]Brügmann, p. 185; V. Vinogradov, *Workers' Control Over Production: Past and Present*, Moscow 1973, pp. 65-66.

[19]A recent interpretation along these lines is that of John Keep (*The Russian Revolution*, p. 265ff.), though after presenting primarily negative evidence on the committees' actions, he concludes on an agnostic note.

[20]Kendall Bailes, *Technology and Society Under Lenin and Stalin*, Princeton 1978, p. 59; Kaplan, p. 129.

[21]Lenin, *Collected Works*, vol. 26, p. 111.

[22]Bailes, *Technology and Society Under Lenin and Stalin*, chapters 1 and 2.

[23]Döring, p. 132.

[24]Quoted in James Bunyan, ed., *The Origin of Forced Labor in the Soviet State, 1917-1921, Documents and Materials*, Baltimore 1967, p. 21. See also the sections of this report reprinted in James Bunyan and H.H. Fisher, eds., *The Bolshevik Revolution, 1917-1918, Documents and Materials*, Palo Alto 1934, pp. 654-55. Six days after this report, dictatorial powers over the rails were invested in the Com-

missar of Ways and Communications.

[25]Quoted in Brügmann, p. 153.

[26]A. Lomov, *Die Produktivität der Arbeit in Sowjet-Russland*, Berlin 1919, p. 5; William Rosenberg, 'Workers and Workers' Control in the Russian Revolution', *History Workshop*, no. 5 (Spring 1978), p. 92.

[27]Lomov, p. 17; Richard Lorenz, 'Wirtschaftspolitische Alternativen der Sowjetmacht im Frühjahr und Sommer 1918', *Jahrbücher für Geschichte Osteuropas*, vol. 15 (1967), p. 233ff.

[28]Carr, *The Bolshevik Revolution*, vol. 2, p. 392ff.

[29]Simon Zagorsky, *La République des Soviets*, Paris 1921, p. 237.

[30]Ward, p. 146; Ferro, *La Révolution de 1917: Octobre*, p. 262ff.; Lomov, p. 4ff.

[31]Döring, p. 111.

[32]The causes for this will be more fully discussed in chapter 5.

[33]These are estimates of Soviet statistician and economist S.G. Strumlin, cited in Brügmann, p. 152. Strumlin regards the physical exhaustion of the workers as the single most important factor affecting productivity at this time.

[34]Zagorsky, *La République des Soviets*, p. 213ff.; Döring, p. 70, notes that in many factories in Petrograd there was a complete turnover every two months, and in some from day to day!

[35]Lomov; see also L.B. Genkin, 'Rozhdeniye Sotsialisticheskoy Distsiplini Truda (konets 1917–leto 1918)', *Istoriya SSSR* (Jan.–Feb. 1965), no. 1, p. 19; Olga Narkiewicz, *The Making of the Soviet State Apparatus*, Manchester 1970, p. 54; Roger Pethybridge, 'The Bolsheviks and Technical Disorder, 1917–1918', *Slavonic and East European Review*, 49:116 (July 1971), p. 414; Lorenz, 'Wirtschaftspolitische Alternativen', p. 234. Lomov was the original Commissar of Justice and then became deputy chairman of the SEC in early 1918. He was a member of the party's left wing.

[36]Quoted in Brügmann, p. 155.

[37]Brügmann, pp. 155–56; Genkin; Rosenberg, 'Workers' Control on the Railroads', D1193ff.; David Mandel, p. 634ff.

[38]Lorenz, *Anfänge*, p. 147; Chauvier, pp. 81–82; Charles Bettelheim, *Class Struggles in the USSR, First Period: 1917–1923*, trans. Brian Pearce, New York 1976, p. 146ff.; for a general review of Bettelheim's book, see my essay 'Popular Movements and Revolutionary Theory in the First Years of Soviet Rule', *Socialist Review*, no. 36 (Nov.–Dec. 1977), pp. 143–60.

[39]These observations are drawn from a wide variety of sources too numerous to cite here. In addition to those already mentioned, see International Labour Office, *Labour Conditions in Soviet Russia*, London 1920, p. 242; M. Philips Price, *My Reminiscences of the Russian Revolution*, London 1921, p. 212.

[40]Brügmann, p. 141.

[41]Ferro, *La Révolution de 1917: Octobre*, pp. 288–89.

[42]Döring, pp. 60–61; 106ff.; Lorenz, *Anfänge*, pp. 100–101.

[43]Brügmann, pp. 186–87; Lorenz, 'Wirtschaftspolitische Alternativen', p. 234.

[44]Quoted in Avrich, 'The Bolshevik Revolution and Workers' Control', p. 50.

[45]Venediktov, p. 82ff. The author, in his attempts to show the correctness of Lenin's actions in this regard, fails to note that neither Lenin's draft nor the actual law eliminated the fundamental ambiguities surrounding workers control, as the conflicting sets of instructions clearly demonstrated.

[46]Buchanan, p. 83.

[47]Brügmann, p. 168.

[48]Brügmann, pp. 177–78, Döring, p. 74 and p. 252, n. 12. It is thus quite erroneous to conclude, on the basis of its role in initiating and staffing the Sec, and on the evidence of some of its members' individual careers in the 1920s, that the Central Council of Factory Committees represented that stratum within Bolshevism that valued above all else the development of the productive forces according to a centralized plan, or 'industrialization at all costs'. See Chris Goodey, 'Factory Committees', p. 46 and passim.

[49]Buchanan, pp. 84–85; Osinsky, in Bunyan and Fisher, pp. 311–312; Lorenz, *Anfänge*, p. 113ff.; Döring, p. 72.

[50]See Bunyan and Fisher, pp. 314–15, for the text of the statute.

[51]Samuel Oppenheim, 'The Supreme Economic Council 1917–1921', *Soviet Studies*, 25:1 (July 1973), pp. 9–10; Buchanan, p. 92; D.A. Baevski, 'Rol' sovnarkhozov i profsoyuzov v organizatsii sotsialisticheskogo promyshlennogo proizvodstva v 1917–1920 gg.', *Istoricheskie Zapiski*, no. 64 (1959), p. 6. An inquiry of August 1919 on the overall composition of the collegia of the *glavki* put it thus: workers 23.8%, middle-level technical and commercial personnel 22.5%, upper-level technical and commercial personnel 29.6%, others 24.5%. Döring, p. 133.

[52]Osinsky, in Bunyan and Fisher, pp. 312–13.

[53]Rosenberg, 'Workers' Control on the Railroads', D1210.

[54]Quoted in David Mandel, p. 650; Buchanan, pp. 101ff., 151ff.; Oppenheim, p. 6ff. Antonov noted at the time, for instance, that the factory committees were subject to a 'chaos of inquiries' emanating from the regional People's Economic Council, the Commissariats, the unions, and other administrative authorities, and, as a result, their response rate to them was extremely low. See Döring, p. 124ff.

As William Rosenberg points out in his discussion of the railroads, 'with the formal demise of workers' control ... this problem of contradictory authorities clearly intensified'. Articles in the rail journals linked falling productivity with the problem of competing (and often revolver-wielding) Bolshevik authorities. And by the fall of 1918, local Bolshevik officials were calling for the restoration of workers' control, 'not for ideological reasons, but because workers themselves knew best how to run the line efficiently, and might obey their own central committees's directives if they were not constantly being countermanded'. See 'Workers' Control on the Railroads', D1207ff.

[55]Döring, pp. 39–40, 71ff.; Baevski, p. 4ff.; Brügmann, p. 177ff.

[56]Buchanan, pp. 95ff., 197, 150ff.

[57]Oppenheim, p. 6; Döring, pp. 100ff., 86ff.

[58]The text of the resolution is in Bunyan, *The Origin of Forced Labor in the Soviet State*, pp. 13–14. See also Kaplan, 183ff.; Brügmann, p. 170.

[59]See Kaplan, pp. 190–91; and Brügmann, pp. 167–68.

[60]Bill Shatov, a former Iww activist in the United States, quoted in Avrich, *The Russian Anarchists*, p. 168.

[61]Quoted in Brinton, *The Bolsheviks and Workers' Control*, p. 31.

[62]Text in Bunyan and Fisher, p. 640.

[63]Quoted in Kaplan, p. 208.

[64]Brügmann, pp. 166–67.

[65]Quoted in Kaplan, p. 216.

[66]Kaplan, p. 211ff.

[67]Ibid., p. 197ff.; Brügmann, pp. 160–61.

[68]Sorenson, *The Life and Death of Soviet Trade Unionism*, p. 59; Kaplan, p. 237ff.; Leonard Schapiro, *The Origin of the Communist Autocracy*, Cambridge,

Mass. 1966, p. 224ff. As many of the most stalwart Bolshevik supporters were drawn into state jobs, and then later into the Red Army, the proportion of opposition parties increased in the factories, although various issues (food, labour controls, political developments), provided fertile ground for labour unrest. In addition, the Bolshevik Party began to lose recruits in early 1918, even before its official decision in the summer to purge 'undesirables'. See Service, p. 70.

[69]Döring, pp. 67–68; Brügmann, pp. 196–97.

[70]Döring, p. 68.

[71]Pankratova, 'Les comités d'usines', p. 59. Even less had the committees effected a painless 'suicide' by the time of the revolution, as Ferro argues in *La Révolution de 1917: Octobre*, p. 283ff. Ferro, indeed, neatly dichotomizes the workers-control movement into those smaller factories seeking to go it alone with *autogestion*, and those larger ones that simply accepted the predominant Bolshevik definition of control, as if there were not a great deal of struggle among the latter (and probably the former) over alternative conceptions of control and coordination.

[72]Avrich, 'The Bolshevik Revolution and Workers Control', p. 68; Lorenz, *Anfänge*, p. 99.

[73]Döring, p. 71.

[74]David Mandel, p. 416.

[75]Buchanan, p. 91.

[76]Devlin, p. 198.

[77]Stephen Cohen, *Bukharin and the Bolshevik Revolution*, New York 1971, p. 60ff.

[78]Lenin, *Collected Works*, vol. 26, pp. 467–68.

[79]Ibid. p. 467.

[80]Ibid. p. 410.

[81]This interpretation differs from that of Lorenz and a number of others that in the early months of the revolution Lenin's policy rested *solely* on the mass enthusiasm of the workers—so much so that he even temporarily lost sight of the leading role of the party. The latter point is certainly exaggerated, considering virtually everything Lenin did in these months. Nor do the two documents Lorenz cites bear out his argument on mass initiative. In the Draft Decree on the Socialization of the People's Economy in December, Lenin is quite clear that control of most industry is to remain in the hands of the capitalists. Nor does he support the more extensive version of workers control being propagated by the Central Council of Factory Committees, or their alternative proposals for an economic superstructure. At best, he is ambivalent on the actual degree of nationalization necessary at that time. The Rough Outline of the Draft Programme of March 1918 is quite radical in its espousal of soviet and economic democracy. But it is unclear whether this is a distant goal or a project for the current period. The latter seems quite unlikely, since, instead of presenting these ideas to the Seventh Party Congress, he chose to publish them in the Left Communist journal. The most likely explanation for what must have appeared a very strange move, given the serious disagreements with the Left over the peace of Brest-Litovsk, was that Lenin was attempting to maintain party unity in face of the Leftists' resignations from Central Committee and SEC posts. In any case, as Lorenz himself recognizes, Lenin had already rejected the theses on economic democracy in internal party discussions, as we shall see below. In this early period Lenin clearly placed great hopes on mass initiative. But he also had relatively well defined limits within which he hoped this would remain, even if he was not always completely clear about the boundaries. See Lorenz, *Anfänge*, pp.

148, 103ff.; Lenin, *Collected Works*, vol. 27, pp. 152–58; Bunyan and Fisher, pp. 316–17.

[82]David Mandel, p. 646.

[83]Deutscher, *Soviet Trade Unions*, p. 17.

[84]Ibid., p. 31.

[85]Zagorsky, *La République des Soviets*, p. 246, claims that there were 417,468 unemployed in the Moscow region alone.

[86]Lorenz, 'Wirtschaftspolitische Alternativen', p. 210; Brügmann, p. 216ff.; Keep, p. 259.

[87]Lenin, *Collected Works*, vol. 27, p. 106.

[88]Ibid., p. 163.

[89]What was essentially a draft of this article had already been presented to a meeting of party leaders on 4 April. See Bunyan and Fisher, pp. 553–60.

[90]Lenin, *Collected Works*, vol. 27, pp. 268–69.

[91]Ibid., p. 269.

[92]Ibid., p. 271.

[93]Ibid., p. 275. In the 'Six Theses on the Tasks of the Soviet Government', there is a brief reference to the 'dictators elected or appointed by Soviet institutions', but the theses were not further elaborated and dictatorship became the rule in practice. In the original draft of 'The Immediate Tasks', Lenin referred explicitly to the right of workers to elect and recall those exercising executive functions, but he later dropped this. Ibid., p. 212.

[94]Ibid., pp. 243–44.

[95]Ibid., p. 244.

[96]Ibid., p. 257.

[97]Ibid., p. 250.

[98]Ibid., pp. 248–49; see also pp. 315–16.

[99]Ibid., pp. 281, 295, 341.

[100]Ibid., p. 340.

[101]Ibid., pp. 294, 339, 335.

[102]Ibid., p. 295.

[103]Ibid., p. 341.

[104]The first issue of the Moscow journal appeared on 20 April, although some of its major theses were presented at the 4 April conference of party leaders referred to above. For selections of the latter, see Bunyan and Fisher, pp. 560–65.

[105]Osinsky, 'Über den Aufbau des Sozialismus', in Fritz Kool and Erwin Oberländer, ed., *Arbeiterdemokratie oder Parteidiktatur*, Olten und Freiburg im Breisgau 1969, p. 105.

[106]Ibid., pp. 104–05, 97–98.

[107]Ibid., pp. 111–12.

[108]Ibid., pp. 110, 116; also, Osinksy, in Bunyan and Fisher, p. 564.

[109]Osinsky, in Kool and Oberländer, pp. 95, 102, 107ff, 118; Osinsky, in Bunyan and Fisher, p. 564. Obviously, this position makes it quite clear that the Left Communists were not hostile to the employment of bourgeois experts as such. This mistaken interpretation can be found in many anti-Leftist commentaries. For example, see Charles Bettelheim, *Class Struggles in the USSR, First Period*, p. 374ff.

[110]Osinsky, in Kool and Oberländer, p. 113ff.

[111]Ibid., p. 116ff.

[112]Ibid., p. 110.

[113]'Theses on the Current Situation', *Kommunist*, no 1, quoted in Robert V.

Daniels, *The Conscience of the Revolution*, New York 1969, p. 87. See also James Bunyan, *Intervention, Civil War, and Communism in Russia: April-December, 1918: Documents and Materials*, Baltimore 1936, p. 395. Bukharin, who played a secondary role among the Left Communists in the economic controversy, considered the whole conception of state capitalism under the dictatorship of the proletariat a theoretical absurdity. See Cohen, *Bukharin and the Bolshevik Revolution*, pp. 75–76.

[114] Lenin, *Collected Works*, vol. 27, p. 341.

[115] Ibid., p. 187, emphasis added.

[116] Ibid., p. 188.

[117] Ibid., p. 329.

[118] Ibid., p. 299.

[119] Ibid., pp. 296, 301. It should be noted that in 'Left-Wing Childishness and the Petty-Bourgeois Mentality', Lenin gave up his state capitalist proposals strictly speaking, after they had been defeated as a result of Left Communist, trade-union and rank-and-file pressure (see below). Hence, in this article he advocates hiring experts purely as technicians and not as capitalists per se. Ibid., p. 349.

[120] Ibid., p. 348.

[121] Lorenz, *Anfänge*, p. 137ff.; Buchanan, pp. 172–73; and Jacques Sadoul, *Notes sur la révolution bolchévique*, Paris 1971, pp. 309–10.

[122] Lenin, *Collected Works*, vol. 27, p. 297 and p. 587, n. 120.

[123] Quoted in Buchanan, p. 195.

[124] Lenin, *Collected Works*, vol. 27, pp. 300–301.

[125] Brügmann, p. 204ff.

[126] Bunyan, *Intervention, Civil War*, pp. 379, 397; Lorenz, 'Wirtschaftspolitische Alternativen', p. 230.

[127] The text of the decree is contained in Bunyan, *Intervention, Civil War*, pp. 397–99; Carr, *The Bolshevik Revolution*, vol. 2, p. 103ff.

[128] Bunyan and Fisher, pp. 615–16; Brügmann, pp. 187–88.

[129] Lenin, *Collected Works*, vol. 27, pp. 388–89 and 594–95, editors' note 148.

[130] For the decree and Shlyapnikov's report, see Bunyan and Fisher, pp. 654–56. Also see Brügmann, pp. 210–11, who notes that the local commissars were often the former chairmen of the rail councils, confirmed by the commissar of ways and communications.

[131] Brügmann, p. 211ff.; Price, pp. 279–80; Lenin, *Collected Works*, vol. 27, pp. 351–52.

[132] Quoted in Carr, *The Bolshevik Revolution*, vol. 2, p. 102.

[133] On this last point, see Venediktov, pp. 591–93; see also Brügmann, p. 191ff., Lorenz, 'Wirtschaftspolitische Alternativen', pp. 231–32; Oppenheim, pp. 14–15.

[134] Carr, *The Bolshevik Revolution*, vol. 2, p. 118; Brügmann, pp. 237–38. As Carr notes, the ratio between highest and lowest in a decree of 19 January 1918, covering the Petrograd metal industry, was three to two, although somewhat higher in other types of work. This represented a notable levelling from pre-February days, although there were often significant differentials in rations.

[135] Brügmann, p. 231. Opponents often referred to Marx's analysis of the exploitative aspects of piece wages, but to my knowledge, he never posed the question of their use during the transition to socialism. See *Capital Volume 1,* Harmondsworth 1976, chapter 21.

[136] As Kaplan notes (pp. 337–38), the establishment of maximum limits was probably also designed to prevent workers from working intensively for short periods

until they accumulated enough money to return to their villages.

[137]Brügmann, p. 241.

[138]Ibid., p. 238ff., Kaplan, p. 236ff.; Zagorsky, *La République des Soviets*, p. 210; Bunyan, *Intervention, Civil War*, pp. 382–83, 397. The introduction of piece wages did not occur everywhere simultaneously, nor were they ever universal. By July 1918, they covered one-quarter of the workers in Petrograd, but still only about one-third of all metal and textile workers by September 1919. In leathers, the figure was 90 per cent.

[139]On Gastev, see Kendall Bailes, 'Alexei Gastev and the Soviet Controversy over Taylorism, 1918–1924', *Soviet Studies*, 29:3 (July 1977), pp. 373–94; also Franziska Baumgarten, *Arbeitswissenschaft und Psychotechnik in Russland*, Munich and Berlin 1924, especially p. 12ff.

[140]Margaret Dewar, *Labour Policy in the USSR, 1917–1928* London 1956, p. 39ff.; Brügmann, p. 225ff.; Kaplan, pp. 339–41.

Chapter 5

[1]Quoted in Boris Brutzkus, 'The Historical Peculiarities of the Social and Economic Development of Russia', in *Class, Status and Power*, Reinhard Bendix and Seymour Lipset, eds., Glencoe, Ill. 1953, p. 125. See also Eric Wolf, *Peasant Wars of the Twentieth Century*, New York 1969, pp. 51ff. As Leroy-Beaulieu has noted, 'it is evident that in the people, obscurely, but down to a great depth, a tradition has survived, a memory of a time when landed property was not yet, or not to any great extent, in the hands of the nobles, when nearly all the meadow lands and forest lands in particular were used indiscriminately and in an undefined way by all.' Quoted by Wolf, p. 57.

[2]On the relative weakness of the landed nobility, see Skocpol, *States and Social Revolutions*, p. 85ff.

[3]Alexander Gerschenkron, 'Agrarian Policies and Industrialization: Russia 1861–1917', *Cambridge Economic History*, vol. 6, part 2, Cambridge 1965, p. 739.

[4]Ibid., p. 778.

[5]Graeme Gill, *Peasants and Government in the Russian Revolution*, New York 1979, p. 10. A *desyatin* is equal to approximately two and one half acres.

[6]Repartitional tenure did not predominate in the Ukrainian, White Russian, Lithuanian, and Baltic provinces. See Francis M. Watters, 'The Peasant and the Village Commune', in *The Peasant in Nineteenth-Century Russia*, Wayne Vucinich ed., Stanford 1968, p. 147; and Dorothy Atkinson, 'The Russian Land Commune and the Revolution', unpublished Ph.D. thesis, Stanford University, 1971, p. 7ff. Strictly speaking, the *mir* and *obshchina* were not identical. The latter never acquired a consistent meaning, and was used predominantly by intellectuals, not peasants. It denoted the collectivist and repartitional aspects that so fascinated Russian intellectuals in the nineteenth century. See Steven Grant, '*Obshchina* and *Mir*', *Slavic Review*, 35:4 (December 1976), pp. 636–51.

[7]Wolf, p. 59.

[8]See the very provocative analysis of Eugene Vinogradoff, 'The "Invisible Hand" and the Russian Peasant', *Peasant Studies Newsletter*, 4:3 (July 1975), pp. 6–19. Although his analysis is tentative, Vinogradoff shows that under conditions in which people and draft animals fiercely competed for scarce land in the face of periodic famine, accumulation beyond a certain modest point could benefit neither the

village nor the individual household. In fact, village inbaitation, the strip system, land repartitioning, and the partitioning of the larger and wealthier households 'all directly aided the peasants in competing for land with their livestock and in using them more efficiently.' This analysis complements and theoretically enriches that of Teodor Shanin, who has amply demonstrated how statistics on differentiation among the Russian peasantry can be highly misleading. The larger households were usually those with more land, according to the various allotment and redivision schemes. Mobility was often multidirectional as well as cyclical, depending not only on redivision itself, but on household partitioning, merger extinction, migration—all of which combined to produce a levelling effect that considerably counterbalanced the cumulative effects of differentiation one might expect from commodity production. In the years after 1917, failure to understand these processes would result in misdirected policies again and again, as we shall see. Both before and after the revolution, 'the peasantry was more remarkable for the depth of its general poverty than for the extent of its differentiation.' Teodor Shanin, *The Awkward Class*, Oxford 1972, p. 21.

[9] Esther Kingston-Mann, 'Marxism and Russian Rural Development', *American Historical Review*, 86:4 (Oct. 1981), pp. 731–52.

[10] Anthony Oberschall's sociological theory of mobilization highlights these factors. See *Social Conflict and Social Movements*, Englewood Cliffs 1973, p. 118ff. Also see Skocpol, *States and Social Revolutions*, p. 112ff.

[11] Geroid Robinson, *Rural Russia Under the Old Regime*, New York 1949, p. 153.

[12] Ibid., chapters 9–10; Harcave, p. 216ff.

[13] Quoted in Robinson, p. 189.

[14] Ibid., p. 194.

[15] Atkinson, 'The Russian Land Commune', p. 50ff.

[16] Dorothy Atkinson, 'The Statistics on the Russian Land Commune, 1905–1917', *Slavic Review*, vol. 32 (1973), p. 775. The author presents considerable statistical evidence to demonstrate the limited effects of the Stolypin reforms, contrary to many earlier views, both Soviet and Western.

[17] A. Tyumenev, quoted in Wolf, p. 68.

[18] Launcelot Owen, *The Russian Peasant Movement, 1906–1917*, New York 1963, p. 184.

[19] Ibid., pp. 186–87.

[20] Graeme Gill analyses these rhythms in great detail.

[21] Owen, p. 172. Voluntary return was probably due to the fact that many separators were not all that well off, and return to the *mir* was the only way to get a piece of the collective action and booty. The richer separators rightly feared total dispossession if they failed to return. Atkinson, 'The Russian Land Commune', p. 150.

[22] Owen, p. 157; Keep, *The Russian Revolution*, p. 217.

[23] Gill, p. 117ff.; Owen, p. 217. Agricultural wage workers have generally been more resistant to self-organization and political mobilization. Without land to fall back on, they are in an extremely vulnerable, high-risk situation, and subject in their everyday activities to direct landlord supervision. And the forms of solidarity available in agricultural wage labour tend not to be as strong as those provided through village community institutions, at least when the latter are pitted against a common target. See Wolf, p. 290; Skocpol, *States and Social Revolution*, p. 116.

[24] Keep, *The Russian Revolution*, p. 157.

[25] Chernov later came to stress the egalitarian more than the collectivist aspects of

the existing *mir*. The latter could be developed in the service of socialism because the former had remained so strong. Radkey, *The Agrarian Foes of Bolshevism*, p. 84, and chapter 2.

[26]Quoted in Carr, *The Bolshevik Revolution*, vol. 2, p. 40.

[27]Quoted in Owen, p. 161.

[28]Keep, *The Russian Revolution*, p. 162ff; Gill, p. 64ff.

[29]Gill, pp. 23ff, 98ff.

[30]Radkey, *The Agrarian Foes of Bolshevism*, pp. 373–74, 437ff.

[31]Lenin, *The Development of Capitalism in Russia*, Moscow 1974, esp. p. 175ff. Lenin's misuse of the available statistics, his inconsistent use of class categories, and his misconceptions of peasant social organization are discussed in Esther Kingston-Mann, *Lenin and the Problem of Marxist Peasant Revolution, 1893–1917*, unpublished manuscript, chapter 3.

[32]Lenin, *Collected Works*, vol. 6, pp. 109–50.

[33]Lenin, *Collected Works*, vol. 13, pp. 291–92. This represents a self-criticism of *The Development of Capitalism in Russia* as well.

[34]Lenin, 'Two Tactics of Social Democracy in the Democratic Revolution', *Collected Works*, vol. 9, pp. 15–140.

[35]Lenin, *Collected Works*, vol. 13, pp. 293, 342ff.

[36]Ibid., vol. 24, p. 291; see also pp. 292, 68, 71–72, 370, 488–89.

[37]Leon Trotsky, 'Results and Prospects', in *The Permanent Revolution and Results and Prospects*, New York 1969, pp. 101–02.

[38]Elements of such an analysis were present in Lenin's writings of 1905 and later, but were not developed. See vol. 9, pp. 236–37; vol. 10, p. 92; vol. 21, p. 402. His shift in 1917 was conditioned by his independent conclusion (since he probably did not read Trotsky's *Results and Prospects* until 1919) that the peasantry could not play an independent political role, and his study of imperialism, which, as Ernest Mandel notes, had led him to the 'conclusion that, in the setting of a world market which had reached the stage of monopoly capitalism, Russian capitalism was doomed to remain under the domination of international finance-capital, and therefore could not but continue to be cramped, maimed, and underdeveloped, with a state power that was reactionary and barbarous'. 'Liebman and Leninism', *Socialist Register 1975*, Ralph Miliband and John Saville, eds., London 1975, p. 99.

[39]Lenin, *Collected Works*, vol. 13, p. 430.

[40]Ibid., vol. 24, p. 169.

[41]Ibid., p. 168.

[42]Ibid., vol. 13, p. 431; vol. 24, pp. 23, 72, 292–93, 451–52, 502ff. See also Atkinson, 'The Russian Land Commune', p. 138. Not all Bolsheviks, however, accepted the category of the 'poorest peasants' as a sociologically and politically meaningful one. See David Mandel, p. 411ff.

[43]Lenin, *Collected Works*, vol. 24, pp. 71, 72; vol. 25, pp. 123ff. Lenin argues that as a result of the war and the shortage of implements, the peasants had begun to realize the necessity of large-scale farming. And he interpreted the 242 Instructions published by the Peasant Soviet in August as implying 'large-scale socialist agriculture or at least social control over integrated small farms, socialist regulation of their economy', although the phrase on the transfer of livestock and implements 'to the exclusive use of the state or a commune', does not at all imply this. See Esther Kingston-Mann, 'Lenin and the Beginnings of Marxist Peasant Revolution: The Burden of Political Opportunity, July-October 1917', *Slavonic and East European Review*, 50:121 (October 1972), p. 597; Lenin, vol. 25, pp. 276–77, 281.

[44]Ibid., vol. 24, pp. 168, 504–05, 69.

[45]Ibid., vol. 25, p. 284.

[46]Ibid., vol. 24, p. 493.

[47]Ibid., vol. 25, p. 285.

[48]Ibid., vol. 26, pp. 333–35.

[49]Text in Bunyan and Fisher, p. 129.

[50]Atkinson, 'The Russian Land Commune', p. 201ff.

[51]According to one estimate, the kulaks lost more than 60 per cent of their pre-revolutionary holdings. Harry Willets, 'Lenin and the Peasants', in *Lenin: The Man, the Theorist, the Leader: A Reappraisal*, Leonard Schapiro and Peter Reddaway eds., New York 1967, p. 224.

[52]Shanin, *The Awkward Class*, pp. 150–51, 159; Atkinson, 'The Russian Land Commune', pp. 155ff, 204ff.

[53]One study notes that in its sample the average village increased in size by some six families (forty persons), and that almost all the returnees and about half of the newcomers were welcomed. This again attests to a very strong egalitarianism and weakly defined sense of private property rights among the Russian peasantry. See Atkinson, 'The Russian Land Commune', p. 156.

[54]See Shanin, *The Awkward Class*, pp. 53–54, 155, 157; Atkinson, 'The Russian Land Commune', p. 158. The estimates on differentiation are taken from a representative sample of villages from twenty-five provinces.

[55]Atkinson, 'The Russian Land Commune', p. 166.

[56]Quoted in Carr, *The Bolshevik Revolution*, vol. 2, p. 57.

[57]Lenin, *Collected Works*, vol. 27, p. 138.

[58]Ibid., p. 430.

[59]Keep, *The Russian Revolution*, p. 429.

[60]Lenin, *Collected Works*, vol. 27, p. 439; see also p. 455.

[61]Atkinson, 'The Russian Land Commune', pp. 170–71. Zinoviev reported that they often were simply appointed by the soviet executive committee or the party organization.

[62]Atkinson, 'The Russian Land Commune', pp. 169–70.

[63]Lenin, *Collected Works*, vol. 28, p. 171.

[64]Narkiewicz, p. 41; Shanin, *The Awkward Class*, p. 149.

[65]Carr, *The Bolshevik Revolution*, vol. 2, p. 153; Seth Singleton, 'The Tambov Revolt (1920–1921)', *Slavic Review*, vol. 25 (1966), pp. 499–500; Lenin, *Collected Works*, vol. 27, pp. 434, 449.

[66]Heiko Haumann, *Beginn der Planwirtschaft*, Düsseldorf 1974, p. 36.

[67]Carr, *The Bolshevik Revolution*, vol. 2, p. 162ff; Robert Abrams, 'The Local Soviets of the RSFSR, 1918–21', unpublished Ph.D. thesis, Columbia University, 1966, p. 297ff.; Lenin, *Collected Works*, vol. 28, pp. 56, 176; vol. 29, pp. 27, 203.

[68]Lenin, ibid., vol. 28, p. 27.

[69]Shanin, *The Awkward Class*, p. 161.

[70]Yuzuru Taniuchi, *The Village Gathering in Russia in the Mid-1920s*, Birmingham 1968, p. 18.

[71]Shanin, *The Awkward Class*, p. 161. A related phenomenon, namely, the very meagre development of agricultural trade unions in this entire period, is discussed by Peter Potichnyj, *Soviet Agricultural Trade Unions, 1917–1970*, Toronto 1972, p. 3ff.

[72]Bunyan and Fisher, pp. 674–76.

[73]Lenin, *Collected Works*, vol. 28, p. 344.

[74]Bunyan, *Intervention, Civil War*, p. 493.

[75]See Robert Wesson, *Soviet Communes*, New Brunswick, New Jersey 1963.

[76]Atkinson, 'The Russian Land Commune', p. 98ff.

[77]Ibid., p. 193. The figures in parentheses represent 'ascribed' *sovkhozy*, which were agricultural enterprises assigned directly to institutions or factories for supplying their own needs.

[78]See, for example, Isaac Steinberg's retrospective analysis in *In The Workshop of the Revolution*, New York 1953, chapter 19, in which he argues that virtually all the peasants 'had truly abandoned the old concepts of private property so as to enter into a new life of common welfare and solidarity. It seemed natural that the peasants, producers of the people's vital goods, would soon forge bonds of friendship with the industrial workers in the cities'. (p. 164). There is no analysis in Steinberg's work of the inherent conflicts between the workers and peasants, given the condition of industry and the historical antagonisms between town and country. Not surprisingly, this romanticization extended to the factory committees and soviets as well (pp. 20–21, 26). But while Steinberg exaggerates the collectivist tendencies of the *mir*, it would be incorrect not to recognize that these aspects often had very deep roots and were not limited simply to land redistribution and taxation. The *mir* often performed social welfare functions (care of widows, collective rebuilding of burned-out huts, emergency food storage); and the organization of artels for collective labour on specific tasks was widely practised before the revolution. See Wesson, p. 44ff.

[79]Speech at the Fifth All-Russian Congress of Soviets, excerpted in Bunyan, *Intervention, Civil War*, p. 208; for Lenin's response, see pp. 209–10. Chernov had pointed to this attitude among the Bolsheviks earlier in 1917. See Kingston-Mann, *Lenin and the Problem of Marxist Peasant Revolution*, p. 220.

[80]Kingston-Mann, ibid., pp. 47–48.

[81]See, for example, *Collected Works*, vol. 32, p. 217; Carr, *The Bolshevik Revolution*, vol. 2, p. 169. In this Lenin differed considerably from Marx himself, for whom the *mir* could very well have become 'a point of support for the socialist regeneration of Russia'. The laws of capitalist development that he laid out in *Capital*, he insisted to his Russian followers, do not necessarily pertain to every existing social formation. His own analysis had been limited to Western Europe, and it was possible that Russia might take quite a different path to socialism than that which follows only in the wake of full-scale capitalist development. For this to happen, however, a number of conditions would have to exist. In order that the *mir* may function as the basis for the socialist regeneration of Russia, he wrote to Vera Zasulich in 1881, 'it would be necessary to remove the harmful influences to which it is imposed on all sides and then guarantee to it normal conditions of free development.' In a draft of this letter he was more explicit: 'if the Russian revolution serves as a signal for a workers' revolution in the West so that the two complement each other, then contemporary Russian land tenure may be the starting point for communist development.' Only in the 1890s did Engels finally conclude that, as Marx had earlier feared, the commune had continued to disintegrate—too far for it to be a source of socialist regeneration. But the twentieth century produced hopes and possibilities much closer to Marx's earlier analysis of the *mir* than to that of Engels, Plekhanov, or other Russian Marxists. The revolution had ruptured the fateful progress of capitalist development; revolutionary state power provided the possibility for more favourable agrarian development; the commune had proven to be far more durable and egalitarian than any Marxists had expected; and a European revolution

was a distinct possibility; indeed, it was a cornerstone of Lenin's entire political strategy. While such a conclusion can only be speculative, it is difficult to imagine that Marx, under such conditions, would not have sought alternatives more favourable to the transformation of the commune from within, rather than its disruption from without. Lenin, in contrast to Marx, never saw the slightest possibility for the transformation of the *mir* in a socialist direction, and treated such suggestions with complete scorn. For useful discussions of Marx's views on the *mir*, see Carr, *The Bolshevik Revolution*, vol. 2, p. 385ff; Martin Buber, *Paths in Utopia*, trans. by R.F.C. Hull, Boston 1949, p. 90ff; and Marx and Engels, *Selected Correspondence*, trans. by Dona Torr, Westport, Conn. 1975, pp. 352–55, 508–10, 513–15.

[82]Boris Kamkov, 'Zur Verhältnis von Stadt und Land', in Gottfried Mergner, ed., *Die russische Arbeiteropposition*, Hamburg 1972, p. 85ff.; 'Organicheskii nedug', in *Teoriya i Praktika Sovetskogo Stroya*, *Vypusk Pervyi*, Berlin n.d. p. 9ff.; Steinberg, *In The Workshop of the Revolution*, pp. 11ff., 107ff.

[83]Steinberg, ibid., p. 46.

[84]Radkey, *The Sickle Under the Hammer*, New York 1963, pp. 141, 153. Steinberg was himself the Commissar of Justice, and another Left SR was second-in-command of the Cheka. They did not, however, shrink from using force against known counter-revolutionaries.

[85]Kamkov, 'Zur Verhältnis von Stadt und Land', p. 89; 'Organicheskii nedug', p. 25ff.

[86]Schapiro, *Origin of the Communist Autocracy*, p. 118ff. As peasant movements in the twentieth century (most notably the Vietnamese) demonstrate, guerrilla warfare may not only have been militarily effective but it may also have facilitated the penetration of revolutionary ideas and organization into the villages. But the cost for Russia would probably have been the capture and destruction of some of its major cities—a price the Bolsheviks, an urban-oriented Marxist party with the support of no major industrial power and supplier of arms, could not have been expected to pay. In such circumstances, not only would victory have been very doubtful, but so also would the kind of socialist society that could have been constructed from the ashes of such a victory. The Left SRs showed little understanding of such realities when they said 'Let the Imperialists occupy Petrograd and Moscow. They will find their grave on the soil on which the revolution grew.' Kamkov, quoted in Steinberg's *Spiridonova: Revolutionary Terrorist*, trans. and ed. by Gwenda David and Eric Mosbacher, London 1935, p. 199. The Makhnovist movement in the Ukraine was one of the few examples in Russia of relatively effective guerrilla warfare combined with attempts at ideological and social transformation of the countryside into a network of democratic agricultural collectives. The almost constant state of warfare, the hostility and cynical manipulation by the Bolsheviks, and the paucity of good studies on the social aspects of the movement, prevent an objective analysis of its possibilities. Let it simply be said that, while the movement often showed tremendous idealism and made significant strides in organizing popular congresses, it failed to interest most peasants in collective forms of labour or political participation beyond the fight against the external oppressors; it showed virtually no comprehension of how to organize a complex urban economy and failed to enlist the support of any significant sector of the urban working class; and the highly erratic and often brutal and dictatorial behaviour of its leaders, including Makhno himself, often belied its stated goals. See Victor Peter, *Nestor Makhno*, Winnipeg 1970; Michael Palij, *The Anarchism of Nestor Makhno, 1918–1921*, Seattle 1976; Peter Arshinov, *History of the Makhnovist Movement (1918–1921)*, trans. by Lorraine and Freddy

Perlman, Detroit and Chicago 1974; Voline, *The Unknown Revolution*, trans, by Holley Cantine and Freddy Perlman, New York 1974, Book III, Part II.

[87]Radkey, *The Sickle Under the Hammer*, pp. 138, 216–17, 104.

[88]Kamkov, at the Fifth Congress of Soviets, in Bunyan, *Intervention, Civil War*, p. 211.

[89]Steinberg, *In the Workshop of the Revolution*, p. 264.

[90]Bunyan, *Intervention, Civil War*, pp. 208–09. It is quite possible, indeed, I would think very probable, that if the Bolsheviks had not instituted the Committees of Poor Peasants and other forms of purely administrative and external controls on the villages, the final break in July would not have been made. The Left SRs did not split over the Land Socialization Law, which contained provisions with which they strongly disagreed, such as the soviets' right to expropriate land for non-agricultural purposes and priority in land allocation for collective farms. They continued to participate in various levels of government, including the Cheka, after the Brest resignations from the Council of People's Commissars. There had been significant opposition to the resignations in their Central Committee, most notably from Spiridonova. The actions against the Germans were not seen as an attack on the Soviet government or the Bolsheviks, as their actual preparations clearly show. And the majority of them later repudiated the assassination. The provocation of the *kombedy* surely helped to create the feeling among the Left SRs that only desperate actions could save a desperate situation. The assassination, however, provided the Bolsheviks an opportune 'excuse for putting an end to the Left Social Revolutionaries as a party', and extirpating their influence from the local soviets. Schapiro, *Origin of the Communist Autocracy*, p. 123; Liebman, *Leninism Under Lenin*, p. 257.

[91]Gill, p. 32ff.

[92]Radkey, *The Agrarian Foes of Bolshevism*, p. 233ff.

[93]Shanin, *The Awkward Class*, p. 186; Atkinson, 'The Russian Land Commune', pp. 179, 183.

[94]T.H. Rigby, *Communist Party Membership in the USSR, 1917–1967*, Princeton 1968, p. 84.

[95]Ibid., pp. 106, 486; Taniuchi, p. 29.

[96]Quoted in Shanin, *The Awkward Class*, pp. 188–89. Yakovlev added that in the past two years not a single Moscow publishing house had brought out anything on the village! See Jan Meijer, 'Town and Country in the Civil War', in Richard Pipes, ed., *Revolutionary Russia*, Garden City, New York 1969, pp. 343–49.

[97]See Franz Schurmann, *Ideology and Organization in Communist China*, 2nd. ed., Berkeley 1968, pp. 423–25. The task would have been considerably more difficult than in China, given the more self-enclosed and solidary nature of the Russian village.

[98]Abrams, passim; Radkey, *The Sickle Under the Hammer*, p. 258ff.

[99]A. Luzhin and M. Rezunov, *Nizovoi sovetskii apparat*, Moscow 1929, quoted in Shanin, *The Awkward Class*, p. 166.

[100]Abrams, passim; Taniuchi, passim.

[101]Lenin, *Collected Works*, vol. 31, p. 505.

[102]Ibid., vol. 29, pp. 31–32, 117, 159–60, 217ff., 246–47, 365ff., 568; vol. 31, p. 506; vol. 32, p. 216.

[103]Heiko Haumann, 'Die russische Revolution und ihre ersten Versuche sozialistischer Wirtschaftspolitik', *Das Argument*, 15:32 (1973), p. 776; Haumann, *Beginn der Planwirtschaft*, p. 33.

[104]Lenin, *Collected Works*, vol. 29, p. 78.

[105]Atkinson, 'The Russian Land Commune', p. 222.

[106]Singleton, p. 499; see also Radkey, *The Unknown Civil War in Soviet Russia*, Stanford 1976.

[107]Service, pp. 78–79.

[108]Abrams, p. 48, n. 2 and chapter 9.

[109]Lenin, *Collected Works*, vol. 27, p. 394.

[110]Meijer, pp. 343, 356, passim.

[111]Meijer (pp. 343ff), also suggests that a tax in kind, similar to the one introduced after the peasant uprisings in 1920–21, was perhaps also a distinct possibility in 1918, and one that might have significantly reduced peasant resistance. 'The total effort to raise a tax in kind would hardly have equalled that involved in the requisitioning and might have established a clearer line of authority in the village.' Such a tax was approved in late October 1918, but never put into effect. The major reason for this seems to have been ideological. During the civil war, the party saw itself as struggling to establish fully communist norms of distribution through state control. And, although the black market functioned extensively and was often tolerated as necessary, any official allowance of free trade was seen as antagonistic to this struggle. Only in 1921 did Lenin recognize this goal as illusory. See Haumann, 'Die russische Revolution', p. 781; *Beginn der Planwirtschaft*, p. 34; Lenin, *Collected Works*, vol. 27, p. 439.

[112]See, for instance, the analysis of Kamkov, considered to be the theoretician of the Left SRs, in 'Organicheskii nedug', p. 22ff. Kamkov's underestimation of such objective factors is paralleled by his overly optimistic reliance on the class consciousness of the peasants and their sense of solidarity with the urban workers. This approach was shared by the anarchists in the Ukraine as well. See Arshinov, pp. 257–58.

Chapter 6

[1]Cohen, *Bukharin*, p. 60. For developments on the military front, see David Footman, *Civil War in Russia*, London 1961.

[2]These and related aspects of Lenin's theory of the state will be discussed in detail in chapter 8.

[3]Lenin, *Collected Works*, vol. 26, p. 49; Andreev, p. 289.

[4]*The Bolsheviks and the October Revolution*: Minutes of the Central Committee of the Russian Social-Democratic Labour Party (Bolsheviks), August 1917—February 1918, trans. Ann Bone, London 1974, p. 132.

[5]Quoted in Bunyan and Fisher, p. 195. In this piece, Lenin argued that, because 'the whole of Europe is with us', there was no need to worry about broadening the political basis of the regime. Ironically, the sailors to whom Lenin threatened to appeal were themselves strong supporters of a coalition government. See also Central Committee Minutes, p. 137.

[6]Brügmann, p. 110ff.; Keep, *The Russian Revolution*, pp. 265–66; David Mandel, p. 587.

[7]I have drawn on numerous detailed accounts of these events, but perhaps the most judicious summary is that of Liebman, *Leninism Under Lenin*, p. 238ff.

[8]Radkey, *The Sickle Under the Hammer*, pp. 71–72.

[9]Anweiler, *The Soviets*, p. 194.

[10]Keep, *The Russian Revolution*, p. 313.

[11]Radkey, *The Sickle Under the Hammer*, pp. 91–92, 396ff.

[12]Ibid., p. 463. Those scholars who have defended the Constituent Assembly against the Bolsheviks hardly even attempt to show how it could have developed effective policies to stem social and economic disintegration in the circumstances. In this regard, Keep is representative. By upholding the Assembly as 'Russia's last hope for civil peace and a pluralistic political order', and yet not disguising the practical bankruptcy and organizational weaknesses of the moderate socialists, he would have his political cake and eat it as a scholar too. See *The Russian Revolution*, p. 337.

[13]Liebman, *Leninism under Lenin*, p. 266; Getzler, *Martov*, chapter 8; Haimson, ed., *The Mensheviks*, part II.

[14]Keep, *The Russian Revolution*, p. 349.

[15]Ibid., pp. 380–81. See chapters 25–27 of this work for a detailed regional analysis of the transfer of power.

[16]Abrams, passim, whose work shows in great detail that a 'transmission belt' relationship between party and local soviets did not exist in these years.

[17]T.H. Rigby, *Lenin's Government: Sovnarkom, 1917–1922*, New York 1979, p. 161ff.

[18]Keep, *The Russian Revolution*, p. 321. Its early deliberations have recently been translated and edited by Keep in *The Debate on Soviet Power*, Oxford 1979.

[19]See Walter Pietsch, *Revolution und Staat: Institutionen als Träger der Macht in Sowjetrussland 1917–1922*, Cologne 1970, chapter 7.

[20]Rigby, *Lenin's Government*, p. 174.

[21]Ibid., p. 43.

[22]The most detailed study of these developments remains that of Pietsch, though Rigby's recent work supplements it in important ways.

[23]As Rosabeth Moss Kanter has shown, even in highly institutionalized systems, all sorts of loyalty criteria are invoked among officials who exercise considerable discretion in an environment of relative uncertainty. In Russia in these years there existed *both* a very high level of uncertainty (the war, the food situation) *and* a very low level of institutionalization, thus placing an especially high premium on loyalty criteria. See her *Men and Women of the Corporation*, New York 1977, chapter 3.

[24]On the changes in party composition, Service's recent work is particularly valuable.

[25]Kaplan, p. 308.

[26]Rigby, *Lenin's Government*, p. 176.

[27]Pietsch, chapter 9. As Pietsch notes, if anything there was a possibility that the party could have been swallowed up in state institutions, rather than vice versa. Local party funds were even dependent on the soviets. See also Abrams, p. 360ff.

[28]Rigby, *Lenin's Government*, pp. 210, 230; Pietsch, chapter 8.

[29]Pietsch, p. 152.

[30]Pierre Sorlin, *The Soviet People and Their Society*, trans. Daniel Weissbort, New York 1968, p. 76. World War I and the civil war together claimed 5 million military victims, and 7.5 million civilians. By 1920 the cities had less people than in 1900, and less workers than in 1880. And these statistics hardly reveal the qualitative misery experienced by the Russian population in these years as a result of disease, displacement, malnutrition, and constant insecurity.

[31]See Roger Pethybridge, *The Social Prelude to Stalinism*, London 1974, chapter 3. Trotsky, the commissar of war, himself often pointed to such factors.

[32]Rigby, *Lenin's Government*, chapters 10 and 11. The relative youth of the peo-

ple's commissars (37 years old on average in 1917) is also striking.

[33]Abrams, p. 372; Pietsch, p. 145; Anweiler, *The Soviets*, p. 220.

[34]Rigby, *Lenin's Government*, p. 238.

[35]Brügmann, p. 245ff.; Döring, p. 147.

[36]Lenin, *Collected Works*, vol. 30, p. 427; also pp. 426, 457.

[37]Ibid., pp. 309–10.

[38]Ibid., vol. 32, pp. 26–27, emphasis added.

[39]Ibid., pp. 33–34.

[40]Ibid., vol. 30, p. 465.

[41]Quoted in Carr, *The Bolshevik Revolution*, vol. 2, p. 193.

[42]Bunyan, *The Origin of Forced Labor*, p. 128ff.; Carr, *The Bolshevik Revolution*, vol. 2, p. 192ff.; Osinsky *et al.*, 'Thesen über die kollegiale und die Einmannleitung (1920)', in Kool and Oberländer, pp. 126–28.

[43]V.Z. Drobizhev, *Glavnii shtab sotsialisticheskoi promyshlennosti*, Moscow 1966, p. 121.

[44]Buchanan, pp. 261–62, 290–91.

[45]Conference resolution, quoted in Bunyan, *Intervention, Civil War*, p. 413; also p. 410ff.

[46]Buchanan, p. 291.

[47]Brügmann, p. 253ff.

[48]Paragraph five of the resolution, in Bunyan, *The Origin of Forced Labor*, p. 28.

[49]Kaplan, pp. 315–16.

[50]Brügmann, pp. 260–62; Bunyan, *The Origin of Forced Labor*, p. 29ff.

[51]Lenin, *Collected Works*, vol. 28, pp. 139–40.

[52]Ibid., vol. 30, p. 109.

[53]Ibid., vol. 28, p. 140; vol. 27, p. 517.

[54]Ibid., vol. 30, p. 456, emphasis added.

[55]Brügmann's claim (p. 262), shared by many other Western commentators, that these developments were primarily the result of the inherent and unremitting drive for party domination, is thus quite one-sided.

[56]Rosenberg, 'Workers' Control on the Railroads', D1213.

[57]Quoted in Buchanan, p. 281; see also Döring, p. 190ff.

[58]Quoted in Carr, *The Bolshevik Revolution*, vol. 2, p. 184; see also Döring, passim; Buchanan, p. 283ff.

[59]Maurice Dobb, *Soviet Economic Development Since 1917*, rev. ed., New York 1966, pp. 111–12; Oppenheim, p. 12.

[60]Carr, *The Bolshevik Revolution*, vol. 2, p. 183.

[61]Sorenson, *Life and Death of Soviet Trade Unionism*, p. 79; Brügmann, p. 248ff.

[62]Lenin, *Collected Works*, vol. 27, p. 408.

[63]Leo Kritsman, *Die heroische Periode der grossen russischen Revolution*, Frankfurt 1971, p. 325.

[64]Ibid., pp. 198–99.

[65]On the development of the electrification project and planning in these years, see especially Heiko Haumann, *Beginn der Planwirtschaft: Elektrifizierung, Wirtschaftsplanung und Entwicklung Sowjetrusslands 1917–1921*, Dusseldorf 1974.

[66]Cited in Dewar, p. 52.

[67]Haumann, *Beginn der Planwirtschaft*, p. 42.

[68]Döring, p. 168.

[69]Zagorsky, *La République des Soviets*, pp. 251–52.

[70]Haumann, 'Die russische Revolution', pp. 774–75; Kritsman, pp. 297–98.

[71]Döring, pp. 168, 154–55, 171ff.

[72]Kritsman (p. 337) claims that by mid-1918 the ratio was already 1:1.9 and by 1920, 1:1.04, but this degree of levelling is surely exaggerated, even when we consider that by 1920 differentials were often in the form of food rations.

[73]Dewar, p. 63ff; Bunyan, *The Origin of Forced Labor*, p. 176ff.

[74]Döring, pp. 170–71.

[75]Statute quoted in Bunyan, *The Origin of Forced Labor*, p. 88.

[76]Rosenberg, 'Workers' Control on the Railroads', D1215–16.

[77]Hans-Theodor Schmidt, *Die sowjetischen Gesellschaftsgerichte*, Cologne 1969, p. 33ff.

[78]Lenin, *Collected Works*, vol. 32, p. 41.

[79]See Kaplan, p. 352ff; Sorenson, *The Life and Death of Soviet Trade Unionism*, p. 149ff.

[80]Lenin, *Collected Works*, vol. 29, p. 427; vol. 30, pp. 285, 517.

[81]Sorenson, *Life and Death of Soviet Trade Unionism*, pp. 148–49; see also Kaplan, p. 359ff.

[82]See the Central Committee's Theses, reprinted in Bunyan, *The Origin of Forced Labor*, pp. 95–101.

[83]Trotsky, *Terrorism and Communism*, Ann Arbor Michigan 1961, p. 134ff. This book represents excerpts from his speeches at the Third Trade Union Congress, the Ninth Party Congress, and the Third PEC Congress. The Menshevik argument that Trotsky attacked, namely that compulsory labour was unproductive, was apparently very well founded. See, for instance, its results on the rails in Rosenberg, 'Workers' Control on the Railroads', D1214.

[84]Lenin, *Collected Works*, vol. 30, p. 508.

[85]Trotsky, *Terrorism and Communism*, pp. 147–48, 158–59.

[86]Nikolai Bukharin, *Economics of the Transformation Period. With Lenin's Critical Remarks*, New York 1971, pp. 117–18, 160 and chapter 10; see also Cohen, *Bukharin*, p. 86ff. Bukharin noted (pp. 131–32) that the military model of coercive discipline did have certain disadvantages, but he apparently had neither the time nor the clarity to elaborate on these.

[87]Ibid., pp. 220–21.

[88]See, for example, Lenin, *Collected Works*, vol. 33, p. 88; and Charles Bettelheim, *Class Struggles in the USSR*, vol. 1, part V, chapter 2.

[89]Lenin, *Collected Works*, vol. 30, p. 144.

[90]Trotsky, *Terrorism and Communism*, p. 147. Arakeheyev was the ill-famed nineteenth-century minister of war who established militarized farming colonies. On the debates on the issue of militarization, see Deutscher, *Soviet Trade Unions*, p. 35ff.; Osinksy, 'Zur Frage der "Militarisierung der Wirtschaft"', in Kool and Oberländer, pp. 141–57.

[91]Quoted in Cohen, *Bukharin*, p. 101.

[92]Jay Sorenson, 'The Workers' Opposition: A Case Study of Factionalism in the Russian Communist Party', unpublished M.A. thesis, Columbia University, 1956, pp. 70–71.

[93]Kaplan p. 287ff.

[94]See, for example, Lenin, *Collected Works*, vol. 30, p. 470; vol. 32, p. 47.

[95]Ibid., vol. 32, pp. 44–45.

[96]Ibid., pp. 20–21.

[97]Ibid., pp. 24–25, 58, 73, 48. In response to Bukharin's criticism, Lenin later

corrected this formulation: 'What I should have said is "A workers' state is an abstraction. What we actually have is a workers' state with this peculiarity, firstly, that it is not the working class but the peasant population that predominates in the country, and, secondly, that it is a workers' state with bureaucratic distortions."

[98]Alexandra Kollontai, *The Workers Opposition*, London 1970, p. 35.

[99]Quoted from the theses presented by the Workers Opposition to the Tenth Party Congress in March 1921, reprinted in an abridged version in Bunyan, *The Origin of Forced Labor*, p. 231. A fuller English translation appears in *Self-Governing Socialism*, Branco Horvat, Mihailo Markovic, and Rudi Supek, eds., vol. 1, White Plains, N.Y. 1975, pp. 173–80. For the complete theses and list of endorsers, see Kool and Oberländer, pp. 170–82.

[100]Kollontai, pp. 23–24, 27.

[101]Excerpted in Bunyan, *The Origin of Forced Labor*, p. 49.

[102]Kollontai, pp. 34–35. Some of the transitional steps to be taken immediately were the strengthening of the lowest cells in the unions (the factory committees), increasing their technical and material resources, full democracy, no one to be appointed to economic organs without the unions' knowledge, no candidate appointed by the unions to be rejected by higher organs, and the full power of recall by the union from which officials are elected. Shlyapnikov's thesis 9, in Horvat, p. 177.

[103]Theses 11 and 13, in Bunyan, *The Origin of Forced Labor*, pp. 234–35; and Kollontai, passim. The unions had themselves become highly bureaucratized, but the Workers Opposition expected this new setup, and especially the revival of the factory committees at the lowest levels, to help undo this.

[104]Kollontai, pp. 16–17, 38ff.

[105]Quoted in Schapiro, *The Origin of the Communist Autocracy*, p. 294.

[106]Barbara Evans Clements, *Bolshevik Feminist: The Life of Alexandra Kollontav*, Bloomington Indiana 1979, p. 204.

[107]For instance, he reduced Osinsky's and Lutovinov's motives to simply 'playing at opposition', and argued that neither they nor Sapronov, Ignatov, and others should be taken seriously, for they do this at every Congress, each trying to outbid the other in promising non-party people more rights. Lenin, *Collected Works*, vol. 32, pp. 35, 51–52. The Democratic Centralists had proposed that the Presidium of the SEC be nominated by the Central Trade Union Council. See also Clements, pp. 195, 202.

[108]Lenin, vol. 32, pp. 50, 49, 245–46. Bukharin, who had formed a 'buffer' or compromise position, was also an object of this attack, for he demanded that trade-union appointees to economic organs be made mandatory, that the party should not be able to veto them.

[109]Ibid., pp. 50, 61, 68, 246, 250–51; see also vol. 28, pp. 424–25.

[110]Paul Avrich, *Kronstadt 1921*, New York 1970, pp. 25, 36.

[111]Lenin, *Collected Works*, vol. 32, pp. 96–97, 65.

[112]The Platform of the Ten reiterated Lenin's basic theses on the gradual transformation of the unions 'into auxiliary organs of the proletarian state and not vice versa', through their participation in state economic organs and their training and political education of the non-party masses. 'Normal' methods of trade-union democracy were to be re-established, but selection of trade-union leaders 'must be under the supervisory control of the party.' The Trotsky-Bukharin platform stressed the greater involvement of the unions in production as opposed to their defence of the consumption interests of their members, but mainly through their integration into existing state organs rather than, as in the Workers Opposition platform, through

the creation of new organs based directly on the unions. On the relation between party and trade-union democracy, their platform is virtually the same as that of the Ten. The various platforms can be found in Bunyan, *The Origin of Forced Labour*.

[113]Clements, p. 300, n. 15.

[114]Service, pp. 144–45, 138.

[115]Kollontai, for instance, was forced to pay for the printing of her pamphlet out of her own pocket. Clements, p. 189. See also Sorenson, *Life and Death of Soviet Trade Unionism*, pp. 98, 116ff.; Sorenson, 'The Workers Opposition', pp. 99–100, 27ff.

[116]Avrich, *Kronstadt*, pp. 111, 136. Avrich's account is the most well-balanced available and, while it is sympathetic to the situation in which the Bolsheviks found themselves in 1921, makes it quite clear that the protests were not a counter-revolutionary plot and that the Bolsheviks made no serious attempt to negotiate. For other accounts, see Ida Mett, *The Kronstadt Uprising*, Montreal 1971; George Katkov, 'The Kronstadt Rising', *St. Anthony's Papers*, no. 6, London, 1959, pp. 9–74.

Chapter 7

[1]All the elements in this reconstruction of Marx's philosophical presuppositions cannot be presented here. For a more elaborate treatment see Habermas, *Knowledge and Human Interests*, trans. by Jeremy Shapiro, Boston 1971, chapters 2 and 3; Habermas, *Towards A Rational Society*, trans. by Jeremy Shapiro, Boston 1970, pp. 80–122; and Albrecht Wellmer, *Critical Theory of Society*, trans. by John Cumming, New York 1971, especially chapter 2.

[2]Helmut Fleischer, *Marxism and History*, trans. by Eric Mosbacher, New York 1973.

[3]Although Marx's terminology on these questions shifts in his work, it has been adequately demonstrated by Avineri that Marx's use of 'true democracy' in his 1843 critique of Hegel is virtually identical to his later concepts of communism and the *Aufhebung des Staats*. Shlomo Avineri, *The Social and Political Thought of Karl Marx*, Cambridge 1970, pp. 33ff., 202ff.

[4]Quoted in Wellmer, p. 80.

[5]Karl Marx, *Writings of the Young Marx on Philosophy and Society*, trans. and ed. by Lloyd D. Easton and Kurt H. Guddat, Garden City New York 1967, p. 250.

[6]Karl Marx, *Capital* Volume 1, Harmondsworth 1976, 71ff.; Easton and Guddat, 277ff.; Trent Schroyer, *The Critique of Domination* New York 1973, pp. 83ff.

[7]Karl Marx, *German Ideology*, ed. by D.J. Arthur, New York 1970, p. 64, emphasis added.

[8]Wellmer, p. 91.

[9]*German Ideology*, p. 87, emphasis added.

[10]For example, in the Preface to *A Contribution to the Critique of Political Economy*, where the same revolutionary dynamic is articulated, although the relations of production are now distinguished from the ideological forms of social interaction. See Karl Marx, *Basic Writings on Politics and Philosophy*, ed. by Lewis Feuer, Garden City, New York 1959, pp. 43–44.

[11]*German Ideology*, pp. 88–89.

[12]Wellmer, p. 94. G.A. Cohen, in *Karl Marx's Theory of History: A Defence* (Oxford 1978), brings forth a great deal of evidence to argue that this technological determinist view of social transformation is the dominant one in Marx, and is a

defensible view at that. For a critique of the latter claim, see Andrew Levine and Erik Olin Wright's review, 'Rationality and Class Struggle', *New Left Review*, no. 123 (September-October 1980), pp. 47-68, which focuses on the untenability of deriving the class capacities necessary for revolutionary tranformation from the development of the productive forces. A more useful and less deterministic view of the forces-relations couplet, though not as strongly articulated in Marx's work, is presented in Fred Block and Larry Hirschorn, 'New Productive Forces and the Contradictions of Contemporary Capitalism', *Theory and Society* 8 (1979), pp. 363-95.

[13]Thus Marx could write in the *Holy Family* (1845): 'It is not a question of what this or that proletarian, or even the whole proletariat itself, imagines the goal to be for the moment. It is a question of what it *is* and what, comfortable to the proletariat's essence, it will be compelled to do historically.' Here class capacity and will become a matter of class essence. Quoted in Karl Marx, *On Revolution*, trans. and ed. by Saul Padover, New York 1971, p. 23.

[14]For example, see Feuer, p. 44; and *Capital* Volume 1, Afterword to the Second German Edition, where Marx favourably quotes a Russian reviewer of his work who characterized it as a scientific analysis of 'social movement as a process of natural history, governed by laws not only independent of human will, consciousness and intelligence, but rather, on the contrary, determining that will, consciousness and intelligence.' Engels as well saw the laws governing human society as 'entirely analogous to that prevailing in the realm of unconscious nature.' Feuer, p. 230. And Marx himself never gave up the idea of a unified science of man and nature, although the epistemological premisses of his method of reflective critique are fundamentally different from those of the sciences of objectified natural processes.

[15]*German Ideology*, p. 93; Wellmer, p. 97.

[16]*German Ideology*, p. 93.

[17]Karl Marx, *Grundrisse*, trans. by Martin Nicolaus, Baltimore 1973, p. 704ff. This argument generally follows Wellmer, who perhaps overemphasizes the positivistic aspects of the *Grundrisse*. See Pier Aldo Rovatti, 'The Critique of Fetishism in Marx's Grundrisse', *Telos*, no. 17 (fall 1977), pp. 87-105, whose argument overlaps Wellmer's, but at the same time reveals the other critical side of the *Grundrisse's* ambiguity on these questions.

[18]*Capital* Volume 1, p. 618, emphasis added.

[19]*Capital* Volume 3, p. 820; *Grundrisse*, p. 706.

[20]See Andrew Arato, 'The Second International: A Reexamination', *Telos*, no. 18 (winter, 1973-74), pp. 2-52. Bettelheim's Maoist critique virtually exempts Marx from a productivist reading, as do the more radical essays in Phil Slater, ed., *Outlines of a Critique of Technology*, Atlantic Highlands New Jersey 1980. Bettelheim, in fact, claims that Lenin too always put ideological struggle ahead of the development of the productive forces, a position that is hardly tenable. See his *Class Struggles in the USSR, First Period: 1917-1923*, pp. 38-39.

[21]Lenin, *Collected Works*, vol. 25, p. 363.

[22]Ibid., p. 362.

[23]Quoted in Ulysses Santamaria and Alain Manville, 'Lenin and the Problem of the Transition', *Telos*, no. 27 (spring 1976), p. 83.

[24]See chapter 4 above and Lenin, *Collected Works*, vol. 32, p. 334.

[25]Ibid., vol. 27, p. 257.

[26]Ibid., vol. 29, p. 427.

[27]Ibid., vol. 36, p. 549. This was written in October 1921, after the war emergency

had receded. On another occasion Lenin modified this approach by arguing that 'without a correct political approach to the matter [of the trade unions] the given class will be unable to stay on top, *and, consequently,* will be unable to solve its *production problems either.*' Ibid., vol. 32, p. 84.

[28]Leon Trotsky, *Terrorism and Communism*, p. 146.

[29]Leon Trotsky, *Marxism and Science*, Colombo, Ceylon, 1973, p. 29.

[30]See chapter 4 above and Lenin, vol. 29, p. 70; Carmen Claudin-Urondo, *Lénine et la révolution culturelle*, Paris 1975, p. 87.

[31]Robert Linhart, *Lénine, les paysans, Taylor*, Paris 1976, p. 111.

[32]Lenin, *On Workers' Control and the Nationalization of Industry*, Moscow 1970, p. 17.

[33]Lenin, *Collected Works*, vol. 33, pp. 245–46, 368–69.

[34]Kendall Bailes, 'Alexei Gastev and the Soviet Controversy over Taylorism, 1918–1924', *Soviet Studies*, 29:3 (1977), pp. 373–94.

[35]Franziska Baumgarten, *Arbeitswissenschaft und Psychotechnik in Russland*, Munich and Berlin 1924, p. 34; also Zenovia Schor, 'Soviet Taylorism Revisited', *Soviet Studies*, 33:2 (April 1981), pp. 246–64.

[36]Trotsky, *Problems of Everyday Life*, New York 1973, pp. 243–44.

[37]See chapter 4 above. Some have argued that this dictatorial control of the labour process derives theoretically from Engels. In his essay 'On Authority', Engels speaks of the 'veritable despotism, independent of all social organization' that modern industry imposes on the worker. While Lenin may have read Engels as implying the dictatorial control of the labour process, the interpretation of this essay as excluding all workers control within the factory is incorrect, for Engels twice refers to the possibility of that authority being delegated by a vote of the majority of the workers in the plant. See Feuer, ed., pp. 483–84. This view is close to the one Lenin had articulated in the original draft of 'Immediate Tasks of the Soviet Government', then later dropped and never returned to. In that draft he also linked the introduction of Taylorism to the reduction of the working day to six hours in order to enable all adult citizens to engage in state administrative activities four hours a day. While the fragmentation of tasks was not questioned, this draft does link the benefits of Taylorism to the abolition of the strict division of labour in state administration and in workplace decision-making. See Linhart, p. 109; Lenin, *Collected Works*, vol. 42, p. 80.

[38]See chapter 6 above.

[39]Lenin, *Collected Works*, vol. 32, p. 81.

[40]Ibid., vol. 31, p. 50.

[41]See chapter 6 above. In *State and Revolution*, p. 84, he also referred to the factory discipline that must pervade the entire society during the socialist transition as not the final aim, but only a foothold necessary to purge society of capitalist exploitation.

[42]Harry Braverman, *Labour and Monopoly Capital*, New York 1974, p. 19.

[43]Santamaria and Manville, p. 87. The authors vacillate on this, wishing on the one hand to postulate a complete break, and on the other, a historical transition. Raniero Panzieri also argues that 'there is no continuity to be asserted, across the revolutionary leap, in the order of techno-economic development.' See Phil Slater, ed., p. 58. Without any continuity, the revolutionary leap could lead only to a counter-revolutionary abyss.

[44]This is the argument of Philip Corrigan, Harvie Ramsay, and Derek Sayer, *Socialist Construction and Marxist Theory*, New York 1978, pp. 46, 55.

[45]The position developed here is close to that of William Leiss, 'Technology and Instrumental Rationality in Capitalism and Socialism,' in Frederick Fleron, ed., *Technology and Communist Culture*, New York 1977, p. 141: 'In opposition to the fashionable thesis concerning the so-called imperatives of technology, I have argued above that there are no imperatives embodied in techniques or in their transfer from one setting to another. There are no imperatives embodied in technologies or their transfer, because technologies do not have a fixed, unidimensional "essence" or character. Rather, they are themselves developing unstable resolutions of diverse and partly contradictory elements. Within technologies there are "mixtures" of means and ends, of techniques and goals, determined in relation to reproductive modes. The formulation of criteria for the selection of techniques and the struggle for the clarification of goals and societal interaction processes are two different but related expressions of the internal dynamics of technological change itself.' This position contrasts to that of Fleron (shared by many Marxist critics), namely, 'that it is not possible to take the master out of the machine he has built as his armor' (p. 474).

[46]The more radical of the recent Marxist analyses of the labour process draw critical impetus from a conception of a classless division of labour that does not adequately formulate the problems of democracy, equality, and the plurality of individual needs, and that offers an overly restrictive conception of the organizational forms for their realization. This complements the restrictive either-or historical approach towards the transformation of the labour process in Russia. See my 'Production and Power in a Classless Society'.

[47]Even *State and Revolution* (p. 79) formulates the question along these lines.

[48]Claudín-Urondo, pp. 95–96.

[49]In the 1920s and 1930s, these tenets were further elaborated by various Soviet theorists who posited a linear, logical, and inexorable development of technology through the various stages until automation reduced the number of manual workers to nil, thus eliminating the division of labour. See Julian Cooper, 'The Scientific and Technical Revolution in Soviet Theory', in Fleron, ed., pp. 146–79.

Chapter 8

[1]Lenin, quoted in Robert V. Daniels, 'The State and Revolution: A Case Study in the Genesis and Transformation of Communist Ideology', *Slavic Review* 12:1 (1953), p. 24.

[2]Lenin, *Collected Works*, vol. 32, p. 41.

[3]Ibid., vol. 32, p. 98, emphasis added.

[4]Ibid., vol. 32, p. 20.

[5]Ibid., vol. 7, pp. 396–97; see also pp. 391–92; vol. 6, pp. 235–52 for the factory metaphor of party discipline. The latter was trenchantly criticized by Rosa Luxemburg, to whom Lenin responded only evasively. As she argued in 1904: 'The "discipline" which Lenin has in mind is implanted in the proletariat not only by the factory but also by the barracks, by modern bureaucratism—in short, by the whole mechanism of the centralized bourgeois state. It is nothing but an incorrect use of the word when at one time one designates as "discipline" two so opposed concepts as the absence of thought and will in a mass of flesh with many arms and legs moving mechanically, and the voluntary coordination of conscious political acts by a social stratum. There is nothing common to the corpselike obedience of a dominated class

and the organized rebellion of a class struggling for its liberation. It is not by linking up with the discipline implanted in him by the capitalist state, by the mere transfer of authority from the hand of the bourgeoisie to that of the Social Democratic central committee but by breaking, uprooting this slavish spirit of discipline that the proletarian can be educated for the new discipline, for the voluntary self-discipline of Social Democracy.' Dick Howard, ed., *Writings of Rosa Luxemburg*, p. 291. Lenin, *Collected Works*, vol. 7, p. 474ff.

[6]Antonio Carlo, 'Lenin on the Party', *Telos*, no. 17 (fall, 1973), p. 12; Lenin, *Collected Works*, vol. 5, p. 473ff.

[7]Lenin, *What Is To Be Done?*, New York 1929.

[8]Louis Menasche, 'Vladimir Ilyich Bakunin: An Essay on Lenin', *Socialist Review*, no. 18 (November/December 1973), p. 30ff.

[9]Lenin, *Collected Works*, vol. 6, pp. 175, 95; vol. 8, p. 453; vol. 9, p. 29. See also Liebman, *Leninism Under Lenin*, p. 29ff.

[10]Quoted in Marcel Liebman, *The Russian Revolution*, pp. 65–66.

[11]Cited in Anweiler, *The Soviets*, p. 78, emphasis added, and p. 76ff.

[12]Quoted in Liebman, *Leninism under Lenin*, pp. 87–88.

[13]Anweiler, *The Soviets*, p. 79.

[14]Solomon Schwarz, p. 181. The latter has the fullest discussion of Bolshevik attitudes towards the soviets in 1905.

[15]Lenin, *Collected Works*, vol. 9, p. 306.

[16]Ibid., vol. 10, pp. 15–28. The 1905 events also altered Lenin's thinking on the party. Now he argued for transforming the party into a mass party, opening the gates to all workers who demonstrated class consciousness, and re-invigorating the elective principle and free discussion as much as possible under continuing autocratic conditions. The authority of the Central Committee should be pruned, that of the Congress expanded. Initiative should be encouraged at all levels. He recognized that the party sometimes lagged behind the masses, and that they could generate their own forms of organization. See, for example, vol. 8, p. 217ff., pp. 409–10; vol.10, p. 29ff., p. 258; vol. 13, p. 105.

[17]Solomon Schwarz, p. 190.

[18]Lenin, *Collected Works*, vol. 10, p. 72.

[19]Ibid., p. 81.

[20]Liebman, *Leninism under Lenin*, p. 53ff.

[21]Lenin, *Collected Works*, vol. 12, pp. 143–44.

[22]Ibid., p. 332, original emphasis. Although he is not explicit, the context of the article clearly suggests that these other organs of state power will be party organs. In this article, Lenin reacts strongly against the idea of mass self-organization. He can see this as implying only the lack of influence of the party, although, to my knowledge, no one was proposing that political programmes be excluded from debate on policy. Here he tends to equate party influence with party hegemony. See also Anweiler, *The Soviets*, p. 82ff.

[23]*Philosophical Notebooks*, vol. 38 of *Collected Works*. This work was important in overcoming his earlier mechanistic materialist epistemology in *Materialism and Empirio-Criticism*. Significantly, however, Lenin commissioned another edition of the latter after the revolution. Klaus-Dieter Seeman, 'Der Versuch einer proletarischen Kulturrevolution in Russland 1917–1922', *Jahrbücher für Geschichte Osteuropas*, 9:1 (1961), p. 212.

[24]Liebman, *Leninism Under Lenin*, pp. 77, 98.

[25]Previously he had concerned himself primarily with Marx's analyses of the

Commune's tactical mistakes. Lenin, *Marxism and the State*, Moscow 1972; Marian Sawyer, 'The Genesis of *State and Revolution*', in *The Socialist Register*, Ralph Miliband and John Saville, ed., London 1977, pp. 209–27.

[26]Anweiler, *The Soviets*, pp. 85–86, 144ff.

[27]Lenin, *Collected Works*, vol. 24, pp. 21–26.

[28]This work was written in July and August 1917, and published only in early 1918, but the notes for it had been prepared during his last months in exile, during his theoretical confrontation with Bukharin.

[29]Karl Marx and Friedrich Engels, *Writings on the Paris Commune*, Hal Draper, ed., New York 1971.

[30]Lenin did not make this a hard and fast rule for the entire transition. See *Collected Works*, vol. 29, pp. 125, 184–85.

[31]In 'Can the Bolsheviks Retain State Power?' Lenin amended this to the *immediate training* of all the unskilled to participate in such administration. Ibid., vol. 26, p. 113.

[32]Lenin, *State and Revolution*, pp. 23–24.

[33]Liebman, *Leninism under Lenin*, pp. 198–99, 205.

[34]Daniel Tarschys, *Beyond the State*, Stockholm 1971, p. 113.

[35]Ralph Miliband, 'The State and Revolution', in *Lenin Today*, Paul Sweezy and Harry Magdoff, *Monthly Review* (1970), p. 80ff.

[36]*Marxism and the State*, pp. 94–95, 82, 86; see also Guy Desolre, 'Le Chapitre VII Inédit de "L' État et la Révolution",' *Revue des Pays de L'Est*, 14:1 (1973), pp. 101–111.

[37]Lenin, *Collected Works*, vol. 25, p. 188. Lenin confuses his argument at this point with talk about moralizing to the proletariat, but in context the meaning is clear enough. See also pp. 174ff., 185ff., 196ff., 253.

[38]Quoted in Anweiler, *The Soviets*, p. 171, see also p. 165ff. Stalin argued that a revolutionary committee or the workers section of the Petrograd soviet could serve the purpose equally well.

[39]Nikolai Bukharin, *The Politics and Economics of the Transition Period*, Kenneth Tarbuck, ed., trans. by Oliver Field, London 1979, p. 51.

[40]Lenin, *Collected Works*, vol. 27, p. 135.

[41]Ibid., vol. 32, p. 86.

[42]Quoted in Deutscher, *The Prophet Armed*, New York 1965, pp. 508–09.

[43]Quoted in Carr, *The Bolshevik Revolution*, vol. 1, p. 229; Lenin, *Collected Works*, vol. 33, p. 495.

[44]Engels, *The Origin of the Family, Private Property and the State*, New York 1972, p. 229; Lenin, *State and Revolution*, p. 8.

[45]Karl Marx and Friedrich Engels, *The Communist Manifesto*, New York 1948, p. 31.

[46]Draper, ed., *Writings on the Paris Commune*, p. 32; *State and Revolution*, p. 66.

[47]Engels to Bebel in Karl Marx, *Critique of the Gotha Programme*, New York 1938, p. 31; also Lenin, *State and Revolution*, pp. 54–55. Engels occasionally adds what, of course, is always implicit, that the state also has the role of 'carrying out the economic revolution'. Quoted in Marx, *Critique of the Gotha Programme*, pp. 107–08, n. 64.

[48]Lenin, *State and Revolution*, p. 75, and *Collected Works*, vol. 25, p. 357.

[49]Marx, *Critique of the Gotha Programme*, p. 8ff.

[50]Lenin, *State and Revolution*, p. 82.

[51]Ibid., pp. 84, 42.

[52]Kaplan, pp. 230, 246, passim.

[53]Engels, in Karl Marx, Friedrich Engels, and V.I. Lenin, *Anarchism and Anarcho-Syndicalism*, New York 1972, p. 27.

[54]Engels to Cuno, ibid., p. 69.

[55]Ibid., p. 168; see also Friedrich Engels, *Anti-Dühring*, New York 1939, p. 306ff., *State and Revolution*, pp. 15–16.

[56]The treatment of divisions within the proletariat in *State and Revolution*, for instance, is glib and offhanded.

[57]Karl Wittfogel, *Oriental Despotism*, New Haven, Connecticut 1957, p. 389ff. See also George Lichtheim, 'Marx and the "Asiatic Mode of Production",' in *St. Anthony's Papers*, no. 14, G.F. Hudson, ed., Carbondale Illinois 1963; Karl Marx, *Pre-Capitalist Economic Formations*, trans. by Jack Cohen, New York 1965.

[58]Ernest Mandel, *The Formation of the Economic Thought of Karl Marx*, trans. by Brian Pearce, New York 1971, p. 131; see also Hal Draper, *Karl Marx's Theory of Revolution*, vol. 1, New York 1977, chapter 22, where Wittfogel's distortions of Marx are clarified.

[59]For example, Engels, *Anti-Dühring*, p. 197ff., where two distinct lines of development of classes are presented, one based on the exercise of common social functions by individuals who gradually form a ruling class.

[60]Lenin, *Collected Works*, vol. 29, pp. 470–83.

[61]Marx and Engels analyse Blanquism as necessarily leading to a dictatorship *over* the proletariat, and Engels speaks briefly of the (non-revolutionary) transfer of the means of production from private capital to direct state control as not abolishing the domination of the working classes. But these insights, as those on Oriental despotism, are never systematically incorporated into their treatments of the future revolution against capital. See Karl Marx and Friedrich Engels, *Werke*, Berlin 1968,vol. 18, p. 529; and Engels, *Anti-Dühring*, pp. 303–04. Whether the analyses of Marx and Engels on Oriental despotism were correct or not is another question entirely, however. See Perry Anderson, *Lineages of the Absolutist State*, London 1974, pp. 462–549.

[62]Lenin, *State and Revolution*, pp. 8–9, 21, 66.

[63]Tarschys, p. 129.

[64]In 'Can the Bolsheviks Retain State Power?', where his romanticization of the administrative competence of the masses is tempered, he also emphasizes the necessity of the new state to enlist the support of the capitalists and their intellectual servants. *Collected Works*, vol. 26, p. 107ff.

[65]*State and Revolution*, p. 83. See also the original version of 'Immediate Tasks', where he argues that during the transition to socialism political tasks occupy a subordinate position to those of economic administration, particularly accounting and control and raising the productivity of labour. *Collected Works*, vol. 42, p. 71.

[66]*State and Revolution*, pp. 38, 84.

[67]Ibid., pp. 43–44.

[68]The only developed example of state administration, that of the sequestering of a rich man's flat to house a poor family, is so simplistically unambiguous that it reveals how much Lenin suppressed questions of politics and political differences where the masses were concerned, in favour of questions of administration. *Collected Works*, vol. 26, pp. 112–123; also *State and Revolution*, pp. 49–50.

[69]Lenin, *Collected Works*, vol. 32, p. 21. Lenin explicitly says that this pertains to all countries. Even the right of recall is seldom if ever linked to the right to re-orient

policy. One gets the sense, especially given the primacy Lenin places on service for workers' wages ('here is shown more clearly than anywhere else, the break from a bourgeois democracy to a proletarian democracy', *State and Revolution*, p. 38), that recall is an instrument for preventing material privilege and opportunism but not for expressing policy changes or disagreements. This would be consistent with Marx, who argues that, as government functions cease to be political, 'elections completely lose their present political character.' Marx, Engels, Lenin, *Anarchism and Anarcho-Syndicalism*, p. 150. One assumes that people will be elected, then, purely on the basis of diligence, efficiency, honesty, and the like.

[70]Engels, ibid., p. 103.

[71]Lenin, *Collected Works*, vol. 33, p. 495; vol. 32, pp. 35–36, 527, n. 1; vol. 31, p. 424.

[72]Miliband, 'The State and Revolution', p. 83ff.

[73]Lenin, *Collected Works*, vol. 32, p. 21; *State and Revolution*, p. 84.

[74]Quoted in Carr, *The Bolshevik Revolution*, vol. 1, p. 236; Lenin, *Collected Works*, vol. 29, p. 559.

[75]Lenin, *Collected Works*, vol. 32, p. 62.

[76]Ibid., vol. 32, p. 21.

[77]It is the party, of course, that plays the role of mediating policy differences, through inner-party debates. But beginning with the Tenth Party Congress and the banning of factions, even this was progressively undermined. This general approach establishes a line of continuity between Lenin's thought and the Jacobin tradition of the French revolution. As Hannah Arendt has argued, in place of the ancient notion of consent, the Jacobin thinkers appropriated Rousseau's *volonté générale*. It was of great relevance, she notes, '… that the very word "consent", with its overtones of deliberate choice and considered opinion, was replaced by the word "will", which essentially excludes all processes of exchange of opinions and an eventual agreement between them. The will, if it is to function at all, must indeed be one and indivisible, "a divided will would be inconceivable"; there is no possible mediation between wills as there is between opinions…. The outstanding quality of this popular will as *volonté générale* was its unanimity, and when Robespierre constantly referred to "public opinion", he meant by it the unanimity of the general will; he did not think of an opinion upon which many publicly were in agreement.' This shift from democratic consent to the undivided general will was paralleled by a shift from concern with the institutional form of the republic and the liberation of the people as citizens to stress on revolutionary administration and liberation of the people as *malheureux*. The assumption of an undivided revolutionary will which is the automatic articulation of the undivided revolutionary interest (and is formed in opposition to each and every particular interest) obviates the necessity for a theory of political/institutional mediation. The revolutionary party becomes the organic expression of this general will; it becomes Rousseau's Sovereign. See Hannah Arendt. *On Revolution*, New York 1963, pp. 69ff.; also Francois George, 'Forgetting Lenin', *Telos*, no. 18 (winter 1973/74), pp. 82–83.

[78]Lenin, *Collected Works*, vol. 27, p. 127; also *Marxism and the State*, p. 28.

[79]*State and Revolution*, pp. 68, 85, 75, 74, 79, 80; also *Collected Works*, vol. 30, p. 517.

[80]*State and Revolution*, p. 78ff.; *Collected Works*, vol. 27, p. 127.

[81]*German Ideology*, p. 53, emphasis added. Although Lenin was not aware of this work, its position on the division of labour is fully consistent with the rest of his own image of pure communism. See also Marx, *Critique of the Gotha Programme*, p. 8ff.

[82]*State and Revolution*, pp. 16–17, 65, 82, 84. Marx, Engels, and Lenin, *On Anarchism and Anarcho-Syndicalism*, p. 168; Engels, *Anti-Dühring*, pp. 306–07. Engels's term *Absterben* invokes a biological metaphor of withering away, while Marx preferred to use *Aufhebung*, a philosophical concept implying the transcendence of the state through the realization of the universal interests represented by it only abstractly as long as it existed in tension with the particularist interests of civil society. Avineri, however, has exaggerated this distinction, which did not lead Marx to differ significantly with Engels's conception of pure communism. Avineri, p. 202ff.

[83]*Grundrisse*, p. 173.

[84]Ibid.

[85]The minimal assumptions for this would be that people would be completely willing to modify their needs to harmoniously match the needs of others, that all such needs would be able to be communicated, and that such communication would be virtually undistorted and instantaneous. Of course, such assumptions are as unwarranted as the 'invisible hand' of Adam Smith, whose theoretical function is similar.

[86]And it is so much clearer today than it was in Marx's time that the natural basis of 'things' as well is not limited.

[87]Marx, *Critique of the Gotha Programme*, p. 10.

[88]As I argue in 'Production and Power in a Classless Society', alternative value standards for the commensuration of socially necessary labour contributions will benecessary even in a possible classless society. The abolition of the class division of labour does not, as Yannick Maignien implies, eliminate the general problem of value. See his *La division du travail manuel et intellectuel*, Paris 1975.

[89]*Critique of the Gotha Programme*, p. 10; *Manifesto of the Communist Party*, p. 31.

[90]I do not wish to draw a rigid distinction between socially necessary and freely disposable time, since people will not necessarily compartmentalize their time strictly and since activities in one area often presuppose certain conditions in the other, and will affect the other as well. Nor do I wish to endorse Marx's own categorization of personally disposable time as the only 'true realm of freedom' (*Capital* Volume 3). Nevertheless, the distinction is an indispensable one for social and political theory, since only on the basis of this can a delimitation of legitimate responsibilities in the area of social labour be made. Likewise, there is a qualitative difference between 'freedom' in one's personal time and 'freedom' within the constraints of socially necessary labour, however democratically the latter may be organized.

[91]Tarschys, p. 67ff., who notes that Marx saw association as self-explanatory, which was not an uncommon position among nineteenth-century thinkers who considered it an inevitable organizing principle in human development.

Chapter 9

[1]Lenin, *Collected Works*, vol. 32, p. 352.

[2]Ibid., vol. 29, p. 183.

[3]Ibid., vol. 31, p. 177.

[4]Ibid., vol. 36, p. 566; see also vol. 28, pp. 394, 405; vol. 29, p. 117, 182ff.; vol. 32, pp. 24, 61, 73.

[5]Moshe Lewin, *Lenin's Last Struggle*, trans. by A.M. Sheridan Smith, New York

1968, p. 124.

[6]Lenin, *Collected Works*, vol. 32, p. 351.

[7]Ibid., p. 205; see also vol. 35, p. 492.

[8]Cited in Draper, *Karl Marx's Theory of Revolution*, p. 555.

[9]Lenin, *Collected Works*, vol. 29, p. 180; also vol. 33, pp. 474, 481; vol. 29, pp. 24, 69, 71, 113, 228ff.; vol. 31, p. 161.

[10]Ibid., vol. 33, pp. 77–78.

[11]Ibid., p. 288.

[12]Ibid., p. 462.

[13]Ibid., p. 78.

[14]Ibid., vol. 32, p. 389; vol. 29, p. 183; vol. 31, p. 421.

[15]Claudín-Urondo, pp. 26–27; see also ibid., vol. 33, p. 72.

[16]Lenin, *Collected Works*, vol. 33, p. 65.

[17]Ibid., vol. 37, p. 452; vol. 28, p. 35ff.; pp. 60–61, 94; vol. 26, pp. 409, 469.

[18]Ibid., vol. 28, p. 424.

[19]Ibid., vol. 27, p. 434.

[20]Ibid., vol. 28, pp. 424, 214; vol. 29, p. 69; vol. 32, p. 50.

[21]Ibid., vol. 39, p. 208.

[22]Ibid., vol. 35, p. 492; also vol. 31, p. 434; vol. 32, pp. 56, 66, 82, 205; vol. 29, p. 70.

[23]Ibid., vol. 33, p. 78; vol. 29, p. 208.

[24]Quoted in Willets, in *Lenin: the Man, the Theorist, the Leader*, Leonard Schapiro and Peter Reddaway, eds., New York 1967, p. 228.

[25]'On Cooperation', vol. 33, pp. 467–75.

[26]Ibid., vol. 31, p. 46ff.

[27]Ibid., vol. 33, p. 192.

[28]Ibid., pp. 256–57.

[29]Ibid., vol. 36, pp. 593ff., 603–04.

[30]Ibid., p. 596; vol. 33, pp. 39–40.

[31]Ibid., vol. 32, p. 100.

[32]Ibid., vol. 33, p. 314.

[33]Ibid., vol. 28, p. 436; vol. 30, pp. 405–06; vol. 31, 420ff.; vol. 32, p. 66; vol. 33, p. 27.

[34]Ibid., vol. 33, p. 40; vol. 30, pp. 300–01; vol. 32, pp. 388, 82; Abrams, p. 290.

[35]Ibid., vol. 29, p. 70, emphasis added.

[36]Quoted in Alfred Meyer, *Leninism*, New York 1962, p. 212.

[37]Lenin, *Collected Works*, vol. 33, pp. 368, 462; vol. 32, p. 61ff.

[38]Ibid., vol. 29, pp. 111–12, 132–33; vol. 31, pp. 288–89, 295; vol. 33, pp. 463–64. For an account of actual developments in education and the arts, see Sheila Fitzpatrick, *The Commissariat of Enlightenment*, Cambridge 1970. Interestingly, Lenin opposed the professionalization of education and the establishment of tracking in the schools, which, due to the shortage of skilled labour after the civil war, was being proposed by a strong lobby within the economic commissariats, the trade unions, and the party itself.

[39]Lenin, *Collected Works*, vol. 33, p. 494.

[40]Lenin, *On Culture and Cultural Revolution*, Moscow 1970, p. 233.

[41]Lenin, *Collected Works*, vol. 33, pp. 474–75, 478–79. For Trotsky and Bukharin as well, the democratization of existing culture was as cornerstone in the struggle against bureaucracy. Bukharin, in fact, saw the demonopolization of education and the overproduction of competent organizers as decisive arguments

against Michels's iron law of oligarchy. See Cohen, *Bukharin*, pp. 143–44.

[42]Claudîn-Urondo, p. 17. The author, however, ignoring some of the more critical moments in Lenin's work, tends to overstate her general thesis. Likewise, she fails to establish exactly how all knowledge, including natural science, is ideological to its core and how, other than the overcoming of the fragmentation of disciplines, science is to be revolutionized. On the inconceivability of a new science predicated on premisses outside the transcendental framework of instrumental action and the cognitive interest of preduction and control of objectified natural processes, see Habermas, *Towards a Rational Society*, especially chapter 6.

[43]Lenin, *Collected Works*, vol. 20, pp. 23–24.

[44]Ibid., vol. 42, p. 217; also vol. 31, pp. 316–17.

[45]Ibid., vol. 33, p. 487.

[46]Ibid., vol. 31, p. 287, emphasis added.

[47]Claudîn-Urondo, pp. 32–33.

[48]For example, Liebman, *Leninism under Lenin*, p. 328, who refers to a caricature of their position by Lunacharsky. Prolecult theorists were quite specific on this point.

[49]This very short and schematic summary of the Prolecult movement draws upon the following works: Richard Lorenz, *Proletarische Kulturrevolution in Sowjet-Russland (1917–1921)*, Munich 1969; Seemann; Fitzpatrick, chapter 5. For a defence of Lenin's views from an orthodox Communist Party point of view, see Georges Cogniot, 'Rupture et continuitë de la tradition culturelle selon Lénine', *La Pensëe* (April, 1970), and Guy Besse *et al.*, *Lënine, la philosophie et la culture*, Paris 1971.

[50]Lenin, *Collected Works*, vol. 29, p. 373.

[51]Trotsky goes much further than Lenin here, when he argues that 'at the foundation of culture lies technology. The decisive instrument in the cultural revolution must be a revolution in technology.' *Problems of Everyday Life*, p. 245; also pp. 29–30.

[52]Lewin, *Lenin's Last Struggle*; Abrams, p. 294. The Saratov City Soviet, for instance, gave workers a guided tour of the soviet institutions, treated them to a few good meals, and sent them back to the factories to tell the other workers how well the fight against bureaucracy was going.

[53]As Robert Michels noted, 'When the leaders are not persons of means and when they have no other source of income, they hold firmly to their positions for economic reasons, coming to regard the functions they exercise as theirs by inalienable right. Especially is this true of manual workers who, since becoming leaders, have lost their aptitude for their former occupation. For them the loss of their positions would be a financial disaster.' *Political Parties*, trans. by Eden and Cedar Paul, New York 1962, p. 207.

[54]Lenin, *Collected Works*, vol. 33, pp. 225–26, original emphasis.

[55]Ibid., vol. 32, p. 353, original emphasis.

[56]Ibid., vol. 32, p. 487ff.

[57]Ibid., 'The Role and Functions of the Trade Unions Under the New Economic Policy', vol. 33, pp. 184–96.

[58]See James Townsend, *Political Participation in Communist China*, Berkeley 1969; also Richard Pfeffer, 'Serving the People and Continuing the Revolution', *China Quarterly*, no. 52 (October/December 1972), for a decidedly pro-Maoist view, which, however, appreciates some of the contradictions inherent in such an approach.

[59]Lenin, *Collected Works*, vol. 32, pp. 361–62.

[60]Lewin, *Lenin's Last Struggle*, p. 122.

[61]Liebman, *Leninism Under Lenin*, p. 323.

[62]Lewin, *Lenin's Last Struggle*, pp. 26–27.

[63]Lenin, *Collected Works*, vol. 36, p. 598. Lenin still naively held that the fusion of government functions was an effective antidote to bureaucracy. Others in the party, including Osinsky, disagreed. See Meyer, p. 202.

[64]Erik Olin Wright, *Class, Crisis and State*, London 1978, p. 221.

[65]Trotsky, *The Revolution Betrayed*, trans. by Max Eastman, New York 1937, pp. 289–90.

[66]And, as I argue in 'Production and Power in a Classless Society', the egalitarian goals of a complex classless society could not be achieved without rational bureaucratic procedures of some sort. The problems of controlling bureaucracies, in contrast to simply abolishing them, will hence persist.

[67]Lenin, *State and Revolution*, p. 43.

[68]Claudîn-Urondo, p. 69.

[69]Lenin, *Collected Works*, vol. 30, p. 456, emphasis added.

Chapter 10

[1]David Montgomery, *Workers' Control in America*, New York 1979, p. 10.

[2]For extensive references on these developments, see my 'Workers Control in the Era of World War I'. A model study for Germany is Jürgen Kocka, *Klassengesellschaft im Kreig, 1914–1918*, Göttingen 1973.

[3]Peter Stearns, *Lives of Labor*, New York 1975; Paul Devinat, *Scientific Management in Europe*, Geneva 1927.

[4]Charles Maier, *Recasting Bourgeois Europe*, Princeton 1975; Peter von Oertzen, *Betriebsräte in der Novemberrevolution*, Düsseldorf 1963.

[5]James Hinton, *The First Shop Stewards' Movement*, London 1973; and Montgomery.

[6]For a general overview of some of the reasons for this, see Roslyn Feldberg, 'Women, Self-Management and Socialism', *Socialist Review*, no. 56 (March-April 1981), pp. 141–52.

[7]Antonio Gramsci, *Selections From Political Writings, 1910–1920*, ed. Quintin Hoare, trans. John Matthews, New York 1977, pp. 263, 110–11, 100–101; also 'Americanism and Fordism', in *Prison Notebooks*, Quintin Hoare and Geoffrey Nowell Smith, eds., New York 1971, pp. 277–318.

[8]See Sergio Bologna, 'Class Composition and the Theory of the Party at the Origin of the Workers' Councils Movement', *Telos*, no. 13 (fall 1972), pp. 4–27; and Karl Heinz Roth, *Die 'andere' Arbeiterbewegung*, Munich 1974.

[9]Branko Pribicevic, *The Shop Stewards' Movement and Workers' Control*, Oxford 1959, p. 164.

[10]Hinton, p. 56.

[11]In fact, skilled workers have at times been the most egalitarian in their conceptions of proper wage differentials. This has been the case in Yugoslavia, for instance. See Bogdan Denitch, *The Legitimation of a Revolution: The Yugoslav Case*, New Haven, Connecticut 1976, p. 174.

[12]Howard Wachtel, *Workers' Management and Workers' Wages in Yugoslavia*, Ithaca 1973; Ian Clegg, *Workers' Self-Management in Algeria*, New York 1971;

Juan Espinosa and Andrew Zimbalist, *Economic Democracy: Workers Participation in Chilean Industry, 1970–1973*, New York 1978; Frank Mintz, *L'Autogestion dans l'Espagne révolutionnaire*, Paris 1970.

[13]Ellen Turkish Comisso argues that this was, in fact, the intention of the Yugoslav reforms from the beginning. *Workers' Control under Plan and Market*, New Haven, Connecticut 1979, p. 55.

[14]For example, in Chile and Yugoslavia. In the former case, workers demanded that experts explain things to them. This, along with other forms of in-plant education, had a mutually reinforcing impact on participation even in the few short years of the socialist experiment. See Andrew Zimbalist, 'Workers Participation in the Management of Socialized Industry: An Empirical Study of the Chilean Experience Under Allende', PhD thesis, Harvard University, 1974, pp. 110, 139, 210 ff.

[15]Other workers control movements in this period and later reveal similar results. See Martin Nile Clark, *Antonio Gramsci and the Revolution that Failed*, New Haven 1977, p. 158ff.; von Oertzen, pp. 172 ff., 119; Mintz; Espinosa and Zimbalist.

[16]Peter Sedgwick, introduction to Victor Serge, *Year One of the Russian Revolution*, Chicago 1972, p. 11.

[17]On the extent of Russia's techological dependence, and the varied forms of transfer, see Anthony Sutton, *Western Technology and Soviet Economic Development, 1917–1930*, Stanford 1968.

[18]Aimée Moutet, 'Les origines du système de Taylor en France: le point de vue patronal (1907–1914)', *Le Mouvement Social*, no. 93 (Oct.–Dec. 1975), p. 39 ff.; Bertrand Abherve, 'Les origins de la grève des métallurgistes parisiens, juin 1919', *Le Mouvement Social*, no. 93, p. 79; Charles Maier, 'Between Taylorism and Technocracy: European Ideologies and the Vision of Industrial Productivity in the 1920s', *The Journal of Contemporary History*, 5:2 (1970), 27–61.

[19]Steve Fraser, 'The "New Unionism" and the "New Economic Policy", in Cronin and Sirianni, eds.

[20]Peter Stearns, *Lives of Labour*, p. 121 ff.

[21]Since the technical and organizational expertise of the Western unions was potentially a great asset, this issue requires further study. Splits in the labour movement and opposition to joint assistance by industrialists may have also impeded such cooperation.

[22]E.H. Carr, *The Interregnum, 1923–24*, Baltimore 1969, p. 89 ff.; *Socialism in One Country, 1924–26*, vol. 1, Baltimore 1970, p. 444; E.H. Carr and R.W. Davies, *Foundations of a Planned Economy, 1926–29*, vol. 1, Baltimore 1974, pp. 549–50; Charles Bettelheim, *Class Struggles in the USSR, Second Period, 1923–1930*, trans. Brian Pearce, New York 1978, p. 251 ff.

[23]Carr and Davies, p. 623.

[24]For example, see M. Argyle, G. Gardner, and F. Cioffi, 'Supervisory Methods Related to Productivity, Absenteeism and Turnover', in Victor Vroom and E. Deci, ed., *Management and Motivation*, Baltimore 1973, pp. 170–191.

[25]Carr and Davies, p. 528, n. 1.

[26]William Dunn, 'The Social Context of Technology Assessment in Eastern Europe', in Fleron, ed., pp. 357–96; also see Denitch. The recent interest of the Chinese in the Yugoslav system reveals some of the limits of the Cultural Revolution's experiments in alternative forms of work discipline, incentives, and participation, which were highly dependent on political and ideological controls (including political controls over wages and consumption), and often resulted in great

organizational confusion and work indiscipline. But the Chinese experience has revealed some of the potential of schemes for job rotation and collective in-plant education. See Stephen Andors, *China's Industrial Revolution*, New York 1977.

[27]Arthur MacEwan, *Revolution and Economic Development in Cuba*, New York 1981.

[28]In both Yugoslavia and Cuba, workplace participation has tended to stimulate or help sustain democratic participation in broader community affairs, and to attenuate commandist methods in the ruling parties.

[29]Sorenson, *The Life and Death of Soviet Trade Unionism*, p. 159.

[30]Andrew Zimbalist, 'The Limits of Work Humanization', *Review of Radical Political Economics*, 7:2 (summer 1975), p. 55 ff.; Evelyn Huber Stephens, *The Politics of Workers' Participation*: *The Peruvian Approach in Comparative Perspective*, New York 1980.

[31]Skocpol, *States and Social Revolutions*, pp. 168–70, emphasis added.

[32]This is consistent with the general theory offered by Oberschall against psychologistic explanations, such as those of Neil Smelser. See Oberschall, *Social Conflict and Social Movements*, p. 172 ff.

[33]Georges Haupt, *Socialism and the Great War*, Oxford 1972, p. 231.

[34]Serge Bricianer, *Pannekoek and the Workers Councils*, trans. Malachy Carroll, St. Louis 1978; Anton Pannekoek, *Workers Councils*, Cambridge, Mass 1970.

[35]Paul Breines, 'Karl Korsch's "Road to Marx"', *Telos*, no. 26 (winter 1975–76), pp. 42–56; Karl Korsch, *Schriften zur Sozialisierung*, Erich Gerlach, ed., Frankfurt am Main 1969.

[36]Von Oertzen, *Betriebsträte*, Reinhard Rürup, Eberhard Kolb, and Gerald Feldman, 'Die Massenbewegungen der Arbeiterschaft in Deutschland am Ende des Ersten Weltkrieges (1917–1920)', *Politische Vierteljahresschrift*, 13 Jahrgang, Heft I (August 1972), pp. 84–105.

[37]Pier Carlo Masini, 'Anarchistes et Communistes dans le mouvement des conseils à Turin:-première après-guerre rouge 1919–1920', *Autogestion*, nos. 26–27 (March–June 1975), pp. 27–53.

[38]Giuseppe Maione, *Il Biennio Rosso*: *Autonomia e spontaneità operaia nel 1919–1920*, Bologna 1975, pp. 86–87.

[39]Martin Nile Clark, *Antonio Gramsci and the Revolution that Failed*, passim. See chapter 12 below.

[40]Besides the works of Hinton and Pribicevic, see Walter Kendall, *The Revolutionary Movement in Britain, 1900–1921*, London 1969, chapter 8.

[41]Karl Korsch, 'Die Arbeitsteilung zwischen körperlicher und geistiger Arbeit und Sozialismus', *Der Arbeiterrat*, no. 24 (1919).

[42]Diego Abad de Santillan, *After the Revolution*: *Economic Reconstruction in Spain Today*, trans. Louis Frank, New York 1937, pp. 74, 42–43, 97. The author did not urge this as a temporary compromise, but argued generally that 'the human rhythm does not make its mark on the machine; it is the rhythm of the machine which determines human progress.' It is particularly significant that this position was put forward precisely when workers control became a reality in Spain, and the Republic had to be defended against fascist attack.

Chapter 11

[1]Antonio Gramsci, *Selections from Political Writings, 1910–1920*, especially pp.

98–108, 260–68.

[2]Bricianer, pp. 99–107.

[3]Ibid., p. 269 ff.; Pannekoek, *Workers Councils*, p. 47, passim. For a similar councilist view, see Paul Mattick, *Anti-Bolshevik Communism*, White Plains, New York 1978, pp. 73–86, 211–230.

[4]James Hinton *The First Shop Stewards' Movement*.

[5]Roger Picard, *Le Mouvement syndical durant la guerre*, Paris 1927, p. 116 ff.; *Le contrôle sur la gestion des enterprises*, Paris 1922; William Oualid and Charles Picquenard, *Salaires et Tarifs*, Paris 1928, p. 420 ff.

[6]Fritz Opel, *Der deutsche Metallarbeiter-Verband während des Ersten Weltkrieges und der Revolution*, Hanover 1958; von Oertzen, *Betriebsräte*, p. 271 ff.

[7]Martin Clark, pp. 36 ff., 80 ff.; Mario Abrate, *La Lotta Sindacale nella Industrializzazione in Italia, 1906–1926*, Turin 1966, chapter 8.

[8]Hinton, chapter 8; Ian McLean, 'Popular Protest and Public Order: Red Clydeside, 1915–1919', in R. Quinalt and J. Stevenson, eds., *Popular Protest and Public Order*, New York 1974, pp. 215–42.

[9]Quoted in Paolo Spriano, *The Occupation of the Factories*, trans. Gwyn Williams, London 1975, p. 91. See also Angelo Tasca's articles in *Antonio Gramsci: Selections from Political Writings, 1910–1920*.

[10]Martin Clark, p. 179.

[11]Rürup, Kolb, and Feldman, p. 100.

[12]Ibid., p. 90 ff.; von Oertzen, *Betriebsräte*. The relative strength of the unions was demonstrated throughout various parts of the former Austro-Hungarian Empire as well. See Jan Svejnar, 'Workers' Participation in Management in Czechoslovakia', paper presented at the First International Conference on Self-Management, Ithaca, New York, June 1975, pp. 1–4.

[13]Karl Mannheim, *Essays on the Sociology of Knowledge*, Paul Kecskemeti, ed., London 1952, p. 283.

[14]See Oberschall, *Social Conflict and Social Movements*, p. 158.

[15]Charles Maier, 'The Two Postwar Eras and the Conditions for Stability in Twentieth Century Western Europe', *American Historical Review*, 86:2 (April 1981), p. 334.

[16]Martin Slater, 'Worker Councils in Italy: Past Developments and Future Projects', in G. David Garson, ed., *Workers' Self-Management in Industry: The West European Experience*, New York 1977, pp. 192–213.

[17]Andrew Martin, 'Sweden: Industrial Democracy and Social Democratic Strategy', in G. David Garson, pp. 49–96.

[18]Eric Batstone, Ian Boraston, and Stephen Frenkel, *Shop Stewards in Action*, Oxford 1977.

[19]Espinosa and Zimbalist, *Economic Democracy*, p. 108 ff.

[20]Evelyn Huber Stephens, *The Politics of Workers' Participation: the Peruvian Approach in Comparative Perspective*, New York 1980.

[21]Clegg, *Workers' Self-Management in Algeria*, p. 45 ff.

[22]Gaston Leval, *Collectives in the Spanish Revolution*, trans. Vernon Richards, London 1975; Sam Dolgoff, ed., *The Anarchist Collectives*, New York 1974.

[23]Such was the case, for instance, in the CGT in France, and was a powerful tendency in the Iww and the CNT. See James Weinstein, 'The Iww and American Socialism, *Socialist Review*, no. 5 (Sept.-Oct. 1970), pp. 3–41; Gerald Meaker, *The Revolutionary Left in Spain, 1914–1923*, Stanford 1974; and Larry Peterson, 'The One Big Union in International Perspective: Revolutionary Industrial Unionism,

1900–1925', in James Cronin and Carmen Sirianni, eds., *Work, Community and Power: the Experience of Labour in Europe and America 1900–25*, Philadelphia 1983.

[24]Erik Olin Wright, *Class, Crisis and State*, p. 235.

[25]Richard Hyman, 'Workers' Control and Revolutionary Theory', *Socialist Register 1974*, Ralph Miliband and John Saville, eds., London 1974, p. 265.

[26]Michael Barratt Brown, Ken Coates, and Tony Topham, 'Workers' Control Versus "Revolutionary" Theory', *Socialist Register 1975*, Ralph Miliband and John Saville, eds., London 1975, p. 299.

[27]Hence the need, as Brown, Coates, and Topham point out (p. 303), for nominations through the unions at the workplace itself, and for report-back and recall procedures.

Epilogue

[1]Rudolf Bahro, *The Alternative in Eastern Europe*, London 1978, p. 116.

[2]Skocpol, *States and Social Revolutions*, p. 225. Despite the criticisms of this conclusion elaborated below, it should be noted that Skocpol's comparative analysis of Russia and China is remarkably insightful, and reveals quite convincingly why a Maoist-type solution was relatively unavailable in Russia, at least in the short run, and likewise why a Stalinist-type solution in agriculture was not feasible in China.

[3]Robert Tucker, 'Stalinism as Revolution from Above', in Tucker, ed., *Stalinism*, New York 1977, p. 88. Tucker cites here James Millar's conclusion from the new data provided in A. A. Barsov's research. See James Millar, 'Mass Collectivization and the Contribution of Soviet Agriculture to the First Five-Year Plan: a Review Article', *Slavic Review*, 33:4 (1974), pp. 750–766.

[4]See especially Moshe Lewin, *Political Undercurrents in Soviet Economic Debates*, Princeton 1974.

[5]Stephen Cohen, 'Bolshevism and Stalinism', in Tucker, ed., *Stalinism*, p. 23; Lewin, *Political Undercurrents*, p. 68 ff.

[6]John Sontag, 'The Soviet War Scare of 1926–27', *The Russian Review*, 34:1 (January, 1975), p. 77.

[7]Alexander Erlich, *The Soviet Industrialization Debate, 1924–28*, Cambridge, Mass. 1967, p. 167 ff.; Moshe Lewin, 'Society, State and Ideology during the First Five-Year Plan', in Sheila Fitzpatrick, ed., *Cultural Revolution in Russia, 1928–1931*, Bloomington, Indiana 1978, p. 52 ff.

[8]Millar, p. 764.

[9]Skocpol, *States and Social Revolutions*, p. 225.

[10]R. W. Davies, *The Socialist Offensive: the Collectivization of Soviet Agriculture, 1929–1930*, Cambridge, Mass. 1980, pp. 412–13.

[11]See Millar; and Michael Ellman, 'Did the Agricultural Surplus Provide the Resources for the Increase in Investment During the First Five-Year Plan?', *Economic Journal*, 85 (Dec. 1975), pp. 844–64.

[12]Alexander Erlich, 'Stalinism and Marxian Growth Models', in Tucker, ed., *Stalinism*, p. 142.

[13]Bailes, *Technology and Society Under Lenin and Stalin*, Part 4. The irrationality that has plagued Soviet-type economics thereafter was presaged in the following case from 1940: 'A professor of the Dnepropetrovsk Metallurgical Institute developed a device for automatically regulating the amount of steel poured in a particular

process. It would have saved millions of rubles in scarce steel, but was applied in only one instance. Other plants rejected it because the device would "ruin" plant output quotas, which were expressed in gross weight, not in the size of the steel sheeting produced. The professor's invention maximized the size while lessening the weight produced. In general, Soviet metal products and machinery were frequently heavier than they needed to be.' Ibid., p. 350.

[14] Lewin, 'Society, State and Ideology During the First Five-Year Plan,' p. 60.

[15] Ibid., pp. 55–56. The phrase is taken from Ordzhonikidze.

[16] Bailes, *Technology and Society Under Lenin and Stalin*, pp. 315–16.

[17] Sheila Fitzpatrick 'Cultural Revolution as Class War', in Fitzpatrick, ed., *Cultural Revolution in Russia*, pp. 8–40; and introduction; also, in the same volume, Gail Warshofsky Lapidus, 'Educational Strategies and Cultural Revolution: the Politics of Soviet Development', p. 93.

[18] Bailes, *Technology and Society Under Lenin and Stalin*, pp. 308–309.

[19] Fitzpatrick, 'Cultural Revolution as Class War', pp. 12, 20.

[20] Bailes, *Technology and Society Under Lenin and Stalin*, p. 324.

[21] Lewin, 'The Social Background of Stalinism', in Tucker, ed., *Stalinism*, p. 117.

[22] Stephen Cohen, 'Bolshevism and Stalinism', pp. 26–27.

[23] Tucker, 'Stalinism as Revolution from Above', p. 89; see also Davis, *The Socialist Offensive*, p. 397.

[24] See especially Moshe Lewin, *Lenin's Last Struggle*; and T. H. Rigby, 'Stalinism and the Mono-Organizational Society', in Tucker, ed., *Stalinism*, p. 67 ff.

Bibliography

Abherve, Bertrand. 'Les Origines de la grève des métallurgistes parisiens, juin 1919. *Le Mouvement Social*, No. 93 (October-December 1975), 75–85.

Abrams, Robert. 'The Local Soviets of the RSFSR, 1918–1921.' Unpublished PhD dissertation, Columbia University 1966.

―――.'Political Recruitment and Local Government: The Local Soviets of the RSFSR, 1918–21.' *Soviet Studies*, Vol. 19, No. 4 (1967–68), 573–80.

Abrate, Mario. *La Lotta sindacale nella industrializzazione in Italia, 1906–1926.* Turin 1966.

Ackelsberg, Martha. 'The Possibility of Anarchism: The Theory and Practice of Non-Authoritarian Organization.' Unpublished PhD dissertation, Princeton University 1976.

Albert, Michael. *What Is To Be Undone*. Boston 1974.

Andors, Stephen. *China's Industrial Revolution*. New York 1977.

Armeson, Robert. *Total Warfare and Compulsory Labour*. The Hague 1964.

Althusser, Louis. *For Marx*. Trans. Ben Brewster. New York 1969.

Anderson, Perry. *Considerations on Western Marxism*. London 1976.

―――. 'The Antinomies of Antonio Gramsci.' *New Left Review*, No. 100 (November 1976–January 1977), 5–78.

―――. *Lineages of the Absolutist State*. London 1974.

―――. *Arguments Within English Marxism*. London 1980.

Andreyev, A. *The Soviets of Workers and Soldiers Deputies on the Eve of the October Revolution*. Moscow 1971.

Anweiler, Oscar. *The Soviets: The Russian Workers, Peasants and Soldiers Councils, 1905–1921*. Trans. Ruth Hein. New York 1974.

Arato, Andrew. 'Reexamining the Second International.' *Telos*, No. 18 (winter, 1973–74), 2–52.

Arendt, Hannah. *On Revolution*. New York 1963.

Arrighi, Giovanni. 'The Class Struggle in Twentieth-century Western Europe.' Paper presented to the Ninth World Congress of Sociology, Uppsala, August 1978.

Arshinov, Peter. *History of the Makhnovist Movement (1918–1921)*. Trans. Lorraine and Freddy Perlman. Detroit, Chicago 1974.

Atkinson, Dorothy. 'The Russian Land Commune and the Revolution.' Unpublished PhD dissertation, Stanford University 1971.

―――. 'The Statistics on the Russian Land Commune, 1905–1917.' *Slavic Review*, Vol. 32 (1973), 773–87.

―――, Alexander Dallin and Gail Warshofsky Lapidus, eds. *Women in Russia*. Stanford 1977.

Avineri, Shlomo. *The Social and Political Thought of Karl Marx*. Cambridge 1970.

Avrich, Paul. *Kronstadt 1921*. New York 1970.

_____. 'Russian Factory Committees in 1917.' *Jahrbücher für Geschichte Osteuropas*, Vol. 11 (1963), 161–82.

_____, ed. *The Anarchists in the Russian Revolution*. Ithaca 1973.

_____. 'The Bolshevik Revolution and Workers Control in Russian Industry.' *Slavic Review*, Vol. 27 (1963), 47–63.

_____. *The Russian Anarchists*. Princeton 1967.

_____. The Russian Revolution and the Factory Committees.' Unpublished PhD dissertation, Columbia University 1961.

Avtorkhanov, Abdurakhman. *The Communist Party Apparatus*. Chicago 1966.

Aya, Rod. 'Theories of Revolution Reconsidered: Contrasting Models of Collective Violence.' *Theory and Society*, 8 (1979), 39–99.

Baevskii, D.A. 'Rol' sovnarkhozov i profsoyuzov v organizatsii sotsialisticheskogo promyshlennogo proizvodstva v 1917–1920 gg.' *Istoricheskie Zapiski*, No. 64 (1959), 3–46.

Bahro, Rudolf. *The Alternative in Eastern Europe*. Trans. David Fernbach. London 1978.

Bailes, Kendall E. 'Alexei Gastev and the Soviet Controversy over Taylorism, 1918–24.' *Soviet Studies*, 29:3 (July 1977), 373–94.

_____. *Technology and Society Under Lenin and Stalin*. Princeton 1978.

Balibar, Etienne. *On the Dictatorship of the Proletariat*. Trans. Grahame Lock. London 1977.

Barfield, Rodney. 'Lenin's Utopianism: *State and Revolution*.' *Slavic Review*, Vol. 30, No. 1 (March 1971), 45–56.

Basil, John Duryea. 'Political Decisions Made by the Menshevik Leaders During the Revolution of 1917.' Unpublished PhD dissertation, University of Washington 1966.

Bassler, Gerhard. 'The Communist Movement in the German Revolution, 1918–1919: A Problem of Historical Typology?' *Central European History*, Vol. 6 (1973), 233–77.

Bater, James. *St. Petersburg: Industrialization and Change*. London 1976.

Batstone, Eric, Ian Boraston and Stephen Frenkel. *Shop Stewards in Action*. Oxford 1977.

Baumgarten, Franziska. *Arbeitswissenschaft und Psychotechnik in Russland*. Munich/Berlin 1924.

Bertrand, Charles, ed. *Revolutionary Situations in Europe, 1917–1922: Germany, Italy, Austria-Hungary*. Montreal 1977.

Besse, Guy, et al. *Lénine, la philosophie et la culture*. Paris 1971.

Bettelheim, Charles. *Class Struggles in the USSR, First Period: 1917–1923*. Trans. Brian Pearce. New York 1976.

_____. *Class Struggles in the USSR, Second Period: 1923–1930*. Trans. Brian Pearce. New York 1978.

_____. *Cultural Revolution and Industrial Organization in China*. New York 1974.

Blair, Thomas. '*The Land to Those Who Work It*.' Garden City 1969.

Block, Fred and Larry Hirschorn. 'New Productive Forces and the Contradictions of Contemporary Capitalism.' *Theory and Society*, 8 (1979), 363–95.

Blum, Jerome. *Lord and Peasant in Russia*. Princeton 1961.

Blumberg, Paul. *Industrial Democracy*. New York 1968.

Bobroff, Anne. 'The Bolsheviks and Working Women, 1905–20.' *Soviet Studies*,

26:4 (1974), 540-67.

Bock, Hans Manfred. *Syndikalismus und Linkskommunismus von 1918–1923*. Meisenheim an Glan, 1969.

Boggs, Carl. *Gramsci's Marxism*. London 1976.

———. 'Marxism, Prefigurative Communism and the Problem of Workers Control.' *Radical America*, Vols. 11–12, Nos. 6–1 (November 1977–February 1978), 99–122.

Boll, Michael. *The Petrograd Armed Workers Movement in the February Revolution*. Washington, DC 1979.

Bologna, Sergio. 'Class Composition and the Theory of the Party at the Origin of the Workers' Councils Movement.' *Telos*, No. 13 (fall 1972), 4–27.

The Bolsheviks and the October Revolution: Minutes of the Central Committee of the Russian Social-Democratic Labour Party (Bolsheviks), August 1917–February 1918. Trans. Ann Bone. London 1974.

Bonnell, Victoria. 'Radical Politics and Organized Labour in Pre-Revolutionary Moscow, 1905–1914.' *Journal of Social History*, 12:2 (March 1979), 282–300.

———. 'Trade Unions, Parties and the State in Tsarist Russia: A Study of Labour Politics in St. Petersburg and Moscow.' *Politics and Society*, 9:3 (1980), 299–322.

Boorstein, Edward. *Allende's Chile*. New York 1977.

Boyd, John. 'The Origins of Order No. 1.' *Soviet Studies*, Vol. 19, No. 3 (January 1968), 359–72.

Brady, Robert. *The Rationalization Movement in German Industry*. Berkeley 1933.

Braverman, Harry. *Labour and Monopoly Capital*. New York 1974.

Breines, Paul. 'Karl Korsch's "Road to Marx".' *Telos*, No. 26 (winter 1975–76), 42–56.

Bricianer, Serge. *Pannekoek and the Workers Councils*. St. Louis 1978.

Brinton, Maurice. *The Bolsheviks and Workers Control*. London 1970.

———. 'Factory Committees and the Dictatorship of the Proletariat.' *Critique*, No. 4 (spring 1975), 78–86.

Broué, Pierre. *Le Parti Bolchévique*. Paris 1963.

——— and Emile Témime. *The Revolution and Civil War in Spain*. Trans. Tony White. Cambridge 1970.

Browder, Robert and Alexander Kerensky, eds. *The Russian Provisional Government of 1917*. Stanford 1961.

Brown, Michael Barratt, Ken Coates and Tony Topham. 'Workers Control versus "Revolutionary Theory".' *The Socialist Register 1975*. London 1975.

Brügmann, Uwe. *Die russischen Gewerkschaften in Revolution und Bürgerkrieg 1917–1919*. Frankfurt am Main 1972.

Brutzkus, Boris. 'The Historical Peculiarities of the Social and Economic Development of Russia.' In *Class, Status and Power*, ed. Reinhard Bendix and Seymour Lipset. Glencoe 1969.

Buber, Martin. *Paths in Utopia*. Trans. R.F.C. Hull. Boston 1958.

Buchanan, Herbert Ray. 'Soviet Economic Policy for the Transition Period: The Supreme Council of the National Economy, 1917–1920.' Unpublished PhD dissertation, Indiana University 1972.

Bukharin, Nikolai. *Economics of the Transformation Period*. New York 1971.

———. *The Politics and Economics of the Transition Period*. Ed. Kenneth Tarbuck, trans. Oliver Field. London 1979.

———. *Historical Materialism*. Ann Arbor 1969.

———. 'The Imperialist Pirate State.' In *The Bolsheviks and the World War*, ed. Olga

Hess Gankin and H.H. Fisher. Stanford 1940.

Bunyan, James and H.H. Fisher, eds. *The Bolshevik Revolution, 1917–1918. Documents and Materials*. Palo Alto 1934.

____, ed. *Intervention, Civil War and Communism in Russia: April–December, 1918: Documents and Materials*. Baltimore 1936.

____, ed. *The Origin of Forced Labour in the Soviet State, 1917–21. Documents and Materials*. Baltimore 1967.

Cammett, John. *Antonio Gramsci and the Origins of Italian Communism*. Stanford 1967.

Cardan, Paul. *From Bolshevism to Bureaucracy*. London n.d.

Carlo, Antonio. 'Lenin on the Party.' *Telos*, No. 17 (fall 1973), 2–40.

Carr, E.H. *Michael Bakunin*. New York 1937.

____. *Socialism in One Country, 1924–1926*. 2 Vols. Baltimore 1970.

____. *The Bolshevik Revolution, 1917–1923*. 3 Vols. Baltimore 1966.

____. *The Interregnum 1923–1924*. Baltimore 1969.

____. *The October Revolution*. New York 1969.

____ and R.W. Davies. *Foundations of a Planned Economy, 1926–29*. Vol. 1. Baltimore 1974.

Carsten, F.L. *Revolution in Central Europe, 1918–1919*. Berkeley 1972.

Castoriadis, Cornelius. *Workers Councils*. London 1972.

Cavalcanti, Pedro and Paul Piccone, eds. *History, Philosophy and Culture in the Young Gramsci*. St. Louis 1975.

Chamberlin, William Henry. *The Russian Revolution*. 2 vols. New York 1965.

Chauvier, Jean-Marie. 'Contrôle ouvrier et "autogestion sauvage" en Russie (1917–1921).' *Revue des Pays de l'Est*, Vol. 14, No. 1 (1973), 71–100.

Chitarin, Attilio. *Lenin e il controllo operaio*. Rome 1973.

Chorley, Catherine. *Armies and the Art of Revolution*. Boston 1973.

Clark, Marjorie Ruth. *A History of the French Labour Movement (1910–1928)* Berkeley 1930.

Clark, Martin. *Antonio Gramsci and the Revolution that Failed*. New Haven 1977.

Clarke, Roger. *Soviet Economic Facts*. New York 1972.

Claudín, Fernando. 'Spain—The Untimely Revolution.' *New Left Review*, No. 74 (July-August 1972), 3–31.

____. 'Democracy and Dictatorship in Lenin and Kautsky.' *New Left Review*, No. 106 (November-December 1977), 59–76.

Claudín-Urondo, Carmen. *Lénine et la révolution culturelle*. Paris 1975.

Clegg, Ian. *Workers Self-Management in Algeria*. New York 1971.

Cliff, Tony. *Lenin*. 2 vols. London 1975, 1976.

____, et al. *Party and Class*. London n.d.

Cogniot, Georges. 'Rupture et continuité de la tradition culturelle selon Lénine.' *La Pensée* (April 1970), 24–37.

Cohen, G.A. *Karl Marx's Theory of History: A Defence*. Oxford 1978.

Cohen, Stephen. *Bukharin and the Bolshevik Revolution*. New York 1971.

Cole, Robert. *Work, Mobility and Participation: A Comparative Study of American and Japanese Industry*. Berkeley 1979.

Collins, D.N. 'A Note on the Numerical Strength of the Red Guard in October 1917.' *Soviet Studies*, Vol. 24, No. 3 (October 1972), 270–80.

Comfort, Richard. *Revolutionary Hamburg*. Stanford 1966.

Comisso, Ellen Turkish. *Workers Control under Plan and Market*. New Haven 1979.

Corrigan, Philip, Harvie Ramsay and Derek Sayer. *Socialist Construction and Marxist Theory*. New York 1978.

Dahl, Robert. *After the Revolution*. New Haven 1970.

Daniels, Robert Vincent. *The Conscience of the Revolution*. New York 1969.

———, ed. *Red October: The Bolshevik Revolution of 1917*. New York 1967.

———. 'The State and Revolution: A Case Study in the Genesis and Transformation of Communist Ideology.' *Slavic Review*, Vol. 12, No. 1 (1953), 22–43.

Davidson, Alastair. *Antonio Gramsci: Towards an Intellectual Biography*. London 1977.

———. 'Gramsci and Lenin 1917–1922.' *Socialist Register 1974*. London 1974, pp. 125–50.

Davies, James, 'Toward a Theory of Revolution.' In *The Sociology of Revolution*, ed. Ronald Ye-Lin Cheng. Chicago 1973.

Davies, R.W. *The Socialist Offensive: The Collectivization of Soviet Agriculture, 1929–1930*. Cambridge 1980.

DeMasi, Guido and Giacomo Marromao. 'Councils and State in Weimar Germany.' *Telos*, No. 28 (summer 1976), 3–35.

Denitch, Bogdan. *The Legitimation of a Revolution: The Yugoslav Case*. New Haven 1976.

Desolre, Guy. 'Le Chapitre VII inédit de l'Etat et la Révolution".' *Revue des Pays de l'Est*, Vol. 14, no. 1 (1973), 101–11.

Deutscher, Isaac. *Heretics and Renegades*. New York 1969.

———. *Stalin: A Political Biography*. New York 1949.

———. *Soviet Trade Unions*. London 1950.

———. *The Prophet Armed*. New York 1965.

———. *The Prophet Unarmed*. New York 1965.

———. *The Prophet Outcast*. New York 1965.

———. *The Unfinished Revolution: Russia 1917–1967*. Oxford 1967.

Devinat, Paul. *Scientific Management in Europe*. Geneva 1927.

Devlin, Robert. 'Petrograd Workers and Workers' Factory Committees in 1917: An Aspect of the Social History of the Russian Revolution.' Unpublished PhD dissertation, State University of New York at Binghamton 1976.

Dewar, Margaret. *Labour Policy in the USSR, 1917–1928*. London 1976.

Dobb, Maurice. *Soviet Economic Development since 1917*, revised ed. New York 1966.

Dolgoff, Sam, ed. *The Anarchist Collectives*. New York 1974.

Döring, Falk. *Organizationsprobleme der russischen Wirtschaft in Revolution und Bürgerkrieg (1918–1920)*. Hanover 1970.

Downs, Charles. 'Comissôes de Moradores and Urban Struggle in Revolutionary Portugal.'· *International Journal of Urban and Regional Research* 4:2 (June 1980), 267–94.

Draper, Hal. *Karl Marx's Theory of Revolution*. Vol. 1. New York 1977.

Drobizhev, V.Z. *Glavnyi shtab sotsialisticheskoi promyshlennosti*. Moscow 1966.

Dubofsky, Melvyn. *We Shall Be All*. New York 1969.

Dunayevskaya, Raya. *Philosophy and Revolution*. New York 1973.

———. 'The Shock of Recognition and the Philosophic Ambivalence of Lenin.' *Telos*, No. 5 (spring 1970), 44–57.

Dutschke, Rudi. *Versuch, Lenin auf die Füsse zu stellen*. Berlin 1974.

Edmondson, Charles. 'The Politics of Hunger: The Soviet Response to Famine, 1921.' *Soviet Studies*, 29:4 (October 1977), 506–18.

Edwards, Stewart. *The Paris Commune 1871*. Chicago 1971.

Eissenstat, Bernard W., ed. *Lenin and Leninism*. Lexington 1971.

Ellis, John. *Armies in Revolution*. London 1973.

Ellison, Herbert. 'The Socialist Revolutionaries.' *Problems of Communism*, Vol. 16 (November-December 1967).

Ellman, Michael. 'Did the Agricultural Surplus Provide the Resources for the Increase in Investment During the First Five-Year Plan?' *Economic Journal*, 85 (December 1975), 844–64.

Elwood, Ralph Carter, ed. *Resolutions and Decisions of the Communist Party of the Soviet Union*. 2 Vols. Toronto 1974.

Emmanuel, Arghiri. 'The State in the Transition Period.' *New Left Review*, Nos. 113–14 (January-April 1979), 111–31.

Engels, Friedrich. *Anti-Dühring*. New York 1939.

_____. *The Origin of the Family, Private Property and the State*. New York 1972.

Erlich, Alexander. *The Soviet Industrialization Debate, 1924–1928*. Cambridge 1967.

Espinosa, Juan and Andrew Zimbalist. *Economic Democracy: Workers Participation in Chilean Industry, 1970–1973*. New York 1978.

Feldberg, Roslyn. 'Women, Self-Management and Socialism.' *Socialist Review*, No. 56 (March-April 1981), 141–52.

Feldman, Gerald. *Army, Industry and Labour in Germany, 1914–1918*. Princeton 1966.

_____. *Iron and Steel in the German Inflation*. Princeton 1977.

_____. 'German Big Business Between War and Revolution: The Origin of the Stinnes-Legien Agreement.' *In Entstehung und Wandel der modernen Gesellschaft*, ed. Gerhard Ritter. Berlin 1970.

Ferro, Marc. *The Russian Revolution of February 1917*. Trans. J.L. Richards. Engelwood Cliffs 1972.

_____. *La Révolution de 1917: Octobre, Naissance d'une société*. Paris 1976.

_____. *The Great War 1914–1918*. Trans. Nicole Stone. London 1973.

_____. 'The Russian Soldier in 1917: Undisciplined, Patriotic and Revolutionary.' *Slavic Review*, Vol. 30 (1970), 483–512.

Fields, Rona. *The Portuguese Armed Forces Movement*. New York 1976.

Fitzpatrick, Sheila, ed. *Cultural Revolution in Russia, 1928–1931*. Bloomington 1978.

_____. *The Commissariat of Enlightenment*. Cambridge 1970.

Fleischer, Helmut. *Marxism and History*. Trans. Eric Mosbacher. New York 1973.

Fleron, Frederick, ed. *Technology and Communist Culture*. New York 1977.

_____ and Lou Jean. 'Administrative Theory as Repressive Political Theory: The Communist Experience.' *Telos*, No. 12 (summer 1972), 63–92.

Footman, David. *Civil War in Russia*. London 1961.

_____. 'Nestor Makhno.' *St. Anthony's Papers*, No. 6, ed. David Footman. London 1959; 75–127.

Frank, André Gunder. 'Long Live Transideological Enterprise! The Socialist Economies in the Capitalist International Division of Labour.' *Review*, Vol. 1, No. 1 (summer 1977), 91–140.

Fraser, Ronald. *Blood of Spain*. New York 1979.

Fraser, Steve. ' "The New Unionism" and the "New Economic Policy" ' in James Cronin and Carmen Sirianni, eds., *Work, Community and Power*, Philadelphia 1933

Fridenson, Patrick. *Histoire des usines Renault.* Paris 1972.

Friedlander, Henry Egon. 'Conflict of Revolutionary Authority: Provisional Government vs. Berlin Soviet, November-December 1918.' *International Review of Social History,* Vol. 7 (1962), 163–75.

Gallo, Max. 'Quelques aspects de la mentalité et du comportement ouvriers dans les usines de guerre, 1914–1918.' *Le Mouvement Social,* No. 56 (July-September 1966), 3–33.

Garson, G. David. *Workers Self-Management in Industry: The West European Experience.* New York 1977.

Genkin, L.B. 'Rozhdeniye Sotsialisticheskoy Distsiplini Truda (konets 1917–leto 1918.' *Istoriya SSSR* (January-February 1965), No. 1, 3–27.

George, Francois. 'Forgetting Lenin.' *Telos,* No. 18 (winter 1973/74), 53–88.

Gerschenkron, Alexander. 'Agrarian Policies and Industrialization: Russia 1861– 1917.' In *Cambridge Economic History of Europe,* Vol. 6, Pt. 2. Cambridge 1965.

Geschichte der Gewerkschaftsbewegung in der UdSSR. Prepared by N.P. Antropow, I.L. Borschtchenko and I.P. Markow. Trans. from the Russian. Berlin 1962.

Getzler, Israel. *Martov.* Cambridge 1967.

——. 'The Mensheviks.' *Problems of Communism,* Vol. 16 (November-December 1967).

Geyer, Dietrich. 'Arbeiterbewegung und "Kulturrevolution" in Russland.' *Vierteljahreshefte für Zeitgeschichte,* Vol. 10 (1962), 43–55.

Gilison, Jerome. *The Soviet Image of Utopia.* Baltimore 1975.

Gill, Graeme. *Peasants and Government in the Russian Revolution.* New York 1979.

Gladkov, I. *Natsionalizatsiya promyshlennosti v SSSR. Sbornik dokumentov i materialov, 1917–1920 gg.* Moscow: 1954.

Goodey, Chris. 'Factory Committees and the Dictatorship of the Proletariat (1918).' *Critique,* No. 3 (Autumn 1974), 27–47.

——. 'Factory Committees and the Dictatorship of the Proletariat: Additional Notes.' *Critique,* No. 5 (autumn 1975), 85–89.

Gordon, David. 'Capitalist Efficiency and Socialist Efficiency.' *Monthly Review,* Vol. 28, No. 3 (July-August 1976), 19–39.

Gorky, Maxim. *Untimely Thoughts.* Trans. Hermann Ermolaev. New York 1968.

Gorz, André. *Socialism and Revolution.* Trans. Norman Denny. Garden City 1973.

——. 'Technical Intelligence and the Capitalist Division of Labour.' *Telos,* No. 12 (summer 1972), 27–41.

——, ed. *The Division of Labour: The Labour Process and Class Struggle in Modern Capitalism.* Atlantic Highlands 1976.

Graham, Lawrence and Harry Mackler, eds. *Portugal Today.* Austin 1979.

Gramsci, Antonio. *Selections from the Prison Notebooks.* Ed. and trans. Quintin Hoare and Geoffrey Nowell-Smith. New York 1971.

——. *Selections from Political Writings 1910–1920.* Ed. Quintin Hoare, trans. John Matthews. New York 1977.

Grant, Steven. '*Obshchina* and *Mir.*' *Slavic Review,* 35:4 (December 1976), 636–51.

Grille, Dietrich. *Lenins Rivale.* Cologne 1966.

Groh, Dieter. *Kritische Geschichtswissenschaft in emanzipatorischer Absicht.* Stuttgart 1973.

Guérin, Daniel. *Anarchism.* Trans. Mary Klopper. New York 1970.

Guroff, Gregory and S. Frederick Starr. 'A Note on Urban Literacy in Russia, 1890–1914.' *Jahrbücher für Geschichte Osteuropas*, Vol. 19 (1971), 520–31.

Gurr, Ted. *Why Men Rebel*. Princeton 1970.

Gutman, Herbert. *Work, Culture and Society in Industrializing America*. New York 1977.

Habermas, Jürgen. *Knowledge and Human Interest*. Trans. Jeremy Shapiro. Boston 1971.

____. *Theory and Practice*. Trans. John Viertel. Boston 1973.

____. *Toward a Rational Society*. Trans. Jeremy Shapiro. Boston 1970.

____. 'Towards a Reconstruction of Historical Materialism.' *Theory and Society*, Vol. 2, No. 3, (fall 1975), 287–300.

Haimson, Leopold. 'Les Menchéviks face à la Révolution d'Octobre: Le Congrès Extraordinaire du RSDRP (Novembre-Decembre 1917).' *Cahiers du Monde Russe et Soviétique* (1973), 5–32.

____, ed. *The Mensheviks*. Trans. Gertrude Vakar. Chicago 1974.

____. 'The Problem of Social Stability in Urban Russia, 1905–1917.' Part One in *Slavic Review*, Vol. 23 (1964), 619–642; Part Two in Vol. 24 (1965), 1–22.

____. 'The Russian Workers Movement on the Eve of the First World War.' Paper delivered at the annual meeting of the American Historical Association, New York, December 1971.

Hammond, Thomas Taylor. *Lenin on Trade Unions and Revolution 1893–1917*. New York 1957.

Harcave, Sidney. *First Blood*. New York 1964.

Harrison, Mark. 'The Problems of Social Mobility among Russian Peasant Households, 1880–1930.' *Journal of Peasant Studies*, Vol. 4, No. 2 (January 1977), 127–61.

Hasegawa, Tsuyoshi. 'The Formation of the Militia in the February Revolution: An Aspect of the Origins of Dual Power.' *Slavic Review*, Vol. 32 (1973), 303–22.

____. 'The Bolsheviks and the Formation of the Petrograd Soviet in the February Revolution.' *Soviet Studies*, Vol. 29, No. 1 (January 1977), 86–107.

____. 'The Problem of Power in the February Revolution of 1917 in Russia.' *Canadian Slavonic Papers*, Vol. 14 (1972), 611–32.

Haumann, Heiko. *Beginn der Planwirtschaft*. Dusseldorf 1974.

____. 'Die russische Revolution und ihre ersten Versuche sozialistischer Wirtschaftspolitik.' *Das Argument*, Vol. 15, No. 82 (1973), 768–803.

____. '"Kriegskommunismus" oder unmittelbarer Aufbau des Sozialismus?' *Jahrbücher für Geschichte Osteuropas*, Vol. 23 (1975), 97–104.

Haupt, Georges and Jean-Jacques Marie. *Makers of the Russian Revolution*. Ithaca 1974.

____. *Socialism and the Great War*. Oxford 1972.

Hinton, James. *The First Shop Stewards Movement*. London 1973.

Hobsbawm, E.J. 'From Social History to the History of Society.' In *Historical Studies Today*, ed. Felix Gilbert and Stephen Graubard. New York 1975.

____. 'Custom, Wages and Workload in Nineteenth-century Industry.' In *Workers in the Industrial Revolution*, ed. Peter Stearns and Daniel Walkowitz. New Brunswick 1974.

Hodgson, Geoff. *Trotsky and Fatalistic Marxism*. Nottingham 1975.

____. *Socialism and Parliamentary Democracy*. Nottingham 1977.

Hogan, Heather. 'The Putilovtsy: A Case Study of Workers' Attitudes During the Russian Revolution.' Unpublished paper, University of Michigan, August 1974.

Homburg, Heidrun. 'Anfänge des Taylorsystems in Deutschland vor dem Ersten Weltkrieg.' *Gesellschaft und Geschichte*, Vol. 4, No. 2 (1978), 170–94.

Horowitz, Daniel. *The Italian Labour Movement*. Cambridge, Mass., 1963.

Horvat, Branko, Mihailo Markovic and Rudi Supek, eds. *Self-Governing Socialism*. Vol. 1. White Plains 1975.

Hosking, Geoffrey A. *The Russian Constitutional Experiment*. Cambridge, Mass., 1973.

Howard, Dick and Karl Klare, eds. *The Unknown Dimension*. New York 1972.

Hunnius, Gerry. 'The Yugoslav System of Decentralization and Self-Management.' In *The Case for Participatory Democracy*, ed. C. George Benello and Dimitri Roussopoulos. New York 1974.

Hyman, Richard. 'Workers Control and Revolutionary Theory.' In *The Socialist Register 1974*. London 1974.

International Labour Office. *Labour Conditions in Soviet Russia*. London 1920.

Itkin, M.L. 'Tsentry fabrichno-zavodskikh komitetov Rossii v 1917 godu.' *Voprosy Istorii*, No. 2 (1974), 21–35.

James, C.L.R. 'Peasants and Workers.' *Radical America*, Vol. 5, No. 6 (November–December 1971), 5–49.

Jasny, Naum. *Soviet Economists of the Twenties*. Cambridge 1972.

Jellinek, Frank. *The Paris Commune of 1871*. New York 1965.

Jenkins, David. *Job Power*. Garden City 1973.

Jessop, Bob. 'Capitalism and Democracy: The Best Possible Shell?' In *Power and the State*, ed. Gary Littlejohn, Barry Smart, John Wakeford and Nira Yuval-Davis. London 1978.

Johnson, R.E. 'Peasant Migration and the Russian Working Class: Moscow at the End of the Nineteenth Century.' *Slavic Review* 35:4 (December 1976), 652–64.

____. 'The Nature of the Russian Working Class: Social Characteristics of the Moscow Industrial Region, 1880–1900.' PhD dissertation, Cornell University 1975.

Kamkov, Boris. 'Organicheskii Nedug.' In *Teoriya i praktika sovetskogo stroya, vypusk pervyi*. Berlin n.d.

____. 'Zum Verhältnis von Stadt und Land.' In *Die russische Arbeiteropposition*, ed. Gottfried Mergner. Hamburg 1972.

Kanter, Rosabeth Moss. *Men and Women of the Corporation*. New York 1977.

Kaplan, Frederick. *Bolshevik Ideology and the Ethics of Soviet Labour*. New York 1968.

Katkov, George. 'The Kronstadt Rising.' *St. Anthony's Papers*, No. 6, ed. David Footman. London 1959, 9–74.

Keep, John L.H. *The Rise of Social Democracy in Russia*. Oxford 1963.

____. *The Russian Revolution*. New York 1976.

____, ed. and trans. *The Debate on Soviet Power*. Oxford 1979.

Kendall, Walter. *The Revolutionary Movement in Britain, 1900–1921*. London 1969.

Kevenhörster, Paul. *Das Rätesystem als Instrument zur Kontrolle politischer und wirtschaftlicher Macht*. Opladen 1974.

Kingston-Mann, Esther. 'Lenin and the Beginnings of Marxist Peasant Revolution: The Burden of Political Opportunity, July-October 1917.' *Slavonic and East European Review*, Vol. 50, No. 121 (October 1972), 570–88.

____. *Lenin and the Problem of Marxist Peasant Revolution, 1893–1917*. Unpublished manuscript, 1980.

_____. 'Marxism and Russian Rural Development.' *American Historical Review*, 86: 4 731-52.

Kluge, Ulrich. *Soldatenräte und Revolution*. Göttingen 1975.

Knei-Paz, Baruch. *The Social and Political Thought of Leon Trotsky*. Oxford 1978.

Kocka, Jürgen. *Klassengesellschaft im Krieg 1914–1918*. Göttingen 1973.

Koenker, Diane. 'Moscow Workers in 1917.' PhD dissertation, University of Michigan 1976.

_____. 'The Evolution of Party Consciousness in 1917: The Case of the Moscow Workers. ' *Soviet Studies*, 30:1 (January 1978), 38–62.

Kolb, Eberhard. *Die Arbeiterräte in der deutschen Innenpolitik 1918–1919*. Dusseldorf 1962.

_____, ed. *Vom Kaiserreich zur Weimarer Republik*. Cologne 1972.

Kollontai, Alexandra. *L'Opposition ouvrière*. Paris 1974.

_____. *The Workers Opposition*. London n.d.

Kool, Fritz and Erwin Oberländer, eds. *Arbeiterdemokratie oder Parteidiktatur*. Olten und Freiburg im Breisgau 1969.

Korpi, Walter. *The Working Class in Welfare Capitalism*. London 1978.

Korsch, Karl. *Schriften zur Sozialisierung*. Frankfurt am Main 1969.

_____. 'What is Socialization? A Program of Practical Socialism.' *New German Critique*, No. 6 (fall 1975), 60–81.

_____. *Marxism and Philosophy*. Trans. and Introduction by Fred Halliday. New York 1970.

Kovanda, Karel. 'Czechoslovak Workers Councils 1968–1979.' *Telos*, No. 28 (summer 1976), 36–54.

Krause, Hartfrid. *USPD*. Frankfurt am Main 1975.

Kritzman, Leo. *Die Heroische Periode der grossen russischen Revolution*. Frankfurt 1971.

_____ and I. Larin. *Wirtschaftsleben und wirtschaftslicher Aufbau in Sowjet-Russland, 1917–1920*. Hamburg 1921.

Laird, Roy. *Collective Farming in Russia*. Lawrence 1958.

Laux, James. *In First Gear: The French Automobile Industry to 1914*. Montreal 1976.

Lavender, William. 'Bolshevik Tactics and Propaganda after the February Revolution, April-November 1917.' Unpublished PhD dissertation, University of Washington 1969.

Leed, Eric. *No Man's Land: Combat and Identity in World War I*. Cambridge 1979.

Lefort, Claude. *Eléments d'une critique de la bureaucratie*. Geneva 1971.

Lenin, V.I. *Collected Works*. London 1964.

Leval, Gaston. *Collectives in the Spanish Revolution*. Trans. Vernon Richards. London 1975.

Levine, Andrew and Erik Olin Wright. 'Rationality and Class Struggle.' *New Left Review*, No. 123 (September-October 1980), 47–68.

Lewin, Moshe. *Lenin's Last Struggle*. Trans. A.M. Sheridan-Smith. New York 1968.

_____. *Russian Peasants and Soviet Power*. Trans. Irene Nove. New York 1975.

_____. *Political Undercurrents in Soviet Economic Debates*. Princeton 1974.

Liberman, Simon. *Building Lenin's Russia*. Chicago 1945.

Lichtheim, George. 'Marx and the "Asiatic Mode of Production".' In *St. Anthony's Papers*, No. 14, ed. G.F. Hudson. Carbondale 1963.

Liebman, Marcel. 'Lenin in 1905: A Revolution that Shook a Doctrine.' In *Lenin Today*. Ed. Paul Sweezy and Harry Magdoff. New York 1970, 57–75.

_____. *Leninism under Lenin*. Trans. Brian Pearce. London 1975.

_____. *The Russian Revolution*. Trans. Arnold Pomerans. New York 1970.

Limon, Didier. 'Lénine et le contrôle ouvrier.' *Autogestion*, No. 4 (December 1967), 65-109.

Lindemann, Albert. *The 'Red Years'*. Berkeley 1974.

Linhart, Robert. *Lénine, les paysans, Taylor*. Paris 1976.

Lomax, Bill. *Hungary 1956*. London 1976.

Lomov, A. *Die Produktivität der Arbeit in Sowjet-Russland*. Berlin 1919.

Lorenz, Richard. *Anfänge der bolschewistischen Industriepolitik*. Cologne 1965.

_____. 'Zur Industriepolitik der provisorischen Regierung.' *Jahrbücher für Geschichte Osteuropas*, Vol. 14 (1966), 367-87.

_____. 'Ergebnisse und Perspektiven der Industrialisierung während der Neuen Ökonomischen Politik.' *Jahrbücher für Geschichte Osteuropas*, Vol. 16 (1968), 212-31.

_____. 'Wirtschaftspolitische Alternativen der Sowjetmacht im Frühjahr und Sommer 1918.' *Jahrbücher für Geschichte Osteuropas*, Vol. 15 (1967), 209-36.

_____. *Proletarische Kulturrevolution in Sowjetrussland (1917-1921)*. Munich 1969.

Lorwin, Val. *The French Labour Movement*. Cambridge, Mass., 1966.

Löwy, Michael. 'From the "Logic" of Hegel to the Finland Station in Petrograd.' *Critique*, No. 6 (spring 1976), 5-15.

Lozovsky, A. *Les Syndicats russes et la nouvelle politique*. Paris 1922.

Lucas, Erhard. *Zwei Formen von Radikalismus in der deutschen Arbeiterbewegung*. Frankfurt am Main 1976.

Lukács, Georg. *Lenin*. Cambridge 1971.

Luxemburg, Rosa. *The Russian Revolution* and *Leninism or Marxism*. Ann Arbor 1961.

_____. *Selected Political Writings*. Ed. and Introduction by Dick Howard. New York 1971.

Lyashchenko, Peter. *History of the National Economy of Russia to the 1917 Revolution*. New York 1949.

MacEwan, Arthur. *Revolution and Economic Development in Cuba*. New York 1981.

_____. 'Incentives, Equality and Power in Revolutionary Cuba.' *Socialist Review*, No. 23 (April 1975), 117-43.

Maier, Charles. *Recasting Bourgeois Europe*. Princeton 1975.

_____. 'Between Taylorism and Technocracy: European Ideologies and the Vision of Industrial Productivity in the 1920s.' *The Journal of Contemporary History*, Vol. 5, No. 2 (1970), 27-61.

_____. 'The Two Post-war Eras and the Conditions for Stability in Twentieth-Century Western Europe.' *American Historical Review* 86:2 (April 1981), 323-48.

Maignien, Yannick. *La division du travail manuel et intellectuel*. Paris 1975.

Maione, Giuseppe. *Il Biennio Rosso*. Bologna 1975.

Mallet, Serge. *La nouvelle classe ouvrière*. Paris 1969.

Male, D.J. *Russian Peasant Organization before Collectivization*. Cambridge 1971.

Mandel, Ernest, ed. *Contrôle ouvrier, conseils ouvriers, autogestion*. 3 Vols. Paris 1973.

_____. 'Liebman and Leninism.' *Socialist Register 1975*. London 1975.

_____. *The Formation of the Economic Thought of Karl Marx*. Trans. Brian Pearce. New York 1971.

_____. 'A Political Interview.' *New Left Review*, No. 100 (November 1976–January

1977), 97–132.

_____. *From Stalinism to Eurocommunism*. London 1978.

Mandel, Mark David. 'The Development of Revolutionary Consciousness Among the Industrial Workers of Petrograd between February and November 1917.' Unpublished PhD dissertation, Columbia University 1978.

Mannheim, Karl. *Essays on the Sociology of Knowledge*. Ed. Paul Kecskemeti. London 1952.

Marcuse, Herbert. *One-Dimensional Man*. Boston 1964.

_____. *Reason and Revolution*. Boston 1960.

_____. *Soviet Marxism*. New York 1961.

Martov, Julian. 'The State and the Socialist Revolution.' *New International Review*, Vol. 1, Nos. 1 and 2 (winter-summer 1977), 11–38, 55–61.

Marwick, Arthur. *The Deluge*. London 1965.

_____. *War and Social Change in the Twentieth Century*. New York 1974.

Marx, Karl, Friedrich Engels and V.I. Lenin. *Anarchism and Anarcho-Syndicalism*. New York 1972.

_____ and Friedrich Engels. *Basic Writings on Politics and Philosophy*. Ed. Lewis Feuer. Garden City 1959.

_____. *Class Struggles in France, 1848–1850*. New York 1964.

_____. *Capital*. Vol. 1. New York 1967.

_____. *Capital*. Vol. 3. Moscow 1966.

_____ and V.I. Lenin. *Civil War in France: The Paris Commune*. New York 1940.

_____. *Critique of the Gotha Programme*. New York 1938.

_____. *Grundrisse*. Trans. Martin Nicolaus. Baltimore 1973.

_____. *On Revolution*. Ed. and trans. Saul Padover. New York 1971.

_____. *Pre-capitalist Economic Formations*. Trans. Jack Cohen. Introduction by E.J, Hobsbawm. New York 1965.

_____ and Friedrich Engels. *Selected Correspondence*. Moscow 1965.

_____ and Friedrich Engels. *The Communist Manifesto*. New York 1948.

_____. *The Eighteenth Brumaire of Louis Bonaparte*. New York 1963.

_____ and Friedrich Engels. *The German Ideology*. Ed. C.J. Arthur. New York 1970.

_____ and Friedrich Engels. *Werke*. Berlin 1968.

_____ and Friedrich Engels. *Writings on the Paris Commune*. Ed. Hal Draper. New York 1971.

_____. *Writings of the Young Marx on Philosophy and Society*. Trans. and ed. Lloyd D. Easton and Kurt H. Guddat. Garden City 1967.

Masini, Pier Carlo. 'Anarchistes et communistes dans le mouvement des conseils à Turin—première après-guerre rouge 1919–1920.' *Autogestion*, Nos. 26–27 (March-June 1974), 27–53.

Mattick, Paul. *Anti-Bolshevik Communism*. White Plains 1978.

Mayer, Arno. *Politics and Diplomacy of Peacemaking*. New York 1967.

Maynard, John. *The Russian Peasant*. New York 1962.

McLean, Iain. 'Popular Protest and Public Order: Red Clydeside, 1915–1919.' In *Popular Protest and Public Order*. Ed. R. Quinalt and J. Stevenson. New York 1974.

McLelland, James C. 'Bolshevik Approaches to Higher Education, 1917–1921.' *Slavic Review*, Vol. 30, No. 4 (December 1971), 818–31.

Meaker, Gerald. *The Revolutionary Left in Spain, 1914–1923*. Stanford 1974.

Medalie, Richard. 'The Communist Theory of the State.' *Slavic Review*, Vol. 18, No. 4 (1959), 510–25.

Menasche, Louis. 'Vladimir Ilyich Bakunin: An Essay on Lenin.' *Socialist Review*, No. 18 (November/December 1973), 9–54.

Mendel, Arthur. 'Peasant and Worker on the Eve of the First World War.' *Slavic Review*, Vol. 24 (1965), 23–33.

Mergner, Gottfried, ed. *Die russische Arbeiteropposition*. Reinback bei Hamburg 1972.

Mett, Ida. *The Kronstadt Uprising*. Montreal 1971.

Meyer, Alfred G. *Leninism*. New York 1962.

Michels, Robert. *Political Parties*. Trans. Eden and Cedar Paul. New York 1962.

Miliband, Ralph. *Marxism and Politics*. Oxford 1977.

_____. 'The State and Revolution.' In *Lenin Today*. Ed. Paul Sweezy and Harry Magdoff. New York 1970.

_____. 'The Coup in Chile.' In *Revolution and Class Struggle*. Ed. Robin Blackburn. Glasgow 1977.

Millar, James. 'Mass Collectivization and the Contribution of Soviet Agriculture to the First Five-Year Plan: A Review Article.' *Slavic Review*, 33:4 (1974), 750–66.

Milligan, Sandra. 'The Petrograd Bolsheviks and Social Insurance, 1914–1917.' *Soviet Studies*, Vol. 20 (1968/1969), 369–74.

Mintz, Frank. *L'Autogestion dans l'Espagne révolutionnaire*. Paris: Belibaste, 1970.

Monds, Jean. 'Workers Control and the Historians: A New Economism.' *New Left Review*, No. 97 (May-June 1976), 81–100.

Montgomery, David. *Workers Control in America*. New York 1979.

Morgan, David. *The Socialist Left and the German Revolution*. Ithaca 1975.

Morris, L.P. 'The Russians, the Allies and the War, February-July 1917.' *Slavonic and East European Review*, Vol. 50, No. 118 (January 1977), 29–48.

Mouffe, Chantal, ed. *Gramsci and Marxist Theory*. London 1979.

Moutet, Aimée. 'Les Origines du système de Taylor en France, le point de vue patronal (1907-1914).' *Le Mouvement Social*, No. 93 (October-December 1975), 15–49.

Narkiewicz, Olga. *The Making of the Soviet State Apparatus*. Manchester 1970.

Nötzold, Jürgen. *Wirtschaftspolitische Alternativen der Entwicklung Russlands in der Ära Witte und Stolypin*. Berlin 1966.

Nove, Alec. *An Economic History of the USSR*. Baltimore 1969.

Nowlin, Bill. 'The Makhnovist Movement.' *Black and Red*, No. 2 (spring 1975), 108–18.

Oberschall, Anthony. *Social Conflict and Social Movements*. Engelwood Cliffs 1973.

Oertzen, Peter von. *Betriebsräte in der Novemberrevolution*. Dusseldorf 1963.

_____. *Die Probleme der wirtschaftlichen Neuordnung und der Mitbestimmung in der Revolution von 1918, unter besonderer Berücksichtigung der Metallindustrie*. Frankfurt am Main 1975.

Oktyabr'skaia revolyutsiia i fabzavkomy. Materialy po istorii fabrichno-zavodskikh komitetov. 3 Vols. Moscow 1927.

Ollman, Bertell. 'Marx's Vision of Communism: A Reconstruction.' *Critique*, No.8 (summer 1977), 4–41.

Opel, Fritz. *Der deutsche Metallarbeiter-Verband während des Erstens Weltkrieges und der Revolution*. Hanover 1958.

Oppenheim, Samuel. 'The Supreme Economic Council, 1917–1921.' *Soviet Studies*, Vol. 25, No. 1 (July 1973), 3–27.

Osipov, G.V., ed. *Industry and Labour in the USSR*. London 1966.

Oualid, Williams and Charles Picquenard. *Salaires et Tarifs*. Paris 1928.

Owen, Launcelot. *The Russian Peasant Movement, 1906-1917*. New York 1963.

Palij, Michael. *The Anarchism of Nestor Makhno*. Washington 1976.

Palmer, Bryan. 'Class, Conception and Conflict: The Thrust for Efficiency. Managerial Views of Labour and Working-Class Rebellion, 1903-1922.' *The Review of Radical Political Economics*, Vol. 7, No. 2 (summer 1975), 31-49.

____. 'Workers Control and Managerial Innovation: A North American Perspective.' Paper presented to the Conference on New Directions in the Labour Process, SUNY-Binghamton, May 1978.

Panitch, Leo. 'Trade Unions and the Corporatist State.' *New Left Review*, No. 125 (January-February 1981), 21-43.

Pankratova, A.M. *Geschichte der Gewerkschaftsbewegung in der UdSSR*. Berlin 1956.

____. 'Les Comités d'usines en Russie à l'époque de la Révolution (1917-1918).' *Autogestion*, No. 4 (December 1967), 3-63.

Pannekoek, Anton. *Lenin as Philosopher*. London 1975.

____. *Workers Councils*. Cambridge, Mass. 1970.

Papayanis, Nicholas. 'Masses révolutionnaires et directions réformistes: Les tensions au cours des grèves des métallurgistes français en 1919.' *Le Mouvement Social*, No. 93 (October-December 1975), 51-73.

Pateman, Carole. *Participation and Democratic Theory*. New York 1970.

Pelikan, Jiři. 'Workers Councils in Czechoslovakia.' *Critique*, Vol. 1, No. 1 (spring 1973), 7-19.

Perrie, Maureen. 'The Social Composition and Structure of the Socialist Revolutionary Party Before 1917.' *Soviet Studies*, Vol. 24 (1972-1973), 223-50.

____. 'The Socialist Revolutionaries on "Permanent Revolution".' *Soviet Studies*, Vol. 24 (1972/1973), 411-13.

Pethybridge, Roger. *The Spread of the Russian Revolution*. London 1972.

____. 'The Bolsheviks and Technical Disorder, 1917-1918.' *Slavonic and East European Review*, Vol. 49, No. 116 (July 1971), 410-24.

____. *The Social Prelude to Stalinism*. New York 1974.

Peter, Victor. *Nestor Makhno*. Winnipeg 1970.

Pfeffer, Richard. 'Serving the People and Continuing the Revolution.' *China Quarterly*, No. 52 (October-December 1972), 620-53.

Picard, Roger. *Le Mouvement syndical durant la guerre*. Paris 1927.

____. *Le contrôle sur la gestion des entreprises*. Paris 1922.

Piccone, Paul. 'Towards an Understanding of Lenin's Philosophy.' *Radical America*, Vol. 4, No. 6 (September-October 1970), 3-20.

Pietsch, Walter. *Revolution und Staat*. Cologne 1969.

Pipes, Richard, ed. *Revolutionary Russia*. Garden City 1969.

____. *Social Democracy and the St. Petersburg Labour Movement, 1885-1897*. Cambridge 1963.

Pons, Alain. 'Lénine et l'utopie.' *Contrepoint*, No. 2 (October 1970).

Portal, Roger. 'The Industrialization of Russia.' In *Cambridge Economic History of Europe*. Vol. 6, Part 2, pp. 801-74. Cambridge 1965.

Pospielovsky, Dimitry. *Russian Police Trade Unionism*. London 1971.

Potichnyj, Peter. *Soviet Agricultural Trade Unions 1917-1970*. Toronto 1972.

Poulantzas, Nicos. *Political Power and Social Classes*. Trans. Timothy O'Hagan. London 1973.

_____. *State, Power, Socialism*. Trans. Patrick Camiller. London 1978.

Pribicevic, Branco. *The Shop Stewards Movement and Workers Control*. Oxford 1959.

Price, M. Philips *My Reminiscences of the Russian Revolution*. London 1921.

Procacci, Giuliano. 'La classe operaia italiana agli inizi del secolo XX.' *Studi Storici*, III, No. 1 (January-March 1962), 3–76.

Prokopovicz, S.N. *Russlands Volkswirtschaft unter den Sowjets*. Zurich 1944.

Przeworski, Adam. 'Social Democracy as a Historical Phenomenon.' *New Left Review*, No. 122 (July-August 1980), 27–58.

_____. 'The Process of Class Formation from Karl Kautsky's *The Class Struggle* to Recent Debates.' *Politics and Society* 7:4 (1977).

Rabehl, Bernd. *Marx und Lenin*. Berlin 1973.

_____. 'Die marxistische Theorie der Transformationsgesellschaft am Beispiel der Entwicklung der Russischen Revolution.' In *Gesellschaftsstrukturen*. Ed. Klaus Meschkat and Oskar Negt. Frankfurt am Main 1973, 214–70.

Rabinowitch, Alexander. *Prelude to Revolution*. Bloomington 1968.

_____ and Janet Rabinowitch, eds. *Revolution and Politics in Russia*. Bloomington 1972.

_____. *The Bolsheviks Come to Power*. New York 1976.

Rachleff, Peter. 'Soviets and Factory Committees in the Russian Revolution.' *Root and Branch*, ed. Jeremy Brecher, et al. Greenwich, Conn. 1975.

Radkey, Oliver Henry. *The Agrarian Foes of Bolshevism*. New York 1958.

_____. *The Election to the Russian Constituent Assembly of 1917*. Cambridge 1950.

_____. *The Unknown Civil War in Soviet Russia*. Stanford 1976.

_____. *The Sickle under the Hammer*. New York 1963.

Raptis, Michel. *Revolution and Counter-revolution in Chile*. London 1974.

Rigby, T.H. *Communist Party Membership in the USSR, 1917–1967*. Princeton 1968.

_____. *Lenin's Government: Sovnarkom, 1917–1922*. New York 1979.

Riskin, Carl. 'Maoism and Motivation: Work Incentives in China.' In *China's Uninterrupted Revolution*. Ed. Victor Nee and James Peck. New York 1975.

Roberts, Paul Craig. '"War Communism": A Re-Examination.' *Slavic Review*, Vol. 29, No. 2 (June 1970), 238–61.

Robinson, Geroid. *Rural Russia Under the Old Regime*. New York 1949.

Rosenberg, Arthur. *A History of Bolshevism*. Trans. Ian F.D. Morrow. Garden City 1967.

_____. *The Birth of the German Republic*. Trans. Ian Morrow. New York 1962.

Rosenberg, William. *Liberals in the Russian Revolution*. Princeton 1974.

_____. 'Workers Control on the Railroads and Some Suggestions Concerning Social Aspects of Labour Politics in the Russian Revolution.' *Journal of Modern History*, supplement, 49:2 (June 1977), D1181–1219.

_____. 'Workers and Workers Control in the Russian Revolution.' *History Workshop*, No. 5 (spring 1978), 89–97.

Roth, Gunther. *The Social Democrats in Imperial Germany*. Totowa 1962.

Roth, Karl Heinz. *Die 'andere' Arbeiterbewegung*. Munich 1974.

Rousseau, Jean-Jacques. *The Social Contract*. Trans. Maurice Cranston. Baltimore 1968.

Rovatti, Pier Aldo. 'The Critique of Fetishism in Marx's *Grundrisse*.' *Telos*, No. 17 (fall 1973), 56–69.

Rowbotham, Sheila. *Women, Resistance and Revolution*. New York 1972.

Rucker, R.D. 'Workers Control of Production in the October Revolution and Civil War.' *Science and Society* 43:2 (summer 1979), 158–85.

Rürup, Reinhard. 'Problems in the German Revolution, 1918–1919.' *The Journal of Contemporary History*, Vol. 3, No. 4 (October 1968), 109–35.

———, Eberhard Kolb and Gerald Fedman. 'Die Massenbewegungen der Arbeiterschaft in Deutschland am Ende des Ersten Weltkrieges (1917–1920).' *Politische Vierteljahresschrift*, Vol. 13 No. 1 (August 1972), 84–105.

———, ed. *Arbeiter-und Soldatenräte im rheinische-westfälischen Industriegebiet.* Wuppertal 1975.

Sablisky, Walter. *The Road to Bloody Sunday.* Princeton 1976.

Sadoul, Jacques. *Notes sur la révolution bolchévique.* Paris 1971.

Salvadori, Massimo. *Karl Kautsky and the Socialist Revolution, 1880–1938.* Trans. Jon Rothschild. London 1979.

Santamaria, Ulysses and Alain Manville. 'Lenin and the Problem of the Transition.' *Telos*, No. 27 (spring 1976), 79–96.

Santillan, Diego Abad de. *After the Revolution: Economic Reconstruction in Spain Today.* Trans. Louis Frank. New York 1937.

Sartan, Yves. 'Les Soviets, la gestion ouvrière et les positions de Lénine dans la révolution russe." *Autogestion*, No. 4 (December 1967), 111–24.

Sawyer, Marian. 'The Genesis of *State and Revolution*.' In *The Socialist Register 1977*. London 1977.

Schapiro, Leonard and Peter Reddaway, eds. *Lenin: the Man, the Theorist, the Leader.* New York 1967.

———. *The Communist Party of the Soviet Union.* New York 1959.

———. *The Origin of the Communist Autocracy.* Cambridge 1966.

Schmidt, Hans-Theodor. *Die sowjetischen Gesellschaftsgerichte.* Cologne 1969.

Schneiderman, Jeremiah. *Sergei Zubatov and Revolutionary Marxism: The Struggle for the Working Class in Tsarist Russia.* Ithaca 1976.

Schorske, Carl. *German Social Democracy, 1905–1917.* Cambridge 1955.

Schroyer, Trent. *The Critique of Domination.* New York 1973.

Schurmann, Franz. *Ideology and Organization in Communist China*, 2nd edition. Berkeley 1968.

Schwartz, Michael. *Radical Protest and Social Structure.* New York 1976.

Schwarz, Solomon M. *The Russian Revolution of 1905.* Trans. Gertrude Vakar. Chicago 1967.

Seemann, Klaus-Dieter. 'Der Versuch einer proletarischen Kulturrevolution in Russland, 1917–1922.' *Jahrbücher für Geschichte Osteuropas*, Vol. 9 (1961), 179–222.

Selitskii, V. Ia. *Massy v bor'be za rabochii kontrol (mart-iyul' 1917 g.).* Moscow 1971.

Serge, Victor. *Memoirs of a Revolutionary 1901–1941.* Trans. Peter Sedgwick. Oxford 1963.

———. *Year One of the Russian Revolution.* Trans. Peter Sedgwick. Chicago 1972.

Service, Robert. *The Bolshevik Party in Revolution: A Study in Organizational Change, 1917–1923.* New York 1979.

Shanin, Teodor. *The Awkward Class.* Oxford 1972.

Singleton, Seth. 'The Tambov Revolt (1920–1921).' *Slavic Review*, Vol. 25 (1966), 497–512.

Sirianni, Carmen. 'Workers Control in the Era of World War I: A Comparative Analysis of the European Experience.' *Theory and Society*, 9:1 (1980), 29–88.

———. 'Production and Power in a Classless Society: A Critical Analysis of the

Utopian Dimensions of Marxist Theory.' *Socialist Review*, No. 59 (September-October 1981), 33–82.

____. 'Popular Movements and Revolutionary Theory in the First Years of Soviet Rule.' *Socialist Review*, No. 36 (November-December 1977), 143–60.

____. Review of Oscar Anweiler's *The Soviets*, *Telos*, No. 24 (summer 1975), 1978–83.

____ and James Cronin, eds. *Work, Community and Power: the Experience of Labour in Europe and America 1900–25,* Philadelphia 1983.

Technology, Community and Class Formation. Philadelphia 1982.

Skočpol, Theda. *States and Social Revolutions in France, Russia and China*. New York 1979.

____. 'Old Regime Legacies and Communist Revolutions in Russia and China.' *Social Forces*, Vol. 55, No. 2 (December 1976), 284–315.

Slater, Phil, ed. *Outlines of a Critique of Technology*. Atlantic Highlands 1980.

Soboul, Albert. *The Sans-Culottes*. Trans. Remy Inglis Hall. Garden City 1972.

Sochor, Zenovia. 'Soviet Taylorism Revisited.' *Soviet Studies*, 33:2 (April 1981), 246–64.

Sontag, John. 'The Soviet War Scare of 1926–27.' *The Russian Review*, 34:1 (January 1975.

Sorenson, Jay. *The Life and Death of Soviet Trade Unionism 1917–1928*. New York 1969.

____. 'The Workers Opposition: A Case Study in Factionalism in the Russian Communist Party.' Unpublished MA thesis, Columbia University 1956.

Sorlin, Pierre. *The Soviet People and Their Society*. Trans. Daniel Weissbort. New York 1968.

Spriano, Paolo. *The Occupation of the Factories*. Trans. Gwyn Williams. London 1975.

Stearns, Peter. *Revolutionary Syndicalism and French Labour*. New Brunswick 1971.

____. *Lives of Labour*. New York 1975.

Steenland, Kyle. 'Two Years of "Popular Unity" in Chile: A Balance Sheet.' *New Left Review*, No. 78 (March-April 1973).

Steinberg, Isaac N. *In the Workshop of the Revolution*. New York 1953.

____. *Spiridonova: Revolutionary Terrorist*. Trans. and ed. Gwenda David and Eric Mosbacher. London 1935.

Stephens, Evelyn Huber. *The Politics of Workers Participation: The Peruvian Approach in Comparative Perspective*. New York 1980.

Sukhanov, N.N. *The Russian Revolution, 1917*. 3 Vols. Trans. Joel Carmichael. London 1955.

Suny, Ronald Grigor. *The Baku Commune 1917–1918*. Princeton 1972.

Sutton, Antony C. *Western Technology and Soviet Economic Development 1917 to 1930*. Stanford 1968.

Svejnar, Jan. 'Workers Participation in Management in Czechoslovakia.' Paper presented to the Second Annual Conference on Self-Management, Cornell University, June 1975.

Sweezy, Paul and Charles Bettelheim. *On the Transition to Socialism*. New York 1971.

Taniuchi, Yuzuru. *The Village Gathering in Russia in the Mid-1920s*. Birmingham 1968.

Tarschys, Daniel. *Beyond the State*. Stockholm 1971.

Tatur, Melanie. '"Wissenschaftliche Arbeitsorganisation": Zur Rezeption des Taylorismus in der Sowjetunion.' *Jahrbücher für Geschichte Osteuropas* 25 (1977), 34–51.

Taub, Rainer. 'Lenin und Taylor. Die Schicksale der "wissenschaftlichen Arbeitsorganisation" in der frühen Sowjetunion.' *Kursbuch*, No. 43 (March 1976), 146–58.

Therborn, Göran. 'The Rule of Capital and the Rise of Democracy.' *New Left Review*, No. 103 (May-June 1977), 3–41.

____. *What Does the Ruling Class Do When It Rules?* London 1978.

Thompson, Edward P. 'Time, Work Discipline, and Industrial Capitalism.' *Past and Present*, No. 38 (December 1967), 56–97.

Tilly, Charles. *From Mobilization to Revolution*. Reading, Mass 1978.

Tomasic, Dinko. *The Impact of Russian Culture on Soviet Communism*. Glenco 1953.

Townsend, James. *Political Participation in Communist China*. Berkeley 1969.

Trotsky, Leon. *Lenin*. Trans. Tamara Deutscher. New York 1971.

____. *Lessons of October*. Trans. John G. Wright. New York 1937.

____. *Literature and Revolution*. Trans. Rose Strunsky. Ann Arbor 1960.

____. *On the Trade Unions*. New York 1969.

____. *1905*. New York 1972.

____. *Problems of Everyday Life*. New York 1973.

____. *Terrorism and Communism*. Ann Arbor 1961.

____. *Marxism and Science*. Colombo 1973.

____. *The Class Nature of the Soviet State*. Trans. Usick Vanzler. London 1968.

____. *The History of the Russian Revolution*. Trans. Max Eastman. Ann Arbor 1957.

____. *The Permanent Revolution and Results and Prospects*. New York 1969.

____. *The Revolution Betrayed*. Trans. Max Eastman. Garden City 1937.

Tucker, Robert, ed. *Stalinism*. New York 1977.

Turin, S.P. *From Peter the Great to Lenin*. London 1935.

Ulam, Adam. *The Bolsheviks*. New York 1965.

Uldricks, Teddy. 'The "Crowd" in the Russian Revolution: Towards Reassessing the Nature of Revolutionary Leadership.' *Politics and Society*, Vol. 4, No. 3 (1974), 397–413.

Urwick, Lyndall. *The Development of Scientific Management in Britain*. London 1938.

Vandervelde, Emile. *Three Aspects of the Russian Revolution*. Trans. Jean Findlay. London 1918.

Venediktov, Anatolii V., *Organizatsiya gosudarstvennoi promyshlennosti v SSSR, Tom I (1917–1920)*. Leningrad 1957.

Vinogradoff, Eugene D. 'The "Invisible Hand" and the Russian Peasant.' *Peasant Studies Newsletter*, Vol. 4, No. 3 (July 1975), 6–19.

Vinogradov, V. *Workers Control Over Production: Past and Present*. Moscow 1973.

Vitak, Robert. 'Workers Control: The Czechoslovak Experience.' In *Socialist Register 1971*. London 1971.

Voline. *The Unknown Revolution 1917–1921*. Trans. Holley Cantine and Freddy Perlman. New York 1974.

Von Laue, Theodore H. 'Russian Labour Between Factory and Field, 1892–1903.' California Slavic Studies, Vol. 3 (1963), 33–65.

____. 'Russian Peasants in the Factory, 1892–1904.' *Journal of Economic History* (1961), 61–80.

____. *Sergei Witte and the Industrialization of Russia.* New York 1963.

Von Loewe, Karl F. 'Challenge to Ideology: The Petrograd Soviet, February 27-March 3, 1917.' *Russian Review*, Vol. 26, No. 2 (April 1967), 164–75.

Vroom, Victor and E. Deci, eds. *Management and Motivation.* Baltimore 1973.

Vucinich, Wayne. *The Peasant in Nineteenth Century Russia.* Stanford 1968.

Wachtel, Howard. *Workers' Management and Workers' Wages in Yugoslavia.* Ithaca 1973.

Wade, Rex. 'The Rajonnye Sovety of Petrograd: The Role of Local Political Bodies in the Russian Revolution.' *Jahrbücher für Geschichte Osteuropas*, Vol. 20 (1972), 226–40.

____. *The Russian Search for Peace, February-October 1917.* Stanford 1969.

Wallerstein, Immanuel. 'Dependence in an Interdependent World: The Limited Possibilities of Transformation within the World Capitalist Economy.' *African Studies Review*, Vol. 17, No. 1 (April 1974), 1–26.

____. 'The Rise and Future Demise of the World Capitalist System: Concepts for Comparative Analysis.' *Comparative Studies in Society and History* (September 1974), 387–415.

Ward, Benjamin. 'Wild Socialism in Russia: The Origins.' *California Slavic Studies*, Vol. 3 (1964), 127–48.

Weber, Henri. 'Eurocommunism, Socialism and Democracy.' *New Left Review*, No. 110 (July-August 1978), 3–14.

Weinstein, James. 'The IWW and American Socialism.' *Socialist Review*, No. 5 (September-October 1970), 3–41.

Wellmer, Albrecht. *Critical Theory of Society.* Trans. John Cumming. New York 1971.

Wesson, Robert. *Soviet Communes.* New Brunswick 1963.

Wetter, Gustav. *Dialectical Materialism.* Trans. Peter Heath. New York 1958.

Wheeler-Bennett, John W. *Brest-Litovsk: The Forgotten Peace.* London 1963.

Wildman, Allan K. *The Making of a Workers' Revolution: Social Democracy, 1891–1903.* Chicago 1967.

Willets, Harry. 'Lenin and the Peasants.' In *Lenin: The Man, the Theorist, the Leader.* Ed. Leonard Schapiro and Peter Reddaway. New York 1967, 211–33.

Williams, Gwyn. *Proletarian Order.* London 1975.

Wittfogel, Karl. *Oriental Despotism.* New Haven 1957.

Wohl, Robert. *French Communism in the Making, 1914–1924.* Stanford 1966.

Wolf, Eric. *Peasant Wars in the Twentieth Century.* New York 1969.

Wright, Erik Olin. *Class, Crisis and the State.* London 1978.

____. 'Varieties of Marxist Conceptions of Class Structure.' *Politics and Society* 9:3 (1980), 323–70.

Zagorsky, Simon. *La République des Soviets.* Paris 1921.

____. *State Control of Industry in Russia During the War.* New Haven 1928.

Zaleski, Eugene. *Planning for Economic Growth in the Soviet Union 1918–1932.* Trans. Marie-Christine MacAndrew and G. Warren Nutter. Chapel Hill 1971.

Zelnik, Reginald. 'Russian Bebels: An Introduction to the Memoirs of Semen Kanatchikov and Matvei Fisher.' *Russian Review*, Vol. 35, No. 3 (July 1976), 249–89, Vol. 35, No. 4 (October 1976), 417–47.

____. 'Russian Workers and the Revolutionary Movement.' *Journal of Social History*, Vol. 6 (winter 1971–72), 214–36.

_____. 'Two-and-a-Half Centuries of Labour History: St. Petersburg/Petrograd/ Leningrad.' *Labour History*, Vol. 33 (1974), 522–27.

Zimbalist, Andrew. 'Worker Participation in the Management of Socialized Industry: An Empirical Study of the Chilean Experience Under Allende.' PhD thesis, Harvard University 1974.

_____. 'The Dynamic of Worker Participation: An Interpretive Essay on the Chilean and Other Experiences.' *Administration and Society*, Vol. 7, No. 1 (May 1975), 43–54.

_____. 'The Development of Workers Participation in Socialist Cuba.' Paper presented at the Second Annual Conference on Workers Self-Management, Cornell University, June 1975.

_____. 'The Limits of Work Humanization.' *Review of Radical Political Economics* 7:2 (summer 1975), 50–9.

Index